From Heaven With Love

E. G. White

A condensation of
The Desire of Ages

Pacific Press Publishing Association
Boise, Idaho
Montemorelos, Nuevo Leon, Mexico
Oshawa, Ontario, Canada

Cover design and cover illustration design by Tim Larson
Cover illustration by Eric Joyner
Illustration after page 160 by Harry Anderson. All other inside
illustrations by John Steel.

This condensation is not a paraphrase. The author's own words are
retained throughout, except when it has been necessary to substitute a
proper noun for a pronoun to avoid confusion, to change a verb tense
to maintain meaning and continuity, or to supply a word or phrase to
make a sentence read more smoothly.

All biblical quotations are from the King James or the Revised
Standard versions of the Bible.

ISBN 0-8163-0651-6

Why You Should Read This Book

In the heart of all people is an inexpressible longing for something they do not naturally possess. This longing, implanted by a merciful God, has been perverted by Satan. He makes people believe that this deep hunger may be satisfied by pleasure, wealth, ease, fame, or power. But those who have been thus deceived by him find that all these things leave the soul unsatisfied.

God designs, however, that this longing shall lead to the One who alone is able to satisfy it. The desire is *of* Him that it may lead *to* Him, the fullness and fulfillment of that desire. That fullness is found in Jesus Christ, the Son of the Eternal God. Haggai calls Him "the Desire of all nations," and we may well call Him "the Desire of all ages," God's Son, sent from heaven with love.

This book sets forth Jesus Christ as the One in whom the deep yearnings of every heart may be satisfied. It is not, however, the purpose of this work to provide a harmony of the Gospels or to set forth in strictly chronological order the important events and wonderful lessons of the life of Christ. Its purpose is to present the love of God as revealed in His Son, the divine beauty of the life of Christ.

In the following pages the author opens before the reader undreamed-of riches from the life of Jesus. New and glorious light flashes forth from many familiar passages of Scripture. Jesus Christ is revealed as the Fullness of the Godhead, the infinitely merciful Saviour of sinners, the Sun of Righteousness, the merciful High Priest, mankind's compelling Example, the Healer of all human maladies and diseases, the tender, compassionate Friend, the Prince of Peace, the Coming King, the culmination and fruition of the desires and hopes of all the ages.

We send forth this book with the prayer that the Holy Spirit will make its words, words of life to millions whose longings and desires are yet unsatisfied.

The Publishers

Contents

1 / Christ Before Coming to Earth

From the days of eternity the Lord Jesus Christ was one with the Father; He was the image of God, the outshining of His glory. To manifest this glory, to reveal the light of God's love, He came to our sin-darkened earth. Therefore it was prophesied of Him, "They shall call His name Immanuel, . . . God with us." Matthew 1:23; cf. Isaiah 7:14.

Jesus was "the Word of God"—God's thought made audible. Not alone for His earthborn children was this revelation given. Our little world is the lesson book of the universe. Both redeemed and unfallen beings will find in the cross of Christ their science and their song. They will see that the glory shining in the face of Jesus is the glory of self-sacrificing love. They will see that the law of life for earth and heaven is the law of self-renouncing love. That love which "seeketh not her own" has its source in the heart of God and is manifested in Jesus, the meek and lowly One.

In the beginning, Christ laid the foundations of the earth. His hand hung the worlds in space and fashioned the flowers of the field. He filled the earth with beauty, and the air with song. See Psalms 65:6; 95:5. Upon all things He wrote the message of the Father's love.

Now sin has marred God's perfect work, yet that handwriting remains. Nothing, save the selfish heart of man, lives unto itself. Every tree and shrub and leaf pours forth that element of life without which neither man nor animal could live; and man and animal, in turn, minister to the life of tree and shrub and leaf. The ocean receives streams from every land, but takes to give. The mists ascending from it fall in showers to water the earth, that it may bring forth and bud. The angels of glory find their joy in giving. They bring light from above and move upon the human spirit to bring the lost into fellowship with Christ.

But turning from all lesser representations, we behold God in Jesus. We see that it is the glory of God to *give*. "I seek not Mine own glory," said Christ, but the glory of Him that sent Me. John 8:50; 7:18. Christ received from God, but He took to give. Through the Son, the Father's life flows out to all; through the Son it returns in joyous service, a tide of love, to the great Source of all. Thus through Christ the circuit of beneficence, the law of life, is complete.

In Heaven This Law Was Broken

Sin originated in self-seeking. Lucifer, the covering cherub, desired to be first in heaven. He sought to draw heavenly beings away from their Creator and win homage to himself. Therefore he misrepresented God, attributing to Him the desire for self-exaltation. He led them to doubt His word, distrust His goodness, and look upon Him as severe and unforgiving. Thus he drew men to join him in rebellion against God, and the night of woe settled down upon the world.

The earth was dark through misapprehension of God. That the world might be brought back to God, Satan's deceptive power was to be broken. This could not be done by force. God desires only the service of love, and love cannot be won by force or authority. Only by love is love awakened. To know God is to love Him; His character must be manifested in contrast to that of Satan. This work only one Being could do. Only He who knew the height and depth of the love of God could make it known.

The plan for our redemption was not a plan formulated after the fall of Adam. It was a revelation of "the mystery which hath been kept in silence through times eternal." Romans 16:25, RV. It was an unfolding of the principles that from eternal ages have been the foundation of God's throne. God foresaw sin's existence and made provision to meet the terrible emergency. He covenanted to give His only-begotten Son, "that whosoever believeth in Him should not perish, but have everlasting life." John 3:16.

Lucifer had said, "I will exalt my throne above the stars of God; . . . I will be like the Most High." But Christ, "being in the form of God, . . . emptied Himself, taking the form of a servant, being made in the likeness of men." Isaiah 14:13, 14; Philippians 2:6, 7, RV.

A Voluntary Sacrifice

Jesus might have retained the glory of heaven. But He chose to step down from the throne of the universe, that He might bring life to the perishing.

Nearly 2000 years ago, a voice was heard in heaven, "A body hast thou prepared Me. . . . Lo, I come (in the volume of the book it is written of Me,) to do Thy will, O God." Hebrews 10:5-7. Christ was about to visit our world, to become incarnate. Had He appeared with the glory that was His before the world was, we could not have endured the light of His presence. That we might behold it and not be destroyed, His glory was shrouded, His divinity veiled with humanity.

This great purpose had been shadowed forth in types and symbols. The burning bush, in which Christ appeared to Moses, revealed God. The lowly shrub, that seemingly had no attractions, enshrined the Infinite. God shrouded His glory that Moses could look upon it and live. So in the pillar of cloud by day and the pillar of fire by night, God's glory was veiled, that finite men might behold it. So Christ was to come "in the likeness of men." He was the incarnate God, but His glory was veiled that He might draw near to sorrowful, tempted men.

Through Israel's weary wandering in the desert, the

symbol of God's presence, the sanctuary, was with them. See Exodus 25:8. So Christ pitched His tent by the side of the tents of men that He might make us familiar with His divine character and life. "The Word became flesh, and tabernacled among us (and we beheld His glory, glory as of the only begotten from the Father), full of grace and truth." John 1:14, RV, margin.

Since Jesus came to dwell with us, we know that God is acquainted with our trials, sympathizes with our griefs, and is the friend of sinners. In the Saviour's life we see *"God* with us."

Satan represents God's law of love as a law of selfishness. He declares it impossible for us to obey its precepts. The fall of our first parents he charges upon the Creator, leading men to look upon God as the author of sin, suffering, and death. Jesus was to unveil this deception. As one of us He was to give an example of obedience. For this He took upon Himself our nature and passed through our experiences. "In all things it behooved Him to be made like unto His brethren." Hebrews 2:17. If we had to bear anything which Jesus did not endure, then on this point Satan would represent the power of God as insufficient for us. Therefore Jesus was "in all points tempted like as we are." Hebrews 4:15. He endured every trial to which we are subject. And He exercised in His own behalf no power not freely offered us. As man, He met temptation and overcame in the strength given Him from God. He made plain the character of God's law, and His life testifies that it is possible for us also to obey the law of God.

By His humanity, Christ touched humanity; by His divinity, He lays hold on the throne of God. As Son of man, He gave us an example of obedience; as Son of God, He gives us power to obey. To us He says, "All power is given unto Me in heaven and in earth." Matthew 28:18. "God with us" is the surety of our deliverance from sin, the assurance of power to obey the law of heaven.

Christ revealed a character the opposite of that of Satan. "Being found in human form He humbled Himself and became obedient unto death, even death on a cross." Philippians 2:8, RSV. Christ took the form of a servant, and offered sacrifice, Himself the priest, Himself the victim. "He was bruised for our iniquities; the chastisement of our peace was upon Him." Isaiah 53:5.

Treated As We Deserve

Christ was treated as we deserve, that we might be treated as He deserves. He was condemned for our sins, in which He had no share, that we might be justified by His righteousness, in which we had no share. He suffered the death which was ours, that we might receive the life which was His. "With His stripes we are healed." Isaiah 53:5.

It was Satan's purpose to bring eternal separation between God and man; but in Christ we become more closely united to God than if we had never fallen. In taking our nature, the Saviour bound Himself to humanity by a tie that is never to be broken. "God so loved the world, that He gave His only-begotten Son." John 3:16. He gave Him, not only to die as our sacrifice; He gave Him to become one of the human family, forever to retain His human nature.

"Unto *us* a child is born, unto *us* a son is given: and the government shall be upon His shoulder." God has adopted human nature in the person of His Son and has carried it to the highest heaven. The "Son of man" shall be called, "Wonderful, Counselor, The mighty God, The everlasting Father, The Prince of Peace." Isaiah 9:6. He who is "holy, harmless, undefiled, separate from sinners" is not ashamed to call us brethren. Hebrews 7:26; 2:11. Heaven is enshrined in humanity, and humanity is enfolded in the bosom of Infinite Love.

The exaltation of the redeemed will be an eternal testimony to God's mercy. "In the ages to come" He will "show the exceeding riches of His grace in His kindness toward us through Christ Jesus" in order that "the manifold wisdom of God" might be made known to "the principalities and the powers in the heavenly places." Ephesians 2:7; 3:10, RV.

Through Christ's work the government of God stands justified. The Omnipotent One is made known as the God of love. Satan's charges are refuted, and his character unveiled. Sin can never again enter the universe. Through eternal ages all are secure from apostasy. By love's self-sacrifice, earth and heaven are bound to the Creator in bonds of indissoluble union.

Where sin abounded, God's grace much more abounds. The earth, the very field Satan claims as his, will be honored above all other worlds in the universe. Here, where the King of glory lived and suffered and died, here the tabernacle of God shall be with men, "and God Himself shall be with them, and be their God." Revelation 21:3. Through endless ages the redeemed will praise Him for His unspeakable gift—Immanuel, "God with us."

2 / The People Who Should Have Welcomed Him

For more than a thousand years the Jewish people had awaited the Saviour's coming. And yet at His coming they knew Him not. They saw in Him no beauty that they should desire Him. See Isaiah 53:2. "He came unto His own, and His own received Him not." John 1:11.

God had chosen Israel to preserve among men the knowledge of His law and of the symbols and prophecies that pointed to the Saviour. The Hebrew people were to reveal God among the nations. In the call of Abraham the Lord had said, "In thee shall all families of the earth be blessed." Genesis 12:3. The Lord declared through Isaiah, "Mine house shall be called an house of prayer for all peoples." Isaiah 56:7, RV.

But Israel fixed their hopes on worldly greatness and followed the ways of the heathen. In vain God sent them warnings by His prophets. In vain they suffered the chastisement of heathen oppression. Every reformation was followed by deeper apostasy.

Had Israel been true to God, He would have made them "high above all nations which He hath made, in praise, and in name, and in honor." "The nations, which shall hear all these statutes," shall say, "Surely this great nation is a wise and understanding people." Deuteronomy 26:19; 4:6.

But because of their unfaithfulness, God's purpose could be wrought only through adversity and affliction. They were brought to Babylon and scattered through the lands of the heathen. While they mourned for the holy temple that was laid waste, through them a knowledge of God was spread among the nations. Heathen systems of sacrifice were a perversion of the system God had appointed; from the Hebrews many learned the meaning of the service divinely ordained and in faith grasped the promise of a Redeemer.

Not a few exiles lost their lives because of their refusal to disregard the Sabbath and to observe heathen festivals. As idolaters were roused to crush out the truth, the Lord brought His servants face to face with kings and rulers, that they and their people might receive the light. The greatest monarchs were led to proclaim the supremacy of the God whom their Hebrew captives worshiped.

During the centuries that followed the Babylonish captivity, the Israelites were cured of the worship of graven images, and their conviction became fixed that their prosperity depended on obedience to the law of God. But with many of the people the motive was selfish. They rendered service to God as the means of attaining national greatness. They did not become the light of the world but shut themselves away in order to escape temptation. God had placed restrictions on association with idolators to prevent them from conforming to the practices of the heathen. But this teaching had been misinterpreted. It was used to build up a wall between Israel and other nations. The Jews were actually jealous lest the Lord should show mercy to the Gentiles!

How They Perverted the Sanctuary Service

After the return from Babylon, all over the country synagogues were erected, where the law was expounded by priests and scribes. But during the captivity, many of the people had received heathen ideas, and these were brought into their religious service.

The ritual service had been instituted by Christ Himself. It was a symbol of Him, full of vitality and spiritual beauty. But the Jews lost the spiritual life from their ceremonies and trusted the sacrifices and ordinances themselves, instead of Him to whom they pointed. To supply that which they had lost, the priests and rabbis multiplied requirements of their own; and the more rigid they grew, the less of the love of God was manifested.

Those who tried to observe the minute and burdensome rabbinical precepts could find no rest from a troubled conscience. Thus Satan worked to discourage the people, to lower their conception of the character of God, and to bring the faith of Israel into contempt. He hoped to establish the claim that the requirements of God could not be obeyed. Even Israel, he declared, did not keep the law.

Expecting a False Messiah

The Jews had no true concept of the Messiah's mission. They did not seek redemption from sin, but deliverance from the Romans. They looked for the Messiah to exalt Israel to universal dominion. Thus the way was prepared to reject the Saviour.

At the birth of Christ the nation was chafing under the rule of foreign masters and was racked with internal strife. The Romans appointed and removed the high priest, and the office was often secured by bribery and even murder. Thus the priesthood became more and more corrupt. The people were subjected to merciless demands and were also heavily taxed by the Romans. Widespread discontent, greed, violence, distrust, and spiritual apathy were eating out the heart of the nation. In their darkness and oppression, the people longed for One who would restore the kingdom to Israel. They had studied the prophecies, but without spiritual insight. Thus they overlooked those scriptures that point to the humiliation of Christ's first advent. They interpreted prophecy in accordance with their selfish desires.

3 / Man's Sin and the "Fullness of the Time"

When Adam and Eve in Eden first heard the promise of the Saviour's coming, they looked for its speedy fulfillment. They welcomed their firstborn son, hoping he might be the Deliverer. But those who first received the promise died without seeing it fulfilled. The promise was repeated through patriarchs and prophets, keeping alive the hope of His appearing; yet He came not. The prophecy of Daniel revealed the time of His advent, but not all rightly interpreted the message. Century after century passed away. The hand of the oppressor was heavy on Israel, and many were ready to exclaim, "The days are prolonged, and every vision faileth." Ezekiel 12:22.

But like the stars in the vast circuit of their appointed path, God's purposes know no haste and no delay. In heaven's council the hour for the coming of Christ had been determined. When the great clock of time pointed to that hour, Jesus was born in Bethlehem.

"When the fullness of the time was come, God sent forth His Son." Galatians 4:4. The world was ripe for the coming of the Deliverer. The nations were united under one government. One language was widely spoken. From all lands the Jews of the dispersion gathered to Jerusalem to the annual feasts. As these returned to the places of their sojourn, they could spread throughout the world the tidings of the Messiah's coming.

The systems of heathenism were losing their hold on the people. Men longed for a religion that could satisfy the heart. Souls looking for light were thirsting for a knowledge of the living God, for some assurance of life beyond the grave.

Many Longed for a Deliverer

The Jews' faith had grown dim, and hope had well-nigh ceased to illuminate the future. To the masses, death was a dread mystery; beyond was uncertainty and gloom. In "the region and shadow of death," men sat unsolaced. With longing they looked for the coming of the Deliverer, when the mystery of the future should be made plain.

Outside of the Jewish nation there were men seeking for truth, and to them the Spirit of Inspiration was imparted. Their words of prophecy had kindled hope in the hearts of thousands of the Gentile world.

For hundreds of years the Scriptures had been translated into the Greek language, then widely spoken throughout the Roman Empire. The Jews were scattered everywhere, and their expectation of the Messiah's coming was to some extent shared by the Gentiles. Among those whom the Jews styled heathen were men who had a better understanding of the Scripture prophecies concerning the Messiah than had the teachers in Israel.

Some who hoped for His coming as a deliverer from sin endeavored to study into the mystery of the Hebrew economy. But the Jews, intent on maintaining the separation between themselves and other nations, were unwilling to impart the knowledge they possessed concerning the symbolic service. The true Interpreter, the One whom all these types prefigured, must come and explain their significance. Lessons must be given to humanity in the language of humanity. Christ must come to utter words clearly understood and to separate truth from the chaff which had made it of no effect.

Among the Jews there were yet steadfast souls through whom a knowledge of God had been preserved. These strengthened their faith by dwelling on the assurance given through Moses, "A Prophet shall the Lord your God raise up unto you of your brethren, like unto me; Him shall ye hear in all things whatsoever He shall say unto you." Acts 3:22. They read how the Lord would anoint One "to preach good tidings unto the meek," "to bind up the brokenhearted, to proclaim liberty to the captives," and to declare the "acceptable year of the Lord." Isaiah 61:1, 2. He would "set judgment in the earth" and the isles would "wait for His law." Isaiah 42:4. Gentiles would come to His light, and kings to the brightness of His rising. See Isaiah 60:3.

The dying words of Jacob filled them with hope: "The scepter shall not depart from Judah, nor a lawgiver from between his feet, until Shiloh come." Genesis 49:10. The waning power of Israel testified that the Messiah's coming was at hand. There was widespread expectation of a mighty prince who should establish his kingdom in Israel and come as a deliverer to the nations.

How Satan Almost Succeeded

"The fullness of the time" had come. Humanity, degraded through ages of transgression, called for the coming of the Redeemer. Satan had been working to make the gulf deep and impassable between earth and heaven. He had emboldened men in sin. It was his purpose to wear out the forbearance of God so that He would abandon the world to satanic jurisdiction.

Satan's strife for supremacy seemed almost wholly successful. It is true that in every generation, even among the heathen, there were men through whom Christ was working to uplift the people from sin. But these men were hated. Many suffered a violent death. The dark shadow Satan had cast over the world grew deeper and deeper.

Satan won his great triumph in perverting the faith of Israel. The heathen had lost a knowledge of God and had become more and more corrupt. So it was with Israel. The principle that man can save himself by his own works lay at the foundation of every heathen religion; it had now become the principle of the Jewish religion.

The Jews defrauded the world by a counterfeit of the gospel. They had refused to surrender themselves to God for the salvation of the world, and they became agents of Satan for its destruction. The people whom God had called to be the pillar and ground of the truth were doing the work Satan desired them to do, taking a course to misrepresent the character of God and cause the world to look upon Him as a tyrant. Priests in the temple lost the significance of the service they performed. They were as actors in a play. Ordinances which God Himself had appointed were made the means of blinding the mind and hardening the heart. God could do no more for man through these channels.

God Pities the Lost World

All the agencies for depraving the souls of men had been put in operation. The Son of God, looking upon the world with compassion, saw how men had become victims of satanic cruelty. Bewildered and deceived, they were moving on in gloomy procession to death in which is no hope of life, toward night to which comes no morning.

The bodies of human beings had become the habitation of demons. The senses, the nerves, the passions, the organs of men, were worked by supernatural agencies in indulgence of the vilest lust. The stamp of demons was impressed on human faces. What a spectacle for the world's Redeemer to behold!

Sin had become a science, and vice a part of religion. Rebellion and hostility were violent against heaven. The unfallen worlds had watched to see God sweep away the inhabitants of earth. And if He should do this, Satan was ready to carry out his plan for securing the allegiance of heavenly beings. He had declared that the principles of God's government make forgiveness impossible. Had the world been destroyed, he would have cast blame on God and spread his rebellion to the worlds above.

But instead of destroying the world, God sent His Son to save it. A way for its recovery was provided. "When the fullness of the time" had come, the Deity poured upon the world a flood of healing grace never to be obstructed or withdrawn till the plan of salvation should be fulfilled. Jesus came to restore in man the image of his Maker, to expel the demons that had controlled the will, to lift us up from the dust, and to reshape the marred character after the pattern of His divine character.

4 / Born in a Stable

The King of glory stooped low to take humanity. His glory veiled, He shunned all outward display. Jesus purposed that no attraction of an earthly nature should call men to His side. Only the beauty of heavenly truth must draw those who would follow Him. He desired men to accept Him on the testimony of the Word of God.

The angels watched to see how the people of God would receive His Son, clothed in the garb of humanity. To the land where the light of prophecy had shone, the angels came. They came unseen to Jerusalem and the ministers of God's house.

Already to Zacharias the priest, as he ministered before the altar, the nearness of Christ's coming had been announced. Already the forerunner was born, and tidings of his birth and the significance of his mission had been spread abroad. Yet Jerusalem was not preparing to welcome her Redeemer.

God had called the Jewish nation to communicate to the world that Christ was to be born of David's line, yet they knew not that His coming was at hand. In the temple the morning and evening sacrifice daily pointed to the Lamb of God, yet even here was no preparation to receive Him. Priests and teachers rehearsed their meaningless prayers and performed the rites of worship, but were not prepared for the revelation of the Messiah. The same indifference pervaded the land of Israel. Hearts selfish and world-engrossed were untouched by the joy that thrilled all heaven. Only a few were longing to behold the Unseen.

This chapter is based on Luke 2:1-20.

Angels attended Joseph and Mary as they journeyed from Nazareth to the city of David. The decree of Rome for enrollment of the peoples of her vast domain had extended to the hills of Galilee. Caesar Augustus became God's agent in bringing the mother of Jesus to Bethlehem. She was of the lineage of David, and the Son of David must be born in David's city. "Out of thee [Bethlehem]," said the prophet, "shall He come forth . . . that is to be ruler in Israel; whose goings forth have been from of old, from the days of eternity." Micah 5:2, margin.

But in the city of their royal line, Joseph and Mary were unrecognized, unhonored. Weary and homeless, they traversed the narrow street to the eastern extremity of town, vainly seeking a resting place for the night. There was no room at the crowded inn. In a rude building where beasts were sheltered, they at last found refuge, and here the Redeemer was born.

The tidings filled heaven with rejoicing. Holy beings from the world of light were drawn to earth. Above the hills of Bethlehem a throng of angels awaited the signal to declare the glad news to the world. The leaders in Israel might have shared the joy of heralding the birth of Jesus. But they were passed by. To those who seek light and accept it with gladness, the bright rays from the throne of God will shine. See Isaiah 44:3; Psalm 112:4.

Only the Shepherds Cared

In the fields where the boy David had led his flock, shepherds keeping watch by night talked together of the promised Saviour and prayed for His coming. And an "angel of the Lord came upon them. . . . And the angel said unto them, Fear not: for, behold, I bring you good tidings of great joy, which shall be to all people. For unto you is born this day in the city of David a Saviour, which is Christ the Lord."

At these words, visions of glory filled the minds of the listening shepherds. The Deliverer has come!

Power, exaltation, triumph, are associated with His coming. But the angel prepared them to recognize their Saviour in poverty and humiliation: "Ye shall find the babe wrapped in swaddling clothes, lying in a manger."

The heavenly messenger had quieted their fears. He had told them how to find Jesus. He had given them time to become accustomed to the divine radiance. Then the whole plain was lighted up with the bright shining of the hosts of God. Earth was hushed, and heaven stooped to listen to the song—

Glory to God in the highest,
And on earth peace, good will toward men.

Oh, that today the human family could recognize that song! The note then struck will swell to the close of time, and resound to the ends of the earth.

As the angels disappeared, the shadows of night once more fell on the hills of Bethlehem. But the brightest picture ever beheld by human eyes remained in the memory of the shepherds. They "said to one another, Let us now go even unto Bethlehem, and see this thing which is come to pass, which the Lord hath made known unto us. And they came with haste, and found Mary, and Joseph, and the babe lying in a manger."

Departing with great joy, they made known the things they had seen and heard. "And all they that heard it wondered at those things which were told them by the shepherds."

Heaven and earth are no wider apart today than when shepherds listened to the angels' song. Angels from the courts above attend the steps of those who come and go at God's command.

In the story of Bethlehem is hidden "the depth of the riches both of the wisdom and knowledge of God." Romans 11:33. We marvel at the Saviour's sacrifice in exchanging the throne of heaven for the manger. Human pride stands rebuked in His presence.

Yet this was but the beginning of His condescension! It would have been an almost infinite humiliation for the Son of God to take man's nature even when Adam stood in innocence in Eden. But Jesus accepted humanity when the race had been weakened by 4000 years of sin. Like every child of Adam He accepted the results of the working of the law of heredity. These results were shown in the history of His earthly ancestors. He came with such a heredity to share our sorrows and temptations and to give us the example of a sinless life.

Satan hated Christ. He hated Him who pledged Himself to redeem sinners. Yet into the world where Satan claimed dominion, God permitted His Son to come, a helpless babe, subject to the weakness of humanity, to meet life's peril in common with every soul, to fight the battle as every child of humanity must fight it—at the risk of failure and eternal loss.

The heart of the human father yearns over his son. He looks into the face of his little child and trembles at the thought of life's peril. He longs to shield him from temptation and conflict. To meet a bitterer conflict and more fearful risk, God gave His only-begotten Son.

"Herein is love." Wonder, O heavens! and be astonished, O earth!

5 / Joseph and Mary Dedicate Jesus

About forty days after the birth of Christ, Joseph and Mary took Him to Jerusalem to present Him to the Lord, and to offer sacrifice. As man's substitute Christ must conform to the law in every particular. He had already been circumcised, as a pledge of His obedience to the law.

As an offering for the mother, the law required a lamb for a burnt offering, and a pigeon or a turtledove for a sin offering. These offerings were to be without blemish, for they represented Christ. He was the "lamb without blemish and without spot." 1 Peter 1:19. He was an example of what God designed humanity to be through obedience to His laws.

The dedication of the firstborn had its origin in earliest times. God had promised to give the Firstborn of heaven to save the sinner. This gift was to be acknowledged in every household by the consecration of the firstborn son. He was to be devoted to the priesthood, as a representative of Christ among men.

What meaning then was attached to Christ's presentation! But the priest did not see through the veil. Day after day he went through the presentation of infants, giving little heed to parents or children, unless he saw some indication of wealth or high rank. Joseph and Mary were poor, and the priest saw only a Galilean man and woman, dressed in the humblest garments.

The priest took the child in his arms and held it up before the altar. After handing it back to its mother, he inscribed the name "Jesus" on the roll. Little did he think, as the babe lay in his arms, that he was enrolling the

This chapter is based on Luke 2:21-38.

name of the Majesty of heaven, the King of glory, the One who was the foundation of the Jewish economy.

This babe was He who declared Himself to Moses as the I AM, He who in the pillar of cloud and of fire had been the guide of Israel. He was the Desire of all nations, the Root and Offspring of David, the Bright and Morning Star. That helpless babe was the hope of fallen humanity. He was to pay the ransom for the sins of the whole world.

But though the priest neither saw nor felt anything unusual, this occasion did not pass without some recognition of Christ. "There was a man in Jerusalem, whose name was Simeon, . . . and the Holy Ghost was upon him. And it was revealed unto him by the Holy Ghost, that he should not see death, before he had seen the Lord's Christ."

Venerable Simeon Recognized Jesus

As Simeon entered the temple, he was deeply impressed that the infant being presented to the Lord was the One he had longed to see. To the astonished priest, he appeared like a man enraptured. He took the child in his arms, while a joy he had never before felt entered his soul. As he lifted the infant Saviour toward heaven, he said, "Lord, now lettest Thou Thy servant depart in peace, according to Thy word: for mine eyes have seen Thy salvation, which Thou hast prepared before the face of all people; a light to lighten the Gentiles, and the glory of Thy people Israel."

While Joseph and Mary stood by, wondering at his words, Simeon said to Mary, "Behold, this child is set for the fall and rising again of many in Israel; and for a sign which shall be spoken against; (yea, a sword shall pierce through thy own soul also,) that the thoughts of many hearts may be revealed."

Also Anna, a prophetess, came in and confirmed Simeon's testimony. Her face lighted up with glory, and she poured out her heartfelt thanks that she had been permitted to behold Christ the Lord.

These humble worshipers had studied the prophecies. But the rulers and priests, though they too had the precious prophecies, were not walking in the way of the Lord, and their eyes were not open to behold the Light of life.

So it is still. The attention of all heaven is centered on events which are undiscerned by religious leaders. Men acknowledge Christ in history, but Christ in the poor and suffering who plead for relief, in the righteous cause that involves poverty and reproach, is no more readily received today than He was nineteen hundred years ago.

As Mary looked upon the child in her arms and recalled the words spoken by the shepherds, she was full of bright hope. Simeon's words called to her mind the prophetic utterances of Isaiah: "The people that walked in darkness have seen a great light: they that dwell in the land of the shadow of death, upon them hath the light shined. . . . For unto us a child is born, unto us a son is given: and the government shall be upon His shoulder: and His name shall be called Wonderful, Counselor, The mighty God, The everlasting Father, The Prince of Peace." Isaiah 9:2-6.

The Anguish Christ's Mother Must Know

Yet Mary did not understand Christ's mission. Simeon had prophesied of Him as a light to lighten the Gentiles, and the angels had announced the Saviour's birth as tidings of joy to all peoples. God desired men to behold Him as the Redeemer of the world. But many years must pass before even the mother of Jesus would understand.

Mary saw not the baptism of suffering by which the Messiah's reign on David's throne must be won. In Simeon's words to Mary, "A sword shall pierce through thy own soul also," God in tender mercy gave to the mother of Jesus an intimation of the anguish that already for His sake she had begun to bear.

"Behold," Simeon had said, "this child is set for the

fall and rising again of many in Israel." They must fall who would rise again. We must fall upon the Rock and be broken before we can be uplifted in Christ. Self must be dethroned. The Jews would not accept the honor that is reached through humiliation. Therefore they would not receive their Redeemer.

"That the thoughts of many hearts may be revealed." In the light of the Saviour's life, the hearts of all, from the Creator to the prince of darkness, are revealed. Satan has represented God as selfish. But the gift of Christ testifies that while God's hatred of sin is as strong as death, His love for the sinner is stronger than death. Having undertaken our redemption, God will spare nothing necessary to the completion of His work. Having collected the riches of the universe, He gives them all into the hands of Christ, and says, Use these gifts to convince man that there is no love greater than Mine. His greatest happiness will be found in loving Me.

How Everyone Will Judge Himself

At the cross of Calvary, love and selfishness stood face to face. Christ had lived only to comfort and bless, and in putting Him to death, Satan manifested the malignity of his hatred against God. The real purpose of his rebellion was to dethrone God and to destroy Him through whom the love of God was shown.

By the life and death of Christ the thoughts of men also are brought to view. The life of Jesus was a call to self-surrender and to fellowship in suffering. All who were listening to the Holy Spirit were drawn to Him. The worshipers of self belonged to Satan's kingdom. In their attitude toward Christ, all would show on which side they stood. And thus everyone passes judgment on himself.

In the day of final judgment, the cross will be presented, and its real bearing will be seen by every mind. Before the vision of Calvary with its mysterious Victim, sinners will stand condemned. Men will see what

The aged prophet Simeon had studied the prophecies. When Joseph and Mary brought Jesus to the temple for dedication, he recognized Jesus as the promised Messiah.

their choice has been. Every question in the controversy will have been made plain. God will stand clear of blame for the existence or continuance of evil. It will be demonstrated that there was no defect in God's government, no cause for disaffection. Both the loyal and the rebellious will declare, "Just and true are Thy ways, Thou King of saints. . . . Thy judgments are made manifest." Revelation 15:3, 4.

6 / "We Have Seen His Star"

"Now when Jesus was born in Bethlehem of Judea in the days of Herod the king, behold, there came wise men from the east to Jerusalem, saying, Where is He that is born King of the Jews? for we have seen His star in the east, and are come to worship Him."

The wise men from the East belonged to a class that comprised wealth and learning. Among these were upright men who studied the indications of Providence in nature and were honored for their integrity and wisdom. Of this character were the wise men who came to Jesus.

As these magi studied the starry heavens, they beheld the glory of the Creator. Seeking clearer knowledge, they turned to the Hebrew Scriptures. In their own land were prophetic writings that predicted the coming of a divine teacher. Balaam's prophecies had been handed down by tradition from century to century. But in the Old Testament the magi learned with joy that the Saviour's coming was near. The whole world was to be filled with a knowledge of the glory of the Lord.

The wise men had seen a mysterious light in the heavens that night when the glory of God flooded the hills of Bethlehem. A luminous star appeared, and lingered in the sky, a phenomenon that excited keen interest. That star was a company of shining angels, but of this the wise men were ignorant. Yet they were impressed that the star was of special import to them.

Could this strange star have been sent as a harbinger

This chapter is based on Matthew 2.

of the Promised One? See Numbers 24:17. The magi had welcomed the light of heaven-sent truth; now it was shed upon them in brighter rays. Through dreams they were instructed to go in search of the newborn Prince.

The Eastern country abounded in precious things, and the magi did not set out empty-handed. The richest gifts the land afforded were borne as an offering to Him in whom all the families of the earth were to be blessed.

A Journey by Night

It was necessary to journey by night in order to keep the star in view, but at every pause for rest the travelers searched the prophecies. The conviction deepened that they were divinely guided. The journey, though long, was a happy one.

They had reached the land of Israel, with Jerusalem in sight, when, lo, the star rested above the temple. With eager steps they pressed onward, confidently expecting the Messiah's birth to be the joyful burden of every tongue. But to their amazement they found their questions called forth no joy, but rather surprise and fear, not unmingled with contempt.

The priests extolled their religion and piety, while they denounced the Greeks and Romans as sinners. The wise men were not idolaters, and in the sight of God they stood far higher than His professed worshipers; yet they were looked upon by the Jews as heathen. Their eager questionings touched no chord of sympathy.

Herod's Jealousy Aroused

The magi's strange errand created an excitement among the people of Jerusalem which penetrated to the palace of King Herod. The wily Edomite was aroused at the intimation of a possible rival. Being of alien blood, he was hated by the people; his only security was the favor of Rome. But this new Prince had a higher claim—He was born to the kingdom.

Herod suspected the priests of plotting with the strangers to excite a tumult and unseat him. Determining to thwart the scheme by superior cunning, he summoned the priests and questioned them in regard to the place of the Messiah's birth.

This inquiry from the usurper of the throne, and made at the request of strangers, stung the pride of the Jewish teachers. The indifference with which they turned to the rolls of prophecy enraged the jealous tyrant. He thought them trying to conceal their knowledge. With an authority they dared not disregard, he commanded them to make a close search and to declare the birthplace of their expected King. "And they said unto him, In Bethlehem of Judea: for it is written by the prophet,

> And thou Bethlehem, land of Judah,
> Art in no wise least among the princes of Judah:
> For out of thee shall come forth a governor,
> Which shall be shepherd of My people Israel." RV

Herod now invited the magi to a private interview. Wrath and fear were raging in his heart, but he preserved a calm exterior, and professed to hail with joy the birth of Christ. He bade his visitors, "Search diligently for the young child; and when ye have found Him, bring me word again, that I may come and worship Him also."

The priests were not as ignorant as they pretended. The report of the angels' visit to the shepherds had been brought to Jerusalem, but the rabbis had treated it as unworthy of notice. They themselves might have been ready to lead the magi to Jesus' birthplace, but instead, the wise men came to call their attention to the birth of the Messiah.

If the reports brought by the shepherds and the wise men were credited, they would disprove the priests' claim to be the exponents of the truth of God. These learned teachers would not stoop to be instructed by heathen. It could not be, they said, that God had passed them by, to communicate with ignorant shepherds or uncircumcised Gentiles. They would not even go to Bethlehem to see whether these things were so. And they led the people to regard the interest in Jesus as fanatical excitement. Here began the rejection of Christ by the priests and rabbis. Their pride and stubbornness grew into a settled hatred of the Saviour.

The wise men departed alone from Jerusalem, the shadows of night falling. But to their great joy they again saw the star, and were directed to Bethlehem. Disappointed by the indifference of the Jewish leaders, they left Jerusalem less confident than when they entered.

No Royal Guard

At Bethlehem they found no royal guard to protect the newborn King. None of the world's honored men were in attendance. Jesus was cradled in a manger, His parents His only guardians. Could this be He who should "raise up the tribes of Jacob," be "a light to the Gentiles," and "salvation unto the end of the earth"? Isaiah 49:6.

"When they were come into the house, they saw the young child with Mary His mother, and fell down, and worshiped Him." They gave their hearts to Him as their Saviour and then poured out their gifts—"Gold, and frankincense, and myrrh." What a faith was theirs!

The wise men, not penetrating Herod's design, prepared to return to Jerusalem to acquaint him with their success. But in a dream they received a message to hold no further communication with him. Avoiding Jerusalem, they set out for their own country by another route.

In like manner Joseph received warning to flee to Egypt with Mary and the child. Joseph obeyed without delay, setting out by night for greater security.

The wise men's inquiries in Jerusalem, the popular interest excited, and even the jealousy of Herod, compelled the attention of the priests and rabbis and directed minds to the prophecies concerning the Messiah and the great event that had taken place.

Satan, bent on shutting out the divine light from the world, used his utmost cunning to destroy the Saviour. But He who never slumbers nor sleeps provided in a heathen land a refuge for Mary and the child Jesus. And through the gifts of the magi from a heathen country, the Lord supplied the means for the journey to Egypt and the sojourn in a land of strangers.

Herod's Terrible Massacre

Herod in Jerusalem impatiently awaited the return of the wise men. As time passed and they did not appear, his suspicions were roused. Had the rabbis penetrated his design and had the magi purposely avoided him? He was maddened at the thought. Through force he would make an example of this child-king.

Soldiers were sent to Bethlehem with orders to put to death all the children of two years and under. The quiet homes of the city of David witnessed scenes that 600 years before had been opened to the prophet: "In Ramah was there a voice heard, lamentation, and weeping, and great mourning, Rachel weeping for her children, and would not be comforted, because they are not."

This calamity the Jews had brought upon themselves. They had rejected the Holy Spirit, their only shield. They had searched for prophecies which could be interpreted to exalt themselves and show how God despised other nations. It was their proud boast that the Messiah was to come as a king and tread down the heathen in His wrath. Thus they excited the hatred of their rulers. Through their misrepresentation of Christ's mission, Satan had purposed to compass the destruction of the Saviour; but instead, it returned on their own heads.

Soon after the slaughter of the innocents, Herod died a fearful death. Joseph, still in Egypt, was now bidden by an angel to return to Israel. Regarding Jesus as the heir of David's throne, Joseph desired to make his home in Bethlehem; but learning that Archelaus reigned in Judea in his father's stead, he feared that the father's designs might be carried out by the son.

Joseph was directed to a place of safety, Nazareth, his former home. Here for nearly thirty years Jesus dwelt, "that it might be fulfilled which was spoken by the prophets, He shall be called a Nazarene." Galilee had a much larger mixture of foreign inhabitants than Judea; thus there was less interest in matters relating especially to the Jews.

Such was the Saviour's reception when He came to earth. God could not trust His beloved Son with men, even while carrying forward His work for their salvation! He commissioned angels to attend and protect Jesus till He should accomplish His mission and die by the hands of those whom He came to save.

7 / The Child Jesus

The childhood and youth of Jesus were spent in a little mountain village. He passed by the homes of wealth and the renowned seats of learning to make His home in despised Nazareth.

"The child grew, and waxed strong in spirit, filled with wisdom: and the grace of God was upon Him." In the sunlight of His Father's countenance, Jesus "increased in wisdom and stature, and in favor with God and man." Luke 2:52. His mind was active and penetrating, with a thoughtfulness and wisdom beyond His years. The powers of mind and body developed gradually, in keeping with the laws of childhood.

As a child, Jesus manifested a loveliness of disposition, a patience that nothing could disturb, and a truthfulness that would never sacrifice integrity. In principle firm as a rock, His life revealed the grace of unselfish courtesy.

The mother of Jesus watched the unfolding of His powers, and sought to encourage that bright, receptive mind. Through the Holy Spirit she received wisdom to cooperate with heavenly agencies in the development of this child who could claim only God as His Father.

In the days of Christ the religious instruction of the young had become formal. Tradition had in a great degree supplanted the Scriptures. The mind was crowded with material that would not be recognized in the higher school of the courts above. Students found no quiet hours to spend with God, to hear His voice speaking to the heart. They turned away from the

This chapter is based on Luke 2:39, 40.

Source of wisdom. That which was regarded as "superior" education was the greatest hindrance to real development of the youth. Their minds became cramped and narrow.

The child Jesus did not receive instruction in the synagogue schools. From His mother and the scrolls of the prophets, He learned of heavenly things. As He advanced to youth, He did not seek the schools of the rabbis. He needed not the education to be obtained from such sources. His intimate acquaintance with the Scriptures shows how diligently His early years were given to the study of God's Word.

Nature Supplemented the Bible

Spread out before Him was the great library of God's created works. He who had made all things studied the lessons His own hand had written in earth and sea and sky. He gathered stores of scientific knowledge from nature—from plants, animals, and man. The parables by which, during His ministry, He loved to teach lessons of truth show how He gathered spiritual teaching from nature and the surroundings of His daily life.

As Jesus was trying to understand the reason of things, heavenly beings were His attendants. From the first dawning of intelligence He was constantly growing in spiritual grace and knowledge of truth.

Every child may gain knowledge as Jesus did. As we try to become acquainted with our heavenly Father, angels will draw near, our minds will be strengthened, our characters elevated and refined. We shall become more like our Saviour. And as we behold the beautiful and grand in nature, our affections go out after God. The spirit is awed, the soul invigorated by coming in contact with the Infinite through His works. Communion with God through prayer develops the mental and moral faculties.

While Jesus was a child, He thought and spoke as a child, but no trace of sin marred the image of God within Him. Yet He was not exempt from temptation.

The inhabitants of Nazareth were proverbial for their wickedness. See John 1:46. It was necessary for Jesus to be constantly on guard in order to preserve His purity. He was subject to all the conflicts we have to meet, that He might be an example to us in childhood, youth, and manhood.

From His earliest years Jesus was guarded by heavenly angels, yet His life was one long struggle against the powers of darkness. The prince of darkness left no means untried to ensnare Jesus with temptation.

Jesus was familiar with poverty, self-denial, and privation. This experience was a safeguard to Him. No aimless hours opened the way for corrupting associations. Neither gain nor pleasure, applause nor censure, could induce Him to consent to a wrong act. He was wise to discern evil, and strong to resist it. Christ, the only sinless One who ever dwelt on earth, for nearly thirty years lived among the wicked inhabitants of Nazareth. This fact is a rebuke to those who think themselves dependent upon place, fortune, or prosperity, to live a blameless life.

As a Carpenter, Christ Honored Work

Jesus had been the Commander of heaven, and angels had delighted to fulfill His word; now He was a willing servant, a loving, obedient son, working in the carpenter's shop with Joseph. He did not employ divine power to lessen His burdens or lighten His toil. He used His physical powers in such a way as to keep in health, that He might do the best work.

He was not willing to be defective, even in handling tools. He was perfect as a workman, as He was perfect in character. By example He taught that work should be performed with exactness and thoroughness and that labor is honorable. God appointed work as a blessing, and only the diligent worker finds the true glory and joy of life. The approval of God rests on children and youth who take their part in the duties of the household, sharing the burdens of father and mother.

Throughout His life Jesus was a constant worker. After He entered on His public ministry, He said, "I must work the works of Him that sent Me, while it is day: the night cometh, when no man can work." John 9:4. Jesus did not shirk care and responsibility, as do many who profess to be His followers. Because they seek to evade this discipline, many are weak, inefficient, nerveless, and almost useless when difficulties are met. The positiveness and strength of character manifested in Christ are to be developed in us, through the same discipline He endured. The grace He received is for us.

Our Saviour shared the lot of the poor. Those who have a true conception of His life will never feel that the rich are to be honored above the worthy poor.

A Cheerful Singer

Often Jesus expressed the gladness of His heart by singing psalms and heavenly songs. Often the dwellers in Nazareth heard His voice raised in praise and song. As his companions complained of weariness, they were cheered by the sweet melody from His lips.

Through those secluded years at Nazareth, His life flowed out in currents of sympathy and tenderness. The aged, the sorrowing, the sin-burdened, children at play, little creatures of the groves, the patient beasts of burden—all were happier for His presence. He whose word upheld the worlds would stoop to relieve a wounded bird. There was nothing beneath His notice, nothing to which He disdained to minister.

Thus He grew in wisdom and stature, in favor with God and man. He showed Himself capable of sympathizing with all. The atmosphere of hope and courage that surrounded Him made Him a blessing in every home. Often on the Sabbath day He was called on to read the lesson from the prophets, and the hearts of the hearers thrilled as new light shone out from the sacred text.

Yet during all the years at Nazareth, He made no exhibition of miraculous power. He assumed no titles. His quiet and simple life teaches an important lesson: the more free the life of the child from artificial excitement, and the more in harmony with nature, the more favorable is it to physical and mental vigor and spiritual strength.

Jesus is our example. In His home life He is the pattern for all children and youth. The Saviour condescended to poverty, that He might teach how closely we in a humble lot may walk with God. His work began in consecrating the lowly trade of the craftsmen who toil for their daily bread.

He was doing God's service just as much when laboring at the carpenter's bench as when working miracles for the multitude. Every youth who follows Christ's example of faithfulness and obedience in His lowly home may also claim these words spoken by the Father: "Behold My Servant, whom I uphold; Mine Elect, in whom My soul delighteth." Isaiah 42:1.

8 / The Passover Visit

Among the Jews the twelfth year was the dividing line between childhood and youth. In accordance with this custom, Jesus made the Passover visit to Jerusalem with Joseph and Mary when He reached the required age.

The journey from Galilee occupied several days, and travelers united in large companies for companionship and protection. The women and aged men rode on oxen or asses over the steep, rocky roads. The stronger men and youth journeyed on foot. The whole land was bright with flowers, and glad with the song of birds. Along the way, fathers and mothers recounted to their children the wonders that God had wrought for His people in ages past, and beguiled their journey with song and music.

Observance of the Passover began with the birth of the Hebrew nation. On the last night of their bondage in Egypt, God directed the Hebrews to gather their families within their own dwellings. Having sprinkled the doorposts with the blood of the slain lamb, they were to eat the lamb, roasted, with unleavened bread and bitter herbs. "It is the Lord's passover." Exodus 12:11. At midnight all the firstborn of the Egyptians were slain. Then the Hebrews went out from Egypt an independent nation. From generation to generation the story of this wonderful deliverance was to be repeated.

The Passover was followed by the seven days' feast of unleavened bread. All the ceremonies of the feast were types of the work of Christ. The slain lamb, the

This chapter is based on Luke 2:41-51.

unleavened bread, the sheaf of first fruits, represented the Saviour. But with most of the people in the days of Christ, this feast had degenerated into formalism. What was its significance to the Son of God!

For the first time the child Jesus looked upon the temple. He saw the white-robed priests performing their solemn ministry, the bleeding victim on the altar of sacrifice. He witnessed the impressive rites of the paschal service. Day by day He saw their meaning more clearly. Every act seemed bound up with His own life. New impulses were awakening within Him. Silent and absorbed, He seemed to be studying out a great problem. The mystery of His mission was opening to the Saviour.

Rapt in contemplation of these scenes, when the paschal services ended, He lingered in the temple courts, and when the worshipers departed from Jerusalem, He was left behind.

In this visit the parents of Jesus wished to bring Him in connection with the great teachers in Israel. They hoped He might be led to reverence the learned rabbis, and give more heed to their requirements. But Jesus in the temple had been taught by God. That which He had received, He began at once to impart.

An apartment connected with the temple was devoted to a sacred school. Here the child Jesus came, seating Himself at the feet of the learned rabbis. As one seeking for wisdom, He questioned these teachers in regard to the prophecies and to events then taking place that pointed to the advent of the Messiah.

His questions suggested deep truths, long obscured, which were vital to salvation. While showing how narrow and superficial was the wisdom of the wise men, every question placed truth in a new aspect. The rabbis spoke of the wonderful elevation which the Messiah's coming would bring to the Jews; but Jesus presented the prophecy of Isaiah and asked the meaning of those scriptures that point to the suffering and death of the Lamb of God. See Isaiah 53.

The doctors turned on Him with questions and were amazed at His answers. With the humility of a child He gave the words of Scripture a depth of meaning that the wise men had not conceived of. If followed, the lines of truth He pointed out would have worked a reformation in the religion of the day; and when Jesus began His ministry, many would have been prepared to receive Him.

In this thoughtful Galilean boy the rabbis discerned great promise. They wanted to have charge of His education; a mind so original must be brought under their molding.

The words of Jesus moved their hearts as they had never before been moved by words from human lips. God was seeking to give light to those leaders. If Jesus had appeared to be trying to teach them, they would have disdained to listen. But they flattered themselves that they were teaching Him—or at least testing His knowledge of the Scriptures. The youthful modesty and grace of Jesus disarmed their prejudices. Their minds opened to the Word of God, and the Holy Spirit spoke to their hearts.

They could see that their expectation of the Messiah was not sustained by prophecy, but they would not admit that they had misapprehended the Scriptures they claimed to teach.

His Parents Become Worried

Meanwhile, in the departure from Jerusalem Joseph and Mary had lost sight of Jesus. The pleasure of traveling with friends absorbed their attention, and they did not notice His absence till night came on. Then they missed the helpful hand of their child. Supposing Him to be with their company, they had felt no anxiety. But now their fears were roused. Shuddering, they remembered how Herod had tried to destroy Him in His infancy. Dark forebodings filled their hearts.

Returning to Jerusalem, they pursued their search. The next day, in the temple, a familiar voice arrested their attention. They could not mistake it—so serious and earnest, yet so full of melody. In the school of the rabbis they found Jesus.

When He was with them again, His mother said, in words that implied reproof, "Son, why hast Thou thus dealt with us? Behold, Thy father and I have sought Thee sorrowing."

"How is it that ye sought Me?" answered Jesus. "Wist ye not that I must be about My Father's business?" As they seemed not to understand, He pointed upward. On His face was a light. Divinity was flashing through humanity. They had listened to what was passing between Him and the rabbis and were astonished at His questions and answers.

Jesus was engaged in the work He had come into the world to do; but Joseph and Mary had neglected theirs. God had shown them high honor in committing to them His Son. But for an entire day they had lost sight of Him, and when their anxiety was relieved, they had not censured themselves but had blamed Him.

It was natural for the parents of Jesus to look upon Him as their own child. His life in many respects was like that of other children, and it was difficult to realize He was the Son of God. The gentle reproof which His words conveyed were designed to impress them with the sacredness of their trust.

In His answer to His mother Jesus showed for the first time that He understood His relation to God. Mary did not understand His words, but she knew He had disclaimed kinship to Joseph and had declared His Sonship to God.

From Jerusalem Jesus returned home with His earthly parents and aided them in their life of toil. For eighteen years He acknowledged the tie that bound Him to the home at Nazareth, and performed the duties of a son, a brother, a friend, and a citizen.

Jesus wished to return from Jerusalem in quietness, with those who knew the secret of His life. By the paschal service God was seeking to remind His people of His wonderful work in their deliverance from Egypt. In this work He desired them to see a promise of deliverance from sin. The blood of Christ was to save their souls. God desired that they should be led to prayerful study in regard to Christ's mission. But as the multitudes left Jerusalem, the excitement of travel and social intercourse often absorbed their attention, and the service they had witnessed was forgotten. The Saviour was not attracted to their company.

Jesus Helps His Mother

Returning from Jerusalem, Jesus hoped to direct Joseph and Mary to the prophecies of the suffering Saviour. On Calvary He sought to lighten His mother's grief; He was thinking of her now. Mary was to witness His last agony, and Jesus desired her to understand His mission, that she might endure when the sword should pierce through her soul. How much better she could have borne the anguish of His death if she had understood the scriptures to which He was now trying to turn her thoughts!

By one day's neglect Joseph and Mary lost the Saviour; but it cost them three days of anxious search to find Him. So with us. By idle talk, evilspeaking, or neglect of prayer, we may in one day lose the Saviour's presence, and it may take many days to find Him and regain the peace we have lost.

We should take heed lest we forget Jesus and pass along unmindful that He is not with us. Absorbed in worldly things, we separate ourselves from Him and from the heavenly angels. These holy beings cannot remain where the Saviour's presence is not desired, and His absence is not marked.

Many attend religious services and are refreshed by the Word of God, but through neglect of meditation and prayer, they lose the blessing, and find themselves more destitute than before they received it. Often they feel that God has dealt hardly with them. They do not see that the fault is their own. By separating themselves from Jesus, they have shut away the light of His presence.

It would be well for us to spend a thoughtful hour each day in contemplation of the life of Christ. We should take it point by point, and let the imagination grasp each scene, especially the closing ones. Thus our confidence in Him will be more constant, our love will be quickened, and we shall be imbued with His spirit. Beholding the beauty of His character, we shall be "changed into the same image from glory to glory." 2 Corinthians 3:18.

9 / Christ's Problems as a Child

Under synagogue teachers, Jewish youth were instructed in the countless regulations which as orthodox Israelites they were expected to observe. But Jesus did not interest Himself in these. From childhood He acted independently of rabbinical laws. The Scriptures were His constant study, and the words, "Thus saith the Lord," were ever on His lips.

He saw that men were departing from the Word of God, and exacting rites that possessed no virtue. In their faithless services they found no peace. They did not know the freedom of spirit that comes by serving God in truth. Though Jesus could not sanction the mingling of human requirements with divine precepts, He did not attack the precepts or practices of the learned teachers. When reproved for His own simple habits, He presented the Word of God in justification of His conduct.

Jesus tried to please those with whom He came in contact. Because He was so gentle and unobtrusive, the scribes and elders supposed He would be easily influenced by their teaching. But He asked for their authority in Holy Writ. He would hear every word that proceeds from the mouth of God, but could not obey the inventions of men. Jesus seemed to know the Scriptures from beginning to end, and He presented them in their true import. The rabbis claimed it was their office to explain them and His place to accept their interpretation.

They knew that no authority could be found in Scripture for their traditions. Yet they were angry because Jesus did not obey their dictates. Failing to convince Him, they sought Joseph and Mary and set before them His noncompliance. Thus He suffered rebuke and censure.

At a very early age, Jesus began to act for Himself in the formation of character. Not even love for His parents could turn Him from obedience to God's Word. But the influence of the rabbis made His life bitter. He had to learn the hard lesson of silence and patient endurance.

His brothers, as the sons of Joseph were called, sided with the rabbis. They regarded the precepts of men more highly than the Word of God, and condemned Jesus' strict obedience to the law of God as stubbornness. Surprised at the knowledge He showed in answering the rabbis, they could not but see that He was an instructor to them. They recognized that His education was of a higher type than their own, but they did not discern that He had access to a source of knowledge of which they were ignorant.

How Jesus Respected All People Alike

Christ found religion fenced in by high walls of seclusion, as too sacred a matter for everyday life. These walls He overthrew. Instead of secluding Himself in a hermit's cell, in order to show His heavenly character, He labored earnestly for humanity. He taught that religion is not meant only for set times and special occasions. This was a rebuke to the Pharisees. It showed that their morbid devotion to personal interest was far from true godliness. This roused their enmity, so they tried to enforce conformity to their regulations.

Jesus had little money to give, but He often denied Himself food in order to relieve those more needy than He. When His brothers spoke harshly to poor, degraded beings, Jesus spoke to them words of encouragement. To those in need He would give a cup of cold water and quietly place His own meal in their hands.

All this displeased His brothers. Being older, they felt He should be under their dictation. They charged Him with thinking Himself superior to them and setting Himself above the teachers, priests, and rulers. Often they tried to intimidate Him, but He passed on, making the Scriptures His guide.

Jesus' Problems With His Family

Jesus' brothers were jealous of Him and manifested decided unbelief and contempt. They could not understand His conduct. Great contradictions presented themselves in Jesus. He was the divine Son of God, and yet a helpless child. As Creator, the earth was His possession, yet poverty marked His life experience. He did not strive for worldly greatness, and in even the lowliest position He was content. This angered His brothers. They could not account for His constant serenity under trial and deprivation.

Jesus was misunderstood by His brothers because He was not like them. In looking to men they had turned away from God, and they had not His power in their lives. The forms of religion they observed could not transform the character. The example of Jesus was to them a continual irritation. He hated sin and could not witness a wrong act without pain impossible to disguise. Because the life of Jesus condemned evil, He was opposed; His unselfishness and integrity were commented on with a sneer. His forbearance and kindness were termed cowardice.

Of the bitterness that falls to the lot of humanity, there was no part Christ did not taste. Some cast contempt on Him because of His birth. Even in childhood He had to meet scornful looks and evil whisperings. If He had responded by an impatient word or look or even one wrong act, He would have failed of being a perfect example. Thus He would have failed of carrying out the plan for our redemption. Had He even admitted that there could be an excuse for sin, Satan would have triumphed, and the world would have been lost. Often He was accused of cowardice for refusing to unite with His brothers in some forbidden act, but His answer was, It is written, "The fear of the Lord, that is wisdom; and to depart from evil is understanding." Job 28:28.

Some felt at peace in His presence; but many avoided Him, rebuked by His stainless life. Young companions enjoyed His presence, but they were impatient at His scruples and pronounced Him narrow and straitlaced. Jesus answered, It is written, "How can a young man keep his way pure? By guarding it according to Thy word. . . . I have laid up Thy word in my heart, that I might not sin against Thee." Psalm 119:9, 11, RSV.

Often He was asked, Why are you bent on being so different from us all? It is written, He said, "Blessed are those who keep His testimonies, who . . . do no wrong, but walk in His ways!" Psalm 119:2, 3, RSV.

When questioned why He did not join in the frolics of the youth of Nazareth, He said, It is written, "I will delight Myself in Thy statutes: I will not forget Thy word." Psalm 119:16.

Jesus did not contend for His rights. He did not retaliate when roughly used, but bore insult patiently. Again and again He was asked, Why do You submit to such despiteful usage, even from Your brothers? It is written, He said, "My son, do not forget My teaching, but let your heart keep My commandments. . . . Let not loyalty and faithfulness forsake you; bind them about your neck, write them on the tablet of your heart. So you will find favor and good repute in the sight of God and man." Proverbs 3:1-4, RSV.

Why He Had to Be Different

Jesus' course of action was a mystery to His parents. He seemed as one set apart. His hours of happiness were found when alone with nature and with God. Early morning often found Him in some secluded place, meditating, searching the Scriptures, or in prayer. From these quiet hours He would return home to take up His duties again.

Mary believed that the holy child born of her was the Messiah, yet she dared not express her faith. Throughout His life she was a partaker in His sufferings. She witnessed with sorrow the trials brought upon Him in His childhood and youth. By her vindication of what she knew to be right in His conduct, she herself was brought into trying positions. She looked upon the associations of the home and the mother's watchcare over her children as vital in the formation of character. The sons and daughters of Joseph knew this, and by appealing to her anxiety tried to correct the practices of Jesus according to their standard.

Mary often remonstrated with Jesus and urged Him to conform to the usages of the rabbis. But He could not be persuaded to change His habits of contemplating the works of God and alleviating suffering. When the priests and teachers required her aid in controlling Jesus, she was greatly troubled; but peace came to her heart as He presented Scripture upholding His practices.

At times she wavered between Jesus and His brothers, who did not believe He was the Sent of God; but evidence was abundant that His was a divine character. His life was as leaven working amid the elements of society. Undefiled, He walked among the thoughtless, the rude, the uncourteous, amid unjust publicans, reckless prodigals, unrighteous Samaritans, heathen soldiers, rough peasants, and the mixed multitude. He spoke a word of sympathy as He saw men weary yet compelled to bear heavy burdens. He repeated to them lessons He had learned from nature of the love and goodness of God.

He taught all to look on themselves as endowed with precious talents. By His own example He taught that every moment of time is to be cherished as a treasure and employed for holy purposes. He passed by no human being as worthless, but sought to inspire with hope the most rough and unpromising, assuring them that they might attain such a character as would make them manifest as the children of God. Often He met those who had no power to break from Satan's snare. To such, discouraged, sick, tempted, and fallen, Jesus would speak words of tenderest pity.

Others He met were fighting a hand-to-hand battle with the adversary of souls. These He encouraged to persevere, for angels of God were on their side and would give them victory. Those whom He helped were convinced that here was One in whom they could trust with perfect confidence.

Jesus was interested in every phase of suffering, and to every sufferer He brought relief, His kind words having a soothing balm. None could say He had worked a miracle, but virtue—the healing power of love—went out from Him. Thus in an unobtrusive way He worked for people from His very childhood.

Yet through childhood, youth, and manhood, Jesus walked alone. In purity and faithfulness, there was none with Him. See Isaiah 63:3. He knew that unless there was a decided change in the principles and purposes of the human race, all would be lost. Filled with intense purpose, He carried out the design of His life that He Himself should be the light of men.

10 / The Voice in the Wilderness

From among the faithful in Israel the forerunner of Christ arose. The aged priest Zacharias and his wife Elisabeth were "both righteous before God," and in their quiet lives the light of faith shone out like a star amid the darkness. To this godly pair was given the promise of a son, who should "go before the face of the Lord to prepare His ways."

Zacharias had gone to Jerusalem to minister for one week in the temple. Standing before the golden altar in the holy place of the sanctuary, suddenly he became conscious of an angel of the Lord "standing on the right side of the altar." For years he had prayed for the coming of the Redeemer; now these prayers were about to be answered.

He was greeted with the joyful assurance: "Fear not, Zacharias: for thy prayer is heard; and thy wife Elisabeth shall bear thee a son, and thou shalt call his name John. . . . He shall be great in the sight of the Lord, and shall drink neither wine nor strong drink; and he shall be filled with the Holy Ghost. . . . And he shall go before Him in the spirit and power of Elias, to turn the hearts of the fathers to the children, and the disobedient to the wisdom of the just, to make ready a people prepared for the Lord. And Zacharias said unto the angel, Whereby shall I know this? for I am an old man, and my wife well stricken in years."

For a moment the aged priest forgot that what God promises, He is able to perform. What a contrast between his unbelief and the faith of Mary, whose answer

This chapter is based on Luke 1:5-23, 57-80; 3:1-18; Matthew 3:1-12; Mark 1:1-8.

to the angel's announcement was, "Behold I am the handmaid of the Lord; let it be to me according to your word." Luke 1:38, RSV.

The birth of a son to Zacharias, like the birth of the child of Abraham, and that of Mary, was to teach a great truth: that which we cannot do will be wrought by the power of God in every believing soul. Through faith the child of promise was given. Through faith spiritual life is begotten, and we are enabled to do the works of righteousness.

Five hundred years before, the angel Gabriel had made known to Daniel the prophetic period which was to extend to the coming of Christ. The knowledge that the end of this period was near had moved Zacharias to pray for the Messiah's advent. Now, the very same angel through whom the prophecy was given had come to announce its fulfillment.

Zacharias Doubted

Zacharias had expressed doubt of the angel's words. He was not to speak again until they were fulfilled. "Behold, you will be silent and unable to speak until the day that these things come to pass, because you did not believe my words, which will be fulfilled in their time." RSV. It was the duty of the priest in this service to pray for pardon of sins and for the coming of the Messiah; but when Zacharias attempted to do this, he could not utter a word. As he came forth from the holy place, his face was shining with the glory of God, and the people "perceived that he had seen a vision in the temple." Zacharias "remained dumb" but through "signs" (RSV) communicated to them what he had seen and heard.

Soon after the birth of the promised child, the father's tongue was loosed. "And all these things were talked about through all the hill country of Judea; and all who heard them laid them up in their hearts, saying, 'What then will this child be?' " RSV. All this called attention to the Messiah's coming.

The Holy Spirit rested upon Zacharias and he proph- esied of the mission of his son:

> Thou, child, shalt be called the prophet of
>   the Highest:
> For thou shalt go before the face of the Lord to
>   prepare His ways; . . .
> To give knowledge of salvation unto His people
> By the remission of their sins.

"And the child grew, and waxed strong in spirit, and was in the deserts till the day of his showing unto Israel." God had called the son of Zacharias to the greatest work ever committed to men. And the Spirit of God would be with him if he heeded the instruction of the angel.

John was to bring to men the light of God. He must impress them with their need of His righteousness. Such a messenger must be holy, a temple for the indwelling Spirit of God. He must have a sound physical constitution, and mental and spiritual strength. Therefore it would be necessary for him to control the appetites and passions.

In the time of John the Baptist, greed for riches and the love of luxury and display had become widespread. Sensuous pleasures, feasting and drinking, were causing physical degeneracy, benumbing spiritual perceptions, and lessening the sensibility to sin. John was to stand as a reformer. By his abstemious life and plain dress he was to rebuke the excesses of his time. Hence the lesson of temperance given to his parents by an angel from the throne of heaven.

In childhood and youth the power of self-control should be acquired. Habits established in early years decide whether a man will be victorious or vanquished in the battle of life. Youth, the sowing time, determines the character of the harvest, for this life and for the life to come.

In preparing the way for Christ's first advent John

was a representative of those who prepare a people for our Lord's second coming. The world is given to self indulgence. Errors and fables abound. All who would perfect holiness in the fear of God must learn temperance and self-control. See 2 Corinthians 7:1. The appetites and passions must be held in subjection to the higher powers of the mind. This self-discipline is essential to that mental strength and spiritual insight which enable us to understand and practice the truths of God's Word.

John's Unusual Education

In the natural order of things the son of Zacharias would have been educated in the rabbinical schools. But since this would have unfitted him for his work, God called him to the desert, that he might learn of nature and nature's God.

John found his home in the barren hills, wild ravines, and rocky caves. Here his surroundings were favorable to habits of simplicity and self-denial. Here he could study the lessons of nature, of revelation, and of Providence. From childhood his mission had been kept before him by his God-fearing parents, and he had accepted the holy trust. The solitude of the desert was a welcome escape from society in which unbelief and impurity had become well-nigh all-pervading. He shrank from constant contact with sin lest he lose the sense of its exceeding sinfulness.

But the life of John was not spent in ascetic gloom or selfish isolation. From time to time he went forth to mingle with men, ever an interested observer of what was passing in the world. Illuminated by the divine Spirit he studied men to understand how to reach their hearts with the message of heaven. The burden of his mission was on him. By meditation and prayer he sought to gird up his soul for the lifework before him.

Although in the wilderness, he was not exempt from temptation. He was assailed by the tempter, but his spiritual perceptions were clear, and through the Holy

Spirit he was able to detect and resist Satan's approaches.

Like Moses amid the mountains of Midian, John was shut in by God's presence. The gloomy and terrible aspect of nature in his wilderness home vividly pictured the condition of Israel. The vineyard of the Lord had become a desolate waste. But above, the dark clouds were arched by the rainbow of promise.

Alone in the silent night he read God's promise to Abraham of a seed numberless as the stars. The light of dawn told of Him who should be as "the light of the morning, when the sun riseth, even a morning without clouds." 2 Samuel 23:4. And in the brightness of noontide he saw the splendor when "the glory of the Lord shall be revealed, and all flesh shall see it together." Isaiah 40:5.

With awed yet exultant spirit he searched in the prophetic scrolls the revelations of the Messiah's coming. Shiloh was to appear before a king should cease to reign on David's throne. Now the time had come. A Roman ruler sat in the palace on Mount Zion. By the sure word of the Lord, already the Christ was born.

Isaiah's Portrayals Studied

Isaiah's rapt portrayals of the Messiah's glory were his study by day and by night. See Isaiah 11:4; 32:2; 62:4. The heart of the lonely exile was filled with the glorious vision. He looked upon the King in His beauty, and self was forgotten. He beheld the majesty of holiness and felt himself to be inefficient and unworthy. He was ready to go forth as Heaven's messenger, unawed by the human, because he had looked upon the Divine. He could stand fearless in the presence of earthly monarchs, because he had bowed low before the King of kings.

John did not fully understand the nature of the Messiah's kingdom, but the coming of a King in righteousness and the establishment of Israel as a holy nation, was the great object of his hope.

He saw his people self-satisfied and asleep in their sins. The message God had given him was to startle them from their lethargy. Before the seed of the gospel could find lodgment, the soil of the heart must be broken up. Before they would seek healing from Jesus, they must be awakened to their danger from the wounds of sin.

God does not send messengers to lull the unsanctified into fatal security. He lays heavy burdens on the conscience of the wrongdoer and pierces the soul with arrows of conviction. Ministering angels present the fearful judgments of God to deepen the sense of need. Then the hand that has humbled in the dust, lifts up the penitent.

On the Edge of Revolution

When the ministry of John began, the nation was verging on revolution. At the removal of Archelaus, Judea had been brought directly under the control of Rome. The tyranny and extortion of the Roman governors, and their efforts to introduce heathen symbols and customs kindled revolt, which had been quenched in the blood of thousands of the bravest of Israel.

Amid discord and strife, a voice was heard from the wilderness, startling and stern yet full of hope: "Repent ye; for the kingdom of heaven is at hand." With a new, strange power it moved the people. Here was an announcement that the coming of Christ was at hand. With the spirit and power of Elijah, John denounced the national corruption and rebuked the prevailing sins. His words were pointed and convincing. The nation was stirred. Multitudes flocked to the wilderness.

John called the people to repentance. As a symbol of cleansing from sin, he baptized them in the waters of the Jordan. Thus he declared that those who claimed to be the chosen people of God were defiled by sin. Without purification of heart they could have no part in the Messiah's kingdom.

Princes and rabbis, soldiers, publicans, and peasants

came to hear the prophet. Many were brought to repentance and received baptism in order to participate in the kingdom he announced.

Many scribes and Pharisees came confessing their sins and asking for baptism. They had led the people to entertain a high opinion of their piety; now the guilty secrets of their lives were unveiled. But John was impressed that many of these men had no real conviction of sin. They were timeservers. As friends of the prophet, they hoped to find favor with the coming Prince. And by receiving baptism they thought to strengthen their influence with the people.

John's Sharp Rebuke to Hypocrites

John met them with the scathing inquiry, "You brood of vipers! Who warned you to flee from the wrath to come? Bear fruit that befits repentance." RSV. Because the Jews had separated themselves from God, they were suffering under His judgments. This was the cause of their bondage to a heathen nation. Because in times past the Lord had shown them great favor, they excused their sins. They flattered themselves that they were better than other men and entitled to His blessings.

John declared to the teachers of Israel that their pride, selfishness, and cruelty showed them to be a deadly curse to the people. In view of the light they had received from God, they were even worse than the heathen. God was not dependent on them for fulfilling His purpose. He could call others to His service.

"And now," said the prophet, "the ax is laid unto the root of the trees: therefore every tree which bringeth not forth good fruit is hewn down, and cast into the fire." If the fruit is worthless, the name cannot save the tree from destruction. John declared to the Jews that if their life and character were not in harmony with God's law, they were not His people.

All who became subjects of Christ's kingdom, he said, would give evidence of faith and repentance.

Kindness and fidelity would be seen in their lives. They would minister to the needy, shield the defenseless, and give an example of virtue and compassion.

"I baptize you with water for repentance, but He who is coming after me is mightier than I, whose sandals I am not worthy to carry; He will baptize you with the Holy Spirit and with fire." RSV. Isaiah had declared that the Lord would cleanse His people "by the spirit of judgment, and by the spirit of burning." Isaiah 4:4.

In all who submit to His power, the Spirit of God will consume sin. See Hebrews 12:29. But if men cling to sin, then the glory of God, which destroys sin, must destroy them. At the second advent of Christ the wicked shall be consumed "with the Spirit of His mouth," and destroyed "with the brightness of His coming." 2 Thessalonians 2:8. The glory of God which imparts life to the righteous will slay the wicked.

In the time of John the Baptist, Christ was about to appear as the revealer of the character of God. His very presence would make manifest to men their sin. Only as they were willing to be purged from sin could they enter into fellowship with Him.

Thus the Baptist declared God's message to Israel. Many gave heed and sacrificed all in order to obey. Not a few cherished the hope that he might be the Messiah. But as John saw the people turning to him, he sought every opportunity of directing their faith to Him who was to come.

Jesus asked John to baptize Him, not because He was a sinner, but because He identified Himself with sinners and wanted to take the steps we must take.

11 / The Baptism of Jesus

The message of the wilderness prophet reached the peasants in the remote hill towns, and the fisher folk by the sea, and in these simple, earnest hearts found its truest response. In Nazareth it was told in the carpentry shop that had been Joseph's, and One recognized the call. His time had come. He bade farewell to His mother and followed His countrymen who were flocking to the Jordan.

Jesus and John the Baptist were cousins, yet they had had no direct acquaintance with each other. Providence had ordered this. No occasion was to be given for the charge that they had conspired together to support each other's claims.

John was acquainted with the events that had marked the birth of Jesus, with the visit to Jerusalem in His boyhood and His sinless life. He believed Him to be the Messiah, but the fact that Jesus had remained in obscurity, giving no special evidence of His mission, gave occasion for doubt. The Baptist, however, waited in faith. It had been revealed to him that the Messiah would seek baptism at his hands, and that a sign of His divine character should then be given.

When Jesus came to be baptized, John recognized in Him a purity of character never before perceived in any man. His very presence was awe-inspiring. This was in harmony with what had been revealed to John regarding the Messiah. Yet how could he, a sinner, baptize the Sinless One? Why should He who needed no repentance submit to a rite that was a confession of guilt to be washed away?

This chapter is based on Matthew 3:13-17; Mark 1:9-11; Luke 3:21, 22.

As Jesus asked for baptism, John drew back, exclaiming, " 'I need to be baptized by You, and do You come to me?' But Jesus answered him, 'Let it be so now; for thus it is fitting for us to fulfill all righteousness.' Then he consented. And when Jesus was baptized, He went up immediately from the water, and behold, the heavens were opened and He saw the Spirit of God descending like a dove, and alighting on Him." RSV.

Sinless Christ Baptized

Jesus did not receive baptism as a confession of guilt on His own account. He identified Himself with sinners, taking the steps that we are to take and doing the work that we must do. His life of suffering and patient endurance after His baptism was also an example to us.

Coming up out of the water, Jesus bowed in prayer on the river bank. He was now entering the conflict of His life. Though He was the Prince of Peace, His coming must be as the unsheathing of a sword. The kingdom He had come to establish was the opposite of that which the Jews desired. He would be looked upon as the enemy and destroyer of the ritual and economy of Israel, condemned as a transgressor, and denounced as Beelzebub. No one on earth had understood Him, and He must still walk alone. His mother and brothers did not comprehend His mission. Even His disciples did not understand Him.

As one with us, He must bear our guilt and woe. The Sinless One must feel the shame of sin. The peace lover must dwell with strife; the truth must abide with falsehood, purity with vileness. Every sin, every discord, every defiling lust was torture to His spirit.

Alone He must tread the path. On Him who had accepted the weakness of humanity the redemption of the world must rest. He saw and felt it all, but His purpose remained steadfast.

The Saviour poured out His soul in prayer. He knew

how sin had hardened the hearts of men, how difficult it would be for them to discern His mission and accept salvation. He pleaded with the Father for power to overcome their unbelief, to break the fetters with which Satan had enthralled them, and in their behalf to conquer the destroyer.

Never before had angels listened to such a prayer. The Father Himself would answer the petition of His Son. The heavens were opened, and upon the Saviour's head descended a dovelike form of purest light.

Few at the Jordan except John discerned the heavenly vision. Yet the solemnity of the divine Presence rested on the assembly. Christ's upturned face was glorified as they had never before seen the face of man. From the open heavens a voice was heard: "This is My beloved Son, in whom I am well pleased."

Endorsed by Heaven

These words were given to inspire faith in those who witnessed the scene and to strengthen the Saviour for His mission. Notwithstanding that the sins of a guilty world were laid on Christ, notwithstanding the humiliation of taking upon Himself our fallen nature, the voice from heaven declared Him to be the Son of the Eternal.

John had been deeply moved. As the glory of God encircled Jesus and the voice from heaven was heard, John knew that it was the world's Redeemer whom he had baptized. With outstretched hand pointing to Jesus, he cried, "Behold the Lamb of God, which taketh away the sin of the world." John 1:29.

None among the hearers, not even the speaker himself, discerned the import of the words, "the Lamb of God." Many of the people of Israel regarded the sacrificial offerings much as the heathen looked on their sacrifices—gifts to propitiate the Deity. God desired to teach them that from His own love comes the gift which reconciles them to Himself.

The word spoken to Jesus, "This is My beloved Son,

in whom I am well pleased,'' embraces humanity. With all our sins and weaknesses, we are not cast aside as worthless. ''He hath made us accepted in the Beloved.'' Ephesians 1:6. The glory that rested on Christ is a pledge of the love of God for us. It tells us of the power of prayer—how the human voice may reach the ear of God, and our petitions find acceptance in the courts of heaven. By sin, earth was cut off from heaven, but Jesus has connected it again with the sphere of glory. The light which fell on the head of our Saviour will fall on us as we pray for help to resist temptation. The voice which spoke to Jesus says to every believing soul, This is My beloved child, in whom I am well pleased.

Our Redeemer has opened the way so that the most sinful, oppressed, and despised, may find access to the Father. All may have a home in the mansions which Jesus has gone to prepare.

12 / The Wilderness Temptation

"Then Jesus was led up by the Spirit into the wilderness to be tempted by the devil. And He fasted forty days and forty nights, and afterward He was hungry." RSV.

Jesus did not invite temptation. He went to the wilderness to be alone, to contemplate His mission. By fasting and prayer He was to brace Himself for the bloodstained path He must travel. But Satan thought this the best time to approach Him.

Mighty issues were at stake. Satan claimed the earth as his and styled himself "the prince of this world." He declared that men had chosen him as their sovereign; through men he held dominion over the world. Christ had come to disprove Satan's claim. As the Son of man, Christ would stand loyal to God. Thus it would be shown that Satan had not gained complete control of the human race, and that his claim to the world was false. All who desired deliverance from his power would be set free.

Satan had known that he did not hold absolute sway over the world. There was seen in men a power that withstood his dominion. See Genesis 3:15. In the sacrifices offered by Adam and his sons he discerned a symbol of communion between earth and heaven. He set himself to intercept this communion. He misrepresented God and misinterpreted the rites that pointed to the Saviour. Men were led to fear God as one who delighted in their destruction. The sacrifices that should have revealed His love were offered only to appease His wrath.

This chapter is based on Matthew 4:1-11; Mark 1:12, 13; Luke 4:1-13.

When God's Written Word was given, Satan studied the prophecies. From generation to generation he worked to blind the people that they might reject Christ at His coming.

At the birth of Jesus, Satan knew that One had come to dispute his dominion. That the Son of God should come to this earth as a man filled him with apprehension. His selfish soul could not understand such love. Since he had lost heaven, he was determined to cause others to share his fall. He would cause them to undervalue heavenly things, and set the heart upon things of earth.

Satan Determined to Prevail

From the time when the Commander of heaven was a babe in Bethlehem, He was continually assailed by the evil one. In the councils of Satan it was determined that He should be overcome.

The forces of evil were set upon His track to engage in warfare against Him, and if possible to prevail over Him.

At the Saviour's baptism, Satan heard the voice of Jehovah testifying to the divinity of Jesus. Now that Jesus had come "in the likeness of sinful flesh" (Romans 8:3), the Father Himself spoke. He had before communicated with humanity *through* Christ; now He communicated with humanity *in* Christ. Now it was manifest that the connection between God and man had been restored.

Satan saw that he must either conquer or be conquered. All the energies of apostasy were rallied against Christ.

Many look on this conflict between Christ and Satan as having no special bearing on their own life. But within every human heart it is repeated. The enticements Christ resisted were those we find so difficult to withstand. With the weight of the sins of the world upon Him, Christ withstood the test on appetite, on the love of the world, and on that love of display which leads to presumption. These were the temptations that overcame Adam and Eve, and that so readily overcome us.

Satan had pointed to Adam's sin as proof that God's law could not be obeyed. In our humanity, Christ was to redeem Adam's failure. But when Adam was assailed by the tempter, none of the effects of sin were upon him. He stood in the strength of perfect manhood, possessing full vigor of mind and body. Surrounded with the glories of Eden, he was in daily communion with heavenly beings.

It was not thus with Jesus when He entered the wilderness to cope with Satan. For 4000 years the race had been decreasing in physical strength, in mental power, and in moral worth; and Christ took upon Him the infirmities of degenerate humanity. Only thus could He rescue man from the depths of degradation.

He Took All Humanity's Liabilities

Many claim that it was impossible for Christ to be overcome by temptation. Then He could not have been placed in Adam's position, nor have gained the victory that Adam failed to gain. If we have in any sense a more trying conflict than had Christ, then He would not be able to succor us. But our Saviour took humanity, with all its liabilities. He took the nature of man, with the possibility of yielding to temptation. We have nothing to bear which He has not endured.

With Christ, as with the holy pair in Eden, appetite was the ground of the first great temptation. Just where the ruin began, the work of our redemption must begin. "When He had fasted forty days and forty nights, He was afterward an hungred. And when the tempter came to Him, he said, If Thou be the Son of God, command that these stones be made bread."

These first words betrayed his character. "If Thou be the Son of God." Here was the insinuation of distrust. If Jesus should do what Satan suggested, it would be an acceptance of the doubt. Satan sought to instill into the mind of Eve the thought that withholding such beautiful fruit was a contradiction of God's love for man. So now the tempter sought to inspire Christ with his own sentiments. *"If* Thou be the Son of God." In his voice was an expression of utter incredulity. Would God treat His own Son thus, leaving Him in the desert with wild beasts, without food, without companions, without comfort? He insinuated that God never meant His Son to be in such a state as this. *"If* Thou be the Son of God," show Thy power. Command that this stone be made bread.

The Temptation to Doubt

The words from heaven, "This is My beloved Son," were still sounding in the ears of Satan. But he was determined to make Christ disbelieve this testimony. The word of God was Christ's assurance of His divine mission; the word declared His connection with heaven. Satan purposed to cause Him to doubt that word. If Christ's confidence in God could be shaken, Satan knew that he could overcome Jesus. He hoped that under the force of despondency and hunger, Christ would lose faith in His Father and work a miracle in His own behalf. Had He done this, the plan of salvation would have been broken.

Satan made the most of his supposed advantage. One of the most powerful of the angels, he said, had been banished from heaven. The appearance of Jesus indicated that He was that fallen angel, forsaken by God and deserted by man. A divine being would sustain his claim by working a miracle: "If Thou be the Son of God, command this stone that it be made bread." Such an act of creative power, urged the tempter, would be conclusive evidence of divinity. It would bring the controversy to an end.

But the Son of God was not to prove His divinity to Satan. Had Christ complied with the suggestion of the enemy, Satan would still have said, Show me a sign that I may believe you to be the Son of God. And

Christ was not to exercise divine power for His own benefit. He had come to bear trial as we must, leaving us an example. His wonderful works were all for the good of others. Strengthened with the memory of the voice from heaven, Jesus rested in His Father's love.

Jesus met Satan with Scripture. "It is written," He said. The weapon of His warfare was the Word of God. Satan demanded of Christ a miracle. But that which is greater than all miracles, a firm reliance on a "Thus saith the Lord," was a sign that could not be controverted. As Christ held to this position, the tempter could gain no advantage.

In the time of greatest weakness Christ was assailed by the fiercest temptations. Thus Satan has taken advantage of the weakness of humanity. See Numbers 20:1-13; 1 Kings 19:1-14. When one is perplexed or afflicted by poverty or distress, Satan is at hand to tempt, to attack our weak points of character, to shake our confidence in God. Often the tempter comes as he came to Christ, arraying before us our weakness. He hopes to discourage the soul and break our hold on God. But if we would meet him as Jesus did, we would escape many a defeat.

Christ said to the tempter, "Man shall not live by bread alone, but by every word that proceedeth out of the mouth of God." In the wilderness more than fourteen hundred years before, God sent His people a constant supply of manna from heaven. This was to teach them that while they trusted in God and walked in His ways He would not forsake them. By the word of God succor had been given to the Hebrew host, and by the same word it had been given to Jesus. He awaited God's time to bring relief. He would not obtain food by following the suggestions of Satan. It is a less calamity to suffer whatever may befall than to depart in any manner from the will of God.

Often the follower of Christ is brought where it appears that obedience to some plain requirement of God will cut off his means of support. Satan would make him believe he must sacrifice his conscientious convictions. But the only thing on which we can rely is the Word of God. See Matthew 6:33. When we learn the power of His Word, we shall not follow the suggestions of Satan in order to obtain food or save our lives. We shall obey God's command and trust His promise.

In the last great conflict with Satan those loyal to God will see every earthly support cut off. Because they refuse to break His law, they will be forbidden to buy or sell. See Revelation 13:11-17. But to the obedient is given the promise, "He shall dwell on high: his . . . bread shall be given him; his water shall be sure." Isaiah 33:16. When the earth shall be wasted with famine, he shall be fed. See Psalm 37:19.

Intemperance Corrupts Morals

In all ages, temptations appealing to the physical nature have been most effectual in corrupting mankind. Through intemperance, Satan works to destroy the mental and moral powers. Thus it becomes impossible for men to appreciate things of eternal worth. Through sensual indulgence Satan seeks to blot from the soul every trace of likeness to God.

Christ declares that before His second coming the condition of the world will be as in the days before the Flood, and as in Sodom and Gomorrah. To us should come home the lesson of the Saviour's fast. Only by the inexpressible anguish Christ endured can we estimate the evil of unrestrained indulgence. Our only hope of eternal life is through bringing our appetites and passions into subjection to the will of God.

In our own strength it is impossible to deny the clamors of our fallen nature. But by passing over the ground man must travel, our Lord has prepared the way for us to overcome. He would not have us intimidated and discouraged. "Be of good cheer," He says; "I have overcome the world." John 16:33.

Let him who is struggling against the power of appetite look to the Saviour in the wilderness of temptation.

See Him in His agony upon the cross, as He exclaimed, "I thirst." His victory is ours.

"The prince of this world cometh," said Jesus, "and hath nothing in Me." John 14:30. Nothing in Him responded to Satan's sophistry. He did not consent to sin. Not even by a thought did He yield to temptation. So it may be with us. Christ's humanity was united with divinity; He was fitted for the conflict by the indwelling of the Holy Spirit. And He came to make us partakers of the divine nature. God reaches for the hand of faith in us to direct it to lay fast hold on the divinity of Christ, that we may attain to perfection of character.

How this is accomplished Christ has shown us. By what means did Christ overcome Satan? By the Word of God. "It is written," He said. And every promise in God's Word is ours. See 2 Peter 1:4. When assailed by temptation, look not to circumstances or to the weakness of self, but to the power of the Word. All its strength is yours. "Thy word," says the psalmist, "have I hid in mine heart, that I might not sin against Thee." "By the word of Thy lips I have kept me from the paths of the destroyer." Psalms 119:11; 17:4.

13 / The Victory

"Then the devil taketh Him up into the holy city, and setteth Him on a pinnacle of the temple, and saith unto Him, If Thou be the Son of God, cast Thyself down: for it is written,

> He shall give His angels charge concerning Thee:
> And in their hands they shall bear Thee up,
> Lest at any time Thou dash Thy foot against
>   a stone."

Satan still appeared as an angel of light, and he made it evident that he was acquainted with the Scriptures. As Jesus used the Word to sustain His faith, the tempter now used it to countenance his deception. Satan urged the Saviour to give still another evidence of His faith.

But again the temptation was prefaced with the insinuation of distrust: "If Thou be the Son of God." Christ was tempted to answer the "if," but He refrained from the slightest acceptance of the doubt.

The tempter thought to take advantage of Christ's humanity, and urge Him to presumption. But while Satan can solicit, he cannot compel to sin. He said, "Cast Thyself down," knowing that he could not cast Him down. Nor could Satan force Jesus to cast Himself down. Unless Christ should consent to temptation, He could not be overcome.

The tempter can never compel us to do evil. The will must consent, faith must let go its hold on Christ, be-

This chapter is based on Matthew 4:5-11; Mark 1:12, 13; Luke 4:5-13.

fore Satan can exercise his power on us. But every sinful desire we cherish is an open door by which he can enter to tempt and destroy us. And every failure on our part gives occasion for him to reproach Christ.

When Satan quoted the promise, "He shall give His angels charge over Thee," he omitted the words, "to keep Thee in all Thy ways"; that is, in all the ways of God's choosing. Jesus refused to go outside the path of obedience. He would not force Providence to come to His rescue, and thus fail of giving man an example of trust and submission.

Jesus declared to Satan, "It is written again, Thou shall not tempt the Lord thy God." God had already testified that Jesus was His Son; now to ask for proof would be putting God's word to the test—tempting Him. We should not present our petitions to God to *prove* whether He will fulfill His word, but *because* He will fulfill it; not to prove that He loves us, but because He loves us. See Hebrews 11:6. Presumption is Satan's counterfeit of faith. Faith claims God's promises and brings forth fruit in obedience. Presumption also claims the promises, but uses them to excuse transgression. Faith would have led our first parents to trust the love of God and obey His commands. Presumption led them to transgress His law, believing that His great love would save them from the consequence of their sin. It is not faith that claims the favor of Heaven without complying with the conditions on which mercy is to be granted.

Venturing on Satan's Ground

If Satan can cause us to place ourselves unnecessarily in the way of temptation, he knows that victory is his. God will preserve all who walk in the path of obedience; but to depart from it is to venture on Satan's ground. The Saviour has bidden us, "Watch ye and pray, lest ye enter into temptation." Mark 14:38.

Often when placed in a trying situation we doubt that the Spirit of God has led us. But it was the Spirit's leading that brought Jesus into the wilderness. When God brings us into trial, He has a purpose to accomplish for our good. Jesus did not presume on God's promises by going unbidden into temptation; neither did He give up to despondency when temptation came upon Him. Nor should we. See 1 Corinthians 10:13; Psalm 50:14, 15.

Jesus was victor in the second temptation, and now Satan manifested himself in his true character—as a mighty angel, though fallen. He avowed himself the leader of rebellion and the god of this world. Placing Jesus on a high mountain, he caused the kingdoms of the world to pass in panoramic view before Him. The sunlight lay on templed cities, marble palaces, fertile fields, and fruit-laden vineyards. The traces of evil were hidden. The eyes of Jesus gazed on a scene of unsurpassed loveliness and prosperity. Then the tempter's voice was heard: "All this will I give Thee. . . . If Thou therefore wilt worship me, all shall be Thine."

Before Christ was a life of sorrow, hardship, and conflict, and an ignominious death. Christ might deliver Himself from the dreadful future by acknowledging the supremacy of Satan. But to do this would be to yield the victory in the great controversy. Should Satan prevail now, it would be the triumph of rebellion.

Christ Could Not Be Bought

When the tempter offered to Christ the kingdom and glory of the world, he was proposing that Christ hold dominion subject to Satan. This was the same dominion on which the hopes of the Jews were set. They desired the kingdom of this world. But Christ declared to the tempter, "Get thee behind Me, Satan: for it is written, Thou shalt worship the Lord thy God, and Him only shalt thou serve." Christ would not be bought. He had come to establish a kingdom of righteousness, and He would not abandon His purpose.

With the same temptation Satan approaches men, and here he has better success than with Christ. He offers them the kingdom of this world on condition that they will sacrifice integrity, disregard conscience, indulge selfishness, and acknowledge his supremacy. Satan says: Whatever may be true in regard to life eternal, to make a success in this world you must serve me. I can give you riches, pleasures, honor, and happiness. Do not be carried away with notions of honesty or self-sacrifice.

Thus multitudes consent to live for self, and Satan is satisfied. But he offers that which is not his to bestow and which is soon to be wrested from him. In return he beguiles them of their title to the inheritance of the sons of God.

Satan Remains a Defeated Foe

In his summary dismissal Satan had proof that Jesus was the Son of God. Divinity flashed through suffering humanity. Writhing with humiliation and rage, Satan was forced to withdraw from the presence of the world's Redeemer. Christ's victory was as complete as had been the failure of Adam.

So we may resist temptation and force Satan to depart from us. Jesus gained the victory through submission and faith in God, and by the apostle He says to us, "Submit yourselves therefore to God. Resist the devil, and he will flee from you. Draw nigh to God, and He will draw nigh to you." James 4:7, 8. "The name of the Lord is a strong tower: the righteous runneth into it, and is safe." Proverbs 18:10. Satan trembles before the weakest soul who finds refuge in that mighty name.

After the foe had departed, Jesus fell exhausted, with the pallor of death on His face. Angels had watched their loved Commander as He had endured the test, greater than we shall ever be called to endure. They now ministered to the Son of God as He lay like one dying. He was strengthened with food, comforted with the assurance that all heaven triumphed in His victory. Warming to life again, His great heart went out in sympathy for man, and He went forth to complete the work He had begun; to rest not until the foe was vanquished and our fallen race redeemed.

Never can the cost of redemption be realized until the redeemed stand with the Redeemer before the throne of God. Then as the glories of the eternal home burst upon our enraptured senses, we shall remember that Jesus left all this for us; that for us He took the risk of failure and eternal loss. "Worthy is the Lamb that was slain to receive power, and riches, and wisdom, and strength, and honor, and glory, and blessing." Revelation 5:12.

14 / We Have Found the Messiah

John the Baptist was now preaching at Bethabara, beyond Jordan, where people daily thronged the banks of the Jordan. The preaching of John had taken a deep hold on the nation. He had not recognized the authority of the Sanhedrin by seeking their sanction, yet interest in his work seemed to continually increase.

The Sanhedrin was made up of priests, rulers, and teachers. In the days of Jewish independence the Sanhedrin was the supreme court of the nation. Though now subordinated by the Roman governors, it still exercised a strong influence in civil as well as religious matters. The Sanhedrin could not well defer an investigation of John's work. Some recalled the revelation made to Zacharias in the temple that had pointed to his child as the Messiah's herald. These things were now called to mind by the excitement concerning the ministry of John.

It was long since Israel had had a prophet. The demand for confession of sin seemed new and startling. Many leaders would not go to hear John lest they be led to disclose the secrets of their lives. Yet his preaching was a direct announcement of the Messiah.

It was well known that the seventy weeks of Daniel's prophecy, covering Messiah's advent, were nearly ended; and all were eager to share in the national glory then expected. Such was the popular enthusiasm that the Sanhedrin would soon be forced either to sanction or to reject John's work. Already it was becoming a

This chapter is based on John 1:19-51.

serious question how to maintain their power over the people. In hope of arriving at some conclusion, they dispatched to the Jordan a deputation of priests and Levites to confer with the new teacher.

A multitude were listening to his words when the delegates approached. With an air of authority designed to impress the people and command the deference of the prophet, the haughty rabbis came. With respect, almost fear, the crowd opened to let them pass. The great men, in their rich robes, in the pride of rank and power, stood before the prophet of the wilderness.

"Who art thou?" they demanded.

Knowing what was in their thoughts, John answered, "I am not the Christ."

"What then? Art thou Elias?"

"I am not."

"Art thou that prophet?"

"No."

"Who art thou? that we may give an answer to them that sent us. What sayest thou of thyself?"

"I am the voice of one crying in the wilderness, Make straight the way of the Lord, as said the prophet Esaias."

Anciently, when a king journeyed through his dominion, men were sent ahead to level the steep places and fill up the hollows, that the king might travel in safety. This custom is employed by the prophet Isaiah to illustrate the work of the gospel. "Every valley shall be exalted, and every mountain and hill shall be made low." Isaiah 40:4. When the Spirit of God touches the soul, it abases human pride. Worldly pleasure, position, and power are seen to be worthless. Then humility and self-sacrificing love are exalted as alone of worth. This is the work of the gospel, of which John's message was a part.

The rabbis continued their questioning: "Why baptizest thou then, if thou be not that Christ, nor Elias, neither that prophet?" The words "that prophet" had reference to Moses. When the Baptist began his ministry, many thought he might be Moses risen from the dead.

It was believed also that before the Messiah's advent, Elijah would personally appear. This expectation John denied, but Jesus afterward said, referring to John, "And if you are willing to accept it, he is Elijah who is to come." Matthew 11:14, RSV. John came in the spirit and power of Elijah, to do such a work as Elijah did. But the Jews did not receive his message. To them he was not Elijah.

Many Today Fail to "See" Christ

Many of those gathered at the Jordan had been present at the baptism of Jesus, but the sign then given had been manifest to but few among them. During the preceding months of the Baptist's ministry, many had refused to heed the call to repentance. Thus when Heaven bore testimony to Jesus at His baptism, they perceived it not. Eyes that had never turned in faith to Him beheld not the revelation of the glory of God; ears that had never listened to His voice heard not the words of witness. So it is now. Often the presence of Christ and ministering angels is manifest in the assemblies of the people, yet many know it not. They discern nothing unusual. But to some the Saviour's presence is revealed. They are comforted, encouraged, and blessed.

The deputies from Jerusalem had demanded of John, "Why baptizest thou?" and they were awaiting his answer. Suddenly, as his glance swept over the throng, his face lighted up, and his whole being was stirred with deep emotion. With outstretched hands he cried, "I baptize with water; but among you stands One whom you do not know, even He who comes after me, the thong of whose sandal I am not worthy to untie." RSV.

The message was distinct and unequivocal, to be carried back to the Sanhedrin. The Messiah was among them! In amazement priests and rulers gazed about them, but He of whom John had spoken was not distinguishable among the throng.

At the baptism of Jesus, John's mind was directed to the words of Isaiah, "He is brought as a lamb to the slaughter." Isaiah 53:7. During the weeks that followed, John studied with new interest the prophecies and the sacrificial service. He saw that Christ's coming had a deeper significance than priests or people had discerned. When he beheld Jesus among the throng on His return from the desert, he waited almost impatiently to hear the Saviour declare His mission; but no word was spoken, no sign given. Jesus did not respond to the Baptist's announcement of Him, but mingled with the disciples of John, taking no measures to bring Himself to notice.

The next day John saw Jesus coming toward him. With the light of the glory of God resting on him, the prophet stretched out his hands, declaring, "Behold, the Lamb of God, who takes away the sin of the world! This is He of whom I said, 'After me comes a man who ranks before me.' . . . I saw the Spirit descend as a dove from heaven, and it remained on Him. . . . He who sent me to baptize with water said to me, . . . 'This is He who baptizes with the Holy Spirit.' And I have seen and have borne witness that this is the Son of God." RSV.

Christ's Appearance Was Undistinguished

Was this the Christ? With awe and wonder the people looked upon the One just declared to be the Son of God. They had been deeply moved by the words of John. He had spoken in the name of God. They had listened to him day after day as he reproved their sins, and the conviction that he was sent of Heaven had strengthened. But who was this One greater than John? In His dress and bearing nothing betokened rank. Apparently He was a simple person, clad in the humble garments of the poor.

Some in the throng had been at Christ's baptism and

had heard the voice of God. But the Saviour's appearance had greatly changed. At His baptism they had seen His countenance transfigured in the light of heaven; now, worn and emaciated, He had been recognized only by John.

But the people saw a face where divine compassion was blended with conscious power. Every glance, every feature of the countenance, was marked with humility, and expressive of unutterable love. He impressed men with a sense of power that was hidden, yet could not be wholly concealed. Was this the One for whom Israel had so long waited?

Jesus came in poverty and humiliation, that He might be our example as well as our Redeemer. If He had appeared with kingly pomp, how could He have taught humility? Where would have been the hope of the lowly in life had Jesus come to dwell as a king among men?

But to the multitude it seemed impossible that the One designated by John should be associated with their lofty anticipations. Many were disappointed and perplexed.

The words so much desired—that Jesus would now restore the kingdom to Israel—had not been spoken. Such a king the priests and rabbis were ready to receive. But one who sought to establish in their hearts a kingdom of righteousness, they would not accept.

John Directs His Followers to Jesus

On the following day, while two disciples were near, John again saw Jesus. Again the face of the prophet was lighted up as he cried, "Behold the Lamb of God!" The disciples did not fully understand. What meant the name that John had given Him—"the Lamb of God"?

Leaving John they went to seek Jesus. One was Andrew, brother of Simon; the other was John the evangelist. These were Christ's first disciples. They followed Jesus—anxious to speak with Him, yet awed and silent, lost in the thought, "Is this the Messiah?"

Jesus knew that the two were following Him. They were the first fruits of His ministry, and there was joy in the heart of the divine Teacher as these souls responded to His grace. Yet turning, He asked only, "What seek ye?"

They exclaimed, "Rabbi [Teacher], . . . where dwellest Thou?" In a brief interview by the wayside they could not receive what they longed for. They desired to be alone with Jesus and hear His words.

"He saith unto them, Come and see. They came and saw where He dwelt, and abode with Him that day."

If John and Andrew had possessed the unbelieving spirit of the priests and rulers, they would not have been learners but critics, to judge His words. But having responded to the Holy Spirit's call in the preaching of John the Baptist, they now recognized the heavenly Teacher. To them the words of Jesus were full of freshness and beauty. A divine illumination was shed upon the Old Testament Scriptures. Truth stood out in new light.

The disciple John was a man of earnest and deep affection, ardent yet contemplative. He had begun to discern "the glory as of the only begotten of the Father, full of grace and truth." John 1:14.

Andrew sought to impart the joy that filled his heart. Going in search of his brother Simon, he cried, "We have found the Messias." Simon also had heard the preaching of John the Baptist, and he hastened to the Saviour. The eye of Christ read his character and life history. His impulsive nature, his loving, sympathetic heart, his ambition and self-confidence, his fall, his repentance, his labors, and his martyr death—the Saviour read it all. He said, "Thou art Simon the son of Jona: thou shalt be called Cephas, which is by interpretation, A stone."

"The next day . . . Jesus . . . findeth Philip and saith to him, Follow Me." Philip obeyed the command, and he also became a worker for Christ.

Philip called Nathanael, who had been among the throng when the Baptist pointed to Jesus as the Lamb of God. As Nathanael looked upon Jesus, he was disappointed. Could this man, who bore the marks of toil and poverty, be the Messiah? Yet the message of John had brought conviction to Nathanael's heart.

Nathanael's Secret Prayers Are Heard

When Philip called him, Nathanael had withdrawn to a quiet grove to meditate on the prophecies concerning the Messiah. He prayed that if the one announced by John was the Deliverer, it might be made known to him. The Holy Spirit rested upon him with assurance that God had visited His people. Philip knew that his friend was searching the prophecies, and while Nathanael was praying under a fig tree, Philip discovered his retreat. They had often prayed together in this secluded spot hidden by the foliage.

The message, "We have found Him, of whom Moses in the law, and the prophets did write," seemed to Nathanael a direct answer to his prayer. But Philip added, "Jesus of Nazareth, the son of Joseph." Prejudice arose in Nathanael's heart, and he exclaimed, "Can there any good thing come out of Nazareth?"

Philip said, "Come and see." Jesus saw Nathanael coming to Him, and said of him, "Behold, an Israelite indeed, in whom is no guile!" In surprise Nathanael exclaimed, "Whence knowest Thou me?" Jesus answered, "Before that Philip called thee, when thou wast under the fig tree, I saw thee."

It was enough. The divine Spirit that had borne witness to Nathanael in his solitary prayer under the fig tree spoke to him in the words of Jesus. Nathanael had come to Christ with an honest desire for truth, and now his desire was met. He said, "Rabbi, Thou art the Son of God; Thou art the King of Israel!"

If Nathanael had trusted to the rabbis for guidance, he would never have found Jesus. It was by seeing and judging for himself that he became a disciple. So today, many trust to human authority. Like Nathanael, we need to study God's Word for ourselves and pray for the enlightenment of the Holy Spirit. He who saw Nathanael under the fig tree will see us in the secret place of prayer. Angels are near to those who in humility seek for divine guidance.

With the calling of John, Andrew, Simon, Philip, and Nathanael, began the foundation of the Christian church. John directed two of his disciples to Christ. Then one of these, Andrew, found his brother. Philip was then called, and he went in search of Nathanael. These examples teach the importance of making direct appeals to our kindred, friends, and neighbors. There are those who have never made a personal effort to bring even one soul to the Saviour.

Many have gone down to ruin who might have been saved if their neighbors, common men and women, had put forth personal effort for them. In the family, the neighborhood, the town where we live, there is work for us to do. No sooner is one converted than there is born within him a desire to make known to others what a precious friend he has found in Jesus.

The Strongest Argument

Philip did not ask Nathanael to accept another's testimony, but to behold Christ for himself. One of the most effective ways of winning souls to Jesus is in exemplifying His character in our daily life. Men may defy our logic or resist our appeals; but a life of love, totally without selfish motives, is an argument they cannot gainsay.

The Word of God, spoken by one who is himself sanctified through it, has a life-giving power attractive to the hearers. When one has received the truth in the love of it, he will make known that which he himself has heard, seen, and handled of the Word of Life. His testimony is truth to the receptive heart, and works sanctification upon the character.

And he who seeks to give light to others will himself

be blessed. "He that watereth shall be watered also himself." Proverbs 11:25. In order to enter into Christ's joy—the joy of seeing souls redeemed by His sacrifice—we must participate in His labors for their redemption.

Nathanael's first expression of faith fell like music on the ears of Jesus. "Because I said to you, I saw you under the fig tree, do you believe? You shall see greater things than these." RSV. The Saviour looked forward with joy to His work in preaching good tidings to the meek, binding up the brokenhearted, and proclaiming liberty to the captives of Satan. He added, "Verily, verily, I say unto you, Hereafter ye shall see heaven open, and the angels of God ascending and descending upon the Son of man."

Here Christ virtually says, On the bank of the Jordan the heavens were opened, and the Spirit descended. But if you believe on Me, your faith will be quickened. You shall see that the heavens are opened, never to be closed. I have opened them to you. The angels of God are ascending, bearing the prayers of the needy and distressed to the Father above, and descending, bringing hope, courage, and life to the children of men.

Angels are ever passing from earth to heaven, and from heaven to earth. Through Christ, by the ministry of His heavenly messengers, every blessing comes from God to us. In taking on Himself humanity, our Saviour unites His interests with those of the fallen sons and daughters of Adam, while through His divinity He grasps the throne of God.

15 / Jesus Attends a Wedding

At a household gathering in a little Galilean village Jesus put forth His power to add joy to a wedding feast. Thus He showed His sympathy with men, and His desire to minister to their happiness. In the wilderness He Himself had drunk the cup of woe; He came forth to give to men the cup of blessing.

There was to be a marriage at Cana. The parties were relatives of Joseph and Mary, and Jesus with His disciples was invited.

Mary, His mother, had heard of the manifestation at the Jordan, at His baptism. The tidings had brought to her mind afresh the scenes that for many years had been hidden in her heart. Mary was deeply stirred by the mission of John the Baptist. Now his connection with Jesus kindled her hopes anew. She had treasured every evidence that Jesus was the Messiah, yet there came to her also doubts and disappointments. She longed for the time when His glory should be revealed.

Death had separated Mary from Joseph, who had shared her knowledge of the mystery of the birth of Jesus. Now there was no one in whom she could confide her hopes and fears. She pondered the words of Simeon, "A sword will pierce through thy own soul also." Luke 2:35. With an anxious heart she awaited Jesus' return.

At the marriage feast she met Him, the same tender, dutiful son. Yet He was not the same. His countenance bore traces of His conflict in the wilderness, and a new expression of dignity and power gave evidence of His

This chapter is based on John 2:1-11.

heavenly mission. With Him was a group of young men who called Him Master. These companions recounted to Mary what they had seen and heard at the baptism and elsewhere.

As the guests assembled, a suppressed excitement pervaded the company. As Mary saw the many glances bent on Jesus she longed to have Him prove that He was the Honored of God.

It was the custom for marriage festivities to continue several days. On this occasion, before the feast ended it was found that the supply of wine had failed. As a relative, Mary had assisted in the feast, and she now said to Jesus, "They have no wine." These words were a suggestion that He might supply their need. But Jesus answered, "Woman, what have I to do with thee? Mine hour is not yet come."

This form of address, abrupt as it seems to us, expressed no coldness or discourtesy. In accordance with Oriental custom, it was used toward persons to whom it was desired to show respect. On the cross, in His last act of tenderness toward His mother, Jesus again addressed her in the same way. Both at the marriage feast and upon the cross, the love expressed in tone, look, and manner interpreted His words.

At His visit to the temple in His boyhood, Christ had said to Mary, "Wist ye not that I must be about My Father's business?" Luke 2:49. Now He repeated the lesson. There was danger that Mary would regard her relationship to Jesus as giving her the right, in some degree, to direct Him in His mission. For thirty years He had been a loving, obedient Son, but now He must go about His Father's work. As Saviour of the world, no earthly ties must hold Him from His mission. This lesson is also for us. No earthly attraction, no ties of human relationship should turn our feet from the path in which God bids us walk.

Mary could find salvation only through the Lamb of God. Her connection with Jesus placed her in no different spiritual relation to Him from that of any other human soul. The Saviour's words make clear the distinction between His relation to her as the Son of man and as the Son of God. The kinship between them in no way placed her on an equality with Him.

"Mine hour is not yet come." As Christ walked among men, He was guided step by step by the Father's will. In saying to Mary that His hour had not yet come, He was replying to her unspoken thought—the expectation she cherished that He would reveal Himself as the Messiah and take the throne of Israel. But the time had not come. Not as a King but as "a man of sorrows and acquainted with grief," Jesus had accepted the lot of humanity.

Mary's Faith Is Rewarded

Though Mary had not a right concept of Christ's mission, she trusted Him implicitly. To this faith He responded. To honor her trust and to strengthen the faith of His disciples, the first miracle was performed. To the disciples the prophecies had made it clear beyond all controversy that Jesus was the Messiah, but they were bitterly disappointed by the unbelief, deep-seated prejudice, and enmity to Jesus displayed by the priests and rabbis. The Saviour's early miracles strengthened the disciples to stand against opposition.

Mary said to those serving at table, "Whatsoever He saith unto you, do it."

Beside the doorway stood six large stone water jars. Jesus told the servants to fill these with water. Then He said, "Draw out now, and bear unto the governor of the feast." Instead of water there flowed forth wine.

Upon tasting that which the servants brought, the ruler of the feast found it superior to any he had ever before drunk. Turning to the bridegroom, he said, "Every man serves the good wine first; and when men have drunk freely, then the poor wine; but you have kept the good wine until now." RSV.

The gifts the world offers may please the eye and fascinate the senses, but they prove unsatisfying. The "wine" turns to bitterness, the gaiety to gloom. That which was begun with songs and mirth ends in weariness and disgust. But the gifts of Jesus are ever fresh and new. The feast that He provides never fails to give satisfaction and joy. There can be no failure of supply. If you abide in Him, a rich gift today ensures the reception of a richer gift tomorrow.

The gift of Christ to the marriage feast was a symbol. The water to fill the jars was brought by human hands, but the word of Christ alone could impart to it life-giving virtue. So with the rites which point to the Saviour's death. Only by the power of Christ, working through faith, do they have efficacy to nourish the soul.

The wine Christ provided for the feast, and which He gave the disciples as a symbol of His own blood, was the pure juice of the grape. To this Isaiah refers when he speaks of the new wine "in the cluster," and says, "Destroy it not; for a blessing is in it." Isaiah 65:8.

Christ in the Old Testament gave the warning, "Wine is a mocker, strong drink is raging: and whosoever is deceived thereby is not wise." Proverbs 20:1. He Himself provided no such beverage. Satan tempts men to indulgence that will becloud reason and benumb the spiritual perceptions, but Christ teaches us to bring the lower nature into subjection. It was Christ who directed that John the Baptist should drink neither wine nor strong drink. He enjoined similar abstinence on the wife of Manoah. And He pronounced a curse on the man who should put the bottle to his neighbor's lips. See Habakkuk 2:15. Christ did not contradict His own teaching. The unfermented wine which He provided for the wedding guests was a wholesome and refreshing drink.

As the guests remarked upon the wine, inquiries were made that drew from the servants an account of the miracle. When at length the company looked for Jesus, He had withdrawn quietly.

Attention now turned to the disciples, who had opportunity to acknowledge their faith in Jesus. They told what they had seen and heard at the Jordan. News of the miracle spread and was carried to Jerusalem. With new interest the priests and elders searched the prophecies pointing to Christ's coming.

Jesus began His work by coming into close sympathy with humanity. While He showed the greatest reverence for the law of God, He rebuked the pretentious piety of the Pharisees, and tried to free the people from the senseless rules that bound them. He was seeking to break down the barriers which separated the different classes of society, that He might bring men together as children of one family.

Jesus reproved self-indulgence, yet He was social in His nature. He accepted the hospitality of all classes, visiting the homes of rich and poor, learned and ignorant, seeking to elevate their thoughts from commonplace life to things that are eternal. No shadow of worldly levity marred His conduct, yet He found pleasure in scenes of innocent happiness. The joy of a Jewish marriage was not displeasing to the Son of man. By attending, Jesus honored marriage as a divine institution.

In both the Old and New Testaments, marriage represents the tender and sacred union that exists between Christ and His people. To the mind of Jesus the gladness of the wedding pointed to the rejoicing of that day when He shall bring home His bride, the redeemed, to the Father's house. "As the bridegroom rejoiceth over the bride, so shall thy God rejoice over thee." "He will rejoice over thee with joy; . . . He will joy over thee with singing." Isaiah 62:5; Zephaniah 3:17. John the apostle wrote: "I heard as it were the voice of a great multitude, . . . saying, . . . Let us be glad and rejoice, and give honor to Him: for the marriage of the Lamb is come, and His wife hath made herself ready." Revelation 19:6, 7.

Jesus reached the hearts of the people by going among them as one who desired their good. He sought them in the streets, in private houses, on boats, in synagogues, by the shores of the lake, and at the marriage feast. He manifested interest in their secular affairs. His strong personal sympathy helped to win hearts. Solitary prayer in the mountains was a preparation for His labor among men in active life. From these seasons He came forth to relieve the sick and to break the chains from the captives of Satan.

By personal contact and association Jesus trained His disciples. Sometimes sitting on the mountainside, sometimes beside the sea, or walking with them by the way, He taught the mysteries of the kingdom of God. He did not sermonize. He did not command His disciples to do this or that, but said, "Follow Me." On His journeys He took them with Him, that they might see how He taught the people.

The example of Christ should be followed by all who preach His Word. We should not seclude ourselves, but must meet all classes where they are. Not alone from the pulpit are the hearts of men touched by divine truth. Another field of labor, fully as promising, is in the home of the lowly, in the mansion of the great, and in gatherings for innocent social enjoyment.

We shall not mingle with the world to unite with them in folly. We should never give sanction to sin by our words or our deeds, our silence or our presence. Wherever we go, we are to carry Jesus with us. We should all become witnesses for Jesus. Social power, sanctified by the grace of Christ, must be improved in winning souls. Let the world see that we desire others to share our blessings and privileges, that religion does not make us unsympathetic or exacting. Let all who have found Christ minister as He did for the benefit of men.

We should never give the world the false impression that Christians are a gloomy, unhappy people. Christ's followers are not statues, but living men and women who are partakers of the divine nature. The light that shines on them they reflect on others in works that are luminous with the love of Christ.

16 / Christ Confronts Corruption in the Temple

"The Jews' Passover was at hand, and Jesus went up to Jerusalem." Jesus had not yet publicly announced His mission, and He mingled unnoticed with the throng. On these occasions, the coming of the Messiah was often the theme of conversation. Jesus knew that the hope of national greatness was to be disappointed, for it was founded on a misinterpretation of Scripture. With deep earnestness He explained the prophecies and tried to arouse the people to a closer study of God's Word.

At Jerusalem during the Passover week large numbers assembled from all parts of Palestine, and even from distant lands. The temple courts were filled with a promiscuous throng. Many were unable to bring with them the sacrifices that were to be offered as typifying the one great Sacrifice. For the convenience of these, animals were bought and sold in the outer court.

Every Jew was required to pay yearly "a ransom for his soul," and the money collected was used for the support of the temple. See Exodus 30:12-16. Besides this, large sums were brought as freewill offerings, to be deposited in the temple treasury. And it was required that all foreign coin be changed for a coin called the temple shekel, which was accepted for the service of the sanctuary. The money changing gave opportunity for fraud and extortion, and it had grown into a disgraceful traffic, which was a source of revenue to the priests.

The worshipers had been taught to believe that if they did not offer sacrifice, the blessing of God would

This chapter is based on John 2:12-22.

Jesus performed His first miracle, turning water into wine, to honor the faith that Mary and His disciples had placed in Him as the Messiah.

not rest on their children or their lands. The dealers demanded exorbitant prices for the animals sold and shared their profits with the priests and rulers, who thus enriched themselves at the expense of the people.

Financial Corruption at the Heart of God's Work

Sharp bargaining, the lowing of cattle, the bleating of sheep, the cooing of doves, mingled with the chinking of coin and angry disputation. So great was the confusion that the words addressed to the Most High were drowned in the uproar. The Jews rejoiced over their temple and regarded a word spoken in its disfavor as blasphemy, but the love of money had overruled their scruples. They had wandered far from the purpose of the service instituted by God Himself. Wherever God manifests His presence, the place is holy. See Exodus 19:12, 13. The precincts of God's temple should have been regarded as sacred. But in the strife for gain, all this was lost sight of.

The priests and rulers should have corrected the abuses of the temple court, and given the people an example of integrity. Instead of studying their own profit, they should have been ready to assist those not able to buy the required sacrifices. But avarice had hardened their hearts.

To this feast came those who were in want and distress—the blind, the lame, the deaf. Some were brought on beds. Many were too poor to purchase the humblest offering for the Lord or even to buy food to satisfy their own hunger. These were greatly distressed by the statements of the priests. The priests boasted of their piety, but they were without sympathy or compassion. The poor, the sick, the dying, awakened no pity in their hearts.

As Jesus came into the temple, He saw the unfair transactions. He saw the distress of the poor, who thought that without shedding of blood there would be no forgiveness for their sins. He saw the sacred, outer court of His temple converted into a place of unholy traffic.

Something must be done. The worshipers offered sacrifices without understanding that they were typical of the only perfect Sacrifice. And among them, unrecognized and unhonored, stood the One symbolized by all their service. He saw that the offerings were perverted and misunderstood. No link bound the priests and rulers to God. Christ's work was to establish an altogether different worship.

With searching glance, Christ took in the scene before Him. With prophetic eye He looked into future years, centuries, and ages. He saw how priests and rulers would forbid the gospel to be preached to the poor, how the love of God would be concealed from sinners, and how men would make merchandise of His grace. Indignation, authority, and power were expressed in His countenance. The attention of the people was attracted to Him. The eyes of those engaged in their unholy traffic were riveted upon His face. They felt that this Man read their inmost thoughts and discovered their hidden motives. Some attempted to conceal their faces.

The sound of traffic and bargaining ceased. The silence became painful. It was as if the assembly were arraigned before the tribunal of God. Looking upon Christ, they beheld divinity flash through humanity. The Majesty of heaven stood as the Judge will stand at the last day—not encircled with the glory that will attend Him then, but with the same power to read the soul. His eye took in every individual. His form seemed to rise above them in commanding dignity, and a divine light illuminated His countenance. His clear, ringing voice—the same that on Mount Sinai proclaimed the law—echoed through the temple: "Take these things hence; make not My Father's house an house of merchandise."

Raising the scourge of cords gathered up on entering the enclosure, Jesus ordered the bargaining company to depart from the temple. With a zeal and severity He had never before manifested, He overthrew the tables of the money-changers. The coins fell, ringing sharply on the marble pavement. None questioned His authority. None dared stop to gather up their ill-gotten gain. Jesus did not smite them with the whip of cords, but in His hand that simple scourge seemed as a flaming sword. Officers of the temple, priests, brokers, and cattle traders, with their sheep and oxen, rushed from the place with the one thought of escaping from the condemnation of His presence.

The Temple Cleansed by the Presence of the Lord

Panic swept over the multitude, who felt the overshadowing of His divinity. Even the disciples trembled, awestruck by the words and manner of Jesus, so unlike His usual demeanor. They remembered that it was written of Him, "Zeal for Thy house has consumed Me." Psalm 69:9, RSV. Soon the courts of the temple were free from unholy traffic. Deep silence and solemnity settled on the scene of confusion. The presence of the Lord had made sacred the temple reared in His honor.

In cleansing the temple, Jesus announced His mission as the Messiah, and entered upon His work. The temple was designed to be an object lesson for Israel and for the world. It was God's purpose that every created being should be a temple for the indwelling of the Creator. Darkened and defiled by sin, the heart of man no longer revealed the glory of the Divine One. But by the incarnation of the Son of God, God dwells in humanity, and through saving grace the heart becomes again His temple.

God designed that the temple at Jerusalem should be a continual witness to the high destiny open to every soul. But the Jews did not yield themselves as holy temples for the Divine Spirit. The courts of the temple, filled with unholy traffic, represented all too truly the temple of the heart, defiled by sensual passion and unholy thoughts. In cleansing the temple, Jesus announced His mission to cleanse the heart from sin—the earthly desires, selfish lusts, and evil habits that corrupt the soul. "The Lord whom you seek will suddenly come to His temple; the Messenger of the covenant in whom you delight. . . . But who can endure the day of His coming, and who can stand when He appears? For He is like a refiner's fire. . . . He will sit as a refiner and purifier of silver, and He will purify the sons of Levi and refine them like gold and silver." Malachi 3:1-3, RSV.

"Know ye not that ye are the temple of God, and that the Spirit of God dwelleth in you? If any man defile the temple of God, him will God destroy; for the temple of God is holy, which temple ye are." 1 Corinthians 3:16, 17.

No man can of himself cast out the evil throng that have taken possession of the heart. Only Christ can cleanse the soul temple. But He will not force an entrance. He says, "Behold, I stand at the door, and knock: if any man hear My voice, and open the door, I will come in to him." Revelation 3:20. His presence will cleanse and sanctify the soul, so that it may be a holy temple unto the Lord, "a dwelling place of God in the Spirit." Ephesians 2:22, RSV.

A Preview of the Final Judgment

Overpowered with terror, the priests and rulers had fled from the temple court and from the searching glance that read their hearts. In this scene Christ saw symbolized the dispersion of the whole Jewish nation for their wickedness and impenitence.

Why did the priests flee? Why did they not stand their ground? He who commanded them to go was a carpenter's son, a poor Galilean. Why did they leave their ill-acquired gain and flee at the command of One whose appearance was so humble?

Christ spoke with the authority of a king, and in His appearance and in the tone of His voice there was that which they had no power to resist. At the word of command they realized their true position as hypocrites and robbers. When divinity flashed through humanity, they felt as if before the throne of the eternal Judge, with their sentence passed on them for time and eternity. For a time many believed Him to be the Messiah. The Holy Spirit flashed into their minds the utterances of the prophets concerning Christ. Would they yield to this conviction?

Repent they would not. They knew they had been guilty of extortion. Because Christ discerned their thoughts they hated Him. His public rebuke was humiliating to their pride, and they were jealous of His growing influence with the people. They determined to challenge Him as to the power by which He had driven them forth.

Slowly and thoughtfully, but with hate in their hearts, they returned to the temple. What a change had taken place! When they fled, the poor remained behind; and these were now looking to Jesus, whose countenance expressed His love and sympathy.

The people pressed into Christ's presence with urgent appeals: Master, bless me. His ear heard every cry. All received attention. Everyone was healed. The hearts of the sufferers were made glad.

As the priests and temple officials witnessed this great work, what a revelation were the sounds that fell on their ears! The people were relating the story of the pain they had suffered, of disappointed hopes, painful days and sleepless nights. When hope seemed dead, Christ had healed them. The burden was so heavy, one said, but I have found a helper. He is the Christ of God, and I will devote my life to His service. Parents said to their children, He has saved your life; lift up your voice and praise Him. Hope and gladness filled the hearts of children and youth, fathers and mothers, friends and spectators. They were restored soul and body, and they returned home proclaiming the love of Jesus.

At the crucifixion of Christ, those who had been healed did not join in crying, "Crucify Him, crucify Him." Their sympathies were with Jesus, for they had felt His wonderful power. They knew Him to be their Saviour. They listened to the apostles, and they became agents of God's mercy and instruments of His salvation.

The crowd that had fled from the temple court slowly drifted back after a time, but their faces expressed irresolution and timidity. They were convinced that in Jesus the prophecies concerning the Messiah were fulfilled. The sin of desecrating the temple rested, in a great degree, on the priests. By their arrangement the court had been turned into a market place. The people were comparatively innocent. But the priests and rulers regarded Christ's mission as an innovation and questioned His right to interfere with what was permitted by the authorities of the temple. They were offended because the traffic had been interrupted, and they stifled the convictions of the Holy Spirit.

The Beginning of the Final Rejection of Christ

The priests and rulers should have seen in Jesus the Anointed of the Lord, for in their hands were the sacred scrolls that described His mission. They knew that the cleansing of the temple was a manifestation of more than human power. Much as they hated Jesus, they could not free themselves from the thought that He might be a prophet sent by God to restore the sanctity of the temple. With a deference born of this fear, they went to Him with the inquiry, "What sign showest Thou unto us, seeing that Thou doest these things?"

Jesus had shown them a sign. In doing the work which the Messiah was to do, He had given convincing evidence of His character. Now He answered them by a parable, showing that He read their malice and saw to what lengths it would lead. "Destroy this temple, and in three days I will raise it up."

In these words He referred not only to the destruction of the Jewish temple and worship, but to His own death—the destruction of the temple of His body. This the Jews were already plotting. As the priests and rulers returned to the temple, they had proposed to kill Jesus and thus rid themselves of the troubler. Yet they took His words as applying only to the temple at Jerusalem, and with indignation exclaimed, "Forty and six years was this temple in building, and wilt Thou rear it up in three days?" Now they felt that Jesus had justified their unbelief, and they were confirmed in their rejection of Him.

Christ knew that His words would be misconstrued by His enemies and turned against Him. At His trial and on Calvary they would be flung at Him. But to explain them now would give His disciples a knowledge of His sufferings and bring on them sorrow which as yet they were not able to bear. And an explanation would prematurely disclose to the Jews the result of their prejudice and unbelief. Already they had entered on a path which they would steadily pursue until He should be led as a lamb to the slaughter.

Christ knew that these words would be repeated. Spoken at the Passover, they would come to the ears of thousands and be carried to all parts of the world. After He had risen from the dead, their meaning would be made plain. To many they would be conclusive evidence of His divinity.

The Saviour's words, "Destroy this temple, and in three days I will raise it up," had a deeper meaning than the hearers perceived. The temple services were typical of the sacrifice of the Son of God. The entire plan of sacrificial worship was a foreshadowing of the Saviour's death to redeem the world. The ritual economy had no value apart from Him. When the Jews sealed their rejection of Christ by delivering Him to death, they rejected all that gave significance to the temple and its services. Its sacredness had departed. It was doomed to destruction. From that day sacrificial offerings were meaningless. In putting Christ to death, the Jews virtually destroyed their temple. When Christ was crucified, the inner veil of the temple was rent in twain from top to bottom, signifying that the great final sacrifice had been made. The system of sacrificial offerings was forever at an end.

"In three days I will raise it up." From the rent sepulcher of Joseph, Jesus came forth a conqueror. By His death and resurrection He became the minister of the "true tabernacle, which the Lord pitched, and not man." Hebrews 8:2. Men reared the Jewish temple; but the sanctuary above was built by no human architect. "The Man whose name is The Branch . . . shall build the temple of the Lord: . . . and He shall bear the glory, and shall sit and rule upon His throne; and He shall be a priest upon His throne." Zechariah 6:12, 13.

The sacrificial service that had pointed to Christ passed away; but the eyes of men were turned to the true sacrifice for the sins of the world. The earthly priesthood ceased; but we look to Jesus, the minister of the new covenant. "The way into the holiest of all was not yet made manifest, while as the first tabernacle was yet standing: . . . but Christ being come an high priest of good things to come, by a greater and more perfect tabernacle, not made with hands, by His own blood He entered in once into the holy place, having obtained eternal redemption for us." Hebrews 9:8-12.

"Wherefore He is able also to save them to the uttermost that come unto God by Him, seeing He ever liveth to make intercession for them." Hebrews 7:25. Though the heavenly sanctuary and our great High Priest would be invisible to human sight, yet the disciples would realize no break in their communion and no diminution of power because of the Saviour's absence. While Jesus ministers in the sanctuary above, He is still by His Spirit the minister of the church on earth. His parting promise is fulfilled, "Lo, I am with you alway, even unto the end of the world." Matthew 28:20. His energizing presence is still with His church.

"We have not an high priest which cannot be touched with the feeling of our infirmities; but was in all points tempted like as we are, yet without sin. Let us therefore come boldly unto the throne of grace, that we may obtain mercy, and find grace to help in time of need." Hebrews 4:15, 16.

17 / Nicodemus Comes to Jesus at Night

Nicodemus, a highly educated and honored member of the national council, had been stirred by the teaching of Jesus. Though rich and learned, he had been strangely attracted by the humble Nazarene. The lessons that had fallen from the Saviour's lips had greatly impressed him, and he desired to learn more.

Christ's exercise of authority in cleansing the temple had roused the hatred of the priests and rulers. Such boldness on the part of an obscure Galilean was not to be tolerated. But not all were agreed on putting an end to His work. Some feared to oppose One so evidently moved by the Spirit of God. They knew that the bondage of the Jews to a heathen nation was the result of their stubbornness in rejecting reproofs from God. They feared that in plotting against Jesus the priests and rulers were following in the steps of their fathers and would bring fresh calamities on the nation. Nicodemus shared these feelings. In a council of the Sanhedrin, he advised caution and moderation. He urged that if Jesus was really invested with authority from God, it would be perilous to reject His warnings. The priests dared not disregard this counsel.

Nicodemus had anxiously studied the prophecies relating to the Messiah. The more he searched, the stronger was his conviction that this was the One who was to come. He had been distressed by the profanation of the temple. He was a witness when Jesus drove out the buyers and the sellers; he saw the Saviour healing the

This chapter is based on John 3:1-17.

sick; he saw their looks of joy, and heard their words of praise. He could not doubt that Jesus of Nazareth was the Sent of God.

He greatly desired an interview with Jesus, but shrank from seeking Him openly. Should his visit come to the knowledge of the Sanhedrin, it would draw upon him scorn and denunciation. He resolved upon a secret interview. Learning by special inquiry the Saviour's place of retirement in the Mount of Olives, he waited until the city was hushed in slumber, and then sought Him.

In the presence of Christ, Nicodemus felt a strange timidity, which he endeavored to conceal. "Rabbi, we know that Thou art a teacher come from God: for no man can do these miracles that thou doest, except God be with him." His words were designed to express and to invite confidence; but they really expressed unbelief. He did not acknowledge Jesus to be the Messiah, only a teacher sent from God.

Jesus bent His eyes on the speaker, as if reading his very soul. He saw before Him a seeker after truth. With a desire to deepen the conviction already resting upon His listener's mind, He came directly to the point, saying kindly, "Verily, verily, I say unto thee, Except a man be born from above, he cannot see the kingdom of God." John 3:3, margin.

Nicodemus had come to enter into a discussion, but Jesus laid bare the foundation principles of truth. He said, You don't need to have your curiosity satisfied, but to have a new heart. You must receive a new life from above before you can appreciate heavenly things. Until this change takes place, it will result in no saving good to discuss with Me My authority or My mission.

Nicodemus had heard the preaching of John the Baptist concerning repentance. Yet the heart-searching message of the Baptist had failed to work in him conviction of sin. He was a strict Pharisee, and prided himself on his good works. He was widely esteemed for his benevolence and felt secure of the favor of God. He was startled at the thought of a kingdom too pure for him to see in his present state.

The figure of the new birth was not wholly unfamiliar to Nicodemus. Converts from heathenism were often compared to children just born. Therefore he must have perceived that the words of Christ were not literal. But as an Israelite he felt that he needed no change. Hence his surprise and irritation at the Saviour's words. The pride of the Pharisee was struggling against the honest desire of the seeker after truth.

Surprised out of his self-possession, he answered in words full of irony, "How can a man be born when he is old?" Like many others, he revealed that nothing in the natural man responds to spiritual things; spiritual things are spiritually discerned.

Raising His hand with quiet dignity, the Saviour pressed the truth home with greater assurance, "Verily, verily, I say unto thee, except a man be born of water and of the Spirit, he cannot enter into the kingdom of God." Nicodemus knew that Christ here referred to the water baptism and the renewing of the heart by the Spirit of God. He was convinced that he was in the presence of the One whom John the Baptist had foretold.

The Mystery of the New Birth Explained

Jesus continued: "That which is born of the flesh is flesh; and that which is born of the Spirit is spirit." By nature the heart is evil. See Job 14:4. No human invention can find a remedy for the sinning soul. "The carnal mind is enmity against God." "Out of the heart proceed evil thoughts, murders, adulteries, fornications, thefts, false witness, blasphemies." Romans 8:7; Matthew 15:19. The fountain of the heart must be purified before the stream can become pure. He who is trying to reach heaven by his own works in keeping the law is attempting an impossibility. The Christian's life is not a modification or improvement of the old, but a transformation of nature, a death to self and sin, and a new life altogether. This change can be brought about only by the Holy Spirit.

Nicodemus was still perplexed, and Jesus used the wind to illustrate His meaning: "The wind bloweth where it listeth, and thou hearest the sound thereof, but canst not tell whence it cometh or whither it goeth; so is every one that is born of the Spirit."

The wind is heard rustling the leaves and flowers, yet it is invisible. So with the work of the Holy Spirit on the heart. A person may not be able to tell the exact time or place or trace the process of conversion, but this does not prove him to be unconverted. By an agency as unseen as the wind, Christ is constantly working on the heart. Little by little, impressions are made that tend to draw the soul to Christ. These may be received through reading the Scriptures or hearing the Word from the living preacher. Suddenly, as the Spirit comes with more direct appeal, the soul gladly surrenders to Jesus. Many call this "sudden conversion," but it is the result of long wooing by the Spirit of God—a patient, protracted process.

Wind produces effects that are seen and felt. So the work of the Spirit on the soul will reveal itself in every act of the one who has felt its saving power. The Spirit of God transforms the life. Sinful thoughts are put away, evil deeds renounced. Love, humility, and peace take the place of anger, envy, and strife. Joy takes the place of sadness. When by faith the soul surrenders to God, that power which no human eye can see creates a new being in the image of God. The beginning of redemption we may know here through personal experience; its results reach through eternal ages.

Nicodemus Begins to See the Light

While Jesus was speaking, some gleams of truth penetrated the ruler's mind. Yet he did not fully understand the Saviour's words. He said wonderingly, "How can these things be?"

"Art thou a master of Israel, and knowest not these things?" Jesus asked. Instead of feeling irritated over the plain words of truth, Nicodemus should have had a humble opinion of himself, because of his spiritual ignorance. Yet Christ spoke with such solemn dignity and earnest love, that Nicodemus was not offended.

But as Jesus explained that His mission was to establish a spiritual instead of a temporal kingdom, His hearer was troubled. Seeing this, Jesus added, "If I have told you earthly things, and ye believe not, how shall ye believe, if I tell you of heavenly things?" Not discerning the nature of Christ's work on earth, Nicodemus could not understand His work in heaven.

The Jews whom Jesus had driven from the temple were zealous to maintain an appearance of holiness, but neglected holiness of heart. Sticklers for the letter of the law, they were constantly violating its spirit. Their great need was that change which Christ had been explaining to Nicodemus—a new moral birth, a cleansing from sin, and a renewing of holiness.

There was no excuse for the blindness of Israel in regard to the work of regeneration. David had prayed, "Create in me a clean heart, O God; and renew a right spirit within me." Through Ezekiel the promise had been given, "A new heart also will I give you, and a new spirit will I put within you: and I will take away the stony heart out of your flesh, and I will give you an heart of flesh. And I will put My Spirit within you, and cause you to walk in My statutes." Psalm 51:10; Ezekiel 36:26, 27.

Nicodemus now began to comprehend the meaning of these scriptures. He saw that the most rigid outward obedience to the mere letter of the law could entitle no man to enter the kingdom of heaven.

Nicodemus was being drawn to Christ. As the Saviour explained to him the new birth, he longed to have this change in himself. How could it be accomplished? Jesus answered the unspoken question: "As Moses lifted up the serpent in the wilderness, even so must the Son of man be lifted up: that whosoever believeth in Him should not perish, but have eternal life.''

The symbol of the uplifted serpent made plain to Nicodemus the Saviour's mission. When the people of Israel were dying from the sting of the fiery serpents, God directed Moses to make a serpent of brass and place it on high in the midst of the congregation. All who would look should live. The serpent was a symbol of Christ. As the image made in the likeness of the destroying serpents was lifted up for their healing, so One made "in the likeness of sinful flesh" was to be their Redeemer. Romans 8:3. God desired to lead the Israelites to the Saviour. Whether for healing of wounds or pardon of sins, they could do nothing for themselves but show their faith in the Gift of God. They were to look and live.

Those who had been bitten by the serpents might have demanded a scientific explanation. But no explanation was given. To refuse to look was to perish. Nicodemus received the lesson and carried it with him. He searched the Scriptures in a new way, not for discussion but to receive life for the soul. He submitted to the leading of the Holy Spirit.

Thousands today need to learn the same truth taught to Nicodemus by the uplifted serpent. "There is none other name under heaven given among men, whereby we must be saved." Acts 4:12. Through faith we receive the grace of God; but faith is not our Saviour. It earns nothing. It is the hand by which we lay hold on Christ, the remedy for sin. We cannot even repent without the aid of the Spirit of God. The Scripture says of Christ, "Him hath God exalted with His right hand to be a Prince and a Saviour, for to give repentance to Israel, and forgiveness of sins." Acts 5:31. Repentance comes from Christ as truly as does pardon.

How, then, are we to be saved? "Behold the Lamb of God, which taketh away the sin of the world." John 1:29. The light shining from the cross reveals the love of God. His love is drawing us to Himself. If we do not resist this drawing, we shall be led to the foot of the cross in repentance for the sins that have crucified the Saviour. Then the Spirit of God through faith produces a new life in the soul. The thoughts and desires are brought into obedience to Christ. The heart, the mind, are created anew in the image of Him who works in us to subdue all things to Himself. Then the law of God is written in the mind and heart, and we can say with Christ, "I delight to do Thy will, O my God." Psalm 40:8.

In the interview with Nicodemus, Jesus unfolded the plan of salvation. In none of His subsequent discourses did He explain so fully, step by step, the work necessary to be done in the hearts of all who would inherit the kingdom of heaven. At the very beginning of His ministry He opened the truth to a member of the Sanhedrin, an appointed teacher of the people. But the leaders of Israel did not welcome the light. Nicodemus hid the truth in his heart, and for three years there was little apparent fruit.

But the words spoken at night in the lonely mountain were not lost. In the Sanhedrin council Nicodemus repeatedly thwarted schemes to destroy Jesus. When at last He was lifted up on the cross, Nicodemus remembered: "As Moses lifted up the serpent in the wilderness, even so must the Son of man be lifted up: that whosoever believeth in Him should not perish, but have eternal life." The light from that secret interview illumined the cross upon Calvary, and Nicodemus saw in Jesus the world's Redeemer.

After the Lord's ascension, when the disciples were scattered by persecution, Nicodemus came boldly to the front. He employed his wealth in sustaining the infant church that the Jews had expected to be blotted out at the death of Christ. In the time of peril he who had been so cautious and questioning was firm as a rock, encouraging the faith of the disciples and furnishing means to carry forward the work of the gospel. He became poor in this world's goods; yet he faltered not in the faith which had its beginning in that night conference with Jesus.

Nicodemus related to John the story of that interview, and by his pen it was recorded for the instruction of millions. The truths there taught are as important today as they were on that solemn night in the shadowy mountain, when the Jewish ruler came to learn the way of life from the lowly Teacher of Galilee.

18 / "He Must Increase, But I Must Decrease"

If John the Baptist had announced himself as the Messiah and raised a revolt against Rome, priests and people would have flocked to his standard. Every consideration that appeals to the ambition of the world's conquerors Satan stood ready to urge upon him. But he had steadfastly refused the splendid bribe. The attention fixed upon him he directed to Another.

Now he saw the tide of popularity turning away from himself to the Saviour. Day by day the crowds about him lessened as the people flocked to hear Jesus. The number of Christ's disciples increased daily.

But the disciples of John looked with jealousy upon the growing popularity of Jesus. They stood ready to criticize His work, and it was not long before they found occasion. A question arose between John's disciples and the Jews as to whether baptism cleansed the soul from sin; they maintained that the baptism of Jesus differed essentially from that of John. Soon they were in dispute with Christ's disciples in regard to the form of words proper to use at baptism, and finally as to their right to baptize at all. The disciples of John came to him with their grievances, saying, "Rabbi, He that was with thee beyond Jordan, to whom thou bearest witness, behold, the same baptizeth, and all men come to Him."

Through these words, Satan brought temptation upon John. If John had expressed disappointment at being superseded, he would have sown seeds of dissension, encouraged envy and jealousy, and seriously impeded the progress of the gospel.

This chapter is based on John 3:22-36.

John had by nature the faults and weaknesses common to humanity, but the touch of divine love had transformed him. He dwelt in an atmosphere uncontaminated with selfishness and ambition. He manifested no sympathy with the dissatisfaction of his disciples, but showed how gladly he welcomed the One for whom he had prepared the way.

He said, "No one can receive anything except what is given him from heaven. You yourselves bear me witness, that I said, I am not the Christ, but I have been sent before Him. He who has the bride is the bridegroom; the friend of the bridegroom, who stands and hears him, rejoices greatly at the bridegroom's voice." RSV. John represented himself as the friend who acted as a messenger between the betrothed parties, preparing the way for the marriage. When the bridegroom had received his bride, the mission of the friend was fulfilled. He rejoiced in the happiness of those whose union he had promoted. So it was John's joy to witness the success of the Saviour's work. He said, "This my joy therefore is fulfilled. He must increase, but I must decrease."

Looking in faith to the Redeemer, John had risen to the height of self-abnegation. He had been only a voice, a cry in the wilderness. Now with joy he accepted silence and obscurity, that the eyes of all might be turned to the Light of life.

The soul of the prophet, emptied of self, was filled with the light of the divine. John said, "He that cometh from above is above all. . . . For He whom God hath sent speaketh the words of God: for God giveth not the Spirit by measure unto Him." Christ could say, "I seek not Mine own will, but the will of the Father which hath sent Me." John 5:30.

So with the followers of Christ. We can receive of heaven's light only as we are willing to be emptied of self and consent to bring into captivity every thought to the obedience of Christ. To all who do this the Holy Spirit is given without measure.

The success of Christ's work, which the Baptist had received with joy, was reported also to the authorities at Jerusalem. The priests and rabbis had been jealous of John's influence as they saw the people leaving the synagogues and flocking to the wilderness. But here was One who had still greater power to attract the multitudes. Those leaders in Israel were not willing to say with John, "He must increase, but I must decrease."

Christ's Example of Avoiding Misunderstanding

Jesus knew that the storm was gathering which would sweep away one of the greatest prophets ever given to the world. Wishing to avoid all occasion for dissension, He quietly withdrew to Galilee. We also, while loyal to truth, should try to avoid all that may lead to misapprehension. Whenever circumstances threaten to cause division, we should follow the example of Jesus and of John the Baptist.

John had been called to lead out as a reformer. But his work was not sufficient to lay the foundation of the Christian church. Another work was to be done, which his testimony could not accomplish. His disciples did not understand this. When they saw Christ coming in to take the work, they were jealous.

The same dangers still exist. God calls a man to do a certain work; and when he has carried it as far as he is qualified, the Lord brings in others to carry it farther. But many feel that the success of the work depends on the first laborer. Jealousy comes in, and the work of God is marred. The one unduly honored is tempted to cherish self-confidence. The people rely on man for guidance and are led away from God.

From time to time the Lord will bring in different agencies through whom His purpose can best be accomplished. Happy are they who are willing for self to be humbled, saying with John the Baptist, "He must increase, but I must decrease."

19 / Jesus and the Woman With Five Husbands

On the way to Galilee Jesus passed through Samaria. It was noon when He reached Jacob's well. Wearied with His journey, He sat down to rest while His disciples went to buy food.

Jews and Samaritans were bitter enemies. To trade with Samaritans in case of necessity was counted lawful by the rabbis; but a Jew would not borrow from a Samaritan, nor receive a kindness, not even a morsel of bread or a cup of water. The disciples, in buying food, were acting in harmony with the custom of their nation. But to ask a favor of the Samaritans did not enter the thought even of Christ's disciples.

As Jesus sat by the well, He was faint from hunger and thirst. The journey had been long, and the sun of noontide beat upon Him. His thirst was increased by the thought of the cool, refreshing water so near; yet He had no rope nor water jar, and the well was deep.

A woman of Samaria approached, and seeming unconscious of His presence, filled her pitcher with water. As she turned to go, Jesus asked for a drink. Such a favor no Oriental would withhold.

The Saviour was seeking to find the key to the woman's heart, and with the tact born of divine love, He asked a favor. Trust awakens trust. The King of heaven came to this outcast soul, asking a service at her hands. He who made the ocean, who controls the waters of the deep, who opened the springs and channels of the earth, was dependent on a stranger's kindness for even a drink of water.

This chapter is based on John 4:1-42.

The woman saw that Jesus was a Jew. In her surprise she forgot to grant His request, but tried to learn the reason for it. "How is it," she asked, "that Thou, being a Jew, askest drink of me, which am a woman of Samaria?"

Jesus answered, "If thou knewest the gift of God, and who it is that saith to thee, Give Me to drink; thou wouldest have asked of Him and He would have given thee living water." Had you asked of Me, I would have given you to drink of the water of everlasting life.

The Woman's Interest Is Awakened

The woman's light, bantering manner began to change. "Sir, Thou hast nothing to draw with, and the well is deep: from whence then hast Thou that living water? Art Thou greater than our father Jacob, which gave us the well, and drank thereof himself?" She saw before her only a thirsty traveler. In her mind she compared Him with Jacob. She was looking backward to the fathers, and forward to the Messiah's coming, while the Messiah Himself was beside her, and she knew Him not. How many thirsty souls are today close by the living fountain, yet looking far away for the wellsprings of life!

With solemn earnestness Jesus said, "Whosoever drinketh of this water shall thirst again: but whosoever drinketh of the water that I shall give him shall never thirst; but the water that I shall give him shall be in him a well of water springing up into everlasting life."

He who seeks to quench his thirst at the fountains of this world will drink only to thirst again. Everywhere men long for something to supply the need of the soul. Only One can meet that want—Christ, "the Desire of all nations." The divine grace which He alone can impart is as living water, purifying, refreshing, and invigorating the soul.

Jesus did not convey the idea that merely one draft of the water of life would suffice. He who tastes of the love of Christ will continually long for more; but he seeks for nothing else. The riches, honors, and pleasures of the world do not attract him. The constant cry of his heart is, More of Thee. Our Redeemer is an inexhaustible fountain. We may drink, and drink again; and ever find a fresh supply.

Jesus had aroused the woman's interest and awakened a desire for the gift of which He spoke. "Sir, give me this water, that I thirst not, neither come hither to draw."

The Dark Secrets of Her Past

Jesus now abruptly turned the conversation. Before this soul could receive the gift He longed to bestow, she must be brought to recognize her sin and her Saviour. Jesus said to her, "Go, call thy husband, and come hither." She answered, "I have no husband." But the Saviour continued, "Thou hast well said, I have no husband: for thou hast had five husbands; and he whom thou now hast is not thy husband: in that saidst thou truly."

The listener trembled. A mysterious hand was turning the pages of her life history. Who was He that could read the secrets of her life? There came to her thoughts of eternity, of the future judgment, when all that is now hidden shall be revealed.

She tried to evade all mention of a subject so unwelcome. "Sir, I perceive that Thou art a prophet." Then, hoping to silence conviction, she turned to points of religious controversy.

Patiently Jesus watched for the opportunity of again bringing the truth home to her heart. "Our fathers worshiped in this mountain," she said, "and Ye say, that in Jerusalem is the place where men ought to worship." Just in sight was Mount Gerizim, a subject of contention between Jews and Samaritans. For many generations the latter people were intermingled with idolaters, whose religion gradually contaminated their own.

When the temple at Jerusalem was rebuilt in the days of Ezra, the Samaritans wished to join the Jews in its erection. This was refused, and bitter animosity sprang up between the two peoples. The Samaritans built a rival temple on Mount Gerizim. But their temple was destroyed by enemies, and they seemed to be under a curse; yet they would not acknowledge the temple at Jerusalem as the house of God, nor admit that the religion of the Jews was superior.

In answer to the woman, Jesus said, "Believe Me, the hour cometh when ye shall neither in this mountain, nor yet at Jerusalem, worship the Father. Ye worship ye know not what: we know what we worship: for salvation is of the Jews." Now Jesus sought to break down the prejudice of this Samaritan against the Jews. Great truths of redemption had been committed to the Jews, and from among them the Messiah was to appear.

Jesus desired to lift the thoughts of His hearer above controversy. "The hour cometh, and now is, when the true worshipers shall worship the Father in spirit and in truth: for the Father seeketh such to worship him. God is a Spirit, and they that worship Him must worship Him in spirit and in truth."

Not by seeking a holy mountain or a sacred temple are men brought into communion with heaven. In order to serve God aright, we must be born of the divine Spirit. This will purify the heart and renew the mind, giving us a willing obedience to all His requirements. This is true worship. It is the fruit of the working of the Holy Spirit. Wherever a soul reaches out after God, there the Spirit's working is manifest, and God will reveal Himself to that soul.

As the woman talked with Jesus, she was impressed with His words. As the past of her life had been spread out before her, she realized her soul thirst, which the waters of the well of Sychar could never satisfy. Nothing had hitherto so awakened her to a higher need. Jesus read the secrets of her life; yet she felt that He was her friend, pitying and loving her. While the purity of His presence condemned her sin, He had spoken no word of denunciation, but had told her of His grace that could renew the soul. The question arose in her mind, Might not this be the long-looked-for Messiah? She said to Him, "I know that Messias cometh, which is called Christ: when He is come, He will tell us all things." Jesus answered, "I that speak unto thee am He."

As the woman heard these words, faith sprang up in her heart. She accepted the wonderful announcement from the lips of the divine Teacher.

This woman was in an appreciative state of mind. She was interested in the Scriptures, and the Holy Spirit had been preparing her to receive more light. Light on Old Testament prophecies was already flashing into her mind. The water of life which Christ gives to every thirsty soul had begun to spring up in her heart.

The plain statement made by Christ to this woman could not have been made to the self-righteous Jews. That which had been withheld from them, and which the disciples were afterward enjoined to keep secret, was revealed to her. Jesus saw that she would make use of her knowledge in bringing others to share His grace.

When the disciples returned from their errand, they were surprised to find their Master speaking with the woman. He had not taken the refreshing draught He desired, and He did not stop to eat the food His disciples had brought. When the woman had gone, the disciples entreated Him to eat. They saw Him silent, His face beaming with light, and they feared to interrupt, but they thought it their duty to remind Him of His physical necessities. Jesus recognized their loving interest and said, "I have meat to eat that ye know not of."

The disciples wondered who could have brought Him food. He explained, "My food is to do the will of Him who sent Me, and to accomplish His work." RSV. To minister to a soul hungering and thirsting for truth was more comforting and refreshing to Him than eating or drinking.

Our Redeemer hungers for the sympathy and love of

those whom He has purchased with His blood. As the mother watches for the smile of recognition from her little child, which tells of the dawning of intelligence, so does Christ watch for the expression of grateful love, which shows that spiritual life is begun in the soul.

The woman had been filled with joy as she listened to Christ's words. Leaving her waterpot, she returned to the city to carry the message to others. She forgot her errand to the well, she forgot the Saviour's thirst, which she had purposed to supply. With heart over-flowing with gladness, she hastened to impart to others the light she had received.

"Come, see a man, which told me all things that ever I did," she said to the men of the city. "Is not this the Christ?" There was a new expression on her face, a change in her whole appearance. "They went out of the city, and came unto Him."

As Jesus still sat at the well side, He looked over the fields of grain spread out before Him, their tender green touched by the golden sunlight. Pointing His disciples to the scene, He employed it as a symbol: "Say not ye, There are yet four months, and then cometh harvest? behold, I say unto you, Lift up your eyes, and look on the fields; for they are white already to harvest." As He spoke, He looked on the groups coming to the well. Here was a harvest ready for the reaper.

The Cycle of Gospel Harvesting

"He that reapeth receiveth wages, and gathereth fruit unto life eternal: that both he that soweth and he that reapeth may rejoice together. And herein is that saying true, One soweth and another reapeth." Those who receive the gospel are to be His living agencies. One scatters the seed; another gathers the harvest; and both rejoice together in the reward of their labor.

Jesus said to the disciples, "I sent you to reap that whereon ye bestowed no labor: other men labored, and ye are entered into their labors." The disciples were entering into other men's labors. An unseen agency had worked silently but effectually to produce the harvest. Christ was about to water the seed with His own blood. His disciples were co-workers with Christ and with holy men of old. By the outpouring of the Spirit at Pentecost, thousands were to be converted in a day. This was the result of Christ's sowing, the harvest of His work.

The Samaritans came and heard Jesus, and believed. Crowding about Him at the well, they plied Him with questions, and eagerly received His explanations of many things that had been obscure to them. Their perplexity began to clear away. Anxious to hear more, they invited Him to their city, and begged Him to remain with them. For two days He tarried in Samaria, and many more believed.

Jesus performed no miracles among them, save in revealing the secrets of her life to the woman at the well. Yet many received Him. In their new joy they said to the woman, "Now we believe, not because of thy saying: for we have heard Him ourselves, and know that this is indeed the Christ, the Saviour of the world."

Christ Breaks Down Walls of Prejudice

Jesus had begun to break down the partition wall between Jew and Gentile, and to preach salvation to the world. He mingled freely with the Samaritans and accepted the hospitality of this despised people. He slept under their roofs, ate with them at their tables, taught in their streets, and treated them with the utmost kindness and courtesy.

In the temple at Jerusalem a low wall separated the outer court from other portions of the sacred building. On this wall were inscriptions stating that none but Jews were allowed to pass this boundary. Had a Gentile presumed to enter the inner enclosure, he would have paid the penalty with his life. But Jesus, the originator of the temple, brought to the Gentiles the salvation which the Jews rejected.

The disciples wondered at the conduct of Jesus. During the two days in Samaria, fidelity to Him kept their prejudices under control; yet in heart they were unreconciled. They were slow to learn that contempt and hatred must give place to pity and sympathy. But after the Lord's ascension, His lessons came back to them with new meaning. They recalled the Saviour's look, His words, the respect and tenderness of His bearing toward these despised strangers. When Peter went to preach in Samaria, he brought the same spirit into his work. When John was called to Ephesus and Smyrna, he remembered the experience at Shechem, and the divine Teacher's own example.

Those who call themselves the Saviour's followers may despise and shun the outcast; but no circumstance of birth or nationality, no condition of life, can turn away His love from any soul, however sinful. The gospel invitation is to be given to all. At Jacob's well Jesus did not neglect the opportunity of speaking to one woman, a stranger living in open sin.

Often He began His lessons with only a few gathered about Him, but one by one the passers-by paused to listen, until a multitude heard with wonder and awe the words of God through the heaven-sent Teacher. There may be only one to hear the message from a worker for Christ today, but who can tell how far reaching will be its influence?

The Samaritan woman proved herself a more effective missionary than His own disciples. Through her a whole cityful were brought to hear the Saviour. Every true disciple is born into the kingdom of God as a missionary. He who drinks of the living water becomes a fountain of life. The receiver becomes a giver. The grace of Christ in the soul is like a spring in the desert, refreshing all and making those who are ready to perish eager to drink of the water of life.

20 / "Except Ye See Signs and Wonders"

The Galileans who returned from the Passover brought back the report of the wonderful works of Jesus. Many of the people lamented the abuse of the temple, and the greed and arrogance of the priests. They hoped that this Man, who had put the rulers to flight, might be the looked-for Deliverer. It was reported that the prophet had declared Himself to be the Messiah.

The news of Christ's return to Cana soon spread throughout Galilee. In Capernaum the tidings attracted the attention of a Jewish nobleman who was an officer in the king's service. A son of the officer was suffering from what seemed to be an incurable disease. When the father heard of Jesus, he determined to seek help from Him. He hoped that a father's prayers might awaken the sympathy of the Great Physician.

On reaching Cana he pressed through a throng to the Saviour's presence. His faith faltered when he saw only a plainly dressed man, dusty and worn with travel. Yet he secured an interview with Jesus, told his errand, and besought the Saviour to accompany him to his home.

Jesus knew that the father had, in his own mind, made conditions concerning his belief in Him. Unless his petition should be granted, he would not receive Him as the Messiah. While the officer waited in an agony of suspense, Jesus said, "Unless ye see signs and wonders, ye will not believe."

The Saviour contrasted the petitioner's questioning unbelief with the simple faith of the Samaritans, who

This chapter is based on John 4:43-54.

asked for no miracle or sign. His word had a convincing power that reached their hearts. Christ was pained that His own people should fail to hear the voice of God speaking to them in His Son.

Yet the nobleman had a degree of faith, for he had come to ask what seemed to him the most precious of all blessings. Jesus desired not only to heal the child, but to make the officer and his household sharers in the blessings of salvation, and to kindle a light in Capernaum. But the nobleman must realize his need before he would desire the grace of Christ. Many of his nation were interested in Jesus from selfish motives. They staked their faith on the granting of temporal favor, but saw not their need of divine grace.

Like a flash of light, the Saviour's words to the nobleman laid bare his heart. He saw that his motives were selfish. His vacillating faith appeared in its true character. In deep distress he realized that his doubt might cost the life of his son. In an agony of supplication he cried, "Sir, come down ere my child die." His faith took hold upon Christ as did Jacob, when, wrestling with the Angel, he cried, "I will not let Thee go, except Thou bless me." Genesis 32:26.

Like Jacob he prevailed. "Go thy way; thy son liveth," Jesus said. The nobleman left the Saviour's presence with a peace and joy he had never known before.

At the same hour the watchers beside the dying child at Capernaum beheld a sudden, mysterious change. The flush of fever gave place to the soft glow of returning health. Strength returned to the feeble, emaciated frame. No signs of his malady lingered about the child. His burning flesh had become soft and moist, and he sank into a quiet sleep. The family were amazed, and great was the rejoicing.

The officer might have reached Capernaum on the evening after his interview with Jesus; but he did not hasten homeward. Not until the next morning did he reach Capernaum. What a homecoming was that!

When he had gone to find Jesus, his heart was heavy with sorrow. How different his feelings now! As he journeyed in the quiet of the early morning, all nature seemed to be praising God with him. While he was still some distance from his dwelling, servants came out to relieve the suspense they were sure he must feel. He showed no surprise at the news they brought, but asked at what hour the child began to mend. They answered, "Yesterday at the seventh hour the fever left him." At the very moment when the father's faith grasped the assurance, "Thy son liveth," divine love touched the dying child.

The father hurried on to greet his son. He clasped him to his heart as one restored from the dead and thanked God again and again for the wonderful restoration.

As the nobleman afterward learned more of Christ, he and all his household became disciples. Tidings of the miracle spread, and in Capernaum the way was prepared for Christ's personal ministry.

Like the afflicted father, we often are led to seek Jesus by the desire for some earthly good; and upon the granting of our request we rest our confidence in His love. The Saviour longs to give a greater blessing than we ask, and He delays the answer that He may show us the evil of our own hearts and our need of His grace. He desires us to renounce the selfishness that leads us to seek Him.

The nobleman wanted to *see* the fulfillment of his prayer before he should believe; but he had to accept the word of Jesus that his request was heard and the blessing granted. Not because we see or feel that God hears us are we to believe. We are to trust His promises. When we have asked for His blessing, we should believe that we receive it, and thank Him that we *have* received it. Then we are to go about our duties, assured that the blessing will be realized when we need it most.

21 / Bethesda and the Sanhedrin

"Now there is at Jerusalem by the sheep market a pool, which is called in the Hebrew tongue Bethesda, having five porches. In these lay a great multitude of impotent folk, of blind, halt, withered."

At certain seasons the waters of this pool were agitated, and it was commonly believed that this was supernatural and that whoever first stepped in would be healed of whatever disease he had. Hundreds of sufferers visited the place; but so great was the crowd when the water was troubled that they trampled underfoot men, women, and children weaker than themselves. Many who succeeded in reaching the pool died on its brink. Shelters had been erected about the place. Some of the sick spent the night in these porches, creeping to the edge of the pool day after day, in hope of relief.

Jesus was again at Jerusalem. Walking alone, in apparent meditation and prayer, He came to the pool. Seeing the wretched sufferers, He longed to exercise His healing power and make every sufferer whole. But it was the Sabbath day, and He knew that such an act of healing would so excite the prejudice of the Jews as to cut short His work.

The Saviour, however, saw one case of supreme wretchedness, a man who had been a helpless cripple for thirty-eight years. His disease was in a great degree the result of his own sin and was looked on as a judgment from God. Alone and friendless and feeling shut out from God's mercy, the sufferer had passed long years of misery. When it was expected that the waters

This chapter is based on John 5.

would be troubled, those who pitied his helplessness would bear him to the porches. But at the favored moment he had no one to help him in. He had seen the rippling of the water, but had never been able to get farther than the edge of the pool. His persistent efforts and continual disappointment were fast wearing away his strength.

The sick man was lying on his mat when a compassionate face bent over him. The hopeful words, "Wilt thou be made whole?" arrested his attention. He felt that in some way he was to have help. But the glow of encouragement soon faded. He remembered how often he had tried to reach the pool. "Sir, I have no man, when the water is troubled, to put me into the pool: but while I am coming, another steppeth down before me."

Jesus did not ask this sufferer to exercise faith in Him. He simply said, "Rise, take up thy bed, and walk." But the man's faith took hold upon that word. Every nerve and muscle in his crippled limbs thrilled with new life. He set his will to obey Christ, and, springing to his feet, he found himself an active man.

The Secret of Spiritual Healing

The man might have stopped to doubt and lost his one chance of healing. But he believed Christ's word, and in acting upon it he received strength. Through the same faith we may receive spiritual healing. By sin our souls have been severed from the life of God and are palsied. Of ourselves we are no more capable of living a holy life than was the impotent man capable of walking. Many who realize their helplessness and long for spiritual life are vainly striving to obtain it. The Saviour is bending over these desponding, struggling ones, saying, "Wilt thou be made whole?"

Do not wait to feel whole. Believe His word, and put your will on the side of Christ. In acting on His word you will receive strength. Whatever may be the evil which binds both soul and body, Christ is able to de-

Called before the Sanhedrin to answer the charge of Sabbath breaking, Jesus showed that His works of healing on the Sabbath were in harmony with the fourth commandment.

liver. He will impart life to the soul "dead in trespasses." Ephesians 2:1.

The restored paralytic stooped to take up his rug and blanket, and, as he straightened himself, he looked around for his Deliverer. But Jesus was lost in the crowd. As he hurried on his way with firm, free step, rejoicing in his new-found strength, he told several of the Pharisees of his cure. He was surprised at the coldness with which they listened.

They interrupted him, asking why he was carrying his bed on the Lord's day. In his joy the man had forgotten it was the Sabbath. He answered boldly, "He that made me whole, said unto me, take up thy bed, and walk." They asked who had done this, but he could not tell. These rulers wished for direct proof that they might condemn Jesus as a Sabbathbreaker. In their judgment He had not only broken the law in healing the sick man on the Sabbath but had committed sacrilege in bidding him to bear away his bed.

Meaningless Requirements

The Jews had so perverted the law with meaningless requirements that they made it a yoke of bondage, and had made its observance an intolerable burden. A Jew was not allowed to kindle a fire nor even light a candle on the Sabbath. As a consequence the people were dependent on the Gentiles for many services which their rulers forbade them to do for themselves. They thought salvation was restricted to the Jews, and that the condition of others, already hopeless, could be made no worse. But God has given no commandments which cannot be obeyed by all.

In the temple Jesus met the man who had been healed. He had come to bring a sin offering and also a thank offering for the great mercy he had received. Jesus made Himself known. The healed man was overjoyed at meeting his Deliverer. Ignorant of the enmity toward Jesus, he told the Pharisees that this was He who had performed the cure. "Therefore did the

Jews persecute Jesus, and sought to slay Him, because He had done these things on the Sabbath day.''

Jesus was brought before the Sanhedrin to answer the charge of Sabbathbreaking. Had the Jews been an independent nation, such a charge would have served their purpose for putting Him to death. But the accusations brought against Christ would have no weight in a Roman court. Other objects, however, they hoped to secure. Christ was gaining an influence greater than their own, and multitudes uninterested in the harangues of the rabbis were attracted by His teaching. He spoke of God, not as an avenging judge, but as a tender father. By His words and works of mercy He was breaking the oppressive power of man-made commandments, and presenting the love of God.

People Gathering to Jesus

In one of the earliest prophecies of Christ it is written, ''The scepter shall not depart from Judah, nor a lawgiver from between his feet, until Shiloh come; and unto Him shall the gathering of the people be.'' Genesis 49:10. The people were gathering to Christ. If the priests and rabbis had not interposed, His teaching would have wrought such a reformation as this world has never witnessed. But these leaders determined to break down the influence of Jesus. Arraignment before the Sanhedrin and open condemnation would aid in effecting this. Whoever dared to condemn the rabbinical requirements was regarded as guilty of treason. On this ground the rabbis hoped to excite suspicion of Christ as trying to overthrow established customs, thus causing division among the people, and preparing the way for complete subjugation by the Romans.

After Satan had failed to overcome Christ in the wilderness, he combined his forces to oppose Christ and thwart His work. He matured his plans to blind the minds of the Jewish people that they might not recognize their Redeemer, imbuing their leaders with his own enmity against the champion of truth. He would lead them to reject Christ and make His life as bitter as possible, hoping to discourage Him in His mission.

Jesus had come to "magnify the law, and make it honorable." Isaiah 42:21. He had come to free the Sabbath from those burdensome requirements that had made it a curse instead of a blessing. For this reason He had chosen the Sabbath for the healing at Bethesda. He could have healed the sick man on any other day, or simply have cured him without bidding him bear away his bed. But He selected the worst case and told the man to carry his bed through the city to publish the great work wrought on him. This would open the way for Him to denounce the restrictions of the Jews in regard to the Lord's day and to declare their traditions void.

Jesus stated that the work of relieving the afflicted was in harmony with the Sabbath law. God's angels are ever ministering to suffering humanity. "My Father worketh hitherto, and I work." All the days are God's, in which to carry out His plans for the human race. If the Jews' interpretation of the law was correct, then He who instituted the Sabbath must put a period to His labor, and stop the never-ending routine of the universe.

Should God forbid the sun to perform its office on the Sabbath? Must He command the brooks to stay from watering fields and forests? Must wheat and corn stop growing? Must trees and flowers put forth no bud nor blossom on the Sabbath?

God could not for a moment stay His hand, or man would faint and die. Man also has work to perform on this day. The sick must be cared for, the wants of the needy supplied. God's holy rest day was made for man; God does not desire His creatures to suffer an hour's pain that may be relieved on the Sabbath.

The Sabbath law forbids secular labor on the rest day of the Lord; the toil that gains a livelihood must cease; no labor for worldly pleasure or profit is lawful on that day. But as God ceased His labor of creating, and rested on the Sabbath, so man is to leave the occupations of daily life and devote those sacred hours to healthful rest, worship, and holy deeds. Christ's healing the sick honored the Sabbath.

But the Pharisees were still more incensed. Jesus had not only broken the law, according to their understanding, but in calling God "His own Father" had declared Himself equal with God. RSV. They accused Him of blasphemy. These adversaries of Christ could only cite their customs and traditions, and these seemed weak and vapid when compared with the arguments Jesus had drawn from the Word of God and the unceasing round of nature. But the rabbis evaded the points He made and sought to stir up anger against Him because He claimed to be equal with God. Had they not feared the people, the priests and rabbis would have slain Jesus on the spot. But popular sentiment in His favor was strong. Many justified His healing of the sufferer at Bethesda.

Jesus Dependent on the Father's Power

Jesus repelled the charge of blasphemy. My authority, He said, is that I am the Son of God, one with Him in nature, will, and purpose. I cooperate with God. "The Son can do nothing of Himself, but what He seeth the Father do." The priests and rabbis were taking the Son of God to task for the very work He had been sent into the world to do. They felt sufficient in themselves, and realized no need of a higher wisdom. But the Son of God was surrendered to the Father's will and dependent on His power. Christ made no plans for Himself. Day by day the Father unfolded His plans. So should we depend upon God that our lives may be the simple outworking of His will.

The words of Christ teach that we should regard ourselves as inseparably bound to our Father in heaven. Whatever our position, we are dependent upon God. He has appointed us our work and has endowed us with means for that work. So long as we surrender the will to

God and trust in His strength and wisdom, we shall be guided in safe paths, to fulfill our appointed part in His plan. But the one who depends upon his own wisdom and power is separating himself from God and fulfilling the purpose of the enemy of God and man.

The Sadducees held that there would be no resurrection of the body, but Jesus told them that one of the greatest works of His Father is raising the dead and that He Himself had power to do the same work. "As the Father raiseth up the dead, and quickeneth them; even so the Son quickeneth whom He will." "The hour is coming, and now is, when the dead shall hear the voice of the Son of God: and they that hear shall live." Christ declared that the power which gives life to the dead was among them, and they were to behold its manifestation. This same resurrection power gives life to the soul and sets men "free from the law of sin and death." Romans 8:2. Through faith the soul is kept from sin. He who opens his heart to Christ becomes a partaker of that mighty power which shall bring forth his body from the grave.

The humble Nazarene rose above humanity, threw off the guise of sin and shame, and stood revealed, the Son of God, One with the Creator of the universe. His hearers were spellbound. No man ever spoke words like His, or bore himself with such kingly majesty. His utterances were clear and plain, fully declaring His mission. "The Father judgeth no man, but hath committed all judgment unto the Son. . . . The Father . . . hath given Him authority to execute judgment also, because He is the Son of man."

The priests and rulers set themselves up as judges to condemn Christ's work, but He declared Himself to be their judge and judge of all the earth. Through Him has come every blessing from God to the fallen race. As soon as there was sin, there was a Saviour. He who has given light to all, He who has followed the soul with tender entreaty, seeking to win it from sin to holiness, is in one its advocate and judge. He who through all the ages has been seeking to wrest the captives from the deceiver's grasp, is the One who will pass judgment on every soul.

Because He has tasted the dregs of human affliction and temptation, and understands the frailties of men; because He has withstood the temptations of Satan and will deal justly and tenderly with the souls that His own blood has been poured out to save—because of this, the Son of man is appointed to execute judgment.

But "God sent not His Son into the world to condemn the world; but that the world through Him might be saved." John 3:17. And before the Sanhedrin Jesus declared, "He that heareth My word, and believeth Him that sent Me, hath eternal life, and cometh not into judgment, but hath passed out of death into life." RV.

Resurrection of Life

"The hour is coming when all who are in the tombs will hear His voice and come forth, those who have done good, to the resurrection of life, and those who have done evil, to the resurrection of judgment." RSV.

The only light that can lighten the gloom of the grave was shining upon Israel. But self-will is blind. Jesus had violated the traditions of the rabbis, and they would not believe.

The time, the place, the intensity of feeling that pervaded the assembly combined to make the words of Jesus before the Sanhedrin the more impressive. The highest religious authorities of the nation were seeking the life of Him who declared Himself the restorer of Israel. The Lord of the Sabbath was arraigned to answer the charge of breaking the Sabbath. His judges looked on Him with astonishment and rage, but His words were unanswerable. He denied the right of priests and rabbis to interfere with His work. He refused to plead guilty to their charges or be catechized by them.

Instead of apologizing, Jesus rebuked the rulers for their ignorance of the Scriptures. He declared that they had rejected the Word of God, inasmuch as they had rejected Him whom God had sent. "Ye search the scriptures, because ye think that in them ye have eternal life; and these are they which bear witness of Me." RV.

The Old Testament Scriptures are irradiated with the glory of the Son of God. So far as it was of divine institution, the entire system of Judaism was a compacted prophecy of the gospel. Through the patriarchal line and the legal economy, heaven's glorious light made plain the footsteps of the Redeemer. In every sacrifice Christ's death was shown. In every cloud of incense His righteousness ascended. In the awful mystery of the holy of holies His glory dwelt.

The Council Fails to Intimidate Jesus

The Jews supposed that in their mere outward knowledge of the Scriptures they had eternal life. But having rejected Christ in His Word, they rejected Him in person. "Ye will not come to Me," He said, "that ye might have life."

The Jewish leaders had studied the teachings of the prophets, not with a sincere desire to know the truth, but with the purpose of finding evidence to sustain their ambitious hopes. When Christ came in a manner contrary to their expectations, they would not receive Him and tried to prove Him a deceiver. The more directly the Saviour spoke to them in His works of mercy, the more determined they were in resisting the light.

Jesus said, "I receive not honor from men." It was not the Sanhedrin's sanction He desired. He was invested with the honor and authority of Heaven. Had He desired it, angels would have come to do Him homage. But for their own sake and for the sake of the nation whose leaders they were, He desired the Jewish rulers to discern His character.

"I am come in My Father's name, and ye receive Me not: if another shall come in his own name, him ye will receive." When others should come, assuming the character of Christ but seeking their own glory, they would be received. Why? Because he who seeks his own glory appeals to the desire for self-exaltation in others. The Jews would receive the false teacher because he flattered their pride. But the teaching of Christ was spiritual and demanded the sacrifice of self; therefore they would not receive it. To them His voice was the voice of a stranger.

Is not the same thing being repeated in our day? Are there not many, even religious leaders, who are rejecting the Word of God that they may keep their own traditions?

"Had ye believed Moses, ye would have believed Me: for he wrote of Me. But if ye believe not his writings, how shall ye believe My words?" If they had listened to the divine voice that spoke through their great leader, Moses, they would have recognized it in the teachings of Christ.

The priests and rabbis saw that their opposition to Jesus was without excuse, yet their murderous hatred was not quenched. Fear seized them as they witnessed the convincing power that attended His ministry, but they locked themselves in darkness.

They had failed to subvert the authority of Jesus or alienate the people, many of whom were convicted by His words. The rulers themselves felt deep condemnation, yet they were determined to take His life. They sent messengers all over the country to warn the people against Jesus as an impostor. Spies were sent to report what He said and did. The precious Saviour was now most surely standing under the shadow of the cross.

22 / The Imprisonment and Death of John

John the Baptist had been first in heralding Christ's kingdom, and he was first also in suffering. From the free air of the wilderness, he was now shut in by the walls of a dungeon, a prisoner in the fortress of Herod Antipas. Herod himself had listened to the Baptist and trembled under the call to repentance. "Herod feared John, knowing that he was a just man and an holy." John denounced his iniquitous alliance with Herodias, his brother's wife. For a time Herod feebly sought to break the chain of lust that bound him; but Herodias fastened him more firmly in her toils and found revenge on the Baptist by inducing Herod to cast him into prison.

The gloom and inaction of his prison life weighed heavily on John. As week after week passed, bringing no change, despondency and doubt crept over him. His disciples brought him tidings of the works of Jesus and how the people were flocking to Him. But why, if this new teacher was the Messiah, did He do nothing to effect the release of John? Doubts which otherwise would never have arisen were suggested to John. Satan rejoiced to see how the words of these disciples bruised the soul of the Lord's messenger. How often the friends of a good man prove to be his most dangerous enemies!

John the Baptist expected Jesus to take the throne of David; and as time passed, and the Saviour made no claim to kingly authority, John became perplexed. He had looked for the high places of human pride and

This chapter is based on Matthew 11:1-11; 14:1-11; Mark 6:17-28; Luke 7:19-28.

137

power to be cast down. The Messiah would thoroughly purge His floor, gather the wheat into His garner, and burn up the chaff with unquenchable fire. See Isaiah 40; Matthew 3. Like Elijah, he looked for the Lord to reveal Himself as a God who would answer by fire.

The Baptist had stood as a fearless reprover of iniquity in high places and low. He had dared to face king Herod with the plain rebuke of sin. And now from his dungeon he watched for the Lion of the tribe of Judah to cast down the pride of the oppressor and to deliver the poor. But Jesus seemed to content Himself with healing and teaching the people. He was eating at the tables of the publicans, while every day the Roman yoke rested more heavily on Israel, while King Herod and his vile paramour worked their will, and the cries of the poor and suffering went up to heaven.

A Terrible Disappointment

All this seemed a mystery. The whisperings of demons tortured John's spirit, and the shadow of a terrible fear crept over him. Could it be that the long-hoped-for Deliverer had not yet appeared? John had been bitterly disappointed in the result of his mission. He had expected that the message from God would have the same effect as when the law was read in the days of Josiah and of Ezra (2 Chronicles 34; Nehemiah 8), that there would follow a deep work of repentance. Had his whole life been sacrificed in vain? Had his work for his own disciples been fruitless? Had he been unfaithful in his mission, that he was now cut off from labor? If the promised Deliverer had appeared and John had been found true to his calling, would not Jesus now overthrow the oppressor's power and set free His herald?

But the Baptist did not surrender his faith in Christ. The voice from heaven, the descending dove, the spotless purity of Jesus, the power of the Holy Spirit that had rested on John as he came into the Saviour's presence, the testimony of the Scriptures—all witnessed that Jesus was the Promised One.

John determined to send a message to Jesus. This he entrusted to two of his disciples, hoping that an interview with the Saviour would confirm their faith. And he longed for some word from Christ spoken directly for himself.

The two disciples came to Jesus with their message: "Art Thou He that should come, or do we look for another?" The question was keenly bitter and disappointing to human nature. If John, the faithful forerunner, failed to discern Christ's mission, what could be expected from the self-seeking multitude?

The Saviour did not at once answer the disciples' question. As they stood wondering at His silence, the sick and afflicted were coming to be healed. The blind, the diseased were eagerly pressing into the presence of Jesus. The voice of the mighty Healer penetrated the deaf ear. A word, a touch of His hand, opened the blind eyes. Jesus rebuked disease and banished fever. His voice reached the ears of the dying, and they arose in health and vigor. While He healed their diseases, the poor peasants and laborers who were shunned by the rabbis as unclean gathered close about Him, and He spoke to them the words of eternal life.

Jesus Presents Evidence

Thus the day wore away, the disciples of John seeing and hearing all. At last Jesus called them to Him and told them to go and tell John what they had witnessed, adding, "Blessed is he, whosoever shall find none occasion of stumbling in Me." RV. The evidence of His divinity was seen; His glory was shown in His condescension to our low estate.

The disciples bore the message, and it was enough. John recalled the prophecy concerning the Messiah, "The Lord hath anointed Me to preach good tidings unto the meek; He hath sent Me to bind up the brokenhearted, to proclaim liberty to the captives." Isaiah 61:1. The works of Christ declared Him to be the Messiah. Jesus was to do His work, not with the clash of arms and the overturning of thrones and kingdoms, but through speaking to the hearts of men by a life of mercy and self-sacrifice.

The principle of the Baptist's own life was the principle of the Messiah's kingdom. But that which was to him convincing evidence of Christ's divinity would be no evidence to the leaders in Israel. John saw that the Saviour's mission could win from them only hatred and condemnation. He, the forerunner, was drinking of the cup which Christ Himself must drain to its dregs.

The Saviour's gentle reproof was not lost upon John. Understanding more clearly now the nature of Christ's mission, he yielded himself to God for life or for death, as should best serve the interests of the cause he loved.

The Saviour's heart went out in sympathy to the faithful witness in Herod's dungeon. He would not leave the people to conclude that God had forsaken John or that his faith had failed in the day of trial. "What went ye out into the wilderness to see?" He said. "A reed shaken with the wind?"

As tall reeds beside the Jordan, the rabbis who had stood as critics of the Baptist's mission were swayed this way and that by the winds of popular opinion. Yet for fear of the people they dared not openly oppose his work. But God's messenger was of no such craven spirit. To Pharisees, Sadducees, King Herod and his court, princes and soldiers, publicans and peasants, John had spoken with equal plainness. He was no trembling reed. In prison he was the same in loyalty to God; in faithfulness to principle he was firm as a rock.

No Man Greater

Jesus continued, "What went ye out for to see? A man clothed in soft raiment? Behold, they which are gorgeously appareled, and live delicately, are in kings' courts." Rich apparel and the luxuries of this life are not the portion of God's servants. The priests and rulers arrayed themselves in rich robes. They were more anxious to gain the admiration of men than to win the approval of God. Their allegiance was not given to God but to the kingdom of this world.

"But what went ye out for to see?" asked Jesus. "A prophet? . . . This is he, of whom it is written,

> Behold, I send My messenger before Thy face,
> Which shall prepare Thy way before Thee."

"I say unto you, among them that are born of women there hath not risen a greater than John the Baptist." In the announcement to Zacharias before the birth of John, the angel had declared, "He shall be great in the sight of the Lord." Luke 1:15. In the estimation of Heaven, what is it that constitutes greatness? Not that which the world counts greatness; not wealth, or rank, or noble descent, or intellectual gifts, in themselves considered. It is moral worth that God values. Love and purity are the attributes He prizes most. John was great in the sight of the Lord when he refrained from seeking honor for himself but pointed all to Jesus as the Promised One. His unselfish joy in the ministry of Christ presents the highest type of nobility ever revealed in man.

More Than a Prophet

John was "more than a prophet." While prophets had seen from afar Christ's advent, to John it was given to behold Him and to present Him to Israel as the Sent of God. The prophet John was the lesser light to be followed by a greater. No other light ever will shine so clearly on fallen man as the teaching and example of Jesus.

Aside from the joy that John found in his mission, his life had been one of sorrow. His was a lonely lot. And he was not permitted to see the result of his own labors. It was not his privilege to be with Christ and behold the light that shone through every word of Christ, shedding glory on the promises of prophecy.

Herod believed John to be a prophet of God and fully

intended to set him at liberty. But he feared Herodias. She knew that by direct measures she could never win Herod's consent to the death of John; hence she resolved to accomplish her purpose by stratagem. On the king's birthday an entertainment was to be given. There would be feasting and drunkenness. Herod might then be influenced according to her will.

When the great day arrived, the king with his lords was feasting and drinking. Herodias sent her daughter into the banquet hall to dance for the guests. Salome was in the first flush of womanhood, and her voluptuous beauty captivated the lordly revelers. A flattering compliment was paid to Herod when this daughter of Israel's priests and princes danced for his guests.

The king was dazed with wine. Passion held sway, and reason was dethroned. He saw only the reveling guests, the banquet, the wine, the flashing lights, and the girl dancing before him. In the recklessness of the moment he desired to make some display that would exalt him before the great men of his realm. With an oath he promised the daughter of Herodias whatever she might ask, even to half of his kingdom.

Salome hastened to her mother. What should she ask? The answer was ready—the head of John the Baptist. Salome shrank from presenting the request, but the determination of Herodias prevailed. The girl returned with the terrible petition: "I want you to give me at once the head of John the Baptist on a platter." RSV.

Herod was astonished and confounded. He was horror-stricken at the thought of taking the life of John. Yet he was unwilling to appear fickle or rash. The oath had been made in honor of his guests, and if one of them had offered a word against the fulfillment of his promise, he would gladly have spared the prophet. He gave them opportunity to speak in the prisoner's behalf. They knew John to be a servant of God. But though shocked at the girl's demand, they were too besotted to remonstrate. No voice was raised to save the life of Heaven's messenger. Upon these men of high positions rested grave responsibilities, yet they had given themselves up to drunkenness. Their heads were turned with the giddy scene of music and dancing, and conscience lay dormant. By their silence they pronounced the sentence of death on the prophet of God, to satisfy the revenge of an abandoned woman.

Herod reluctantly commanded the execution of the prophet. Soon the head of John was brought in. Never more would that voice be heard calling men to repentance. The revels of one night cost the life of one of the greatest of the prophets.

How often have the innocent been sacrificed through the intemperance of those who should have been guardians of justice! He who puts the intoxicating cup to his lips makes himself responsible for all the injustice he may commit under its besotting power. Those who have jurisdiction over the lives of their fellowmen should be held guilty of a crime when they yield to intemperance. They need full command of their physical, mental, and moral powers that they may possess vigor of intellect, and a high sense of justice.

Herodias exulted in her revenge and flattered herself that Herod's conscience would no longer be troubled. But no happiness resulted. Her name became abhorred, while Herod was tormented by remorse. He was constantly seeking to find relief from a guilty conscience. As he recalled John's self-denial, his solemn, earnest appeals, his sound judgment in counsel, and then remembered how he had come to his death, Herod could find no rest. In the affairs of state, receiving honors from men, he bore a smiling face while he concealed an anxious heart oppressed with fear. He was convinced that God had witnessed the revelry of the banqueting room, that He had seen the exultation of Herodias, and the insult she offered to the severed head of her reprover.

When Herod heard of the works of Christ, he thought God had raised John from the dead. He was in constant fear that John would avenge his death by condemning him and his house. Herod was reaping the result of sin—"a trembling heart, and failing eyes, and a languishing soul. . . . In the morning you shall say, 'Would it were evening!' and at evening . . . 'Would it were morning!' because of the dread which your heart shall fear." Deuteronomy 28:65-67, RSV. No torture is keener than a guilty conscience which gives no rest day nor night.

The Reason Christ Did Not Deliver John

Many minds question why John the Baptist should have been left to languish and die in prison. But this dark providence can never shake our confidence in God when we remember that John was but a sharer in the sufferings of Christ. All who follow Christ will wear the crown of sacrifice. Satan will war against the principle of self-sacrifice wherever it is manifested.

Satan had been unwearied in his efforts to draw away the Baptist from a life of unreserved surrender to God; but he had failed. In the temptation in the wilderness, Satan had been defeated. Now he determined to bring sorrow upon Christ by striking John. The One whom he could not entice to sin he would cause to suffer.

Jesus did not interpose to deliver His servant. He knew that John would bear the test. Gladly would the Saviour have come to brighten John's dungeon gloom with His own presence. But He was not to imperil His own mission. For the sake of thousands who in after years must pass from prison to death, John was to drink the cup of martyrdom. As the followers of Jesus should languish in lonely cells, or perish by the sword, the rack, or the fagot, apparently forsaken by God and man, what a stay to their hearts would be the thought that John the Baptist had passed through a similar experience!

John was not forsaken. He had the companionship of heavenly angels, who opened to him the prophecies concerning Christ and the precious promises of Scripture. To John, as to those that came after him, was given the assurance, "Lo, I am with you always, to the close of the age." Matthew 28:20, RSV.

God never leads His children otherwise than they would choose to be led, if they could see the end from the beginning, and discern the purpose they are fulfilling as coworkers with Him. Not Enoch, who was translated to heaven, not Elijah, who ascended in a chariot of fire, was greater or more honored than John the Baptist, who perished alone in the dungeon. "Unto you it is given in the behalf of Christ, not only to believe on Him, but also to suffer for His sake." Philippians 1:29. Of all the gifts that Heaven can bestow upon men, fellowship with Christ in His sufferings is the most weighty trust and the highest honor.

23 / How Daniel Identified Jesus as the Christ

The Messiah's coming had been first announced in Judea. On the hills of Bethlehem the angels had proclaimed the birth of Jesus. To Jerusalem the magi had come in search of Him.

If the leaders in Israel had received Christ, He would have honored them as His messengers to carry the gospel to the world. But Israel knew not the time of her visitation. The jealousy and distrust of the Jewish leaders had ripened into open hatred, and the hearts of the people were turned away from Jesus. The Sanhedrin was bent upon His death; therefore Jesus departed from Jerusalem, from the people who had been instructed in the law, and turned to another class to proclaim His message.

In every succeeding generation, the history of Christ's withdrawal from Judea has been repeated. When the Reformers preached the word of God, they had no thought of separating from the established church; but the religious leaders would not tolerate the light, and those that bore it were forced to seek another class who were longing for truth. In our day few professed followers of the Reformers are listening for the voice of God, ready to accept truth in whatever guise it may be presented. Often those who follow in the steps of the Reformers are forced to turn away from churches they love in order to declare the plain word of God. Many are obliged to leave the church of their fathers that they may render obedience.

The people of Galilee presented a more favorable

field for the Saviour's work. Less under the control of bigotry, their minds were more open for the reception of truth. The province was the home of a much larger mixture of people of other nations than was Judea.

As Jesus traveled through Galilee, teaching and healing, multitudes came, many even from Judea. Enthusiasm ran so high it was necessary to take precautions lest the Roman authorities be aroused to fear an insurrection. Hungering and thirsting souls feasted upon the grace of a merciful Saviour.

Prophet Daniel Foretold Christ's Ministry

The burden of Christ's preaching was, "The time is fulfilled, and the kingdom of God is at hand: repent ye, and believe the gospel." Mark 1:15. The gospel message as given by the Saviour was based on the prophecies. The "time" which He declared fulfilled was the period made known to Daniel. "Seventy weeks," said the angel Gabriel, "are determined upon thy people and upon thy Holy City, to finish the transgression, and to make an end of sins, and to make reconciliation for iniquity, and to bring in everlasting righteousness, and to seal up the vision and prophecy, and to anoint the Most Holy." Daniel 9:24. A day in prophecy stands for a year. Ezekiel 4:6. The seventy weeks, or 490 days, represent 490 years.

A starting point for this period is given: "Know therefore and understand, that from the going forth of the commandment to restore and to build Jerusalem unto the Messiah the Prince shall be seven weeks, and threescore and two weeks," sixty-nine weeks, or 483 years. Daniel 9:25.

The commandment to restore and build Jerusalem, as completed by the decree of Artaxerxes Longimanus (see Ezra 6:14; 7:1, 9, RSV), went into effect in the autumn of 457 B.C. From this time 483 years extend to the autumn of A.D. 27. According to the prophecy, this period was to reach to the Messiah, the Anointed One. In A.D. 27, Jesus at His baptism received the anointing of the Holy Spirit and soon afterward began His ministry. Then the message was proclaimed, "The time is fulfilled."

Then, said the angel, "He shall confirm the covenant with many for one week [seven years]." For seven years after the Saviour entered on His ministry, the gospel was to be preached especially to the Jews; for three and a half years by Christ Himself, and afterward by the apostles. "In the midst of the week He shall cause the sacrifice and the oblation to cease." Daniel 9:27. In the spring of A.D. 31, Christ the true sacrifice was offered on Calvary. Then the veil of the temple was rent in twain, showing that the sacredness and significance of the sacrificial service had departed. The time had come for the earthly sacrifice and oblation to cease.

The one week—seven years—ended in A.D. 34. Then, by stoning Stephen, the Jews finally sealed their rejection of the gospel. The disciples, scattered by persecution, "went everywhere preaching the word" (Acts 8:4); and shortly after, Saul the persecutor was converted, and became Paul, the apostle to the Gentiles.

The time of Christ's coming, His anointing by the Holy Spirit, His death, and the giving of the gospel to the Gentiles were definitely pointed out. It was the privilege of the Jews to understand these prophecies and to recognize their fulfillment in the mission of Jesus. Referring to the prophecy given to Daniel in regard to their time, Christ said to His disciples, "Whoso readeth, let him understand." Matthew 24:15. After His resurrection He explained to them in "all the prophets" "the things concerning Himself." Luke 24:27. The Saviour had spoken through the prophets and "testified beforehand the sufferings of Christ, and the glory that should follow." 1 Peter 1:11.

It was Gabriel, the angel next in rank to the Son of God, who came with the divine message to Daniel. It was Gabriel whom Christ sent to open the future to

John; and a blessing is pronounced on those who read and hear the words of the prophecy, and keep the things written therein. See Revelation 1:3. God's blessing will attend the reverent, prayerful study of the prophetic scriptures.

As the message of Christ's first advent announced the kingdom of His grace, so the message of His second advent announces the kingdom of His glory. And the second message, like the first, is based on the prophecies. The Saviour Himself has given signs of His coming, and He says, "Take heed to yourselves, lest at any time your hearts be overcharged with surfeiting, and drunkenness, and cares of this life, and so that day come upon you unawares." "Watch ye therefore, and pray always, that ye may be accounted worthy to escape all these things that shall come to pass, and to stand before the Son of man." Luke 21:34, 36.

The Jews misinterpreted the Word of God and knew not the time of their visitation. The years of the ministry of Christ and His apostles they spent in plotting the destruction of the Lord's messengers. Earthly ambitions absorbed them. So today the kingdom of this world absorbs men's thoughts, and they take no note of the rapidly fulfilling prophecies and the tokens of the swift-coming kingdom of God. While we are not to know the hour of our Lord's return, we may know when it is near. "Therefore let us not sleep, as do others; but let us watch and be sober." 1 Thessalonians 5:6.

24 / "Is Not This the Carpenter's Son?"

Across the bright days of Christ's ministry in Galilee, one shadow lay—the people of Nazareth rejected Him. "Is not this the carpenter's son?" they said. Matthew 13:55. During His youth, Jesus had worshiped among His brethren in the synagogue at Nazareth. Since the opening of His ministry He had been absent from them, but as He again appeared, their expectation was excited to the highest pitch. Here were the familiar faces He had known from infancy. Here were His mother, His brothers and sisters, and all eyes were turned on Him as He entered the synagogue on the Sabbath and took His place among the worshipers.

In the regular service the elder exhorted the people still to hope for the Coming One, who would bring in a glorious reign and banish all oppression. He sought to encourage his hearers by rehearsing the evidence that the Messiah's coming was near. He kept prominent the thought that He would appear at the head of armies to deliver Israel.

When a rabbi was present he was expected to deliver the sermon, and any Israelite might give the reading from the prophets. Upon this Sabbath Jesus was requested to take part in the service. He "stood up to read; and there was given to Him the book of the prophet Isaiah." RSV. The scripture He read was understood as referring to the Messiah:

> The Spirit of the Lord is upon Me,
> Because He hath anointed Me to preach the
>   gospel to the poor.

This chapter is based on Luke 4:16-30.

> He hath sent Me to heal the brokenhearted,
> To preach deliverance to the captives,
> And recovering of sight to the blind,
> To set at liberty them that are bruised,
> To preach the acceptable year of the Lord.

"And He closed the book, and gave it back to the attendant, and sat down; and the eyes of all in the synagogue were fixed on Him. . . . And all spoke well of Him, and wondered at the gracious words which proceeded out of His mouth." RSV.

Explaining the words He had read, Jesus spoke of the Messiah as a reliever of the oppressed, a healer of the afflicted, restoring sight to the blind, and revealing the light of truth. The wonderful import of His words thrilled the hearers with a power they had never felt before. The tide of divine influence broke every barrier down. As their hearts were moved by the Holy Spirit, they responded with fervent amens and praises to the Lord.

But when Jesus announced, "This day is this scripture fulfilled in your ears," they were suddenly recalled to think of the claims of Him who had been addressing them. They, children of Abraham, had been represented as being in bondage, prisoners to be delivered from the power of evil, in darkness, and needing the light of truth. Their pride was offended. Jesus' work for them was to be altogether different from what they desired. Their deeds might be investigated too closely. They shrank from inspection by those clear, searching eyes.

Who is this Jesus? they questioned. He who had claimed the glory of the Messiah was the son of a carpenter. They had seen Him toiling up and down the hills. They were acquainted with His brothers and sisters, and knew His life and labors. They had seen Him develop from childhood to manhood. Although His life had been spotless, they would not believe He was the Promised One. They opened the door to doubt, and their hearts became harder for having been momentarily softened. With intense energy Satan worked to fasten them in unbelief.

They had been stirred by the conviction that it was their Redeemer who addressed them. But Jesus now gave them evidence of His divinity by revealing their secret thoughts. "No prophet is acceptable in his own country. But in truth, I tell you, there were many widows in Israel in the days of Elijah, when the heaven was shut up three years and six months, when there came a great famine over all the land; and Elijah was sent to none of them but only to Zarephath, in the land of Sidon, to a woman who was a widow. And there were many lepers in Israel in the time of the prophet Elisha; and none of them was cleansed, but only Naaman the Syrian." RSV.

The servants whom God had chosen were not allowed to labor for a hardhearted, unbelieving people. In the days of Elijah, Israel had rejected the Lord's messengers. Thus God found a refuge for His servant in a heathen land, with a woman who did not belong to the chosen people. But this woman's heart was open to the greater light that God sent through His prophet.

For the same reason in Elisha's time the lepers of Israel were passed by. But Naaman, a heathen nobleman, was in a condition to receive the gifts of God's grace. He was not only cleansed from leprosy but blessed with a knowledge of the true God. The heathen who choose the right as far as they can distinguish it are in a more favorable condition than those who profess to serve God but disregard light, and by their daily life contradict their profession.

Jesus Set Their Real Condition Before Them

The words of Jesus to His hearers struck at the root of their self-righteousness. Every word cut like a knife as their real condition was set before them. They now scorned the faith with which Jesus had at first inspired them. They would not admit that He who had sprung from poverty and lowliness was other than a common man. Their unbelief bred malice. In wrath they cried out against the Saviour. Fierce national pride was aroused, and His words were drowned in a tumult of voices. Their prejudices offended, they were ready to commit murder.

The assembly broke up, and laying hands on Jesus they thrust Him from the synagogue and out of the city. Eager for His destruction, they hurried Him to the brow of a precipice, intending to cast Him down head-long. Shouts filled the air. Some were casting stones at Him when suddenly He disappeared. Heavenly messengers were with Him in the midst of that maddened throng and conducted Him to safety.

So, in all ages, the confederacy of evil is arrayed against Christ's faithful followers; but armies of heaven encamp about all who love God, to deliver them. In eternity we shall know that messengers from God attended our steps from day to day.

Not without one more call to repentance could Jesus give up His hearers in the synagogue. Toward the close of His ministry in Galilee, He again visited the home of His childhood. The fame of His preaching and miracles had filled the land. None in Nazareth could now deny that He possessed more than human power. About them were whole villages in which He had healed all the sick.

Again as they listened to His words the Nazarenes were moved by the Divine Spirit. But even now they would not admit that this Man, brought up among them, was greater than themselves. Still there rankled the bitter memory that while He had claimed to be the Promised One, He had really denied them a place with Israel; for He had shown them less worthy of God's favor than a heathen man and woman. Though they questioned, "Whence hath this Man this wisdom, and these mighty works?" (Matthew 13:54), they would not receive Him as the Christ of God. Because of their unbelief, the Saviour could not work many miracles among them, and reluctantly He departed, never to return.

Unbelief, having once been cherished, continued to control the men of Nazareth, the Sanhedrin, and the nation. Their rejection of the Holy Spirit culminated in the cross of Calvary, in the destruction of their city, in the scattering of the nation.

Christ longed to open to Israel the precious treasures of truth! But they clung to their creed and useless ceremonies. They spent their money for chaff and husks, when the bread of life was within their reach. Again and again Christ quoted from the prophets, and declared, "This day is this scripture fulfilled in your ears." If they had honestly searched the Scriptures, bringing their theories to the test of God's Word, Jesus need not have declared, "Behold, your house is left unto you desolate." Luke 13:35. The calamity that laid their proud city in ruins might have been averted.

But the lessons of Christ demanded repentance. If they accepted His teachings, their practices must be changed, and their cherished hopes relinquished. They must go contrary to the opinions of the great thinkers and teachers of the time.

The Jewish leaders were filled with spiritual pride. They loved the highest seats in the synagogue. They were gratified with the sound of their titles on the lips of men. As real piety declined, they became more jealous for their traditions and ceremonies. Their minds darkened by selfish prejudice, they could not harmonize the power of Christ's convicting words with the humility of His life. His poverty seemed wholly inconsistent with His claim to be the Messiah. Why was He so unpretending? If He was what He claimed to be, why was He satisfied to be without the force of arms? How could the power and glory so long anticipated bring the nations as subjects to the city of the Jews?

But it was not simply the absence of outward glory in His life that led the Jews to reject Jesus. He was the embodiment of purity, and they were impure. His sincerity revealed their insincerity, and discovered iniquity to them in its odious character. Such a light was unwelcome. They could have borne the disappointment of their ambitious hopes better than Christ's reproof of their sins, and the reproach they felt even from the presence of His purity.

25 / The Call by the Sea

Day was breaking over the Sea of Galilee. The disciples, weary with a night of fruitless toil, were still in their fishing boats on the lake. Jesus had come to spend a quiet hour by the waterside in the early morning. He hoped for a little rest from the multitude that followed Him day after day. But soon the people began to gather, so that He was pressed on all sides.

To escape the pressure Jesus stepped into Peter's boat and told him to pull out a little from the shore. Here He could be better seen and heard by all, and from the boat He taught the multitude on the beach. He who was the Honored of heaven was declaring the great things of His kingdom in the open air to the common people. The lake, the mountains, the spreading fields, the sunlight flooding the earth, all illustrated His lessons and impressed them on the mind. And no lesson fell fruitless. Every message came to some soul as the word of eternal life.

To such as this the prophets had looked forward, and wrote:

> The land of Zebulun and the land of Naphtali,
> Toward the sea, beyond Jordan,
> Galilee of the Gentiles,
> The people which sat in darkness
> Saw a great light,
> And to them which sat in the region and shadow
>   of death
> To them did light spring up. RV

This chapter is based on Matthew 4:15-22; Mark 1:16-20; Luke 5:1-11.

156

Looking down the ages, Jesus saw His faithful ones in prison and judgment hall, in temptation, loneliness, and affliction. In the words spoken to those gathered about Him on the shores of Gennesaret, He was speaking also to these other souls the words that would come as a message of hope in trial, comfort in sorrow, and light in darkness. That voice speaking from the fisherman's boat would be heard speaking peace to human hearts to the close of time.

The discourse ended, Jesus told Peter to launch out into the sea and let down his net for a draught. But Peter was disheartened. All night he had taken nothing. During the lonely hours, he had thought of John the Baptist languishing in his dungeon, of the prospect before Jesus and His followers, of the ill success of the mission to Judea, and of the malice of the priests and rabbis. As he watched by the empty nets, the future seemed dark with discouragement. "Master, we have toiled all the night, and have taken nothing: nevertheless at Thy word I will let down the net."

After toiling all night without success, it seemed hopeless to cast the net into the clear waters of the lake, but love for their Master moved the disciples to obey. Simon and his brother let down the net. As they attempted to draw it in, so great was the quantity of fish that they were obliged to summon James and John to their aid. When the catch was secured, both boats were so heavily laden that they were in danger of sinking.

Unholiness Revealed

This miracle, above any other he had ever witnessed, was to Peter a manifestation of divine power. In Jesus he saw One who held all nature under His control. Shame for his unbelief, gratitude for the condescension of Christ, above all, the sense of his uncleanness in the presence of infinite purity, overwhelmed him. Peter fell at the Saviour's feet, exclaiming, "Depart from me; for I am a sinful man, O Lord."

It was the same presence of divine holiness that had caused the prophet Daniel to fall as one dead before the angel. See Daniel 10:8. Isaiah exclaimed, "Woe is me! for I am undone; because I am a man of unclean lips, . . . for mine eyes have seen the King, the Lord of hosts." Isaiah 6:5. Thus it has been with all who have been granted a view of God's greatness and majesty.

The Saviour answered Peter, "Fear not; from henceforth thou shalt catch men." After Isaiah had beheld the holiness of God and his own unworthiness, he was entrusted with the divine message. After Peter had been led to self-renunciation, he received the call to work for Christ.

The disciples had witnessed many of Christ's miracles, and had listened to His teaching, but none had entirely forsaken their former employment. The imprisonment of John the Baptist had been a bitter disappointment. If such were the outcome of John's mission, they could have little hope for their Master, with the religious leaders combined against Him. It was a relief to return for a short time to their fishing. But now Jesus called them to forsake their former life and unite their interests with His. Peter had accepted the call. On reaching shore, Jesus bade the three others, "Follow Me, and I will make you fishers of men." Immediately they left all and followed Him.

Sacrifice Rewarded

Before asking them to leave their fishing boats, Jesus had given them the assurance that God would supply their needs. The use of Peter's boat had been richly repaid. He who is "rich unto all that call upon Him," has said, "Give, and it shall be given unto you; good measure, pressed down, and shaken together, and running over." Romans 10:12; Luke 6:38. In this measure He had rewarded Peter's service. And every sacrifice made in His ministry will be recompensed. See Ephesians 3:20; 2:7.

During that sad night on the lake, separated from

Christ, the disciples were pressed hard by unbelief. But His presence kindled faith, and brought joy and success. So with us; apart from Christ our work is fruitless, and it is easy to distrust and murmur. But when we labor under His direction, we rejoice in the evidence of His power. He inspires us with faith and hope. He whose word could gather fishes from the sea can also impress human hearts and draw them so that His servants may become "fishers of men."

Christ was abundantly able to qualify humble and unlearned men for the position for which He had chosen them. The Saviour did not despise education; when controlled by the love of God, intellectual culture is a blessing. But the wise men of His time were so self-confident that they could not become colaborers with the Man of Nazareth. They scorned to be taught by Christ. The first thing to be learned by all who would become workers with God is the lesson of self-distrust; then they are prepared to have imparted to them the character of Christ. This is not to be gained through education in scientific schools.

How True Servants Are Educated

Jesus chose unlearned fishermen because they had not been schooled in the erroneous customs of their time. They were men of native ability, and they were humble and teachable. In the common walks of life many a man is patiently treading the round of daily toil, unconscious that he possesses powers which, if called into action, would raise him to equality with the world's most honored men. The touch of a skillful hand is needed to arouse those dormant faculties. Such men Jesus called to be His colaborers. When the disciples came forth from the Saviour's training, they had become like Him in mind and character.

The highest work of education is to impart that vitalizing energy received through the contact of mind with mind, and soul with soul. Only life can beget life. What a privilege, then, was theirs who for three years were in daily contact with that divine life! John the disciple says, "From His fulness have we all received, grace upon grace." John 1:16, RSV. The lives of these men, the characters they developed, and the mighty work wrought through them, are a testimony to what God will do for all who are teachable and obedient. There is no limit to the usefulness of one who, putting self aside, makes room for the working of the Holy Spirit upon his heart, and lives a life wholly consecrated to God. If men will endure the necessary discipline, God will teach them hour by hour, and day by day. He takes men as they are and educates them for His service, if they will yield themselves to Him. The Spirit of God, received into the soul, will quicken all its faculties. The mind devoted unreservedly to God develops harmoniously and is strengthened to comprehend and fulfill His requirements. The weak character becomes one of steadfastness.

Continual devotion establishes so close a relation between Jesus and His disciple that the Christian becomes like Him in mind and character. He will have clearer and broader views, his discernment will be more penetrative, his judgment better balanced. He is enabled to bear much fruit to the glory of God. Christians in humble life have obtained an education in the highest of all schools. They have sat at the feet of Him who spoke as "never man spake."

Jesus chose uneducated fishermen to be His disciples because they were humble and teachable and had not been schooled in the false customs of their time.

26 / Busy and Happy Days at Capernaum

In the intervals of His journeys to and fro, Jesus dwelt at Capernaum on the shores of the Sea of Galilee, and it came to be known as "His own city." Matthew 9:1. The shores of the lake and the hills that at a little distance encircle it, were dotted with towns and villages. The lake was covered with fishing boats. Everywhere was the stir of busy, active life.

Being on the highway from Damascus to Jerusalem and Egypt, and to the Mediterranean Sea, people from many lands passed through Capernaum. Here Jesus could meet all nations and all ranks, and His lessons would be carried to other countries. Investigation of the prophecies would be excited, attention would be directed to the Saviour, and His mission would be brought before the world. Angels were preparing the way for His ministry, moving upon men's hearts and drawing them to the Saviour.

In Capernaum the nobleman's son whom Christ had healed was a witness to His power. The court official and his household joyfully testified of their faith. When it was known that the Teacher Himself was among them, the whole city was aroused. On the Sabbath the people crowded the synagogue until great numbers had to turn away.

All who heard the Saviour "were astonished at His doctrine: for His word was with power." "He taught them as one having authority, and not as the scribes." Luke 4:32; Matthew 7:29. The teaching of the scribes and elders was cold and formal. They professed to ex-

This chapter is based on Mark 1:21-38; Luke 4:31-44.

plain the law, but no inspiration from God stirred their own hearts or the hearts of their hearers.

Jesus' work was to present the truth. His words shed a flood of light upon the teachings of the prophets. Never before had His hearers perceived such depth of meaning in the Word of God.

Jesus made truth beautiful by presenting it in the most direct and simple way. His language was pure, refined, and clear as a running stream. His voice was as music to those who had listened to the monotonous tones of the rabbis.

No Doubts or Hesitancy

He spoke as one having authority. The rabbis spoke with doubt and hesitancy, as if Scripture might be interpreted to mean one thing or exactly the opposite. But Jesus taught Scripture as of unquestionable authority. Whatever His subject, it was presented with power.

Yet He was earnest, rather than vehement. In every theme God was revealed. Jesus sought to break the spell of infatuation which keeps men absorbed in earthly things. He placed the things of this life in their true relation as subordinate to those of eternal interest; but He did not ignore their importance. He taught that a knowledge of divine truth prepares men better to perform the duties of everyday life. Conscious of His relationship to God, He yet recognized His unity with every member of the human family.

He knew "how to speak a word in season to him that is weary." Isaiah 50:4. He had tact to meet prejudiced minds and to surprise them with illustrations that won their attention. His illustrations were taken from the things of daily life, and although simple, they had a wonderful depth of meaning. The birds, the lilies, the seed, the shepherd, the sheep—with these objects Jesus illustrated immortal truth; and ever afterward when His hearers chanced to see these things, they recalled His lessons.

Christ never flattered men or praised them for their clever inventions; but deep, unprejudiced thinkers received His teaching and found that it tested their wisdom. The highly educated were charmed with His words, and the uneducated were always profited. He made even the heathen to understand that He had a message for them.

Even amid angry enemies He was surrounded with an atmosphere of peace. The loveliness of His character, the love expressed in look and tone, drew to Him all who were not hardened in unbelief. Afflicted ones felt that He was a faithful and tender friend, and they desired to know more of the truths He taught. They longed that the comfort of His love might be with them continually.

Jesus watched the countenances of His hearers. Faces that expressed interest gave Him satisfaction. As the arrows of truth pierced through the barriers of selfishness, working contrition and gratitude, the Saviour was glad. When His eye recognized faces He had seen before, His countenance lighted up with joy. When truth plainly spoken touched some cherished idol, He marked the change of countenance which told that the light was unwelcome. When He saw men refuse the message of peace, His heart was pierced to the very depths.

In the synagogue Jesus was interrupted while speaking of His mission to set free the captives of Satan. A madman rushed from among the people, crying out, "Let us alone; what have we to do with Thee, thou Jesus of Nazareth? art Thou come to destroy us? I know Thee who Thou art; the Holy One of God."

All was confusion and alarm. The attention of the people was diverted from Christ, and His words were unheeded. But Jesus rebuked the demon, saying, "Hold thy peace, and come out of him. And when the devil had thrown him in the midst, he came out of him, and hurt him not."

The mind of this wretched sufferer had been darkened by Satan, but in the Saviour's presence, he was roused to long for freedom from Satan's control. But the demon resisted. When the man tried to appeal to Jesus for help, the evil spirit put words in his mouth, and he cried out in an agony of fear.

The demoniac partially comprehended that he was in the presence of One who could set him free; but when he tried to come within reach of that mighty hand, another's will held him, another's words found utterance through him. The conflict between the power of Satan and his own desire for freedom was terrible.

The demon exerted all his power to retain control of his victim. It seemed that the tortured man must lose his life in the struggle with the foe that had been the ruin of his manhood. But the Saviour spoke with authority and set the captive free. The man stood before the wondering people happy in the freedom of self-possession. Even the demon had testified to the divine power of the Saviour. The eye that had so lately glared with the fire of insanity now beamed with intelligence and overflowed with grateful tears.

The people exclaimed, "What is this? a new teaching! With authority He commands even the unclean spirits, and they obey Him." Mark 1:27, RSV.

This man had been fascinated by the pleasures of sin and had thought to make life a grand carnival. He did not dream of becoming a terror to the world and the reproach of his family. He thought his time could be spent in innocent folly. But intemperance and frivolity perverted his nature, and Satan took absolute control of him. When he would have sacrificed wealth and pleasure to regain his lost manhood, he had become helpless in the grasp of the evil one. Satan had taken possession of all his faculties. When once the wretched man was in his power, the fiend became relentless in his cruelty. So with all who yield to evil; the fascinating pleasure of their early career ends in despair or the madness of a ruined soul.

The same evil spirit controlled the unbelieving Jews,

but with them he assumed an air of piety. Their condition was more hopeless than that of the demoniac, for they felt no need of Christ and were therefore held fast under the power of Satan.

Christ's personal ministry among men was the time of greatest activity for the forces of the kingdom of darkness. For ages Satan had been seeking to control the bodies and souls of men, to bring upon them sin and suffering; then he had charged all this misery on God. Jesus was revealing to men the character of God, breaking Satan's power, and setting his captives free. Love and power from heaven were moving the hearts of men, and the prince of evil was aroused. At every step he contested the work of Christ.

Satan Works Under Disguise

So it will be in the final conflict between righteousness and sin. While new life and power are descending on the disciples of Christ, a new life is energizing the agencies of Satan. With subtlety gained through centuries of conflict, the prince of evil works under disguise, clothed as an angel of light. Multitudes are "giving heed to seducing spirits and doctrines of devils." 1 Timothy 4:1.

The leaders and teachers of Israel were neglecting the only means by which they could have withstood evil spirits. It was by the Word of God that Christ overcame the wicked one. By their interpretation the Jewish leaders made God's Word express sentiments that God had never given. They disputed over technicalities, and practically denied essential truths. Thus God's Word was robbed of its power, and evil spirits worked their will.

History is repeating. With the open Bible before them, many religious leaders of our time are destroying faith in it as the Word of God. They dissect the Word, and set their own opinions above its plainest statements. This is why infidelity runs riot, and iniquity is rife.

Those who turn from the plain teaching of Scripture and the convicting power of God's Holy Spirit are inviting the control of demons. Criticism and speculation have opened the way for spiritism to gain a foothold even in the professed churches of our Lord Jesus Christ. Side by side with the preaching of the gospel, agencies are at work which are lying spirits. Many a man tampers with these merely from curiosity, but seeing evidence of more than human power, he is lured on until he is controlled by the mysterious power of a will stronger than his own. The defenses of the soul are broken down. Secret sin or master passion may hold him a captive as helpless as the demoniac of Capernaum. Yet his condition is not hopeless.

He can overcome by the power of the Word. If we desire to know and to do God's will, His promises are ours: "You will know the truth, and the truth will make you free." "If any man's will is to do His will, he shall know whether the teaching is from God." John 8:32; 7:17, RSV. Through faith in these promises every man may be delivered from the snares of error and the control of sin.

There Is Hope for Every Lost Person

None have fallen so low, none are so vile, but that they can find deliverance in Christ. The demoniac could utter only the words of Satan, yet the heart's unspoken appeal was heard. No cry from a soul in need, though it fail of words, will be unheeded. Those who will consent to enter into covenant relation with the God of heaven are invited by the Saviour, "Let him take hold of My strength, that he may make peace with Me; and he shall make peace with Me." Isaiah 27:5. Angels of God will contend for that soul with prevailing power. "Can . . . the captives of a tyrant be rescued? . . . I will contend with those who contend with you, and I will save your children." Isaiah 49:24, 25, RSV.

While the congregation in the synagogue were still spellbound, Jesus withdrew to the home of Peter for a little rest. But here also a shadow had fallen. The mother of Peter's wife lay sick, stricken with a "great fever." Jesus rebuked the disease, and the sufferer arose and ministered to the Master and His disciples.

Tidings of the work of Christ spread rapidly throughout Capernaum. For fear of the rabbis, the people dared not come for healing on the Sabbath; but no sooner had the sun disappeared below the horizon, than the inhabitants of the city pressed toward the humble dwelling that sheltered Jesus. The sick were brought into the Saviour's presence.

Hour after hour they came and went, for none could know whether tomorrow would find the Healer still among them. Never before had Capernaum witnessed a day like this. The air was filled with the voice of triumph and shouts of deliverance. The Saviour rejoiced in His power to restore the sufferers to health and happiness.

It was far into the night when the multitude departed, and silence settled down on the home of Simon. The long, exciting day was past, and Jesus sought rest. But while the city was still wrapped in slumber, "a great while before day, . . . [the Saviour] went out, and departed into a solitary place, and there prayed."

Jesus often dismissed His disciples to visit their homes and rest; but He gently resisted their efforts to draw Him away from His labors. All day He toiled, and at eventide or in the early morning, He went to the mountains for communion with His Father. Often He passed the entire night in prayer and meditation, returning at daybreak to His work among the people.

Early in the morning, Peter and his companions came to Jesus, saying that already the people were seeking Him. The authorities at Jerusalem were seeking to murder Him; even His own townsmen had tried to take His life; but at Capernaum He was welcomed with enthusiasm, and the hopes of the disciples kindled anew. It might be that among the liberty-loving Galileans were to be found the supporters of the new kingdom. With surprise they heard Christ's words, "Let us go on to the next towns, that I may preach there also; for that is why I came out." Mark 1:38, RSV. Jesus was not satisfied to attract attention to Himself as a wonder worker or healer. While the people were eager to believe that He had come as a king, to establish an earthly reign, He desired to turn their minds away from the earthly to the spiritual.

And the wonder of the careless crowd jarred upon His spirit. The homage the world gives to position, or wealth, or talent was foreign to the Son of man. None of the means men employ to win allegiance did Jesus use. It had been prophesied of Him, "He will not cry or lift up His voice, or make it heard in the street; . . . He will faithfully bring forth justice." Isaiah 42: 2, 3, RSV.

In the life of Jesus, no noisy disputation, no ostentatious worship, no act to gain applause was ever witnessed. Christ was hid in God, and God was revealed in the character of His Son.

The Sun of Righteousness did not burst upon the world in splendor, to dazzle the senses with His glory. Quietly and gently the daylight dispels the darkness and wakes the world to life. So did the Sun of Righteousness arise, "with healing in His wings." Malachi 4:2.

27 / The First Leper to Be Cleansed by Christ

Of all diseases known in the East, leprosy was most dreaded. Its incurable and contagious character and its horrible effect on its victims filled the bravest with fear. Among the Jews it was regarded as a judgment on account of sin, and hence "the finger of God." It was looked upon as a symbol of sin.

Like one already dead, the leper was shut out from the habitations of men. Whatever he touched was unclean. The air was polluted by his breath. One suspected of having the disease must present himself to the priests. If pronounced a leper, he was doomed to associate only with those similarly afflicted. The law was inflexible. Kings and rulers were not exempt.

Away from friends and kindred, the leper must bear the curse. He was obliged to publish his calamity and sound the alarm, warning all to flee his contaminating presence. The cry, "Unclean! Unclean!" coming in mournful tones from the lonely exile was a signal heard with fear and abhorrence.

News of Christ's work reached many of these sufferers, kindling a gleam of hope. But since the days of Elisha such a thing had never been known as the cleansing of one upon whom this disease had fastened. There was one man, however, in whose heart faith began to spring up. Yet how could he present himself to the Healer? And would Christ heal him? Would He notice one suffering the judgment of God? Would He pronounce a curse on him?

The leper thought of all that had been told him of Je-

This chapter is based on Matthew 8:2-4; 9:1-8, 32-34; Mark 1:40-45; 2:1-12; Luke 5:12-28.

sus. Not one who had sought His help had been turned away. The wretched man determined to find the Saviour. It might be that he could cross His path in some byway along the mountain roads or as He was teaching outside the towns. This was his only hope.

The leper was guided to the Saviour as He taught beside the lake. Standing afar off, the leper caught a few words from the Saviour's lips. He saw Him laying His hands on the sick, the lame, the blind, the paralytic, and those dying of various maladies rose up and praised God for their deliverance. Faith strengthened in his heart. He drew nearer. The restrictions laid on him, and the fear with which all men regarded him were forgotten. He thought only of the blessed hope of healing.

He was a loathsome spectacle, his decaying body horrible to look upon. At sight of him the people fell back in terror, crowding upon one another in their eagerness to escape from contact with him. Some tried to prevent him from approaching Jesus, but he neither saw nor heard them. He saw only the Son of God. Pressing to Jesus, he cast himself at His feet with the cry, "Lord, if Thou wilt, Thou canst make *me* clean."

Jesus replied, "I will; be thou clean," and laid His hand on him.

Immediately a change passed over the leper. His flesh became healthy, the nerves sensitive, the muscles firm. The rough, scaly surface disappeared, and a soft glow, like that upon the skin of a healthy child, took its place.

With urgency Christ enjoined on the man the necessity of silence and prompt action. Jesus said to him, "See thou say nothing to any man: but go thy way, show thyself to the priest, and offer for thy cleansing those things which Moses commanded, for a testimony unto them." Had the priests known the facts concerning the healing, their hatred of Christ might have led them to render a dishonest sentence. Jesus desired the man to present himself at the temple before rumors of the healing had reached them. Thus an impartial decision could be secured, and the restored leper would be permitted to unite once more with his family and friends.

The Saviour also knew that if the healing of the leper were noised abroad, other sufferers from this disease would crowd about Him, and the cry would be raised that the people would be contaminated. Many lepers would not use the gift of health as a blessing to themselves or others. And by drawing lepers about Him, He would give occasion for the charge that He was breaking down the restrictions of the law. Thus His preaching would be hindered.

A multitude had witnessed the healing of the leper and were eager to learn of the priests' decision. When the man returned to his friends, there was great excitement. The man made no effort to conceal his cure. It would indeed have been impossible to conceal, but the leper published the matter, conceiving that only the modesty of Jesus laid this restriction on him. He did not understand that every such manifestation made the priests and elders more determined to destroy Jesus. The restored man rejoiced in the vigor of manhood and felt it impossible to refrain from giving glory to the Physician who had made him whole. But his act in blazing abroad the matter caused the people to flock to Him in such multitudes that He was forced for a time to cease His labors.

Every act of Christ's ministry was far-reaching in its purpose. He left untried no means by which the priests and teachers, shut in by prejudice and tradition, might be reached. In sending the healed leper to the priests, He gave them a testimony calculated to disarm their prejudices. The Pharisees had asserted that Christ was opposed to the law, but His direction to the cleansed leper to present an offering according to the law disproved this charge. Christ gave evidence of His love for humanity, His respect for the law, and His power to deliver from sin and death.

The same priests who condemned the leper to banishment certified his cure publicly. And the healed man, reinstated in the congregation, was a living witness for his Benefactor. Joyfully he magnified the name of Jesus. Opportunity was granted the priests to know the truth. During the Saviour's life, His mission seemed to call forth little response of love from them, but after His ascension "a great company of the priests were obedient to the faith." Acts 6:7.

How Christ Cleanses the Soul From Sin

The work of Christ in cleansing the leper is an illustration of His work in cleansing the soul from sin. The man who came to Jesus was "full of leprosy." The disciples sought to prevent their Master from touching him. But in laying His hand on the leper, Jesus received no defilement. His touch imparted life-giving power.

Thus it is with the leprosy of sin—deadly, impossible to be cleansed by human power. "From the sole of the foot even unto the head there is no soundness in it; but wounds, and bruises, and putrefying sores." Isaiah 1:6. But Jesus has healing virtue. Whoever will fall at His feet, saying in faith, "Lord, if You will, You can make me clean," shall hear the answer, "I will; be clean." RSV.

In some instances of healing, Jesus did not at once grant the blessing sought. In the case of the leper, no sooner was the appeal made than it was granted. When we pray for earthly blessings, the answer may be delayed, or God may give us something other than we ask. But not so when we ask for deliverance from sin. It is His will to cleanse us, make us His children, and enable us to live a holy life. Christ "gave Himself for our sins, that He might deliver us from this present evil world, according to the will of God and our Father." Galatians 1:4. "If we ask anything according to His will He hears us. And if we know that He hears us in whatever we ask, we know that we have obtained the requests made of Him." 1 John 5:14, 15, RSV.

In the healing of the paralytic at Capernaum, Christ again taught the same truth. To manifest His power to forgive sins, the miracle was performed. Like the leper, this paralytic had lost all hope. His disease was the result of a life of sin, and his sufferings were embittered by remorse. He had appealed to the Pharisees and doctors, but they coldly pronounced him incurable and abandoned him to the wrath of God.

Seeing no prospect of aid from any quarter, the palsied man had sunk into despair. Then he heard of Jesus. Friends encouraged him to believe that he too might be cured if he could be carried to Jesus.

The Burden of Sin

It was not physical restoration he desired so much as relief from the burden of sin. If he could receive the assurance of forgiveness and peace with Heaven, he would be content to die. The dying man had no time to lose. He besought his friends to carry him on his bed to Jesus, and this they gladly undertook to do. But so dense was the crowd where the Saviour was that it was impossible for the sick man and his friends even to come within hearing of His voice.

Jesus was teaching in the house of Peter, His disciples close about Him. And "there were Pharisees and doctors of the law sitting by, which were come out of every town of Galilee, and Judea, and Jerusalem" as spies. Outside thronged the multitude, the eager, the reverent, the curious, the unbelieving. "And the power of the Lord was present to heal." But the Pharisees and doctors did not discern the Spirit's presence. They felt no need, and the healing was not for them. "He hath filled the hungry with good things; and the rich He hath sent empty away." Luke 1:53.

The bearers of the paralytic tried to push their way through the crowd, but in vain. Must the sick man relinquish hope? At his suggestion his friends bore him to the top of the house and, breaking up the roof, let him down at the feet of Jesus.

The Saviour saw the pleading eyes fixed upon Him. He understood the case. While the paralytic was at home, the Saviour had brought conviction to his conscience. When he repented of his sins, the life-giving mercies of the Saviour first blessed his longing heart. Jesus had watched the first glimmer of faith grow stronger with every effort to come into His presence.

Now, in words that fell like music on the sufferer's ear, the Saviour said, "Son . . . thy sins be forgiven thee." The burden of despair rolled from the sick man's soul; the peace of forgiveness shone out on his countenance. His pain was gone, his whole being was transformed. The helpless paralytic was healed, the guilty sinner pardoned!

In simple faith he accepted the words of Jesus. He urged no further request, but lay in blissful silence. The people looked on with awe.

The rabbis recollected how the man had appealed to them for help, and they, refusing him hope or sympathy, had declared he was suffering the curse of God for his sins. They marked the interest with which all were watching the scene and felt a terrible fear of losing their influence over the people. Looking into one another's faces they read the same thought—something must be done to arrest the tide of feeling. Jesus had declared the sins of the paralytic forgiven. The Pharisees could present this as blasphemy, a sin worthy of death. "It is blasphemy! Who can forgive sins but God alone?" RSV.

Fixing His glance on them, Jesus said, "Why do you question thus in your hearts? Which is easier, to say to the paralytic, 'Your sins are forgiven,' or to say, 'Rise, take up your pallet and walk?' But that you may know that the Son of man has authority on earth to forgive sins"—he said to the paralytic—"I say to you, rise, take up your pallet and go home." RSV.

Then he who had been borne on a litter to Jesus rose to his feet with the elasticity and strength of youth. Every organ of his body sprang into activity. The glow of health succeeded the pallor of approaching death. "And immediately he arose, took up the bed, and went forth before them all; insomuch that they were all amazed, and glorified God, saying, We never saw it on this fashion."

Creative power restored health to that decaying body. The same voice that spoke life to man created from the dust of the earth spoke life to the dying paralytic. And the same power that gave life to the body had renewed the heart. Christ bade the paralytic arise and walk, "that ye may know that the Son of man hath power on earth to forgive sins."

Spiritual Healing Often Precedes Physical Healing

Thousands today suffering from physical disease, like the paralytic, long for the message, "Thy sins are forgiven." Sin is the foundation of their maladies. The Healer of the soul alone can impart vigor to the mind and health to the body.

Jesus still has the same life-giving power as when on earth He healed the sick and spoke forgiveness to the sinner. He "forgiveth all thine iniquities"; He "healeth all thy diseases." Psalm 103:3; see 1 John 3:8; John 1:4-10; 10:10; 1 Corinthians 15:45.

As the man who had been cured passed through the multitude bearing his burden as if it were a feather's weight, the people fell back to give him room. With awestricken faces they whispered softly among themselves, "We have seen strange things today."

The Pharisees were dumb with amazement and overwhelmed with defeat. Disconcerted and abashed, they recognized but did not confess the presence of a superior being. From the home of Peter, where they had seen the paralytic restored, they went away entrenched in unbelief to invent new schemes for silencing the Son of God.

In the home of the healed paralytic there was great rejoicing. His family gathered round with tears of joy, scarcely daring to believe their eyes. The flesh that had been shrunken and leaden-hued was now fresh and ruddy. He walked with a firm, free step. Joy and hope were written on his countenance. Purity and peace had taken the place of the marks of sin and suffering. This man and his family were ready to lay down their lives for Jesus. No doubt dimmed their faith in Him who had brought light into their darkened home.

28 / Matthew: From Tax Collector to Apostle

Roman officials in Palestine were hated. The fact that taxes were imposed by a foreign power was a continual irritation, a reminder to the Jews that their independence had departed. And the taxgatherers, the publicans, were not merely instruments of Roman oppression, they were extortioners on their own account, enriching themselves at the expense of the people. A Jew who accepted this office was despised and classed with the vilest of society.

To this class belonged Levi-Matthew, who was to be called to Christ's service. Matthew had listened to the Saviour's teaching, and as the Spirit of God revealed his sinfulness he longed to seek help from Christ; but accustomed to the exclusiveness of the rabbis, he had no thought that this Great Teacher would notice him.

Sitting at his toll booth one day, the publican saw Jesus approaching. Great was his astonishment to hear the words addressed to himself, "Follow Me."

Matthew "left all, rose up, and followed Him." There was no hesitation, no questioning, no thought of the lucrative business to be exchanged for poverty and hardship. It was enough for him to be with Jesus, to listen to His words, and unite with Him in His work.

So it was when Jesus bade Peter and his companions follow Him. Immediately they left their boats and nets. Some had friends dependent on them for support, but when they received the Saviour's invitation, they did not inquire, How shall I live, and sustain my family? When afterward Jesus asked them, "When I sent you

This chapter is based on Matthew 9:9-17; Mark 2:14-22; Luke 5:27-39.

without purse, and scrip, and shoes, lacked ye anything?" they could answer, "Nothing." Luke 22:35.

To Matthew in his wealth, and to Andrew and Peter in their poverty, the same test was brought. At the moment of success, when the nets were filled with fish, and the impulses of the old life were strongest, Jesus asked the disciples at the sea to leave all for the gospel. So every soul is tested as to whether the desire for temporal good or for fellowship with Christ is stronger.

No one can succeed in the service of God unless his whole heart is in the work. No one who makes any reserve can be the disciple of Christ, much less His colaborer. When men and women appreciate the great salvation, the self-sacrifice seen in Christ's life will be seen in theirs. Wherever He leads the way, they will follow.

The call of Matthew excited great indignation. For Christ to choose a publican as one of His immediate attendants was an offense against religious, social, and national customs. By appealing to prejudice the Pharisees hoped to turn popular feeling against Jesus. But among the publicans widespread interest was created. In the joy of his new discipleship, Matthew made a feast at his house and called together his relatives, friends, and former associates. Not only were publicans included, but many others who were proscribed by their more scrupulous neighbors.

External Distinctions Meant Nothing

The entertainment was given in honor of Jesus, and He did not hesitate to accept. He well knew it would give offense to the Pharisaic party and also compromise Him in the eyes of the people. But no question of policy could influence His movements.

Jesus sat as an honored guest at the table of the publicans. By sympathy and social kindliness He showed that He recognized the dignity of humanity; and men longed to become worthy of His confidence. New impulses were awakened, and the possibility of a new life opened to these outcasts of society.

Not a few were impressed who did not acknowledge the Saviour until after His ascension. When 3000 were converted in a day, there were among them many who first heard the truth at the table of the publicans. To Matthew himself the example of Jesus at the feast was a constant lesson. The despised publican became one of the most devoted evangelists, following in his Master's steps.

Attempt to Alienate Disciples

The rabbis seized the opportunity of accusing Jesus, but chose to work through the disciples. By arousing their prejudices they hoped to alienate them from their Master. "Why eateth your Master with publicans and sinners?" they questioned.

Jesus did not wait for the disciples to answer, but Himself replied: "They that be whole have no need of a physician, but they that are sick; . . . I am not come to call the righteous, but sinners to repentance." The Pharisees claimed to be spiritually whole, and therefore in no need of a physician, but they regarded the publicans and Gentiles as perishing from diseases of the soul. Then was it not His work, as a physician, to go to the very class that needed His help?

Jesus said to the rabbis, "Go ye and learn what that meaneth, I will have mercy, and not sacrifice." They claimed to expound the Word of God, but they were wholly ignorant of its spirit.

The Pharisees, silenced for the time but more determined in their enmity, next tried to set the disciples of John the Baptist against the Saviour. These Pharisees had pointed in scorn to the Baptist's simple habits and coarse garments and had declared him a fanatic. They had tried to stir up the people against him. The Spirit of God had moved upon the hearts of these scorners, convicting them of sin, but they had declared that John possessed a devil.

Now when Jesus came mingling with the people, eating and drinking at their tables, they accused Him of being a glutton and a winebibber. They would not consider that Jesus was eating with sinners in order to bring the light of heaven to those who sat in darkness. They would not consider that every word dropped by the divine Teacher was living seed that would germinate and bear fruit to the glory of God. They had determined not to accept the light, and although they had opposed the mission of the Baptist, they were now ready to court the friendship of his disciples, hoping to secure their cooperation against Jesus. They represented that Jesus was setting at nought the ancient traditions, and they contrasted the austere piety of the Baptist with Jesus feasting with publicans and sinners.

The disciples of John were at this time in great sorrow. With their beloved teacher in prison, they passed their days in mourning. And Jesus was making no effort to release John, and even appeared to cast discredit on his teaching. If John had been sent by God, why did Jesus and His disciples pursue a course so widely different?

The disciples of John thought there might be some foundation for the charges of the Pharisees. They observed many rules prescribed by the rabbis. Fasting was practiced by the Jews as an act of merit; the most rigid fasted two days every week. The Pharisees and John's disciples were fasting when the latter came to Jesus with the inquiry, "Why do we and the Pharisees fast oft, but Thy disciples fast not?"

Tenderly Jesus answered. He did not try to correct their erroneous concept of fasting, but only to set them right in regard to His own mission. John the Baptist himself had said, "He who has the bride is the bridegroom; the friend of the bridegroom, who stands and hears him, rejoices greatly at the bridegroom's voice; therefore this joy of mine is now full." John 3:29, RSV. The disciples of John could not fail to recall these words of their teacher. Taking up the illustration, Jesus said, "Can ye make the children of the bridechamber fast, while the bridegroom is with them?"

The Prince of heaven was among His people. The greatest gift of God had been given to the world. Joy to the poor, for He had come to make them heirs of His kingdom. Joy to the rich, for He would teach them to secure eternal riches. Joy to the ignorant, for He would make them wise unto salvation. Joy to the learned, for He would open to them deeper mysteries than they had ever fathomed. This was not a time for the disciples to mourn and fast. They must open their hearts to receive the light of His glory, that they might shed light on those who sat in darkness and in the shadow of death.

A Heavy Shadow

It was a bright picture, but across it lay a heavy shadow which Christ's eye alone discerned. "The days will come when the bridegroom shall be taken away from them, and then shall they fast." When they should see their Lord betrayed and crucified, the disciples would mourn and fast.

When He should come forth from the tomb, their sorrow would be turned to joy. After His ascension, through the Comforter He would still be with them, and they were not to spend their time mourning. Satan desired them to give the impression that they had been deceived and disappointed. But by faith they were to look to the sanctuary above where Jesus was ministering for them; they were to open their hearts to the Holy Spirit and rejoice in the light of His presence. Yet days of trial would come. When Christ was not personally with them and they failed to discern the Comforter, then it would be more fitting for them to fast.

The Scripture describes the fast that God has chosen—"to loose the bands of wickedness, to undo the heavy burdens, and to let the oppressed go free, and that ye break every yoke"; to "draw out thy soul to the hungry, and satisfy the afflicted soul." Isaiah 58:6, 10. Here is set forth the character of the work of Christ. Whether fasting in the wilderness or eating with publicans, He was giving His life for the redemption of the lost. The true spirit of devotion is shown in the surrender of self in willing service to God and man.

Continuing His answer to the disciples of John, Jesus spoke a parable: "No one puts a piece of unshrunk cloth on an old garment, for the patch tears away from the garment, and a worse tear is made." Matthew 9:16, RSV. An attempt to blend the tradition and superstition of the Pharisees with the devotion of John would only make more evident the breach between them.

Nor could the principles of Christ's teaching be united with the forms of Pharisaism. Christ was to make more distinct the separation between the old and the new. "Neither is new wine put into old wineskins; if it is, the skins burst, and the wine is spilled, and the skins are destroyed; but new wine is put into fresh wineskins, and so both are preserved." Matthew 9:17, RSV. Skin bottles used as vessels to contain new wine, after a time became dry and brittle, and were then worthless to serve the same purpose again. The Jewish leaders were fixed in a rut of ceremonies and traditions. Their hearts had become like dried-up wine skins. Satisfied with a legal religion, it was impossible for them to become the depositaries of living truth. They did not desire that a new element should be brought into their religion. The faith that works by love and purifies the soul could find no place for union with the religion of the Pharisees, made up of ceremonies and the injunctions of men. To unite the teachings of Jesus with the established religion would be vain. The vital truth of God, like wine, would burst the old decaying bottles of the Pharisaical tradition.

New Bottles for New Wine

The Saviour turned away from the Pharisees to find others who would receive the message of heaven. In untutored fishermen, in the publican at the market place, in the woman of Samaria, in the common people who heard Him gladly, He found His new bottles for the new wine. Those souls who gladly receive the light which God sends are His agencies for imparting truth to the world.

The teaching of Christ, represented by new wine, was not new doctrine but that which had been taught from the beginning. But to the Pharisees, Christ's teaching was new in almost every respect, and it was unrecognized and unacknowledged.

"No man having drunk old wine straightway desireth new: for he saith, The old was better." The truth given through patriarchs and prophets shone out in new beauty in the words of Christ. But the scribes and Pharisees had no desire for the precious new wine. Until emptied of old traditions and practices, they had no place in mind or heart for the teachings of Christ.

The Peril of Cherished Opinion

This proved the ruin of the Jews, and it will prove the ruin of many in our day. Rather than give up some cherished idea or idol of opinion, many refuse the truth which comes from the Father of light. They insist on being saved in some way by which they may perform some important work. When they see there is no way of weaving self into the work, they reject the salvation provided.

A legal religion is a loveless, Christless religion. Fasting or prayer actuated by a self-justifying spirit is an abomination in the sight of God. Our own works can never purchase salvation. To those who do not know their spiritual destitution comes the message, "For you say, I am rich, I have prospered, and I need nothing; not knowing that you are wretched, pitiable, poor, blind, and naked. Therefore I counsel you to buy from Me gold refined by fire, that you may be rich, and white garments to clothe you and to keep the shame of your nakedness from being seen." Revelation 3:17, 18, RSV. Faith and love are the gold. But with many, the gold has become dim, the rich treasure lost. The righteousness of Christ is a robe unworn, a fountain untouched.

"The sacrifices of God are a broken spirit: a broken and a contrite heart, O God, thou wilt not despise." Psalm 51:17. When self is renounced, then the Lord can make man a new creature. New bottles can contain new wine. The love of Christ will animate the believer with new life. In him the character of Christ will be manifest.

29 / Jesus Rescues the Sabbath

The Sabbath was hallowed at creation. As ordained for man, it had its origin when "the morning stars sang together, and all the sons of God shouted for joy." Job 38:7. Earth was in harmony with heaven. "God saw everything that He had made, and, behold, it was very good"; and He rested in the joy of His completed work. Genesis 1:31.

Because He had rested on the Sabbath, "God blessed the seventh day, and sanctified it" (Genesis 2:3)—set it apart to a holy use. It was a memorial of the work of creation, and thus a sign of God's power and love.

All things were created by the Son of God. "All things were made by Him; and without Him was not anything made that was made." John 1:3. And since the Sabbath is a memorial of the work of creation, it is a token of the love and power of Christ.

The Sabbath brings us into communion with the Creator. In the song of the bird, the sighing of the trees, and the music of the sea, we still may hear His voice who talked with Adam in Eden. And as we behold His power in nature, we find comfort, for the Word that created all things is that which speaks life to the soul. He "who commanded the light to shine out of darkness, hath shined in our hearts, to give the light of the knowledge of the glory of God in the face of Jesus Christ." 2 Corinthians 4:6.

"Look unto Me and be ye saved, all the ends of the earth: for I am God, and there is none else." Isaiah

45:22. This is the message written in nature, which the Sabbath is appointed to keep in memory. When the Lord told Israel to hallow His Sabbaths, He said, "They shall be a sign between Me and you, that ye may know that I am the Lord your God." Ezekiel 20:20.

The people of Israel had knowledge of the Sabbath before they came to Sinai. On the way, the Sabbath was kept. When some profaned it, the Lord reproved them, "How long refuse ye to keep My commandments and My laws?" Exodus 16:28.

The Sabbath was not for Israel merely, but for the world. Like the other precepts of the Decalogue, it is of imperishable obligation. Of that law Christ declares, "Till heaven and earth pass, one jot or one tittle shall in nowise pass from the law." Matthew 5:18. So long as the heavens and the earth endure, the Sabbath will continue as a sign of the Creator's power. And when Eden shall bloom on earth again, God's holy rest day will be honored by all beneath the sun. "From one Sabbath to another" the inhabitants of the glorified new earth shall go up "to worship before Me, saith the Lord." Isaiah 66:23.

The Sign of True Conversion

But in order to keep the Sabbath holy, men must themselves be holy. Through faith they must become partakers of the righteousness of Christ. When the command was given to Israel, "Remember the Sabbath day, to keep it holy" (Exodus 20:8), the Lord said also to them, "Ye shall be holy men unto Me." Exodus 22:31.

As the Jews departed from God and failed to make the righteousness of Christ their own by faith, the Sabbath lost its significance to them. Satan worked to pervert the Sabbath, because it is the sign of the power of Christ. The Jewish leaders surrounded God's rest day with burdensome requirements. In the days of Christ its observance reflected the character of selfish and arbitrary men rather than the character of the loving heavenly Father. The rabbis virtually represented God as giving laws impossible for men to obey. They led the people to look on God as a tyrant, and to think that the Sabbath made men hardhearted and cruel. It was the work of Christ to clear away these misconceptions. Jesus did not conform to the rabbis' requirements, but went straight forward, keeping the Sabbath according to the law of God.

A Sabbath Lesson

One Sabbath, as the Saviour and His disciples passed through a field of ripening grain, the disciples began to gather the heads of grain and to eat the kernels after rubbing them in their hands. On any other day this would have excited no comment, for a person passing through a field, an orchard, or a vineyard, was at liberty to gather what he desired to eat. See Deuteronomy 23:24, 25. But to do this on the Sabbath was held to be an act of desecration. Gathering the grain was a kind of reaping, the rubbing of it in the hands a kind of threshing.

The spies at once complained to Jesus, "Behold, Thy disciples do that which is not lawful to do on the Sabbath day." Mark 2:24.

When accused of Sabbathbreaking at Bethesda, Jesus defended Himself by affirming His Sonship to God, declaring He worked in harmony with the Father. Now that the disciples were attacked, He cited Old Testament examples of acts performed on the Sabbath by those who were in the service of God.

In the Saviour's answer to His accusers there was an implied rebuke for their ignorance of the Sacred Writings: "Have you not read what David did when he was hungry, he and those who were with him: how he entered the house of God, and took and ate the bread of the Presence, which it is not lawful for any but the priests to eat?" "And He said unto them, The Sabbath was made for man, and not man for the Sabbath." "Or have you not read in the law how on the Sabbath the priests in the temple profane the Sabbath, and are guiltless? I tell you, something greater than the temple is here." "The Son of man is Lord of the Sabbath." Luke 6:3, 4, RSV; Mark 2:27, 28; Matthew 12:5, 6, 8, RSV.

If it was right for David to satisfy his hunger by eating the bread set apart to a holy use, then it was right for the disciples to pluck grain on the Sabbath. Again, the priests in the temple performed greater labor on the Sabbath than on other days. The same labor in secular business would be sinful, but they were performing rites that pointed to the redeeming power of Christ, and their labor was in harmony with the Sabbath.

The object of God's work in this world is the redemption of man. Therefore that which is necessary to do on the Sabbath in the accomplishment of this work is in accord with the Sabbath law. Jesus then crowned His argument by declaring Himself the "Lord of the Sabbath"—One above all questions and all law. This infinite judge acquitted the disciples of blame, appealing to the very statutes they were accused of violating.

Jesus declared that in their blindness His enemies had mistaken the object of the Sabbath. He said, "If ye had known what this meaneth, I will have mercy, and not sacrifice, ye would not have condemned the guiltless." Matthew 12:7. Their heartless rites could not supply the lack of that integrity and tender love which characterize the true worshiper of God.

Jesus Deliberately Heals on the Sabbath

Sacrifices were in themselves of no value. They were a means, not an end. Their object was to direct men to the Saviour, to bring them into harmony with God. It is the service of love that God values. When this is lacking, mere ceremony is an offense to Him. So with the Sabbath. When the mind was absorbed with wearisome rites, the object of the Sabbath was thwarted. Its mere outward observance was a mockery.

On another Sabbath, Jesus saw in the synagogue a man who had a withered hand. The Pharisees watched, eager to see what He would do. The Saviour did not hesitate to break down the wall of traditional requirements that barricaded the Sabbath.

Jesus told the afflicted man to stand forth, and asked, "Is it lawful to do good on the Sabbath or to do evil? to save life, or to kill?" Mark 3:4. It was a maxim among the Jews that failure to do good when one had opportunity, was to do evil; to neglect to save life was to kill. Thus Jesus met the rabbis on their own ground. "But they were silent. And He looked at them with anger, grieved at the hardness of heart, and said to the man, 'Stretch out your hand.' He stretched it out, and his hand was restored." Verse 5, RSV.

When questioned, "Is it lawful to heal on the Sabbath?" Jesus answered, "What man of you, if he has one sheep and it falls into a pit on the Sabbath, will not lay hold of it and lift it out? Of how much more value is a man than a sheep! So it is lawful to do good on the Sabbath." Matthew 12:10-12, RSV.

Greater Care Shown Animals

The spies dared not answer Christ. They knew He had spoken the truth. Rather than violate traditions, they would leave a man to suffer, while they would relieve a brute because of the loss to the owner if it were neglected. Greater care was shown for dumb animals than for man. This illustrates the working of all false religions. They originate in man's desire to exalt himself above God, but result in degrading man below the brute. Every false religion teaches its adherents to be careless of human needs, sufferings, and rights. The gospel places a high value on humanity as the purchase of the blood of Christ, and teaches a tender regard for the wants and woes of man. See Isaiah 13:12.

The Pharisees were hunting Jesus' life with bitter hatred, while He was saving life and bringing happiness to multitudes. Was it better to slay upon the Sabbath, as they were planning to do, than to heal the afflicted, as He had done?

In healing the withered hand, Jesus condemned the custom of the Jews, and left the fourth commandment standing as God had given it. "It is lawful to do well on the Sabbath days," He declared. By sweeping away senseless restrictions, Christ honored the Sabbath, while those who complained of Him were dishonoring God's holy day.

Those who hold that Christ abolished the law teach that He broke the Sabbath and justified His disciples in doing the same. Thus they are taking the same ground as did the caviling Jews. In this they contradict Christ Himself, who declared, "I have kept My Father's commandments, and abide in His love." John 15:10. Neither the Saviour nor His followers broke the Sabbath. Looking upon a nation of witnesses who were seeking occasion to condemn Him, He could say unchallenged, "Which of you convicts Me of sin?" John 8:46, RSV.

"The Sabbath was made for man, and not man for the Sabbath," Jesus said. The Ten Commandments, of which the Sabbath forms a part, God gave to His people as a blessing. See Deuteronomy 6:24. Of all who keep "the Sabbath from polluting it," the Lord declares, "even them will I bring to My holy mountain, and make them joyful in My house of prayer." Isaiah 56:6, 7.

"The Son of man is Lord also of the Sabbath." These words are full of instruction and comfort. Because the Sabbath was made for man, it is the Lord's day. It belongs to Christ. For "all things were made by Him; and without Him was not any thing made that was made." John 1:3. Since Christ made all things, He made the Sabbath. By Him it was set apart as a memorial of creation. It points to Him as both Creator and Sanctifier. It declares that He who created all things is the Head of the church and that by His power we are reconciled to God. He said, "I gave them My Sabbaths, to be a sign between Me and them, that they might know that I am the Lord that sanctify them"— make them holy. Ezekiel 20:12. The Sabbath is a sign of Christ's power to make us holy. And it is given to all whom Christ makes holy, as a sign of His sanctifying power.

To all who receive the Sabbath as a sign of Christ's creative and redeeming power, it will be a delight. See Isaiah 58:13, 14. Seeing Christ in it, they delight themselves in Him. While it calls to mind the lost peace of Eden, it tells of peace restored through the Saviour. And every object in nature repeats His invitation, "Come unto Me, all ye that labor and are heavy laden, and I will give you rest." Matthew 11:28.

30 / Christ Ordains
Twelve Apostles

"And He went up into the hills, and called to Him those whom He desired; and they came to Him. And He appointed twelve, to be with Him, and to be sent out to preach." RSV.

Beneath the sheltering trees of the mountainside, a little distance from the Sea of Galilee, the Twelve were called to the apostolate, and the Sermon on the Mount was given. In training His disciples Jesus chose to withdraw from the confusion of the city to the quiet of the fields and hills, as more in harmony with the lessons of self-abnegation He desired to teach. And during His ministry He loved to gather the people about Him under the blue heavens, on some grassy hillside, or on the beach beside the lake. Here He could turn His hearers from the artificial to the natural. In the growth and development of nature, they could learn precious lessons of divine truth.

The first step was now to be taken in the organization of the church that after Christ's departure was to be His representative on earth. No costly sanctuary was at their command, but the Saviour led His disciples to the retreat He loved, and in their minds the sacred experiences of that day were forever linked with the beauty of mountain, vale, and sea.

Jesus had called His disciples that He might send them forth to declare to the world what they had seen and heard of Him. Their office, the most important to which human beings had ever been called, was second

This chapter is based on Mark 3:13-39; Luke 6:12-16.

Jesus chose the quiet scenes of nature, away from the confusion of the city, as the ideal place to teach His disciples.

only to that of Christ Himself. They were to work with God for the saving of the world.

The Saviour knew the character of the men He had chosen; their weaknesses and errors were open before Him. He knew the perils through which they must pass; and His heart yearned over these chosen ones. Alone on a mountain He spent the entire night in prayer for them, while they were sleeping at the foot of the mountain. With the first light of dawn He summoned them to meet Him.

John and James, Andrew and Peter, with Philip, Nathanael, and Matthew, had been more closely connected with Jesus in active labor than the others. Peter, James, and John stood in still nearer relationship to Him, witnessing His miracles and hearing His words. The Saviour loved them all, but John's was the most receptive spirit. Younger than the others, with more of a child's confiding trust, he opened his heart to Jesus. Thus he came more into sympathy with Christ, and through him the Saviour's deepest spiritual teaching was communicated to His people.

Slow to Believe

Philip was the first to whom Jesus addressed the distinct command, "Follow Me." He had heard John the Baptist's announcement of Christ as the Lamb of God. He was a sincere seeker for truth, but was slow of heart to believe, as his announcement of Him to Nathanael shows. Though Christ had been proclaimed by the voice from heaven as the Son of God, to Philip He was "Jesus of Nazareth, the son of Joseph." John 1:45. Again, when the 5000 were fed, Philip's lack of faith was shown. It was to test him that Jesus questioned, "Whence shall we buy bread, that these may eat?" Philip's answer, on the side of unbelief, grieved Jesus: "Two hundred pennyworth of bread is not sufficient for them, that every one of them may take a little." John 6:5, 7. Philip had seen Jesus' works and felt His power, yet he had not faith.

When the Greeks inquired of Philip concerning Jesus, he did not seize the opportunity of introducing them to the Saviour, but went to tell Andrew. Again, in those last hours before the crucifixion, the words of Philip were such as to discourage faith. When Thomas said, "Lord, . . . how can we know the way?" the Saviour answered, "I am the Way. . . . If ye had known Me, ye would have known My Father also." From Philip came the response of unbelief: "Lord, show us the Father, and it sufficeth us." John 14:5-8.

In happy contrast to Philip's unbelief was the child-like trust of Nathanael, whose faith took hold upon unseen realities. Yet Philip was a student in the school of Christ, and the divine Teacher bore patiently with his unbelief and dullness. When the Holy Spirit was poured out on the disciples, Philip taught with an assurance that carried conviction to the hearers.

While Jesus was preparing the disciples for ordination, one who had not been summoned urged his presence among them. Judas Iscariot, a professed follower of Christ, came forward, soliciting a place in this inner circle. By joining the apostles he hoped to secure a high place in the new kingdom. He was of commanding appearance, of keen discernment and executive ability, and the disciples commended him to Jesus as one who would greatly assist Him in His work. If Jesus had repulsed Judas, they would have questioned the wisdom of their Master. However, the after-history of Judas would show the danger of allowing worldly consideration to have weight in deciding the fitness of men for the work of God.

Yet Judas felt the influence of that divine power which was drawing souls to the Saviour. Jesus would not repulse this soul while even one desire was reaching toward the light. The Saviour read the heart of Judas; He knew the depths of iniquity to which, unless delivered by the grace of God, he would sink. In connecting this man with Himself, He placed him where he might, day by day, be brought in contact with His own unselfish love. If he would open his heart to Christ, even Judas might become a subject of the kingdom of God.

God takes men as they are and trains them for His service, if they will be disciplined and learn of Him. Through the knowledge and practice of the truth, through the grace of Christ, they may become transformed into His image.

Judas had the same opportunities as had the other disciples. But the practice of the truth was at variance with his desires and purposes, and he would not yield in order to receive wisdom from Heaven.

Tenderly the Saviour dealt with him who was to be His betrayer! Jesus presented before Judas the heinous character of greed. Many a time the disciple realized that his character had been portrayed and his sin pointed out; but he would not confess and forsake his unrighteousness. He continued to follow fraudulent practices. Lesson after lesson fell unheeded on the ears of Judas.

Judas Without Excuse

With divine patience Jesus bore with this erring man, even while giving him evidence that He read his heart as an open book. He presented before him the highest incentives for right doing; but evil desires, revengeful passions, dark and sullen thoughts were cherished, until Satan had full control.

If Judas had been willing to wear the yoke of Christ, he might have been among the chief of the apostles. But he chose his own selfish ambitions and thus unfitted himself for the work God would have given him to do.

All the disciples had serious faults when Jesus called them. John and his brother were called "the sons of thunder." Any slight shown to Jesus aroused their indignation. Evil temper, revenge, criticism, were all in John, the beloved disciple. But day by day he beheld the tenderness and forbearance of Jesus and heard His lessons of humility and patience. He opened his heart to the divine influence and learned to wear the yoke of Christ.

Jesus reproved and cautioned His disciples but John and his brethren did not leave Him. They continued to the end to share His trials and to learn the lessons of His life. By beholding Christ, they became transformed in character.

The apostles differed widely in habits and disposition. There were the publican, Levi-Matthew; the fiery zealot Simon; generous, impulsive Peter; mean-spirited Judas; Thomas, truehearted, yet timid and fearful; Philip, inclined to doubt; the ambitious, out-spoken sons of Zebedee, with their brethren. These were brought together, all with inherited and cultivated tendencies to evil. But in Christ they were to learn to become one in faith, in doctrine, in spirit. They would have their differences of opinion, but while Christ was abiding in the heart, there could be no dissension. The lessons of the Master would lead to the harmonizing of all differences, till the disciples would be of one mind and one judgment. Christ is the great center, and they would approach one another in proportion as they approached the center.

Ordained for Sacred Work

Jesus gathered the little band close about Him, and kneeling in the midst of them and laying His hands on their heads, offered a prayer dedicating them to His sacred work.

As His representatives among men, Christ does not choose angels who have never fallen, but human beings, of like passions with those they seek to save. Christ took upon Himself humanity. It required both the divine and the human to bring salvation to the world. So with the servants and messengers of Christ. Humanity lays hold on divine power, Christ dwells in the heart by faith; and through cooperation with the divine, the power of man becomes efficient for good.

He who called the fishermen of Galilee is still calling men to His service. However imperfect and sinful we may be, the Lord offers us apprenticeship to Christ. Uniting with Him, we may work the works of God.

"We have this treasure in earthen vessels, to show that the transcendent power belongs to God and not to us." 2 Corinthians 4:7, RSV. It is manifest that the power which works through the weakness of humanity is the power of God. Thus we believe that the power which can help others as weak as ourselves can help us.

Those who are themselves "compassed with infirmity" should be able to "have compassion on the ignorant, and on them that are out of the way." Hebrews 5:2. There are souls perplexed with doubt, weak in faith, and unable to grasp the Unseen; but a friend whom they can see, coming in Christ's stead, can be a connecting link to fasten their trembling faith on Christ.

Man must be the channel to communicate with man. And when we give ourselves to Christ, angels rejoice that they may speak through our voices to reveal God's love.

31 / The Sermon on the Mount

Christ seldom gathered His disciples alone to receive His words. It was His work to reach the multitudes, in words of warning, entreaty, and encouragement, seeking to uplift all who would come to Him.

The Sermon on the Mount, though given especially to the disciples, was spoken in the hearing of the multitude. After the ordination of the apostles, Jesus went to the seaside. In the early morning people had begun to assemble. "When they had heard what great things He did," they "came to hear Him, and to be healed of their diseases; . . . there went virtue out of Him, and healed them all." Mark 3:8; Luke 6:17-19.

The narrow beach did not afford even standing room, and Jesus led the way back to the mountainside. Reaching a level space that offered a pleasant gathering place, He seated Himself on the grass, and the disciples and the multitude followed His example.

The disciples sat close beside Him, eager to understand the truths they were to make known to all lands and all ages. They believed that the kingdom was soon to be established.

A feeling of expectancy pervaded the multitude also. As the people sat on the green hillside, their hearts were filled with thoughts of future glory. Scribes and Pharisees looked forward to the day when they should have dominion over the hated Romans and possess the riches and splendor of the world's great empire. Poor peasants and fishermen hoped to hear that their

This chapter is based on Matthew 5 to 7.

wretched hovels, scanty food, and fear of want were to be exchanged for mansions and ease. They hoped that Israel was soon to be honored before the nations as the chosen of the Lord, and Jerusalem exalted as the head of a universal kingdom.

Christ Disappointed the Hope of Worldly Greatness

In the Sermon on the Mount Christ sought to undo the work that had been wrought by false education and to give His hearers a right conception of His kingdom. Without combating their ideas of the kingdom of God, He told them the conditions of entrance therein, leaving them to draw their own conclusions as to its nature. Happy are they, He said, who recognize their spiritual poverty and feel their need of redemption. Not to the spiritually proud is the gospel revealed, but to those who are humble and contrite.

The proud heart strives to earn salvation; but both our title to heaven and our fitness for it are found in the righteousness of Christ. The Lord can do nothing toward the recovery of man until he yields himself to the control of God. Then he can receive the gift God is waiting to bestow. From the soul that feels his need, nothing is withheld. See Isaiah 57:15.

"Blessed are they that mourn: for they shall be comforted." The mourning of which He speaks does not consist in melancholy and lamentation. We often sorrow because our evil deeds bring unpleasant consequences, but real sorrow for sin is the result of the working of the Holy Spirit. The Spirit brings us in contrition to the foot of the cross. By every sin Jesus is wounded afresh; and as we look on Him whom we have pierced, we mourn for sins that have brought anguish on Him. Such mourning will lead to the renunciation of sin. This sorrow binds the penitent to the Infinite One. The tears of the penitent are the raindrops that precede the sunshine of holiness, heralding a joy which will be a living fountain in the soul. See Jeremiah 3:12, 13; Isaiah 61:3.

For those also who mourn in trial and sorrow there is comfort. Through affliction God reveals to us the plague spots in our characters, that by His grace we may overcome. Unknown chapters in regard to ourselves are opened to us, and the test comes, whether we will accept the reproof and counsel of God. When in trial, we should not rebel or worry ourselves out of the hand of Christ. The ways of the Lord appear dark and joyless to our human nature, but His ways are ways of mercy, and the end is salvation.

God's word for the sorrowing is, "I will turn their mourning into joy, and will comfort them, and make them rejoice from their sorrow." Jeremiah 31:13.

A Calm Spirit Glorifies God

"Blessed are the meek." The difficulties we encounter may be much lessened by that meekness which hides itself in Christ. If we possess the humility of our Master, we shall rise above slights, rebuffs, and annoyances. They will cease to cast a gloom over the spirit. He who under abuse fails to maintain a calm spirit robs God of His right to reveal in him His own perfection of character. Lowliness of heart is the strength that gives victory to the followers of Christ.

Those who reveal the meek and lowly spirit of Christ may be looked on with scorn by the world, but they are of great value in God's sight. The poor in spirit, the humble in heart, whose highest ambition is to do God's will—these will be among that number who have washed their robes and made them white in the blood of the Lamb.

"Blessed are they which do hunger and thirst after righteousness; for they shall be filled." The sense of unworthiness will lead the heart to hunger for righteousness. All who long to bear the likeness of the character of God shall be satisfied. Love will expand the soul, giving it a capacity for higher attainments, for increased knowledge of heavenly things, so that it will not rest short of the fullness.

The merciful shall find mercy, and the pure in heart shall see God. Every impure thought impairs the moral sense and tends to obliterate the impressions of the Holy Spirit. The Lord may and does forgive the repenting sinner; but though forgiven, the soul is marred. All impurity of speech or thought must be shunned by him who would have clear discernment of spiritual truth.

But the words of Christ cover more than freedom from sensual impurity, more than freedom from that ceremonial defilement which the Jews so rigorously shunned. Selfishness prevents us from beholding God. Until we have renounced self-seeking, we cannot understand Him who is love. Only the unselfish heart, the humble and trustful spirit, shall see God as "merciful and gracious, longsuffering, and abundant in goodness and truth." Exodus 34:6.

"Blessed are the peacemakers." The world is at enmity with the law of God; sinners are at enmity with their Maker. As a result they are at enmity with one another. Human plans will fail of producing peace, because they do not reach the heart. The only power that can create true peace is the grace of Christ. When this is implanted in the heart, it will cast out the evil passions that cause strife and dissension.

The Multitudes Were Amazed

The people had come to think that happiness consisted in the possession of the things of this world, and that fame and honor were to be coveted. It was very pleasing to be called "Rabbi" and to be extolled as wise and religious. But Jesus declared that earthly honor was all such persons would ever receive. A convincing power attended His words. Many were convinced that this remarkable Teacher was actuated by the Spirit of God.

After explaining how true happiness may be obtained, Jesus pointed out the duty of His disciples. He knew that they would often be insulted, and their testimony rejected. The humble men who listened to His words were to bear calumny, torture, imprisonment, and death, and He continued:

"Blessed are they which are persecuted for righteousness' sake: for theirs is the kingdom of heaven. Blessed are ye, when men shall revile you, and persecute you, and shall say all manner of evil against you falsely, for My sake. Rejoice, and be exceeding glad: for great is your reward in heaven: for so persecuted they the prophets which were before you."

The world loves sin and hates righteousness, and this was the cause of its hostility to Jesus. The light of Christ sweeps away the darkness that covers their sins, and the need of reform is made manifest. Those who yield to the Holy Spirit begin war with themselves; those who cling to sin war against the truth and its representatives.

Thus Christ's followers are accused as troublers of the people. But it is fellowship with God that brings them the world's enmity. They are treading the path trodden by the noblest of earth. Each fiery trial is God's agent for their refining. Each conflict will add to the joy of their final triumph. Having this in view, the test of their faith will be cheerfully accepted rather than dreaded.

"Ye are the salt of the earth." Do not withdraw yourselves from the world in order to escape persecution. You are to abide among men, that the savor of divine love may be as salt to preserve the world from corruption. If those who serve God were removed from the earth, this world would be left to destruction. The wicked owe even the blessings of this life to the presence in the world of God's people whom they despise and oppress. But if Christians are such in name only, they are like salt that has lost its savor. Through misrepresentation of God they are worse than unbelievers.

"Ye are the light of the world." Salvation is like sunshine; it belongs to the whole world. The religion of the Bible is not to be confined between the covers of a book, nor within the walls of a church. It is to sanctify the daily life and manifest itself in all our social relations. The principles of righteousness must be enshrined in our hearts. The consistent life, the unswerving integrity, the benevolent spirit, the godly example—these are the mediums through which light is conveyed to the world.

Jesus knew that spies stood ready to seize every word that might be wrested to serve their purpose. He said nothing to unsettle faith in the institutions committed through Moses. Christ Himself had given both the moral and the ceremonial law. He did not come to destroy confidence in His own instruction. While He set aside false interpretations of the law, He carefully guarded against yielding up the vital truths committed to the Hebrews.

To the Pharisees the Saviour's words sounded like heresy. As He swept away the rubbish under which truth had been buried, they thought He was sweeping away the truth itself. He read their thoughts, and answered them, saying, "Think not that I am come to destroy the law, or the prophets: I am not come to destroy, but to fulfill." His mission was to vindicate the sacred claims of that law which they charged Him with breaking. If the law of God could have been changed or abrogated, then Christ need not have suffered the consequences of our transgression. He came to explain the relation of the law to man, and to illustrate its precepts by His life of obedience.

Obedience Leads to Joy

God loves mankind. To shield us from the results of transgression, He has revealed the principles of righteousness. When the law is received in Christ, it lifts us above the power of natural desires and tendencies, above temptations that lead to sin. God gave us the precepts of the law that in obeying them we might have joy.

At Sinai, God made known to men the holiness of

His character, that by contrast they might see the sinfulness of their own. The law was given to convict them of sin, and reveal their need of a Saviour. This work it is still to do. As the Holy Spirit reveals to men their need of Christ's cleansing blood and justifying righteousness, the law is still an agent in bringing us to Christ, that we may be justified by faith. "The law of the Lord is perfect, converting the soul." Psalm 19:7.

"Till heaven and earth pass, one jot or one tittle shall in no wise pass from the law, till all be fulfilled." The sun shining, and the solid earth are God's witnesses that His law is eternal. Though they may pass away, the divine precepts shall endure. The system of types that pointed to Jesus as the Lamb of God was to be abolished at His death, but the Decalogue is as immutable as the throne of God.

The Saviour's life of obedience proved that the law could be kept in humanity and showed the excellence of character that obedience would develop. On the other hand, all who break God's commandments sustain Satan's claim that the law cannot be obeyed. To admit them to heaven would again bring in discord and rebellion, and imperil the well-being of the universe. No one who willfully disregards one principle of the law shall enter the kingdom of heaven.

The greatest deception of the human mind in Christ's day was that a mere assent to the truth constitutes righteousness. In all human experience a theoretical knowledge of the truth has been proved to be insufficient for the saving of the soul. It does not bring forth the fruits of righteousness.

A jealous regard for what is termed theological truth often accompanies a hatred of genuine truth as made manifest in life. The darkest chapters of history are burdened with the record of crimes committed by bigoted religionists. The Pharisees thought themselves the greatest religionists of the world, but their so-called orthodoxy led them to crucify the Lord of glory. Many profess faith in the truth; but if it does not make them sincere, kind, patient, forbearing, heavenly-minded, it is a curse to its possessors, and through their influence it is a curse to the world.

The Depth and Breadth of God's Law

Jesus took up the commandments separately and showed how far-reaching their principles are. He declared that by the evil thought or lustful look the law of God is transgressed. The least injustice is breaking the law. He who gives hatred a place in his heart is setting his feet in the path of the murderer.

The Jews cultivated a spirit of retaliation. In their hatred of the Romans they gave utterance to hard denunciations, training themselves to do terrible deeds. There is an indignation that is justifiable, even in the followers of Christ. When they see God dishonored and the innocent oppressed, a righteous indignation stirs the soul. Such anger is not sin. But bitterness and animosity must be banished from the soul if we would be in harmony with heaven.

God's ideal for His children is higher than the highest human thought can reach. "Be ye, therefore, perfect, even as your Father which is in heaven is perfect." This command is a promise. The plan of redemption contemplates our complete recovery from the power of Satan. Christ always separates the contrite soul from sin. He has made provision that the Holy Spirit shall be imparted to every repentant soul, to keep him from sinning.

Temptations Are Not Excuses

Satan's temptations are not to be accounted an excuse for one wrong act. There is no excuse for sinning. A holy temper, a Christlike life, is accessible to every repenting, believing child of God.

As the Son of man was perfect in His life, so His followers are to be perfect in their lives. Jesus was in all things made like unto His brethren. He became flesh, even as we are. He shared the lot of man; yet He was the blameless Son of God. He was God in the flesh. His character is to be ours.

Christ is the ladder that Jacob saw, the base resting on the earth, the topmost round reaching heaven. If that ladder had failed by a single step of reaching the earth, we should have been lost. But Christ reaches us where we are. He took our nature and overcame, that we, through taking His nature, might overcome. Made "in the likeness of sinful flesh" (Romans 8:3), He lived a sinless life. Now He bids us by faith in Him attain to the glory of the character of God.

We are to be perfect, even as our "Father which is in heaven is perfect."

Jesus had shown in what righteousness consists and had pointed to God as its source. Now He turned to practical duties. Let nothing be done to attract attention or win praise to self. Give in sincerity, for the benefit of the suffering poor. In prayer, commune with God. In fasting, go not with the heart filled with thoughts of self.

Service rendered in sincerity of heart has great recompense. "Thy Father which seeth in secret will reward thee openly." By the life we live through the grace of Christ the character is formed. The attributes of the character of Christ are imparted, and the image of the Divine begins to shine forth. Men and women who walk and work with God are surrounded with the atmosphere of heaven. For these souls the kingdom of God has begun.

"No man can serve two masters." Bible religion is not one influence among many others; it is to pervade the whole life.

"If therefore thine eye be single, thy whole body will be full of light. But if thine eye be evil, thy whole body shall be full of darkness." He who desires to know the truth must be willing to accept all that it reveals. To be wavering and halfhearted in allegiance to truth is to choose error and satanic delusion.

Worldly policy and the principles of righteousness

do not blend into each other, like the colors of the rainbow. Between the two a clear line is drawn by God. The likeness of Christ stands out as distinct from that of Satan, as midday in contrast with midnight. And only those who live the life of Christ are His coworkers.

All who have chosen God's service are to rest in His care. Christ pointed to the birds flying in the heavens, and to the flowers of the field, and asked: "Are you not of more value than they?" RSV. The little brown sparrow is watched over. The flowers, the grass, share the notice of our heavenly Father. The great Master Artist has taken thought for the lilies, making them outshine the glory of Solomon. How much more does He care for man, who is the image and glory of God. As the sunbeam imparts to the flowers their delicate tints, so God imparts to the soul the beauty of His own character.

In the book of God's providence, the volume of life, we are each given a page. That page contains every particular of our history. God's children are never absent from His mind. "Therefore do not be anxious about tomorrow." RSV. God does not give His children all the directions for their life journey at once. He tells them just as much as they can remember and perform. Strength and wisdom imparted are for the present emergency.

"Judge not, that ye be not judged." Do not think yourself better than other men and set yourself up as their judge. Since you cannot discern motive, you are incapable of judging another. In criticizing him, you are passing sentence on yourself; for you show that you are a participant with Satan, the accuser of the brethren. See 2 Corinthians 13:5; 1 Corinthians 11:31.

The good tree will produce good fruit. So the fruit borne in the life testifies as to the character. Good works can never purchase salvation, but they are an evidence of the faith that works by love and purifies the soul. The reward is not bestowed because of our merit, yet it will be in proportion to the work done through grace.

Thus Christ set forth the principles of His kingdom. To impress the lesson, He added an illustration. It is not enough to hear My words; by obedience you must make them the foundation of your character. If you build on human theories, your house will fall. By the winds of temptation and trial it will be swept away. But these principles that I have given will endure. Receive Me; build on My words.

"Every one then who hears these words of mine and does them will be like a wise man who built his house upon the rock; and the rain fell, and the floods came, and the winds blew and beat upon that house, but it did not fall, because it had been founded on the rock." RSV.

32 / An Army Officer
Asks Help for His Servant

Christ was grieved that His own nation should require outward signs of His Messiahship. But He marveled that the centurion who came to Him did not even ask Him to come in person to perform the miracle. "Speak the word only, and my servant shall be healed."

The centurion's servant, stricken with palsy, lay at the point of death. Among the Romans, servants were slaves, bought and sold and treated with abuse and cruelty. But the centurion, tenderly attached to his servant, greatly desired his recovery. He believed that Jesus could heal him. The reports he heard had inspired him with faith.

This Roman was convinced that the Jews' religion was superior to his own. He had broken through the prejudice and hatred that separated the conquerors from the conquered, and had shown kindness to the Jews. In the teaching of Christ he found that which met the need of the soul. All that was spiritual within him responded to the Saviour's words. But he felt unworthy to come into the presence of Jesus, and appealed to the Jewish elders to request the healing of his servant. They were acquainted with the Great Teacher, and would, he thought, know how to approach Him so as to win His favor. As Jesus entered Capernaum, He was met by a delegation of the elders. They urged that "he was worthy for whom He should do this: for he loveth our nation, and he hath built us a synagogue."

This chapter is based on Matthew 8:5-13; Luke 7:1-17.

Jesus immediately set out for the officer's home; but, pressed by the multitude, He advanced slowly. The centurion, in his self-distrust, sent Him the message, "Lord, . . . I am not worthy that Thou shouldest come under my roof." But the Saviour kept on His way. Venturing at last to approach Him, the centurion said, "Neither thought I myself worthy to come unto Thee." "Speak the word only, and my servant shall be healed. For I am a man under authority, having soldiers under me: and I say to this man, Go, and he goeth; and to another, Come, and he cometh; and to my servant, do this, and he doeth it." As I represent the power of Rome, and my soldiers recognize my authority, so You represent the power of the Infinite God, and all created things obey Your word. You can command the disease to depart, and it shall obey. You can summon heavenly messengers to impart healing virtue. Speak but the word, and my servant shall be healed.

"When Jesus heard these things, He marveled at him, and turned Him about, and said unto the people that followed Him, I say unto you, I have not found so great faith, no, not in Israel." And to the centurion He said, "As thou hast believed, so be it done unto thee. And his servant was healed in the selfsame hour."

In their self-righteousness the Jewish elders commended the centurion because of the favor he had shown to "our nation." But the centurion said of himself, "I am not worthy." He trusted not to his own goodness. His faith took hold on Christ in His true character, the Friend and Saviour of mankind.

When Satan tells you that you are a sinner, tell him that Christ came into the world to save sinners. The plea that we may urge now and ever is our utterly helpless condition that makes His redeeming power a necessity.

> In my hand no price I bring;
> Simply to Thy cross I cling.

The Jews saw in Jesus nothing to be desired. But the centurion, educated in the idolatry of Rome, seemingly cut off from spiritual life by education and surroundings, and shut out by the bigotry of the Jews—this man perceived truth to which the children of Abraham were blind. The "Light, which lighteth every man that cometh into the world" (John 1:9) had shone upon him, and he had discerned the glory of the Son of God. To Jesus this was an earnest of the gathering of souls from all nations to His kingdom.

A Dead Man Raised to Life

More than twenty miles from Capernaum lay the village of Nain, and thither Jesus next bent His steps. All along the way the people came, bringing their sick for healing, and ever hoping that He would make Himself known as the King of Israel. A glad, expectant company followed Him up the rocky path toward the gate of the mountain village.

As they drew near, a funeral train was seen proceeding to the place of burial. On an open bier in front was the body of the dead. Filling the air with their wailing cries, the mourners gathered to show sympathy for the bereaved.

The deceased was the only son of his mother, and she a widow. The lonely mourner was following to the grave her sole earthly support and comfort. "When the Lord saw her, He had compassion on her." As she moved on blindly, weeping, He came close beside her and gently said, "Weep not."

"He came and touched the bier." To Jesus contact with death could impart no defilement. The bearers stood still, and the mourners gathered, hoping against hope. One was present who had vanquished demons; was death also subject to His power?

In clear, authoritative voice the words were spoken, "Young man, I say unto thee, Arise." That voice pierced the ears of the dead. The young man opened his eyes. Jesus took him by the hand, and lifted him up, and mother and son united in a long, joyous embrace. The multitude looked on in silence, as if in the very presence of God. Then they "glorified God, saying, That a great prophet is risen up among us, and that God hath visited His people." The funeral train returned to Nain as a triumphal procession.

He who stood beside the sorrowing mother at Nain is touched with sympathy for our grief. His word is no less efficacious now than when spoken to the young man of Nain. See Matthew 28:18. To all who believe on Him, He is still a living Saviour.

The mother's son was called forth to this earthly life, to endure its sorrows and to pass again under the power of death. But Jesus comforts our sorrow for the dead with a message of infinite hope: "I am He that liveth, and was dead; and, behold, I am alive forevermore, . . . and have the keys of hell and of death." Revelation 1:18.

Satan cannot hold in spiritual death one soul who in faith receives Christ's word of power. "Awake thou that sleepest, and arise from the dead." Ephesians 5:14. The word of God which bade the first man live, still gives life. Christ's word, "Young man, I say unto thee, Arise," gave life to the youth of Nain. So that word, "Arise from the dead," is life to the soul that receives it.

And "if the Spirit of Him that raised up Jesus from the dead dwell in you, He that raised up Christ from the dead shall also quicken your mortal bodies." Romans 8:11; see 1 Thessalonians 4:16, 17. This is the word wherewith He bids us comfort one another.

33 / How Jesus Related to Family Problems

The sons of Joseph were far from being in sympathy with Jesus in His work. The reports in regard to His life and labors filled them with dismay. They heard that He devoted entire nights to prayer, that through the day He was thronged by people, and did not even take time to eat. His friends felt He was wearing Himself out; they were unable to account for His attitude toward the Pharisees; and some feared that His reason was becoming unsettled.

His brothers felt keenly the reproach that came upon them through their relation to Jesus. They were indignant at His denunciation of the Pharisees. He must be persuaded to cease this manner of labor, and they induced Mary to unite with them, thinking that His love for her might prevail on Him to be more prudent.

The Pharisees had reiterated the charge, "He casteth out devils through the prince of the devils." Matthew 9:34. Christ told them that those who spoke against Him, not discerning His divine character, might receive forgiveness; through the Holy Spirit they might see their error and repent. But he who rejects the work of the Holy Spirit is placing himself where repentance cannot come to him. When men willfully reject the Spirit, and declare it to be from Satan, they cut off the channel by which God can communicate with them.

The Pharisees did not themselves believe the charge they brought against Jesus. Those dignitaries had

This chapter is based on Matthew 12:22-50; Mark 3:20-35.

213

heard the Spirit's voice in their own hearts declaring Him to be the Anointed of Israel. In His presence they had realized their unholiness and longed for righteousness. But after rejecting Him, it would be too humiliating to receive Him as the Messiah. To avoid acknowledging truth, they tried to dispute the Saviour's teaching. They could not prevent Him from working miracles, but they did everything in their power to misrepresent Him. Still the convicting Spirit of God followed them, and they had to build up barriers to withstand the mightiest agency that can be brought to bear upon the human heart.

God does not blind the eyes of men or harden their hearts. He sends them light to correct their errors; by rejection of this light the eyes are blinded and the heart hardened. Often the process is almost imperceptible. But when one ray of light is disregarded, there is a partial benumbing of spiritual perceptions, and the second revealing of light is less clearly discerned. So the darkness increases, until it is night in the soul. Thus it had been with these Jewish leaders. They attributed the work of the Holy Spirit to Satan. In doing this they deliberately chose deception, and henceforth were controlled by Satan's power.

Closely connected with Christ's warning in regard to the sin against the Holy Spirit is a warning against idle and evil words. Words are an indication of character. "Out of the abundance of the heart the mouth speaketh." Words also have power to react on the character. Men are influenced by their own words. Often under a momentary prompting by Satan, they give utterance to that which they do not really believe; but the expression reacts on the thoughts, and they come to believe what was spoken at Satan's instigation. Having once expressed an opinion or decision, often they are too proud to retract it. They try to prove themselves right, until they believe they are.

It is dangerous to utter a word of doubt, dangerous to question and criticize light. Careless and irreverent criticism reacts upon the character, fostering irreverence and unbelief. Many a man has gone on until he was ready to criticize and reject the Holy Spirit. Jesus said, ''Every idle word that men shall speak, they shall give account thereof in the day of judgment. For by thy words thou shalt be justified, and by thy words thou shalt be condemned.''

Then Jesus added a warning to those who had been impressed by His words, but had not surrendered themselves for the indwelling of the Holy Spirit. ''When the unclean spirit is gone out of a man, he walketh through dry places, seeking rest, and findeth none. Then he saith, I will return unto my house from whence I came out; and when he is come, he findeth it empty, swept, and garnished. Then goeth he, and taketh with himself seven other spirits more wicked than himself, and they enter in and dwell there.''

Many in Christ's day, as today, through the grace of God were set free from evil spirits that held dominion over the soul. They rejoiced in the love of God but did not surrender themselves to God daily, that Christ might dwell in the heart; and when the evil spirit returned, with ''seven other spirits more wicked than himself,'' they were wholly dominated by the power of evil.

A New Power Takes Possession

When the soul surrenders to Christ, a new power takes possession of the heart. A change is wrought which man can never accomplish for himself. The soul that is yielded to Christ becomes His own fortress, which he holds in a revolted world, and He intends that no authority shall be known in it but His own. A soul thus kept by heavenly agencies is impregnable to the assaults of Satan.

But unless we yield ourselves to the control of Christ, we shall be dominated by the wicked one. It is not necessary deliberately to choose the kingdom of darkness in order to come under its dominion. We have only to neglect to ally ourselves with the kingdom of light. If we do not cooperate with heavenly agencies, Satan will make the heart his abiding place. The only defense against evil is the indwelling of Christ in the heart through faith in His righteousness. Unless vitally connected with God, we can never resist self-love and temptation to sin. We may for a time leave off bad habits, but without moment by moment surrender to Christ and a continual communion, we are at the mercy of the enemy, and shall do his bidding in the end.

"The last state of that man is worse than the first. Even so shall it be also unto this wicked generation." There are none so hardened as those who have slighted the invitations of mercy. The most common manifestation of the sin against the Holy Spirit is in persistently slighting Heaven's invitation to repent.

In rejecting Christ the Jewish people committed the unpardonable sin; and by refusing the invitation of mercy, we may commit the same error. We put the Prince of life to shame before Satan and before the heavenly universe when we refuse to listen to His delegated messengers, and instead listen to agents who would draw the soul away from Christ. So long as one does this, he can find no pardon, and will finally lose all desire to be reconciled to God.

Christ's Real Brethren

While Jesus was still teaching the people, His disciples brought the message that His mother and brothers were outside and desired to see Him. "But He replied to the man who told Him, 'Who is My mother, and who are My brothers?' and stretching out His hand toward His disciples, He said, 'Here are My mother and My brothers! For whoever does the will of My Father in heaven is My brother, and sister, and mother.' " RSV.

All who receive Christ by faith are united to Him by a tie closer than human kinship. As a believer and doer of His words, His mother was more nearly and savingly related to Him than through her natural relationship. His brothers would receive no benefit from their connection with Him unless they accepted Him as their personal Saviour.

Their unbelief was a part of the bitterness of that cup of woe which He drained for us.

The enmity kindled in the human heart against the gospel was most painful to Jesus in His home. His brothers looked on Him as in need of their counsel. They thought that if He would speak things acceptable to the Pharisees, He would avoid disagreeable controversy. They thought He was beside Himself in claiming divine authority. They knew that the Pharisees were seeking occasion to accuse Him, and they felt He had given them sufficient occasion.

They could not fathom the mission He came to fulfill, and therefore could not sympathize with Him in His trials. Their coarse, unappreciative words showed that they had no true perception of His character. Instead of comforting Him, their spirit and words wounded His heart. His sensitive nature was tortured, His motives misunderstood, His work uncomprehended.

His brothers often presumed to think that they could teach Him who understood all truth. They freely condemned that which they could not understand. They thought they were vindicating God, when God was with them in the flesh, and they knew Him not.

These things made Jesus' path thorny. So pained was Christ by the misapprehension in His own home that it was a relief to go where it did not exist. He loved to visit the home of Lazarus, Mary, and Martha, for in the atmosphere of faith and love His spirit had rest. Yet often He could find relief only in being alone and communing with His Father.

Those who are called to endure misapprehension and distrust for Christ's sake in their own homes may find comfort in the thought that Jesus endured the same. He bids them find companionship in Him and relief in communion with the Father.

Those who accept Christ are not left as orphans, to bear trials alone. As members of the heavenly family, He bids them call His Father their Father. He has toward them an exceeding tenderness, far surpassing what our father or mother felt toward us in our helplessness.

When through poverty a Hebrew had been forced to sell himself as a bondservant, the duty of redeeming him fell to the one nearest of kin. See Leviticus 25:25, 47-49; Ruth 2:20. So the work of redeeming us fell on Him who is "near of kin" to us. Christ became our kinsman. Closer than father, mother, brother, friend, or lover is the Lord our Saviour. We cannot understand this love, but we can know it to be true in our own experience.

34 / His Yoke Is Easy and His Burden Light

"Come unto Me, all ye that labor and are heavy-laden, and I will give you rest." The Saviour left none to feel shut out from His care and love. He looked upon the distressed and heart-burdened, those whose hopes were blighted and who with earthly joys were seeking to quiet the longing of the soul, and He invited all to find rest in Him.

Tenderly He told the toiling people, "Take My yoke upon you, and learn of Me; for I am meek and lowly in heart: and ye shall find rest unto your souls."

In these words Christ is speaking to every human being. Whether they know it or not, all are weighed down with burdens that only Christ can remove. The heaviest burden is the burden of sin. If we were left to bear this, it would crush us. But the Sinless One has taken our place. "The Lord has laid on Him the iniquity of us all." Isaiah 53:6. He has borne the burden of our guilt. The burden of care and sorrow also He will bear.

The Elder Brother of our race is by the eternal throne. He knows by experience the weaknesses of humanity, our wants, and the strength of our temptations, for He was in all points tempted like as we are, yet without sin. Are you tempted? He will deliver. Are you weak? He will strengthen. Are you ignorant? He will enlighten. Are you wounded? He will heal. "He healeth the broken in heart, and bindeth up their wounds." Psalm 147:3.

Whatever your anxieties and trials, spread out your

This chapter is based on Matthew 11:28-30.

case before the Lord. Your spirit will be braced for endurance. The way will be opened to disentangle yourself from embarrassment and difficulty. The heavier your burdens, the more blessed the rest in casting them upon the Burden Bearer.

The rest that Christ offers depends on conditions, but these are plainly specified. They are those with which all can comply.

"Take My yoke upon you." The yoke is an instrument of service. Cattle are yoked for labor, and the yoke is essential that they may labor effectually. By this illustration Jesus teaches that we are called to service. We are to take upon us His yoke.

The yoke is the law of God, in the new covenant written in the heart. It binds the human worker to the will of God. If we were left to go just where our will would lead us, we should fall into Satan's ranks. Therefore God confines us to His will.

The yoke of service Christ Himself has borne in humanity. He said, "I came down from heaven, not to do Mine own will, but the will of Him that sent Me." John 6:38. Love for God, zeal for His glory, and love for fallen humanity brought Jesus to earth. This was the controlling power of His life. This principle He bids us adopt.

What Makes Us So Tired

Many whose hearts are aching under a load of care have chosen the world's service, accepted its perplexities, adopted its customs. Thus their life is made a weariness. To gratify worldly desires, they wound the conscience and bring upon themselves an additional burden of remorse. Our Lord desires them to lay aside this yoke of bondage. He says, "My yoke is easy, and My burden is light." He bids them seek first the kingdom of God and His righteousness. Worry is blind and cannot discern the future, but in every difficulty Jesus has His way prepared to bring relief. Our heavenly Father has a thousand ways to provide for us, of which we know nothing. Those who make the service and honor of God supreme will find perplexities vanish and a plain path before their feet.

"Learn of Me," says Jesus, "for I am meek and lowly in heart: and ye shall find rest." We are to enter the school of Christ and learn from Him. Redemption is that process by which the soul is trained for heaven. This training means emancipation from ideas, habits, and practices gained in the school of the prince of darkness.

In the heart of Christ there was perfect peace. He was never elated by applause nor dejected by censure or disappointment. Amid opposition and cruel treatment, He was still of good courage. But many of His followers have an anxious, troubled heart, because they are afraid to trust God. They shrink from the consequences of complete surrender to Him. But unless they make this surrender, they cannot find peace.

When we are born from above, the same mind will be in us that was in Jesus. Then we shall not be seeking the highest place. We shall desire to sit at the feet of Jesus, and learn of Him. We shall understand that the value of our work is in proportion to the impartation of the Holy Spirit. Trust in God brings holier qualities of mind, so that in patience we may possess our souls.

How His Yoke Makes the Work Easy

The yoke is placed on the oxen to aid in drawing the load, to lighten the burden. So with the yoke of Christ. When our will is swallowed up in the will of God, we shall find life's burden light. He who walks in the way of God's commandments walks with Christ, and in His love the heart is at rest. When Moses prayed, "Show me now Thy ways, that I may know Thee," the Lord answered, "My presence will go with thee, and I will give thee rest." Exodus 33:13.

Those who take Christ at His word, and surrender their lives to His ordering, will find peace. Nothing of the world can make them sad when Jesus makes them glad by His presence. "Thou wilt keep him in perfect peace, whose mind is stayed on Thee: because he trusteth in Thee." Isaiah 26:3.

Our lives may seem a tangle, but as we submit to the wise Master Worker, He will bring out the pattern of life and character that will be to His own glory. And that character which expresses the glory—the character—of Christ will be received into the Paradise of God.

As through Jesus we enter into rest, heaven begins here. We respond to His invitation, Come, learn of Me, and thus we begin the life eternal. Heaven is a ceaseless approaching to God through Christ. The more we know of God, the more intense will be our happiness. As we walk with Jesus in this life, we may be filled with His love, satisfied with His presence. All that human nature can bear, we may receive here.

35 / The Stilling of the Storm

It had been an eventful day. Beside the Sea of Galilee Jesus had spoken His first parables, explaining the nature of His kingdom and the manner in which it was to be established. He had likened His work to that of the sower; the development of His kingdom to the growth of the mustard seed and the effect of leaven in meal. The final separation of the righteous and the wicked He had pictured in parables of the wheat and tares and the fishing net. The precious truths He taught had been illustrated by the hidden treasure and the pearl of great price.

As evening came on, the crowds still pressed upon Him. Day after day He had ministered to them, scarcely pausing for food or rest. Now the close of day found Him so utterly wearied that He sought retirement in some solitary place across the lake. He bade His disciples accompany Him thither.

After He had dismissed the multitude, they took Him into the boat and hastily set off. But other fishing boats lying near the shore were quickly crowded with people who followed Jesus, eager still to see and hear Him.

The Saviour, overcome with weariness and hunger, lay down in the stern of the boat and soon fell asleep. The evening had been calm and pleasant, but suddenly darkness overspread the sky, and a fierce tempest burst upon the lake.

The waves, lashed into fury by howling winds, dashed fiercely over the boat and threatened to engulf

This chapter is based on Matthew 8:23-34; Mark 4:35-41; 5:1-20; Luke 8:22-39.

it. Those hardy fishermen had guided their craft safely through many a storm, but now their strength and skill availed nothing. Helpless in the grasp of the tempest, they saw their boat filling.

Jesus Cared

Absorbed in their efforts to save themselves they had forgotten that Jesus was on board. Now, seeing only death before them, they remembered at whose command they had set out to cross the sea. In Jesus was their only hope. "Master, Master!" But their voices were drowned by the roaring of the tempest, and there was no reply. Doubt and fear assailed them. Was He who had conquered disease and demons, and even death, powerless to help His disciples now? Was He unmindful of their distress?

Again they called, but there was no answer except the shrieking of the angry blast. Apparently they were to be swallowed up by the hungry waters.

Suddenly a flash of lightning pierced the darkness, and they saw Jesus lying asleep, undisturbed by the tumult. In amazement they exclaimed, "Master, carest Thou not that we perish?"

Their cry aroused Jesus. As the lightning's glare revealed Him, they saw the peace of heaven in His face; they saw in His glance tender love, and they cried, "Lord, save us: we perish."

Never did a soul utter that cry unheeded. As the disciples grasped their oars to make a last effort, Jesus rose. While the tempest raged and the waves broke over them, He lifted His hand and said to the angry sea, "Peace, be still."

The billows sank, the clouds rolled away, and the stars shone forth. The boat rested on a quiet sea. Then Jesus asked sorrowfully, "Why are you afraid? Have you no faith?" RSV.

A hush fell upon the disciples. Terror and despair had seized the occupants of the boats that had set out to accompany Jesus. The storm had driven the boats

The One who stilled the wind and calmed the waves of Galilee has the power to quiet the storms that break on our lives too.

into close proximity, and all on board beheld the miracle. The people whispered among themselves, "What manner of man is this, that even the winds and the sea obey Him?"

When Jesus was awakened to meet the storm, there was no trace of fear in word or look. But He rested not in possession of almighty power. It was not as "Master of earth and sea and sky" that He reposed in quiet. That power He had laid down. "I can of Mine own self do nothing." John 5:30. He trusted in the Father's might. It was in faith—faith in God's love and care— that Jesus rested, and the power of that word which stilled the storm was the power of God.

So we are to rest in the care of our Saviour. The disciples' fear in time of danger revealed their unbelief. They forgot Jesus, and only when they turned to Him could He give them help.

How often when tempests of temptation gather we battle with the storm alone. We trust to our own strength till we are ready to perish. Then we remember Jesus, and if we call upon Him to save us, we shall not cry in vain. He never fails to give us the help we need. If we have the Saviour in our hearts, there is no need of fear. The Redeemer will deliver us from danger in the way that He knows best.

"The wicked are like the troubled sea." Isaiah 57:20. Sin has destroyed our peace. The masterful passions of the heart no human power can control. We are as helpless here as were the disciples to quiet the raging storm. But however fierce the tempest, those who turn to Jesus with the cry, "Lord, save us," will find deliverance. His grace quiets the strife of human passion, and in His love the heart is at rest. "He made the storm be still, and the waves of the sea were hushed. Then they were glad because they had quiet; and He brought them to their desired haven." Psalm 107:29, 30, RSV. "Being justified by faith, we have peace with God through our Lord Jesus Christ." Romans 5:1.

In the early morning the Saviour and His companions came to shore. The light of the rising sun touched sea and land with the benediction of peace. But as they stepped on the beach, their eyes were greeted by a sight more terrible than the fury of the tempest. Two madmen rushed on them as if to tear them to pieces. Hanging about these men were parts of chains they had broken in escaping from confinement. Their flesh was torn and bleeding. Their eyes glared out from under their long and matted hair. Demons possessed them, and they looked more like wild beasts than like men.

The disciples fled in terror; but presently they turned to look for Jesus. He was standing where they had left Him. He who had stilled the tempest did not flee. When the men, foaming at the mouth, approached Him, Jesus raised that hand which had beckoned the waves to rest, and the men could come no nearer.

With authority Jesus commanded the unclean spirits to come out of them. His words penetrated the darkened minds of the unfortunate men. They realized dimly that One was near who could save them from the tormenting demons. But when their lips were opened to entreat His mercy, the demons spoke through them, crying vehemently, "What have I to do with Thee, Jesus, Thou Son of God most high? I beseech Thee, torment me not."

Jesus asked, "What is thy name?" And the answer was, "My name is Legion: for we are many." The demons begged Jesus not to send them out of the country. On a mountainside not far distant a great herd of swine was feeding. Into these the demons asked to be allowed to enter. Immediately the herd rushed madly down the cliff, plunged into the lake, and perished.

Meanwhile a marvelous change had come over the demoniacs. Light had shone into their minds. Their eyes beamed with intelligence. With glad voices the men praised God for deliverance.

From the cliff the keepers of the swine had seen all that had occurred, and they hurried away to publish the news to their employers. In fear and amazement the whole population flocked to meet Jesus. The demoniacs had been the terror of the country. No one had been safe to pass where they were. Now these men were clothed and in their right mind, listening to Jesus' words and glorifying Him who had made them whole. But the people did not rejoice. The loss of the swine seemed greater than the deliverance of these captives of Satan.

The owners of the swine were absorbed in earthly things and cared not for the great interests of spiritual life. Jesus desired to break the spell of selfish indifference, that they might accept His grace. But indignation for their temporal loss blinded their eyes to the Saviour's mercy.

Superstition Excited Fears

The manifestation of supernatural power excited the fears of the people. Further calamities might follow from having this Stranger among them. Those who had crossed the lake with Jesus told of their peril in the tempest and how the wind and the sea had been stilled. But their words were without effect. In terror the people pleaded with Jesus to go away, and He complied, taking ship at once for the opposite shore.

The people of Gergesa were so fearful of endangering their earthly interests that He who had vanquished the prince of darkness before their eyes was treated as an intruder, and the Gift of heaven was turned from their doors. Still there are many who refuse to obey Christ's word because obedience would involve the sacrifice of some worldly interest. Lest His presence cause pecuniary loss, many reject His grace and drive His Spirit from them.

But the restored demoniacs desired the company of their Deliverer. In His presence they felt secure from the demons that had tormented their lives and wasted their manhood. As Jesus was about to enter the boat, they kept close to His side and begged Him to keep them near Him. But Jesus told them to go home and tell what great things the Lord had done for them.

Here was a work for them to do—to go to a heathen home and tell of the blessing they had received from Jesus. It was hard for them to be separated from the Saviour. Difficulties were sure to beset them. Long isolation from society seemed to disqualify them for the work He had indicated. But as soon as Jesus pointed out their duty, they were ready to obey. They went throughout Decapolis, everywhere declaring His power to save and describing how He had freed them from the demons. In doing this work they could receive a greater blessing than if they had remained in His presence. In working to spread the "good news" of salvation we are brought near to the Saviour.

The two restored demoniacs were the first missionaries Christ sent to preach in the region of Decapolis. For only a few moments these men had been privileged to hear the teachings of Christ. But they bore in their own persons the evidence that Jesus was the Messiah. They could tell what they knew, what they had seen and heard and felt of the power of Christ. This is what everyone can do whose heart has been touched by the grace of God. See 1 John 1:1-3.

If we have been following Jesus step by step, we shall have something to tell concerning the way in which He has led us: how we have tested His promise, and found the promise true. This is the witness for which our Lord calls us.

Though the people of Gergesa had not received Jesus, He did not leave them to the darkness they had chosen. They had not heard His words. They were ignorant of that which they were rejecting. Therefore He again sent light to them by those to whom they would not refuse to listen.

The destruction of the swine roused the whole country as nothing else could have done and directed attention to Christ. The men He healed remained as witnesses to His power, channels of light, messengers of the Son of God. A door was opened throughout that region. When Jesus returned to Decapolis, thousands heard the message. Even the working of evil is overruled for good.

The demoniacs of Gergesa, dwelling in the place of graves, in bondage to uncontrolled passions and loathsome lusts, represent what humanity would become if given up to satanic jurisdiction. Satan's influence is constantly exerted on men to control the mind and incite to violence and crime. He darkens the intellect and debases the soul. Whenever men reject the Saviour's invitation, they are yielding themselves to Satan. Multitudes in the home, in business, and even in church are doing this today. Because of this, violence and crime overspread the earth, and moral darkness enshrouds the habitations of men. Satan leads men to worse and worse evils, till utter depravity and ruin are the result. The only safeguard against his power is the presence of Jesus. Before men and angels Satan has been revealed as man's enemy and destroyer; Christ, as man's friend and deliverer.

God has called us to be "conformed to the image of His Son." Romans 8:29. And souls that have been degraded into instruments of Satan are still through Christ transformed into messengers of righteousness and sent forth to tell "what great things the Lord hath done for thee."

36 / The Touch of Faith Brings Healing

Returning from Gergesa to the western shore of Lake Galilee, Jesus found a multitude gathered to receive Him. He remained by the seaside for a time, teaching and healing, and then went to the house of Levi-Matthew to meet the publicans at the feast. Here Jairus, the ruler of the synagogue, found Him. In great distress he exclaimed, "My little daughter lieth at the point of death: I pray Thee, come and lay Thy hands on her, that she may be healed; and she shall live."

Jesus set out at once with the ruler for his home. The disciples were surprised at His compliance with the entreaty of the haughty rabbi, yet they accompanied their Master and the people followed. Jesus and His companions advanced slowly, for the crowd pressed Him on every side. The anxious father was impatient, but Jesus stopped now and then to relieve suffering, or to comfort a troubled heart.

While they were on the way, a messenger pressed through the crowd, bearing the news that Jairus' daughter was dead. The word caught the ear of Jesus. "Fear not: believe only, and she shall be made whole."

Together they hurried to the ruler's home. Already hired mourners and flute players were filling the air with their clamor. Jesus tried to silence them: "Why make ye this ado, and weep? the damsel is not dead, but sleepeth." They were indignant at the words of the Stranger. They had seen the child in the embrace of death. Requiring them all to leave, Jesus took the fa-

This chapter is based on Matthew 9:18-26; Mark 5:21-43; Luke 8:40-56.

ther and mother of the maiden, and Peter, James, and John, and entered the chamber of death.

Jesus approached the bedside, and, taking the child's hand in His own, pronounced softly, in the familiar language of her home, "Damsel, I say unto thee arise."

Instantly a tremor passed through the unconscious form. The eyes opened widely as if from sleep, and the maiden gazed with wonder on the group beside her. She arose, and her parents clasped her in their arms, and wept for joy.

On the way to the ruler's house, Jesus had met a poor woman who for twelve years had suffered from a disease that made her life a burden. She had spent all her means on physicians and remedies, only to be pronounced incurable. But her hopes revived when she heard of Christ. If she could only go to Him she would be healed. In weakness and suffering she came to the seaside where He was teaching, and tried to press through the crowd, but in vain. She followed Him from the house of Levi-Matthew, but was still unable to reach Him. She had begun to despair when He came near where she was.

She was in the presence of the Great Physician! But amid the confusion she could not speak to Him or catch more than a passing glimpse of Him. Fearful of losing her one chance of relief, she pressed forward, saying to herself, "If I may but touch His garment, I shall be whole." As He was passing, she reached forward and succeeded in barely touching the border of His garment. In that one touch was concentrated the faith of her life; and instantly her pain and feebleness gave place to the vigor of perfect health.

With grateful heart she tried to withdraw from the crowd, but suddenly Jesus stopped. Looking about, He asked in a voice distinctly heard above the confusion, "Who touched Me?" Jostled on all sides, as he was, it seemed a strange inquiry.

Peter, ever ready to speak, said, "Master, the multitude throng Thee and press Thee, and sayest Thou, Who touched Me?" Jesus answered, "Somebody hath touched Me: for I perceive that virtue is gone out of Me." The Saviour could distinguish the touch of faith from the casual contact of the careless throng. Such trust should not be passed without comment. He would speak to the humble woman words of comfort, words that would be a blessing to His followers to the close of time.

Looking toward the woman, Jesus insisted on knowing who had touched Him. Finding concealment vain, she came forward, trembling. With grateful tears she told of her suffering and how she had found relief. Jesus said, "Daughter, . . . thy faith hath made thee whole; go in peace." He gave no opportunity for superstition to claim healing virtue for touching His garments. Through the faith which took hold on His divine power, the cure was wrought.

Living Faith Brings Healing

To talk of religion in a casual way, to pray without soul hunger and living faith, avails nothing. A nominal faith, which accepts Christ merely as the Saviour of the world, can never bring healing to the soul. Faith is not mere intellectual assent to truth. It is not enough to believe *about* Christ; we must believe *in* Him. Saving faith is a transaction by which those who receive Christ join themselves in covenant relation with God. Genuine faith means an increase of vigor, a confiding trust, by which the soul becomes a conquering power.

After healing the woman, Jesus desired her to acknowledge the blessing she had received. The gifts which the gospel offers are not to be enjoyed in secret. Our confession of His faithfulness is Heaven's chosen agency for revealing Christ to the world. That which will be most effectual is the testimony of our own experience. See Isaiah 43:12. Acknowledgments of His grace, when supported by a Christlike life, have irresistible power that works for the salvation of souls.

When the ten lepers came to Jesus for healing, they were cleansed; but only one returned to give Him glory. How many still do the same thing! The Lord raises up the sick, He delivers men from peril, He commissions angels to save them from calamity, to guard them from pestilence and destruction (Psalm 91:6); yet they are unmindful of His great love. By ingratitude they close their hearts against the grace of God.

It is for our own benefit to keep every gift of God fresh in our memory. Thus faith is strengthened. Let us, then, remember the loving-kindness of the Lord. And as we review God's dealings with us, let us declare, "What shall I render unto the Lord for all His benefits toward me?" Psalm 116:12.

37 / The First Evangelists

The apostles had accompanied Jesus on foot through Galilee. They had walked and talked with the Son of God and learned how to work for humanity. As Jesus ministered to the multitudes, His disciples were eager to lighten His labor. They assisted in bringing the afflicted ones to the Saviour and promoting the comfort of all. They watched for interested hearers and explained the Scriptures to them.

But they needed an experience in laboring alone. They were still in need of much instruction and patience. Now, while He was personally with them to counsel and correct them, the Saviour sent them forth as His representatives.

The disciples had often been perplexed by the teaching of the priests and Pharisees, but they had brought their perplexities to Jesus. He had strengthened their confidence in God's Word and in a great measure had set them free from their bondage to tradition. When they were separated from Him, every look and word came back to them. Often when in conflict with enemies of the gospel, they repeated His words.

Calling the Twelve about Him, Jesus told them to go out two and two through the towns and villages. Thus they could counsel and pray together, each one's strength supplementing the other's weakness.

Evangelistic work would be far more successful if this example were more closely followed.

The disciples were to enter into no controversy as to whether Jesus was the Messiah; but in His name they were to "heal the sick, cleanse the lepers, raise the

This chapter is based on Matthew 10; Mark 6:7-11; Luke 9:1-6.

dead, cast out devils: freely ye have received, freely give.''

Jesus devoted more time to healing the sick than to preaching. Wherever He went, the objects of His compassion were rejoicing in health. His voice was the first sound that many had ever heard, His name the first word they had ever spoken, His face the first they had ever looked upon. As He passed through the towns and cities, He was like a vital current, diffusing life and joy.

The followers of Christ are to labor as He did. We are to feed the hungry, comfort the suffering, and inspire hope in the hopeless. The love of Christ, manifested in unselfish ministry, will be more effective in reforming the evildoer than will the sword or court of justice. Often the heart will melt under the love of Christ. Through His servants, God desires to be a Comforter such as the world knows not.

The disciples on their first missionary tour were to go only to ''the lost sheep of the house of Israel.'' If the Jews would receive the gospel, God purposed to make them His messengers to the Gentiles. Therefore they were first to hear the message.

On this first tour the disciples were to go only where Jesus had been before them and had made friends. Their preparation for the journey was to be simple. They were not to adopt the dress of religious teachers, nor use apparel to distinguish them from the humble peasants. They were not to call the people together for public service; their efforts were to be in house-to-house labor. In every place they were to accept the hospitality of those who would welcome them as if entertaining Christ Himself, entering the dwelling with the beautiful salutation, ''Peace be to this house.'' Luke 10:5. That home would be blessed by their prayers, their songs of praise, and the opening of the Scriptures in the family circle. The message they had to bear was the word of eternal life, and the destiny of men depended upon their reception or rejection of it. See Matthew 10:14, 15.

"Behold," said Jesus, "I send you forth as sheep in the midst of wolves: be ye therefore wise as serpents, and harmless as doves." Christ did not suppress one word of truth, but He spoke it always in love. He was never rude, never gave needless pain to a sensitive soul. He did not censure human weakness. He fearlessly denounced hypocrisy and iniquity, but tears were in His voice as He uttered His scathing rebukes. Every soul was precious in His eyes.

The servants of Christ need to have close communion with God, lest under provocation self rise up and they pour forth a torrent of words that are not as dew or the still showers that refresh the withering plants. God's servants are to fix their eyes on Christ's loveliness. Then they can present the gospel with divine tact. And the spirit that is kept gentle under provocation will speak more effectively in favor of truth than any argument, however forcible.

We Must Meet Opposition

Continuing His instruction to His disciples, Jesus said, "Beware of men." They were not to put implicit confidence in those who knew not God, and open to them their counsels; for this would give Satan's agents an advantage. Man's inventions often counterwork God's plans. God is dishonored and the gospel betrayed when His servants depend on the counsel of men who are not under the guidance of the Holy Spirit.

"They will deliver you up to councils, . . . and you will be dragged before governors and kings for My sake, to bear testimony before them and the Gentiles." RSV. The servants of Christ will be brought before the great men of the world, who, but for this, might never hear the gospel. They have listened to false charges concerning the faith of Christ's disciples, and often their only means of learning its real character is the testimony of those who are brought to trial for their faith. "It shall be given you," said Jesus, "in that same hour what ye shall speak. For it is not ye that speak, but the

Spirit of your Father which speaketh in you." Those who reject the truth will stand to accuse the disciples. But the Lord's children are to reveal the meekness of their divine Example. Thus rulers and people will see the contrast between Satan's agents and the representatives of Christ.

The servants of Christ were to prepare no set speech to present when brought to trial. The Holy Spirit would bring to their remembrance the very truths that would be needed. The knowledge obtained by diligent searching of the Scriptures would be flashed into the memory. But if any had neglected to acquaint themselves with the words of Christ, they could not expect the Holy Spirit to bring His words to their remembrance.

What to Do When Persecution Comes

The disciples of Christ would be betrayed even by members of their own households: "Ye shall be hated of all men for My name's sake: but he that shall endure unto the end, the same shall be saved." But He bade them not to expose themselves unnecessarily to persecution. He Himself often left one field of labor for another in order to escape from those who were seeking His life. So His servants were not to be discouraged by persecution, but to seek a place where they could still labor for souls.

But whatever the danger, Christ's followers must scorn concealment. They cannot remain uncommitted until assured of safety in confessing the truth. Jesus said, "What I tell you in darkness, that speak ye in light: and what ye hear in the ear, that preach ye upon the housetops."

Jesus never purchased peace by compromise. His heart overflowed with love for the whole human race, but He was never indulgent to their sins. He was too much their friend to remain silent while they were pursuing a course that would ruin their souls. He labored that man should be true to himself, true to his higher, eternal interest. The servants of Christ, called to the same work, should beware lest, in seeking to prevent discord, they surrender truth. Real peace can never be secured by compromising principle. And no man can be true to principle without exciting opposition. Jesus told His disciples, "Fear not them which kill the body, but are not able to kill the soul." Their only fear should be lest they surrender truth and thus betray the trust with which God has honored them.

Satan works to fill men's hearts with doubt. He tempts them to sin, and then to regard themselves as too vile to approach their heavenly Father. The Lord understands all this. Jesus assures His disciples of God's sympathy, that not a sigh is breathed, not a pain felt, not a grief pierces the soul, but the throb vibrates to the Father's heart.

The Bible shows us God in His high and holy place (Isaiah 57:15), not inactive, not in silence and solitude, but surrounded by thousands of holy intelligences waiting to do His will. Through channels we cannot discern, He is in active communication with every part of His dominion, including this speck of a world. God is bending from His throne to hear the cry of the oppressed. To every sincere prayer He answers, "Here am I." He uplifts the distressed and downtrodden. In every temptation and trial the angel of His presence is near to deliver.

Jesus continued: As you confess Me before men, so I will confess you before God and the holy angels. You are to be My witnesses upon earth; so I will be your representative in heaven. The Father beholds not your faulty character, but He sees you clothed in My perfection. And everyone who shares My sacrifice for the lost shall be a sharer in the glory and joy of the redeemed.

He who would confess Christ must have Christ abiding in him. The disciples might speak fluently on doctrines, but unless they possessed Christlike meekness and love, they were not confessing Him. A spirit contrary to the spirit of Christ would deny Him. Men may deny Christ by evilspeaking, by foolish talking, by words that are untruthful or unkind. They may deny Him by shunning life's burdens, by conforming to the world, by uncourteous behavior, by justifying self, by cherishing doubt, and borrowing trouble. And "whosoever shall deny Me before men, him will I also deny before My Father which is in heaven."

The Saviour said, "I have not come to send peace, but a sword." This strife is not the effect of the gospel, but of opposition to it. Of all persecution, the hardest to bear is in the home, the estrangement of dearest earthly friends. But Jesus declared, "He that loveth father or mother more than Me is not worthy of Me: and he that loveth son or daughter more than Me is not worthy of Me. And he that taketh not his cross, and followeth after Me, is not worthy of Me."

"He that receiveth you, receiveth Me, and he that receiveth Me receiveth Him that sent Me." No act of kindness shown in His name will fail to be rewarded. He includes the feeblest and lowliest of the family of God. "Whosoever shall give to drink unto one of these little ones a cup of cold water only in the name of a disciple, verily I say unto you, he shall in no wise lose his reward."

Thus the Saviour ended His instruction. The chosen Twelve went out, as He had gone, "to preach the gospel to the poor, . . . to heal the brokenhearted, to preach deliverance to the captives, and recovering of sight to the blind." Luke 4:18.

38 / Christ and the Twelve Take a Vacation

On returning from their missionary tour, "the apostles returned to Jesus, and told Him all that they had done and taught. And He said to them, 'Come away by yourselves to a lonely place, and rest a while.' " RSV.

The disciples' intimate relationship with Jesus encouraged them to lay before Him their favorable and unfavorable experiences as evangelists. As they frankly told Christ of their experiences, He saw that they needed much instruction. He saw, too, that they needed rest.

But where they then were they could not obtain privacy, "for there were many coming and going, and they had no leisure so much as to eat." The people were thronging after Christ, anxious to be healed and eager to listen to His words. He seemed to many to be the fountain of all blessings.

But now Christ longed for retirement, for He had much to say to His disciples. In their work at times they had been much troubled to know what to do. They needed now to go to a place of retirement where they could hold communion with Jesus and receive instruction for future work. They had been putting their whole souls into labor for the people, and this was exhausting their physical and mental strength. It was their duty to rest.

As the disciples had seen the success of their labors, they were in danger of taking credit to themselves, of cherishing spiritual pride, and falling under Satan's temptations. They must learn that their strength was

This chapter is based on Matthew 14:1, 2, 12, 13; Mark 6:30-32; Luke 9:7-10.

not in self, but in God. They needed to commune with Christ, with nature, and with their own hearts.

It was about this time that Jesus received tidings of the Baptist's death. This brought vividly before Him the end to which His own steps were tending. Priests and rabbis were watching, spies hung upon His steps, and plots for His ruin were multiplying.

News reached Herod of Jesus and His work. "This is John the Baptist," he said; "he is risen from the dead"; and he expressed a desire to see Jesus. Herod was in constant fear lest a revolution unseat him and break the Roman yoke from the Jewish nation. Among the people the spirit of insurrection was rife. It was evident that Christ's public labors in Galilee could not long continue, and He longed to be apart for a season from the confusion of the multitude.

With saddened hearts the disciples of John had borne his mutilated body to its burial. Then "they went and told Jesus." These disciples had been envious of Christ and had doubted His divine mission because He did not set the Baptist at liberty. But now they longed for consolation in their great sorrow and for guidance as to their future work. They came to Jesus and united their interest with His.

At the northern end of the lake was a lonely region, beautiful with the fresh green of spring. For this place they set out in their boat. The scenes of nature were in themselves a rest, grateful to the senses. Here they could listen to Christ without the angry interruptions, retorts, and accusations of the scribes and Pharisees.

Rest Refreshed Them

The time Christ and His disciples spent in retirement was not devoted to pleasure seeking. They talked together regarding the work of God and the possibility of greater efficiency. Christ corrected their errors and made plain to them the right way of approaching the people. They were vitalized by divine power, and inspired with hope and courage.

When Jesus said that the harvest was great and the laborers few, He did not urge ceaseless toil, but said, "Pray ye therefore the Lord of the harvest, that He will send forth laborers into His harvest." Matthew 9:38. God would not have a few weighted with responsibilities while others have no burden, no travail of soul.

Christ's words of compassion are spoken to His workers today, "Come ye yourselves apart . . . and rest a while." It is not wise to be always under the strain of ministering to men's spiritual needs, for in this way personal piety is neglected and soul and body are overtaxed. Self-denial is required, but care must be exercised lest Satan take advantage of human weakness, and the work of God be marred.

As activity increases and men become successful in doing any work for God, there is a tendency to pray less and to have less faith. We lose sight of our dependence on God and seek to make a savior of activity. It is Christ's power which does the work. We must take time for meditation, prayer, and study of the Word. Only the work accomplished with much prayer, and sanctified by the merit of Christ, will in the end prove efficient for good.

Never Too Busy to Talk With God

No other life was so crowded with labor as was that of Jesus; yet how often He was found in prayer! Again and again are found records such as these: "Rising up a great while before day, He went out, and departed into a solitary place, and there prayed." "Great multitudes came together to hear, and to be healed by Him of their infirmities. And He withdrew Himself into the wilderness, and prayed." "And it came to pass in those days, that He went out into a mountain to pray, and continued all night in prayer to God." Mark 1:35; Luke 5:15, 16; 6:12.

The Saviour found it necessary to turn aside from a life of ceaseless activity and contact with human needs to seek unbroken communion with His Father. As one with us, He was wholly dependent on God. In the secret place of prayer He sought divine strength that He might go forth braced for duty and trial. Jesus endured struggles and torture of soul. In communion with God He could unburden the sorrows that were crushing Him. As a man, He supplicated the throne of God till His humanity was charged with a heavenly current that should connect humanity with divinity. He received life from God that He might impart life to the world. His experience is to be ours.

If today we would take time to go to Jesus and tell Him our needs, we should not be disappointed. He is the Wonderful Counselor. We are invited to ask wisdom of Him. He "giveth to all men liberally, and upbraideth not." Isaiah 9:6; James 1:5.

Everyone needs a personal experience in obtaining a knowledge of the will of God. We must individually hear Him speaking to the heart. When every other voice is hushed and in quietness we wait before Him, the silence of the soul makes more distinct the voice of God. See Psalm 46:10. Here alone can true rest be found. The soul thus refreshed will reveal a divine power that will reach men's hearts.

39 / "Give Ye Them to Eat"

This rare season of peaceful quietude was soon broken. The disciples thought they would not be disturbed, but as soon as the multitude missed the divine Teacher, they inquired, "Where is He?" Some had noticed the direction where He and His disciples had gone. Many went by land, others in their boats, to meet them. The Passover was at hand, and pilgrims on their way to Jerusalem gathered to see Jesus, until there were assembled 5000 men besides women and children.

From the hillside Jesus looked upon the multitude, and "was moved with compassion toward them, because they were as sheep not having a shepherd." Leaving His retreat, He found a convenient place where He could minister to them.

The people listened to words of mercy from the Son of God, words that were as balm to their souls. The healing of His divine hand brought life to the dying and ease and health to those suffering with disease. The day seemed like heaven on earth, and they were unconscious of how long it had been since they had eaten anything.

At length the sun was sinking in the west, and yet the people lingered. Jesus had labored all day without food or rest, but He could not withdraw Himself from the multitude that pressed upon Him.

The disciples finally urged that for their own sake the people should be sent away. Many had eaten nothing since morning. In surrounding towns they might buy

This chapter is based on Matthew 14:13-21; Mark 6:32-44; Luke 9: 10-17; John 6:1-13.

food. But Jesus said, "Give ye them to eat." Turning to Philip, He questioned, "Whence shall we buy bread, that these may eat?" This He said to test the faith of the disciple. Philip looked over the sea of heads, and answered that two hundred pennyworth* of bread would not be nearly enough, so that each of them might have a little.

Jesus inquired how much food could be found among the company. "There is a lad here," said Andrew, "which hath five barley loaves, and two small fishes: but what are they among so many?" Jesus directed that these be brought to Him and that the disciples seat the people on the grass in parties of fifty or a hundred, that all might witness what He was about to do. When this was accomplished, Jesus "looked up to heaven, and blessed, and broke the loaves, and gave them to the disciples to set before the people; and He divided the two fish among them all. And they all ate and were satisfied. And they took up twelve baskets full of broken pieces and of the fish." RSV. He who taught the people the way to secure peace and happiness was just as thoughtful of their temporal necessities as of their spiritual need.

Christ never worked a miracle except to supply a genuine necessity, and every miracle was to lead the people to the tree of life. The simple food passed round by the disciples contained a whole treasure of lessons. Humble fare had been provided; the fishes and barley loaves were the daily food of the fisherfolk. Christ could have spread a rich repast, but food prepared merely for the gratification of appetite would have conveyed no lesson for their good. Never did people enjoy luxurious feasts as this people enjoyed the rest and simple food which Christ provided so far from human habitations.

If men today were simple in their habits, living in

---

*The "penny," or denarius, was equivalent to the daily wage of a common laborer. See Matthew 20:1, 2.

harmony with nature's laws, there would be an abundant supply for the human family. There would be fewer imaginary wants, and more opportunities to work in God's ways. But selfishness and indulgence of unnatural taste have brought sin and misery into the world.

To that great throng, weary and hungry, the simple fare was an assurance not only of Jesus' power, but of His tender care for them in the common needs of life. The Saviour has not promised His followers luxuries. Their fare may be plain, even scanty; their lot may be shut in by poverty. But His word is pledged that their need shall be supplied, and He has promised that which is far better than worldly good—the comfort of His own presence.

In the production of earth's harvests, God is working a miracle every day. Through natural agencies the same work is accomplished that was wrought in the feeding of the multitude. Men prepare the soil and sow the seed, but life from God causes the seed to germinate. It is God who every day feeds millions from earth's harvest fields. Men ascribe the working of His power to natural causes or to human instrumentality. Man is glorified in place of God, and His gracious gifts are made a curse instead of a blessing. God desires us to recognize Him in His gifts. To accomplish this, the miracles of Christ were performed.

A Valuable Lesson in Ecology

After the multitude had been fed, there was an abundance of food left. But Jesus said, "Gather up the fragments that remain, that nothing be lost." The lesson was twofold. Nothing is to be wasted. Let everything be gathered up that will relieve earth's hungry ones. And there should be the same carefulness in spiritual things. The people wanted their friends at home to share in the bread that Christ had blessed. So those who were at the feast were to give to others the bread that comes down from heaven, to satisfy the hunger of the soul. They were to repeat what they had learned of the wonderful things of God. Nothing was to be lost.

The miracle of the loaves teaches dependence upon God. When Christ fed the 5000, food was not nigh at hand. Here He was, in the wilderness. But He knew that the large multitude would feel hungry and faint, for He was one with them in their need for food. They were far from home, and many were without means to purchase food. The providence of God had placed Jesus where He was; and He depended on His heavenly Father for the means to relieve the necessity.

We too are to depend on God. We are not to plunge into difficulties and misuse the faculties God has given us. But when, after following His directions, we are brought into strait places, we are to seek help from Him who has infinite resources at His command. He will keep every soul that is brought into perplexity through trying to keep the way of the Lord.

How We Often Repeat Andrew's Unbelief

Christ has bidden us, "Go ye into all the world, and preach the gospel to every creature." Mark 16:15. But how often our faith fails us, as we see how great is the need and how small the means in our hands. Like Andrew, often we hesitate, unwilling to give all that we have, fearing to spend and to be spent for others. But Jesus has bidden us, "Give ye them to eat." Behind His command is the same power that fed the multitude beside the sea.

In Christ's act is wrapped up a deep spiritual lesson for all His workers. Christ received from the Father; He imparted to the disciples; they imparted to the multitude; and the people to one another. So all who are united to Christ will receive from Him the bread of life and impart it to others. Jesus took the small loaves, and although there was but a small portion for His own disciples, He did not invite them to eat, but began to distribute to them, bidding them serve the people. The food multiplied in His hands; and the hands of the disciples, reaching out to Christ, were never empty. After the people had been supplied, Christ and His disciples ate together of the Heaven-supplied food.

The disciples were the channel of communication between Christ and the people. The most intelligent, the most spiritual, can bestow only as they receive. We can impart only what we receive from Christ; and we can receive only as we impart to others. And the more we impart, the more we shall receive.

Too often the worker for Christ fails to realize his personal responsibility. He is in danger of shifting his burden on organizations instead of relying on Him who is the source of all strength. Successful work for Christ depends not so much on talent as on earnest, dependent faith. In place of shifting your responsibility on someone you think is more richly endowed than you are, work according to your ability. When the question comes home to your heart, "Whence shall we buy bread, that these may eat?" let not your answer be the response of unbelief. When people are destitute of the bread of life, shall we send for someone from afar to come and feed them? Christ said, "Make the men sit down," and He fed them there. So when you are surrounded by souls in need, know that Christ is there. Bring your barley loaves to Jesus. The little that is wisely used in the service of the Lord will increase in the very act of imparting.

The Lord says, "Give, and it will be given to you." "He who supplies seed to the sower and bread for food will supply and multiply your resources and increase the harvest of your righteousness. You will be enriched in every way for great generosity." Luke 6:38; 2 Corinthians 9:10, 11, RSV.

40 / A Night on the Lake

Seated on the grassy plain in the twilight of the spring evening, the people ate the food Christ provided. The miracle of the loaves appealed to everyone in that vast multitude. God had fed Israel with manna in the desert, and who was this that had fed them that day but He whom Moses had foretold? They said one to another, "This is of a truth the Prophet that should come into the world."

That crowning act was assurance that the long-looked-for Deliverer was among them. This was He who would make Judea an earthly paradise, a land flowing with milk and honey. He could break the power of the hated Romans. He could heal the soldiers wounded in battle. He could supply whole armies with food. He could give to Israel the long-sought dominion!

The people were ready at once to crown Him king. They saw that He made no effort to secure honor to Himself, and they feared He would never urge His claim to David's throne. Consulting together, they agreed to take Him by force and proclaim Him the king of Israel. The disciples united with the multitude in declaring the throne of David the rightful inheritance of their Master. Let the arrogant priests and rulers be forced to honor Him who came clothed with the authority of God.

But Jesus saw what was on foot. Violence and insurrection would follow, and the work of the spiritual kingdom would be hindered. Without delay the move-

This chapter is based on Matthew 14:22-33; Mark 6:45-52; John 6: 14-21.

ment must be checked. Calling His disciples, Jesus bade them take the boat and return at once to Capernaum, leaving Him to dismiss the people.

Never before had a command from Christ seemed so impossible. This seemed the golden opportunity to establish their beloved Master on the throne of Israel. It was hard for them to go away by themselves and leave Jesus alone on that desolate shore. They protested, but Jesus now spoke with an authority He had never before assumed toward them. In silence they turned toward the sea.

Jesus now commanded the multitude to disperse, and His manner was so decisive that they dared not disobey. In the very act of advancing to seize Him, their steps were stayed. The kingly bearing of Jesus and His few quiet words of command frustrated their designs. They recognized in Him a power above all earthly authority, and without question they submitted.

Left alone, Jesus "went up into a mountain apart to pray." For hours He prayed for power to reveal to men the divine character of His mission, that Satan might not blind their understanding and pervert their judgment. He knew that His days on earth were nearly ended, and that few would receive Him. His disciples were to be grievously tried, their long-cherished hopes disappointed. In place of His exaltation to the throne of David, they were to witness His crucifixion. This was to be indeed His true coronation; but they did not discern this, and without the Holy Spirit the faith of the disciples would fail. For them He poured out His supplications with bitter agony and tears.

The disciples had not put off immediately from land, hoping that Jesus would come. But as darkness was fast gathering, they "entered into a ship, and went over the sea toward Capernaum." They murmured because they had not been permitted to proclaim Him king. They blamed themselves: if they had been more persistent, they might have accomplished their purpose.

Unbelief was taking possession of their minds and hearts. Love of honor had blinded them. They were eager to see Jesus exalted as they thought He should be. Were they always to be accounted followers of a false prophet? Why did not He who possessed such power reveal Himself in His true character, and make their way less painful? Why had He not saved John the Baptist from a violent death? Thus the disciples reasoned until they brought on themselves great spiritual darkness. They questioned, Could Jesus be an impostor, as the Pharisees asserted?

The Storm Within the Disciples' Hearts

The memory of that precious, glorious day should have filled them with faith and hope, but they had forgotten it all. Their thoughts were stormy and unreasonable, and the Lord gave them something else to afflict their souls and occupy their minds. God often does this when men create burdens and troubles for themselves. The disciples had no need to make trouble. Already danger was fast approaching.

A violent tempest had been stealing upon them, and they were unprepared for it. It was a sudden contrast, and when the gale struck they were afraid. They forgot their disaffection, unbelief, and impatience. Everyone worked to keep the boat from sinking. In ordinary weather the journey required but a few hours; but now they were driven farther from the point they sought. Until the fourth watch of the night they toiled at the oars. Then the weary men gave themselves up for lost. Helpless, they longed for the presence of their Master.

The Watcher on the shore saw those fear-stricken men battling with the tempest. With deepest solicitude His eyes followed the storm-tossed boat with its precious burden; for these men were to be the light of the world. When their hearts were subdued, their unholy ambition quelled, and in humility they prayed for help, it was given them.

At the moment when they believed themselves lost,

a gleam of light revealed a mysterious figure approaching on the water. But the One who had come for their help, they counted as an enemy. Terror overpowered them. Hands that had grasped the oars with muscles like iron let go. The boat rocked at the will of the waves; all eyes were riveted on this vision of a man walking on the white-capped billows of the foaming sea.

They thought it a phantom that omened their destruction, and they cried out for fear. Jesus advanced as if He would pass them, but they recognized Him and entreated His help. His voice silenced their fear, "It is I; be not afraid."

As soon as they could credit the wondrous fact, Peter cried out, "Lord, if it be Thou, bid me come unto Thee on the water. And He said, Come."

Peter's Self-Exaltation and His Fall

Looking unto Jesus, Peter walked securely; but as he glanced back toward his companions in the boat, his eyes were turned from the Saviour. The waves rolled high and he was afraid. For a moment Christ was hidden from view, and his faith gave way. He began to sink. But while the billows talked with death, Peter lifted his eyes from the angry waters, and cried, "Lord, save me." Jesus grasped the outstretched hand, saying, "O thou of little faith, wherefore didst thou doubt?"

Walking side by side, Peter's hand in that of his Master, they stepped into the boat together. Peter was now subdued and silent. Through unbelief and self-exaltation he had nearly lost his life.

When trouble comes, how often we look on the waves, instead of keeping our eyes on the Saviour! The proud waters go over our souls. Jesus does not call us to follow Him and then forsake us. "Fear not," He says. "When thou passest through the waters, I will be with thee; and through the rivers, they shall not overflow thee. . . . I am the Lord thy God, the Holy One of Israel, thy Saviour." Isaiah 43:1-3.

In this incident on the sea Jesus desired to reveal to Peter that his safety was in constant dependence on divine power. Amid the storms of temptation he could walk safely only as he should rely on the Saviour. Where he thought himself strong, Peter was weak. Had he learned the lesson in that experience on the sea, he would not have failed when the great test came upon him.

Day by day God instructs His children. By the circumstances of daily life He is preparing them to act their part upon that wider stage to which His providence has appointed them. We may now suppose that our feet stand secure, and that we shall never be moved. We may say with confidence, Nothing can shake my faith in God and in His Word. But Satan is planning to take advantage of our hereditary and cultivated defects. Only through realizing our own weakness and looking steadfastly to Jesus can we walk securely.

No sooner had Jesus taken His place in the boat than the wind ceased, "and immediately the ship was at the land whither they went." The disciples and others on board bowed at the feet of Jesus with thankful hearts, saying "Of a truth Thou art the Son of God!"

41 / The Crisis in Galilee

Christ knew that a turning point in His history was reached. Multitudes who desired to exalt Him to the throne today would turn from Him tomorrow. Disappointment of selfish ambition would turn love to hatred, and praise to curses.

Yet He took no measures to avert the crisis. From the first He had held out no hope of earthly rewards. Of those now connected with Him, many had been attracted by hope of a worldly kingdom. These must be undeceived.

Early next morning the people flocked to Bethsaida in great numbers. Those who had left Jesus the preceding night returned, expecting to find Him still there; for there had been no boat by which He could pass to the other side. But their search was fruitless.

Meanwhile He had arrived at Gennesaret, after an absence of but one day. Those who had come from Bethsaida learned from His disciples how He had crossed the sea. The fury of the storm, the many hours of adverse winds, Christ walking on water, His reassuring words, the adventure of Peter, the sudden stilling of the tempest and landing of the boat, all were faithfully recounted to the wondering crowd. Not content with this, many hoped to receive from Christ's own lips a further account of the miracle.

Jesus did not gratify their curiosity. He sadly said, "Ye seek Me, not because ye saw the miracles, but because ye did eat of the loaves, and were filled. Labor not for the meat which perisheth, but for that meat

This chapter is based on John 6:22-71.

which endureth unto everlasting life.'' Seek not merely for material benefit, but for spiritual food.

For the moment the interest of the hearers was awakened. ''What shall we do, that we might work the works of God?'' Their question meant, What shall we do that we may deserve heaven? What price are we required to pay in order to obtain the life to come?

Jesus answered, ''This is the work of God, that ye believe on Him whom He hath sent.'' The price of heaven is Jesus. The way to heaven is through faith in the Lamb of God.

Selfish Hopes Unfulfilled

Jesus had done the very work prophecy had foretold the Messiah would do, but the people had not witnessed what their selfish hopes had pictured as His work. In the days of Moses Israel had been fed with manna forty years, and far greater blessings were expected from the Messiah. Why could Jesus not give health, strength, and riches to all His people, free them from their oppressors, and exalt them to power and honor? He claimed to be the Sent of God, yet refused to be Israel's king. This was a mystery they could not fathom. Did He dare not assert His claims because He Himself doubted the divine character of His mission?

Half mockingly a rabbi questioned: ''What sign showest Thou then, that we may see, and believe Thee? what dost Thou work? Our fathers did eat manna in the desert; as it is written, He gave them bread from heaven to eat.''

''Then said Jesus unto them, Verily, verily, I say unto you, Moses gave you not that bread from heaven.'' The giver of the manna was standing among them. Christ Himself had led the Hebrews and had daily fed them with the bread from heaven. That food was a type of the real bread from heaven. The life-giving Spirit is the true manna. ''For the bread of God is that which comes down from heaven, and gives life to the world.'' RSV.

Still thinking it was temporal food, some exclaimed, "Lord, evermore give us this bread." Jesus then spoke plainly, "I am the bread of life."

Moses had said, "Man doth not live by bread only, but by every word that proceedeth out of the mouth of the Lord." Deuteronomy 8:3. And Jeremiah had written, "Thy words were found, and I did eat them; and Thy word was unto me the joy and rejoicing of mine heart." Jeremiah 15:16. The teaching of the prophets made plain the spiritual lesson in the miracle of the loaves. Had Christ's hearers in the synagogue understood the Scriptures, they would have understood His words, "I am the bread of life." As the multitude had received physical strength from the bread He had given them the day before, so from Christ they might receive spiritual strength unto eternal life. "He that cometh to Me," He said, "shall never hunger; and he that believeth on Me shall never thirst." But he added, "Ye also have seen Me, and believe not."

They had seen Christ by the witness of the Holy Spirit, by the revelation of God to their souls. The living evidences of His power had been before them day after day, yet they asked for still another sign. If they were not convinced by what they had seen and heard, it was useless to show them more marvelous works. Unbelief will ever find excuse for doubt, and will reason away the most positive proof.

Again Christ appealed to those stubborn hearts: "Him that cometh to Me I will in nowise cast out." All who received Him in faith, He said, should have eternal life. No longer need men mourn in hopeless grief over their dead. "This is the will of Him that sent Me, that everyone which seeth the Son, and believeth on Him, may have everlasting life: and I will raise him up at the last day."

But the leaders were offended. "Is not this Jesus, the son of Joseph, whose father and mother we know? How is it then that He saith, I came down from heaven?" Referring scornfully to the lowly origin of

Like Peter, we often take our eyes from Jesus and begin to sink into life's troubles. But when we call for help, He always reaches out, grasps our hands, and lifts us up.

Jesus, they contemptuously alluded to His family as being poor and lowly. The claims of this uneducated carpenter, they said, were unworthy of their attention. On account of His mysterious birth they insinuated that He was of doubtful parentage.

Jesus did not attempt to explain the mystery of His birth, as He had made no answer to the questions concerning His crossing the sea. Voluntarily He had made Himself of no reputation and taken the form of a servant. But His words and works revealed His character.

The prejudice of the Pharisees had its root in the perversity of their hearts. Every word and act of Jesus aroused antagonism in them; for the spirit they cherished could find in Him no answering chord.

"No one can come to Me, except the Father which hath sent Me draw him. . . . It is written in the prophets, And they shall be all taught of God. Every man therefore that hath heard, and hath learned of the Father, cometh unto Me." None will ever come to Christ, save those who respond to the drawing of the Father's love. But God is drawing all hearts unto Him, and only those who resist His drawing will refuse to come to Christ. Those who had learned of God had been listening to His Son, and in Jesus of Nazareth they would recognize Him who had declared the Father.

When Heaven Begins

"Verily, verily, I say unto you, He that believeth on Me hath everlasting life." And Jesus said, "I will raise him up at the last day." Christ became one flesh with us, that we might become one spirit with Him. By virtue of this union we are to come forth from the grave, because through faith His life has become ours. Those who see Christ and receive Him into the heart, have everlasting life. Through the Spirit, Christ dwells in us; and the Spirit of God, received by faith, is the beginning of life eternal.

The manna which the fathers ate in the wilderness did not prevent death nor insure immortality, but the bread of heaven would nourish the soul unto everlasting life. The Saviour said, "This is the bread which cometh down from heaven, that a man may eat thereof, and not die." Only through dying could Christ impart life to men, and He points to His death as the means of salvation: "The bread that I will give is My flesh, which I will give for the life of the world."

In the symbol of the Passover lamb the Jews did not discern the Lord's body. The same truth was taught in the words of Christ, but it was still undiscerned.

Now the rabbis exclaimed angrily, "How can this Man give us His flesh to eat?" To some extent they comprehended the meaning of Jesus, but by misconstruing His words, hoped to prejudice the people against Him.

Christ reiterated the truth in yet stronger language: "Verily, verily, I say unto you, Except ye eat the flesh of the Son of man, and drink His blood, ye have no life in you. Whoso eateth My flesh, and drinketh My blood, hath eternal life; and I will raise him up at the last day. For My flesh is meat indeed, and My blood is drink indeed. He that eateth My flesh, and drinketh My blood, dwelleth in Me, and I in him."

What food is to the body, Christ must be to the soul. Food cannot benefit us unless it becomes a part of our being. So a theoretical knowledge will do us no good. We must feed upon Christ. His life, His love, His grace, must be assimilated.

"As the living Father hath sent Me, and I live by the Father: so he that eateth Me, even he shall live by Me." So fully was Jesus surrendered to the will of God that the Father alone appeared in His life. Although tempted in all points like as we are, He stood untainted by the evil that surrounded Him. Thus we also are to overcome as Christ overcame.

Are you a follower of Christ? Then all that is written concerning the spiritual life may be attained through uniting yourself to Jesus. Has your first love grown cold? Accept again the love of Christ. Eat of His flesh, drink of His blood, and you will become one with the Father and with the Son.

By ritual law the Jews were forbidden to taste blood, and they now construed Christ's language into sacrilegious speech. Many even of the disciples said, "This is an hard saying; who can hear it?"

The Saviour answered them: "Doth *this* offend you? What and if ye shall see the Son of man ascend up where He was before? It is the spirit that quickeneth; the flesh profiteth nothing: the words that I speak unto you, they are spirit, and they are life."

Life in the Word

The life of Christ that gives life to the world is in His word. By His word Jesus healed disease and cast out demons; by His word He stilled the sea and raised the dead. The whole Bible is a manifestation of Christ, and the Saviour desired to fix the faith of His followers on the word. When His visible presence should be withdrawn, the word must be the source of their power.

As our physical life is sustained by food, so our spiritual life is sustained by the Word of God. As we must eat for ourselves, so we must receive the Word for ourselves. We should carefully study the Bible, asking God for the aid of the Holy Spirit, that we may understand His Word. We should take one verse, ascertain the thought God has put in that verse for us, and dwell upon the thought until it becomes our own.

In His promises and warnings, Jesus means me. God so loved the world, that He gave His Son, that *I* by believing in Him, might not perish, but have everlasting life. The experiences related in God's Word are to be *my* experiences. Prayer and promise are *mine*. "I am crucified with Christ: nevertheless I live; yet not I, but Christ liveth in me: and the life which I now live in the flesh I live by the faith of the Son of God, who loved me, and gave Himself for me." Galatians 2:20. As faith thus assimilates the principles of truth, they become a part of the being and the motive power of the life. The Word molds the thoughts and enters into the development of character.

God will make precious revelations to His hungering, thirsting people. As they feed on His Word, they find it is spirit and life. The Word destroys the natural, earthly nature, and imparts a new life in Christ. The Holy Spirit comes as a Comforter. By God's grace, the disciple becomes a new creature. Love takes the place of hatred, and the heart receives the divine similitude. This is eating the Bread that comes down from heaven.

Christ knew the character of those who claimed to be His disciples, and His words tested their faith. He declared that they were to believe and act on His teaching and be conformed to His character. This involved the relinquishment of cherished ambitions. It required complete surrender to Jesus. They were called to become self-sacrificing, meek and lowly in heart, to walk in the narrow path traveled by the Man of Calvary.

Christ's Words Alienate Many

The test was too great. The enthusiasm of those who had sought to take Jesus by force and make Him king grew cold. This discourse had opened their eyes. No earthly rewards were to be realized from connection with Him. They had welcomed His miracle-working power but would not come into sympathy with His self-sacrificing life. If He would not obtain their freedom from the Romans, they would have nothing to do with Him.

Jesus told them plainly, "There are some of you that believe not," adding, "Therefore said I unto you, that no man can come unto Me, except it were given unto him of My Father." If they were not drawn to Him, it was because their hearts were not open to the Holy Spirit.

By the public rebuke of their unbelief, these disciples were still further alienated from Jesus. Wishing to wound the Saviour and gratify the malice of the Pharisees, they turned their backs on Him and left Him with disdain. They had made their choice; they walked no more with Jesus.

By the words of truth, the chaff was being separated from the wheat. See Matthew 3:12. Because they were too self-righteous to receive reproof, many turned away. Souls are tested today as were those disciples in the synagogue at Capernaum. When truth is brought home to the heart, they see the need of an entire change, but are not willing to take up the self-denying work. They go away offended, murmuring, "This is an hard saying; who can hear it?"

Truth Is Unwelcome

When the crowds follow and the multitudes are fed and the shouts of triumph are heard, their voices are loud in praise; but when God's Spirit reveals sin and bids them leave it, they turn their backs on the truth.

As those disaffected disciples turned away, a different spirit took control of them. They could see nothing attractive in Christ whom they had once found so interesting. They misinterpreted His words, falsified His statements, and impugned His motives, gathering up every item that could be turned against Him. Such indignation was stirred up by these false reports that His life was in danger.

The news spread swiftly that by His own confession Jesus of Nazareth was not the Messiah. Thus in Galilee the popular feeling turned against Him, as, the year before, it had been in Judea. Israel rejected their Saviour because they wanted the food which perishes, not that which endures unto everlasting life.

With a yearning heart, Jesus saw those who had been His disciples depart. His compassion unappreciated, His love unrequited, His salvation rejected—this filled Him with inexpressible sorrow. Such developments as these made Him "a man of sorrows, and acquainted with grief." Isaiah 53:3.

Without attempting to hinder those who were leaving, Jesus turned to the Twelve and said, "Will ye also go away?"

Peter replied by asking, "Lord, to whom shall we go? Thou hast the words of eternal life. And we believe and are sure that Thou art that Christ, the Son of the living God."

"To whom shall we go?" The disciples had found more peace and joy since they had accepted Christ than in all their previous lives. How could they go back to those who scorned and persecuted the Friend of sinners?

"To whom shall we go?" To the darkness of unbelief, the wickedness of the world? Peter expressed the faith of the disciples—"Thou art that Christ." To be destitute of a Saviour was to be adrift on a dark and stormy sea.

Every word and act of Jesus had its definite purpose in the work of our redemption. While we cannot now comprehend the ways of God, we can discern His great love which underlies all His dealings with men. He who lives near to Jesus will recognize the mercy that tests the character and brings to light the purpose of the heart.

Love Under All His Dealings

Jesus knew what would be the result of His words. He foresaw that His agony in Gethsemane, His betrayal and crucifixion would be to His beloved disciples a most trying ordeal. Had no previous test been given, many actuated by merely selfish motives would have been connected with them. When their Lord was condemned, when the multitude who had hailed Him as their king hissed at Him and reviled Him, when the jeering crowd cried, "Crucify Him!"—these self-seeking ones would, by renouncing their allegiance to Jesus, have brought on the disciples a bitter, heart-burdening sorrow in addition to their grief and disappointment in the ruin of their fondest hopes. The example of those who turned from Him might have carried others with them. But Jesus brought about this crisis while by His personal presence He could still strengthen the faith of His true followers.

Compassionate Redeemer, who in the full knowledge of the doom that awaited Him, tenderly smoothed the way for the disciples, prepared them for their crowning trial, and strengthened them for the final test!

42 / Christ Foretells a Great Uprooting

The mission of the Twelve, indicating the extension of Christ's work, had excited anew the jealousy of the leaders at Jerusalem. The spies sent to Capernaum in the early part of Christ's ministry were put to confusion, but now another deputation was sent to watch His movements and find some accusation against Him.

As before, the ground of complaint was His disregard of traditional precepts professedly designed to guard the observance of the law. Among the observances most strenuously enforced was ceremonial purification. Neglect of the forms to be observed before eating was accounted a heinous sin.

The life of those who tried to observe the rabbinical requirements was one long struggle against ceremonial defilement. While the people were occupied with trifling observances, their attention was turned away from the great principles of God's law.

Christ and His disciples did not observe ceremonial washings. The spies did not, however, make a direct attack on Christ, but came to Him with criticism of His disciples: "Why do Thy disciples transgress the tradition of the elders? for they wash not their hands when they eat bread."

Jesus made no attempt to defend Himself or His disciples. He proceeded to show the spirit that actuated these sticklers for human rites. He gave them an example of what they were repeatedly doing: "Full well ye reject the commandment of God," He said, "that ye may keep your own tradition. For Moses said, Honor

This chapter is based on Matthew 15:1-20; Mark 7:1-23.

thy father and thy mother; and, Whoso curseth father or mother, let him die the death; but ye say, If a man shall say to his father or mother, It is Corban, that is to say, a gift, by whatsoever thou mightest be profited by me; he shall be free. And ye suffer him no more aught for his father or his mother." An undutiful child had only to pronounce the word *Corban* over his property, and he could retain it for his own use during his lifetime, and after his death it was to be appropriated to the temple service. Thus he was at liberty to dishonor and defraud his parents, under cover of a pretended devotion to God.

Jesus commended the poor woman who gave her all to the temple treasury. But the apparent zeal for God on the part of the priests and rabbis was a pretense to cover a desire for self-aggrandizement. Even the disciples of Christ were not wholly free from inherited prejudice and rabbinical authority. By revealing the true spirit of the rabbis, Jesus sought to free all who were really desirous of serving God.

"Ye hypocrites, well did Esaias prophesy of you, saying, This people draweth nigh unto Me with their mouth, and honoreth Me with their lips; but their heart is far from Me. In vain they do worship Me, teaching for doctrines the commandments of men." Christ declared that by placing their requirements above the divine precepts, the rabbis were setting themselves above God. Jesus explained that defilement comes not from without, but from within. Purity and impurity pertain to the soul.

The Rage of the Spies

The disciples noted the rage of the spies and heard the half-muttered words of dissatisfaction and revenge. They told Christ, hoping that He might conciliate the enraged officials: "Knowest thou that the Pharisees were offended, after they heard this saying?"

He answered, "Every plant, which My heavenly Father hath not planted, shall be rooted up." The customs and traditions so highly valued by the rabbis could not endure the testing of God. Every human invention that has been substituted for the commandments of God will be found worthless in that day when "God shall bring every work into judgment, with every secret thing, whether it be good, or whether it be evil." Ecclesiastes 12:14.

Even among Christians are found institutions and usages that have no better foundation than the traditions of the fathers. Men cling to their traditions and hate those who show them their error. In this day, when we are bidden to call attention to the commandments of God and the faith of Jesus, we see the same enmity as was manifested in the days of Christ. Of the remnant people of God it is written, "The dragon was wroth with the woman, and went to make war with the remnant of her seed, which keep the commandments of God, and have the testimony of Jesus Christ." Revelation 12:17.

But "every plant, which My heavenly Father hath not planted, shall be rooted up." In place of the authority of the so-called fathers of the church, God bids us accept the word of the eternal Father, the Lord of heaven and earth. Here alone is truth unmixed with error. "In vain they do worship Me, teaching for doctrines the commandments of men."

43 / Christ Breaks Down Racial Barriers

After the encounter with the Pharisees Jesus withdrew from Capernaum and crossed Galilee to the hill country on the borders of Phoenicia. Looking westward He could see the ancient cities of Tyre and Sidon with their heathen temples. Beyond was the Mediterranean, over which the messengers of the gospel were to bear its glad tidings to the centers of the world's empire. The work before Him now was to prepare His disciples for their mission.

"Behold, a Canaanite woman from that region came out and cried, 'Have mercy on me, O Lord, Son of David; my daughter is severely possessed by a demon.' " RSV. The people of this district were idolaters, despised and hated by the Jews. The woman who now came to Jesus was a heathen, and therefore was excluded from the advantages the Jews daily enjoyed.

Tidings of Christ's work had penetrated to this region. This woman had heard of the prophet, who, it was reported, healed all manner of diseases. Hope sprang up in her heart. Inspired by a mother's love, she determined to present her daughter's case to Him. He must heal her child. At times she was tempted to think, What can this Jewish teacher do for me? But the word had come, He heals all manner of diseases, whether those who come for help are rich or poor.

Christ knew that this woman was longing to see Him, and He placed Himself in her path. By ministering to her sorrow, He could give a living representation

This chapter is based on Matthew 15:21-28; Mark 7:24-30.

of the lesson He designed to teach. For this He had brought His disciples to this region. He desired them to see the ignorance existing in cities and villages close to Israel. The people who had been given the truth made no effort to help souls in darkness. The partition wall which Jewish pride had erected shut even the disciples from sympathy with the heathen world. These barriers were to be broken down.

Christ received this representative of a despised race with the cold and heartless manner in which the Jews would treat such a case. But the woman did not lose faith. As He passed on, as if not hearing her, she followed, continuing her supplications. Annoyed, the disciples asked Jesus to send her away. They saw that their Master treated her with indifference, and they supposed that the prejudice of the Jews against the Canaanites was pleasing to Him.

But it was a pitying Saviour who answered: "I am not sent but unto the lost sheep of the house of Israel." Although this answer appeared to be in accordance with the prejudice of the Jews, it was an implied rebuke to the disciples, which they afterward understood as reminding them of what He had often told them—that He came to the world to save all who would accept Him.

The woman urged her case with increased earnestness, bowing at Christ's feet, and crying, "Lord, help me." Jesus, still apparently rejecting her entreaties, answered, "It is not meet to take the children's bread, and to cast it to dogs." This was virtually asserting that it was not right to lavish on strangers and aliens from Israel the blessings brought to the favored people of God. This answer would have utterly discouraged a less earnest seeker. But the woman saw that her opportunity had come.

Beneath the apparent refusal of Jesus, she saw a compassion He could not hide. "Truth, Lord, yet the dogs eat of the crumbs which fall from their masters' table." Even dogs are not left unfed! So, while there were many blessings given to Israel, was there not also a blessing for her? She was looked on as a dog, and had she not, then, a dog's claim to a crumb from His bounty? If she may have the privilege of a dog, she was willing to be regarded as a dog; and she immediately acknowledged Jesus as the Redeemer, as being able to do all that she asked of Him.

Faith in Christ Gives Her a Tremendous Argument

The Saviour was satisfied. He had tested her faith. He had shown that she who had been regarded as an outcast from Israel was no longer an alien, but a child in God's household. As a child it was her privilege to share in the Father's gifts. Christ now granted her request and finished the lesson to the disciples. Turning to her with a look of pity and love, He said, "O woman, great is thy faith: be it unto thee even as thou wilt." From that hour her daughter became whole. The woman departed, acknowledging her Saviour, and happy in the granting of her prayer.

It was for this miracle that Jesus went to the borders of Tyre and Sidon. He wished to relieve the afflicted woman and at the same time leave an example of mercy for the benefit of His disciples when He would no longer be with them. He wished to lead them to be interested in working for others besides their own people.

Jesus longed to unfold the deep mysteries of the truth, that the Gentiles should be fellow heirs with the Jews, and "partakers of His promise in Christ by the gospel." Ephesians 3:6. In rewarding the faith of the centurion at Capernaum and preaching to the inhabitants of Sychar, He had already given evidence that He did not share the intolerance of the Jews. But now Jesus brought the disciples in contact with a heathen, whom they regarded as having no reason to expect favor from Him. He would show that His love was not to be circumscribed to race or nation.

When He said, "I am not sent but to the lost sheep of

the house of Israel,'' He stated the truth. This woman was one of the lost sheep that Israel should have rescued. The work they had neglected, Christ was doing.

This act opened the minds of the disciples more fully to the labor that lay before them among the Gentiles. They saw souls bearing sorrows unknown to those more highly favored, longing for help from the mighty Healer, hungering for truth. Afterward, when the partition wall between Jew and Gentile was broken down by the death of Christ, this lesson had a powerful influence on the representatives of Christ.

The Saviour's visit to Phoenicia and the miracle there performed had a yet wider purpose. Today, the same pride and prejudice have built strong walls of separation between different classes of men. Multitudes feel virtually shut away from the gospel. But let them not feel that they are shut away from Christ.

In faith the woman of Phoenicia flung herself against the barriers piled up between Jew and Gentile. Against discouragement, regardless of appearances, that might have led her to doubt, she trusted the Saviour's love. Thus Christ desires us to trust in Him. The blessings of salvation are for every soul. Nothing but his own choice can prevent any man from becoming a partaker of the promise in Christ by the gospel.

Caste is hateful to God. In His sight the souls of all men are of equal value. He ''hath made of one blood all nations of men, . . . that they should seek the Lord, if haply they might . . . find Him, though He be not far from every one of us.'' All are invited to come to Him and live. ''The same Lord over all is rich unto all that call upon Him. For whosoever shall call upon the name of the Lord shall be saved.'' Acts 17:26, 27; Romans 10:12, 13.

44 / The True Sign

In Decapolis, where the demoniacs of Gergesa had been healed, the people had constrained Jesus to depart. But they had listened to the messengers He left behind. As He came again into that region, a crowd gathered, and a deaf, stammering man was brought to Him. Taking him apart, Jesus put His fingers in his ears and touched his tongue. He sighed at thought of the ears that would not be open to the truth, the tongues that refused to acknowledge the Redeemer. At the word, "Be opened," the man's speech was restored.

Jesus went up into a mountain, and there the multitude flocked to Him, bringing their sick and lame. He healed them all; and the people, heathen as they were, glorified the God of Israel. For three days they thronged about the Saviour, sleeping at night in the open air, and through the day pressing to hear the words of Christ and see His works.

At the end of three days their food was spent. Jesus would not send them away hungry, and He called on His disciples to give them food. At Bethsaida they had seen how their little store availed for feeding the multitude; yet they did not now bring forward their all, trusting His power to multiply it for the hungry crowds. Again the disciples revealed their unbelief. Those He fed at Bethsaida were Jews; these were Gentiles and heathen. Jewish prejudice was still strong in the hearts of the disciples. "Where are we to get bread enough in the desert to feed so great a crowd?" RSV.

But obedient to His word they brought Him what

This chapter is based on Matthew 15:29-39; 16:1-12; Mark 7:31-37; 8:1-21.

they had—seven loaves and two fishes. The multitude were fed, seven large baskets of fragments remaining. Four thousand men, besides women and children, were thus refreshed.

Then with His disciples, Jesus crossed the lake to Magdala. In the border of Tyre and Sidon His spirit had been refreshed by the confiding trust of the Syrophoenician woman. The heathen people of Decapolis had received Him with gladness. Now as He landed once more in Galilee, where most of His works of mercy had been performed, He was met with contemptuous unbelief.

The Aristocracy of the Nation Challenge Christ

The two sects—Pharisees and Sadducees—had been at bitter enmity, but now they united against Christ, asking for a sign from heaven. When Israel went out to battle with the Canaanites at Bethhoron, the sun had stood still at Joshua's command. Some such sign was demanded of Jesus. But no mere external evidence could benefit them.

"O ye hypocrites," said Jesus, "ye can discern the face of the sky,"—by studying the sky they could foretell the weather—"but can ye not discern the signs of the times?" Christ's own words, spoken with the power of the Holy Spirit, were the sign God had given. The song of the angels to the shepherds, the star that guided the wise men, the voice from heaven at His baptism were witnesses for Him.

"And He sighed deeply in His spirit, and saith, Why doth this generation seek after a sign?" "There shall no sign be given unto it, but the sign of the prophet Jonas." As the preaching of Jonah was a sign to the Ninevites, so Christ's preaching was a sign to His generation. But what a contrast in the reception of the word! The people of the great heathen city humbled themselves; the high and lowly together cried to the God of heaven, and His mercy was granted them. "The men of Nineveh shall rise in judgment with this generation," Christ had said, "and shall condemn it: because they repented at the preaching of Jonas; and, behold, a greater than Jonas is here." Matthew 12:41.

Every miracle Christ performed was a sign of His divinity, but to the Pharisees these works of mercy were a positive offense. The Jewish leaders looked with heartless indifference on human suffering. In many cases their oppression had caused the affliction that Christ relieved. Thus His miracles were to them a reproach.

The True Evidence That Christ Came From God

That which led the Jews to reject the Saviour was the highest evidence of His divine character: His miracles were for the blessing of humanity. His life revealed the character of God. He did the works and spoke the words of God. Such a life is the greatest of all miracles.

Many in our day, like the Jews, cry, Show us a sign; work a miracle. Christ does not impart to us power to vindicate ourselves or satisfy the demands of unbelief and pride. But is it not a miracle that we can break from the bondage of Satan? Enmity against Satan is not natural to the human heart. It is implanted by the grace of God. When one who has been controlled by a stubborn, wayward will yields himself to the drawing of God's heavenly agencies, a miracle is wrought; so also when a man who has been under strong delusion comes to understand moral truth. The change in human hearts, the transformation of human characters, is a miracle that reveals an ever-living Saviour. In preaching the Word of God, the sign that should be manifest now and always is the presence of the Holy Spirit, to make the Word a regenerating power to those that hear.

Those who desired a sign from Jesus had hardened their hearts. They would not see that His mission was in fulfillment of the Scriptures. "If they hear not Moses and the prophets, neither will they be persuaded, though one rose from the dead." Luke 16:31.

Turning from the group of cavilers, Jesus reentered the boat with His disciples. In sorrowful silence they again crossed the lake. On reaching the farther side, Jesus said, "Take heed and beware of the leaven of the Pharisees and of the Sadducees." The Jews had been taught to regard leaven as a type of sin. In their sudden departure from Magdala the disciples had forgotten to take bread. They understood Christ as warning them not to buy bread of a Pharisee or Sadducee. Their lack of spiritual insight often led to misconception of His words.

Now Jesus reproved them for thinking that He who had fed thousands with a few fishes and barley loaves could have referred in that solemn warning to merely temporal food. There was danger that the crafty reasoning of the Pharisees and Sadducees would leaven His disciples with unbelief.

The disciples were inclined to think that their Master should have granted the demand for a sign in the heavens. He was able to do this, and such a sign would put His enemies to silence. They did not discern the hypocrisy of the cavilers. Months afterward, Jesus repeated the same teaching. "Beware ye of the leaven of the Pharisees, which is hypocrisy." Luke 12:1.

Self-Deception of Egocentric Motivation

Leaven works imperceptibly, changing the meal to its own nature. So if hypocrisy is allowed in the heart, it permeates the character and life. A striking example was the practice of Corban, by which a neglect of filial duty was concealed under a pretense of liberality to the temple. The scribes and Pharisees concealed the real tendency of their doctrines, instilling them artfully into the minds of their hearers. This deceptive teaching made it hard for the people to receive the words of Christ.

The same influences are working through those who try to explain the law of God to make it conform to their practices. This class do not attack the law openly, but put forward speculative theories that undermine its principles. They explain it so as to destroy its force.

The hypocrisy of the Pharisees was the product of self-seeking. This led them to pervert and misapply the Scriptures. This subtle evil even the disciples of Christ were in danger of cherishing. The followers of Jesus were influenced in a great degree by the reasoning of the Pharisees, often vacillating between faith and unbelief. Even the disciples had not in heart ceased to seek great things for themselves. This spirit prompted the strife as to who should be greatest. This made them so little in sympathy with Christ's mission of self-sacrifice. As leaven will cause corruption, so the self-seeking spirit, cherished, works the defilement and ruin of the soul.

Today, as of old, how widespread is this subtle, deceptive sin! How often our service to Christ is marred by the secret desire to exalt self! How ready the thought of self-gratulation and the longing for human approval! The love of self, the desire for an easier way than God has appointed, leads to the substitution of human theories and traditions for the divine precepts.

The religion of Christ is sincerity itself. Zeal for God's glory is the motive implanted by the Holy Spirit, and only the power of God can banish self-seeking and hypocrisy. This change is the sign of His working. When the faith we accept destroys selfishness and pretense, when it leads us to seek God's glory and not our own, we may know that it is of the right order. "Father, glorify Thy name" (John 12:28) was the keynote of Christ's life, and if we follow Him this will be the keynote of our life.

45 / The Foreshadowing of the Cross

Even before Christ took humanity upon Him, He saw the whole length of the path He must travel to save that which was lost. Every pang that rent His heart, every insult heaped on His head, every privation He was called to endure was open to His view before He laid aside His crown and royal robe and stepped down from the throne to clothe His divinity with humanity. He knew the anguish that would come upon Him, and yet He said, "Lo, I come: in the volume of the book it is written of Me, I delight to do Thy will, O My God: yea, Thy law is within My heart." Psalm 40:7, 8.

His earthly life, so full of toil and self-sacrifice, was cheered by the prospect that by giving His life, He would win back the world to its loyalty to God. Although the baptism of blood must first be received; although the sins of the world were to weigh upon His innocent soul; although the shadow of an unspeakable woe was upon Him; yet for the joy set before Him, He chose to endure the cross.

The time was near when the chosen companions of His ministry must see Him whom they loved and trusted hung upon the cross of Calvary. Soon He must leave them to face the world without the comfort of His visible presence. Bitter hate and unbelief would persecute them, and He desired to prepare them for their trials.

Jesus and His disciples had now come into one of the towns about Caesarea Philippi. They were beyond Galilee, in a region where idolatry prevailed. Around

This chapter is based on Matthew 16:13-28; Mark 8:27-38; Luke 9: 18-27.

them were represented forms of superstition that existed in all parts of the world. Jesus desired that a view of these things might lead the disciples to feel their responsibility to the heathen.

He was about to tell them of the suffering that awaited Him. But first He prayed that their hearts might be prepared to receive His words. He did not at once communicate that which He desired to impart, but gave them opportunity to confess their faith in Him. He asked, "Whom do men say that I the Son of man am?"

Sadly the disciples acknowledged that Israel had failed to recognize their Messiah. The multitudes at Bethsaida had desired to proclaim Him king of Israel. Many were ready to accept Him as a prophet, but they did not believe Him to be the Messiah.

Jesus now put a second question, relating to the disciples themselves: "But whom say ye that I am?" Peter answered, "Thou art the Christ, the Son of the living God."

From the first, Peter had believed Jesus to be the Messiah. Many others who had accepted Christ began to doubt as to John's mission when he was imprisoned and put to death, and they now doubted that Jesus was the Messiah. Many who had expected Jesus to take His place on David's throne left Him when they perceived that He had no such intention. But the vacillating course of those who praised yesterday and condemned today did not destroy the faith of the true follower of the Saviour. Peter declared, "Thou art the Christ, the Son of the living God." He waited not for kingly honors to crown his Lord, but accepted Him in His humiliation.

Peter had expressed the faith of the Twelve. Yet the opposition of the priests and rulers still caused them great perplexity. They did not see their way clearly. Their early training, the teaching of the rabbis, the power of tradition, still intercepted their view of truth. Precious rays of light shone on them, yet often they were like men groping among shadows. But on this day, the Holy Spirit rested on them in power. Beneath the guise of humanity they discerned the glory of the Son of God.

Jesus answered Peter, saying, "Blessed art thou, Simon Bar-Jona: for flesh and blood hath not revealed it unto thee, but My Father which is in heaven."

The truth which Peter had confessed is the foundation of the believer's faith. But through no wisdom or goodness of his own had it been revealed to Peter. The fact that Peter discerned the glory of Christ was an evidence that he had been "taught of God." See Psalm 25:14; John 6:45.

Jesus continued: "I say also unto thee, Thou art Peter, and upon this rock I will build My church; and the gates of hell shall not prevail against it." The word Peter signifies a stone—a rolling stone. Peter was not the rock on which the church was founded. The gates of hell did prevail against him when he denied his Lord with cursing and swearing. The church was built on One against whom the gates of hell could not prevail.

Christ Is the Rock

Moses had pointed to the Rock of Israel's salvation. See Deuteronomy 32:4. The psalmist had sung of "the rock of my strength." Psalm 62:7. Isaiah had written, "Thus saith the Lord God, Behold, I lay in Zion for a foundation a stone, a tried stone, . . . a sure foundation." Isaiah 28:16. Peter himself applies this prophecy to Jesus: "For you have tasted the kindness of the Lord. Come to Him, to that living stone, rejected by men but in God's sight chosen and precious; and like living stones be yourselves built into a spiritual house." 1 Peter 2:3-5, RSV. "Other foundation can no man lay than that is laid, which is Jesus Christ." 1 Corinthians 3:11. "Upon this rock," said Jesus, "I will build my church." Christ founded His church on the living Rock—Himself, His own body, for us broken and bruised. Against the church built on this foundation, the gates of hell shall not prevail.

How feeble the church appeared when Christ spoke these words! There was only a handful of believers, against whom the power of demons and men would be directed, yet they were not to fear; they could not be overthrown.

Peter had expressed the truth which is the foundation of the church's faith, and Jesus now honored him as the representative of the body of believers. "I will give unto thee the keys of the kingdom of heaven: and whatsoever thou shalt bind on earth shall be bound in heaven: and whatsoever thou shalt loose on earth shall be loosed in heaven."

"The keys of the kingdom of heaven" are the words of Christ. All the words of Holy Scripture are His. These words have power to open and to shut heaven. The work of those who preach God's Word is a savor of life unto life or of death unto death.

The Saviour did not commit the work of the gospel to Peter individually. Later, repeating the words spoken to Peter, He applied them to the church, and also to the Twelve as representatives of the body of believers. If Jesus had delegated any special authority to one disciple above the others, we should not find them so often contending as to whom should be the greatest. They would have honored the one chosen. Instead of appointing one to be their head, Christ said, "Be not ye called Rabbi." "Neither be ye called masters: for one is your Master, even Christ." Matthew 23:8, 10.

"The head of every man is Christ." God, who put all things under the Saviour's feet, "gave Him to be the head over all things to the church, which is His body, the fullness of Him that filleth all in all." 1 Corinthians 11:3; Ephesians 1:22, 23. The church is built on Christ as its foundation. It is not to depend on man or be controlled by man. Many claim that a position of trust in the church gives them authority to dictate what other men shall believe and do. The Saviour declares, "All ye are brethren." Matthew 23:8. Upon no finite being can we depend for guidance. The Rock of faith is the living presence of Christ in the church. Those who think themselves the strongest will prove to be the weakest, unless they make Christ their efficiency. See Jeremiah 17:5; Psalm 2:12.

Jesus charged the disciples to tell no man that He was the Christ. The people, and even the disciples, had so false a conception of the Messiah that a public announcement would give them no true idea of His character or work.

The Disciples Had Not Envisioned a Cross to Come

The disciples still expected Christ to reign as a temporal prince. They believed that He would not always remain in obscurity and that the time was near when He would establish His kingdom. That Christ would be rejected by His own nation, condemned as a deceiver, and crucified as a malefactor—such a thought the disciples had never entertained. Jesus must open to His disciples the conflict before them. He was sad as He anticipated the trial.

Hitherto He had refrained from making known to them anything relative to His sufferings and death. In His conversation with Nicodemus He had said, "As Moses lifted up the serpent in the wilderness, even so must the Son of man be lifted up: that whosoever believeth in Him should not perish, but have eternal life." John 3:14, 15. But the disciples did not hear this. Now the time had come for the veil that hid the future to be withdrawn: "From that time forth began Jesus to show unto His disciples, how He must go unto Jerusalem, and suffer many things of the elders and chief priests and scribes, and be killed, and be raised again the third day."

Speechless with grief and amazement, the disciples listened. Christ had accepted Peter's acknowledgment of Him as the Son of God, and now His words pointing to His suffering and death seemed incomprehensible. Peter could not keep silent. He laid hold on his Master, as if to draw Him back from His impending doom: "Be it far from Thee, Lord: this shall not be unto Thee."

Peter loved his Lord; but Jesus did not commend him for the desire to shield Him from suffering. Peter's words were not a help and solace to Jesus in the great trial before Him. They were not in harmony with God's purpose of grace toward a lost world, nor with the lesson of self-sacrifice that Jesus had come to teach by His own example. The impression which his words would make was directly opposed to that which Christ desired to make on the minds of His followers, and the Saviour was moved to utter one of the sternest rebukes that ever fell from His lips: "Get behind Me, Satan! You are a hindrance to Me; for you are not on the side of God, but of men." RSV.

Satan Was Trying to Get at Christ

Satan was trying to discourage Jesus and turn Him from His mission, and Peter was giving voice to the temptation. The prince of evil, the author of the thought, was behind that impulsive appeal. Satan had offered Christ the dominion of the world on condition of forsaking the path of humiliation and sacrifice. Now he was seeking to fix Peter's gaze on earthly glory, that he might not behold the cross. Through Peter, he was again pressing the temptation on Jesus.

But the Saviour heeded it not; His thought was for His disciple. Satan had interposed between Peter and his Master. The words of Christ were spoken to the one trying to separate him from his Redeemer: "Get behind Me, Satan." Let Me come face to face with Peter, and I may reveal to him the mystery of My love.

It was a bitter lesson, which Peter learned but slowly: the path of Christ lay through agony and humiliation. But in the heat of the furnace fire the disciple was to learn its blessing. Long afterward he wrote, "Rejoice in so far as you share Christ's sufferings, that you may also rejoice and be glad when His glory is revealed." 1 Peter 4:13, RSV.

Jesus now explained to His disciples that His own life of self-abnegation was an example of what theirs should be: "If any man will come after Me, let him deny himself, and take up his cross daily, and follow Me." The cross, associated with the power of Rome, was the most cruel and humiliating form of death. Criminals were required to bear the cross to the place of execution. Often as it was laid on their shoulders, they resisted with desperate violence, until they were overpowered. To the disciples Jesus' words, though dimly comprehended, pointed to their submission to death for the sake of Christ.

No more complete self-surrender could the Saviour's words have pictured. But all this He had accepted for them. He left the heavenly courts for a life of reproach and insult, and a death of shame. He who was rich in heaven's priceless treasure, became poor, that through His poverty we might be rich. We are to follow in the path He trod.

Love for souls means crucifixion of self. He who is a child of God should look on himself as a link in the chain let down to save the world, one with Christ, going forth with Him to seek and save the lost. The Christian has consecrated himself to God, and in character he is to reveal Christ to the world.

"Whosoever will save his life shall lose it; but whosoever shall lose his life for my sake and the gospel's, the same shall save it." Selfishness is death. The heart, failing to send its lifeblood to the hand and the head, would quickly lose its power. So is the love of Christ diffused through every part of His mystical body. We are members one of another, and the soul that refuses to impart will perish. "What is a man profited," said Jesus, "if he shall gain the whole world, and lose his own soul? or what shall a man give in exchange for his soul?"

Christ pointed the disciples to His coming in glory with the hosts of heaven. Then He said, "He shall reward every man according to his works." And for their encouragement He promised, "Verily I say unto you, There be some standing here, which shall not taste of death, till they see the Son of man coming in His kingdom."

But the disciples did not comprehend His words. Their eyes were fixed on the poverty, humiliation, and suffering. Were they not to see their Lord exalted to the throne of David? Could it be that Christ was to be despised, rejected, and put to death? Sadness oppressed their hearts, for it seemed incomprehensible that the Son of God should be subjected to such cruel humiliation. Why should He voluntarily go to Jerusalem to meet the treatment He was there to receive? How could He resign Himself to such a fate, and leave them in greater darkness than they were groping in before He revealed Himself to them?

In the region of Caesarea Philippi, the disciples reasoned that Christ had nothing to fear from the hatred of the Jews or from the power of the Romans. Why not work there? Why give Himself up to death? If He was to die, how could His kingdom be established so firmly that the gates of hell should not prevail against it? This was indeed a mystery.

They were even now journeying toward the city where all their hopes were to be crushed. They talked together in low, sorrowful tones in regard to the future. Perhaps some unforeseen circumstance might avert the doom which seemed to await their Lord. Thus they doubted, hoped, and feared for six long, gloomy days.

46 / Jesus Transfigured

Evening was drawing on as Jesus called to His side Peter, James, and John, and led them far up a lonely mountainside. They had spent the day traveling and teaching, and the climb added to their weariness. Soon the sun disappeared, and the travelers were wrapped in darkness. The gloom of their surroundings seemed in harmony with their sorrowful lives, around which clouds were gathering.

The disciples did not venture to ask Christ whither He was going, or for what purpose. He had often spent entire nights in the mountains in prayer; He was at home with nature and enjoyed its quietude. Yet the disciples wondered why their Master should lead them up this toilsome ascent when they were weary and when He too needed rest.

Presently Christ told them that they were to go no farther. Stepping a little aside from them, the Man of Sorrows poured out His supplication with tears. He prayed for strength to endure the test in behalf of humanity. He must gain a fresh hold on Omnipotence, for only thus could He contemplate the future. And He poured out His heart-longings for His disciples, that their faith might not fail. The dew was heavy on His bowed form, but He heeded it not. So the hours passed slowly by.

At first the disciples united their prayers with His, but after a time they fell asleep. Jesus had told them of His sufferings, and had longed to lighten their grief by an assurance that their faith had not been in vain. Not

This chapter is based on Matthew 17:1-8; Mark 9:2-8; Luke 9:28-36.

all, even of the Twelve, could receive the revelation He desired to give. Only the three who were to witness His anguish in Gethsemane had been chosen to be with Him in the mount. Now His prayer was that they might witness a manifestation that would comfort them in the hour of His supreme agony with the knowledge that He was of a surety the Son of God and that His shameful death was part of the plan of redemption.

His prayer was heard. Suddenly the heavens opened, and holy radiance descended upon the mount, enshrouding the Saviour's form. Divinity from within flashed through humanity and met the glory coming from above. Arising from His prostrate position, Christ stood in godlike majesty. His countenance shone "as the sun," and His garments were "white as light."

The disciples, awaking, gazed in fear and amazement on the radiant form of their Master. As they became able to endure the wondrous light, they saw beside Jesus two heavenly beings—Moses, who on Sinai had talked with God; and Elijah, to whom the high privilege was given never to come under the power of death.

Because of his sin at Meribah, it was not for Moses to enter Canaan. Not for him was the joy of leading Israel into the inheritance of their fathers. A wilderness grave was the goal of forty years of toil and heart-burdening care. Moses passed under the dominion of death, but he did not remain in the tomb. Christ Himself called him forth to life. See Jude 9.

Moses on the mount of transfiguration represented those who shall come forth from the grave at the resurrection of the just. Elijah, who had been translated to heaven without seeing death, represented those living at Christ's second coming, who will be "changed, in a moment, in the twinkling of an eye, at the last trump." 1 Corinthians 15:51, 52. Jesus was clothed as He will appear when He shall come the second time "in the glory of His Father with the holy angels." Mark 8:38;

see Hebrews 9:28. Upon the mount the future kingdom of glory was represented in miniature—Christ the King, Moses a representative of the risen saints, and Elijah of the translated ones.

Peter Seriously Misunderstands

The disciples rejoiced that the meek and lowly One, who had wandered to and fro a helpless stranger, was honored by the favored ones of heaven. They believed that Elijah had come to announce that the kingdom was about to be set up on earth. Here they longed to tarry. Peter exclaimed, "Master, it is good for us to be here: and let us make three tabernacles; one for Thee, and one for Moses, and one for Elias." The disciples were confident that Moses and Elijah had been sent to protect their Master and establish His authority as king.

But before the crown must come the cross. Bearing the weakness of humanity, burdened with its sorrow and sin, Jesus walked alone in the midst of men. As the darkness of the coming trial pressed upon Him, He was in loneliness of spirit, in a world that knew Him not. Even His loved disciples had not comprehended His mission. In the world He had created, He was in solitude. Now heaven had sent messengers; not angels, but men who had endured suffering and sorrow, and who could sympathize with the Saviour.

Moses and Elijah had been colaborers with Christ. They had shared His longing for the salvation of men. Moses had pleaded for Israel: "Yet now, if Thou wilt forgive their sin—; and if not, blot me, I pray thee, out of Thy book which Thou hast written." Exodus 32:32. Elijah had known loneliness of spirit, as for three years and a half of famine he had borne the nation's hatred and woe. Alone he had fled to the desert in anguish and despair. These men had come to commune with Jesus concerning His suffering and to comfort Him. The salvation of every human being was the burden of their interview.

Overcome with sleep, the disciples heard little of

what passed between Christ and the heavenly messengers. They had not received what God desired to give them—a knowledge of the sufferings of Christ and the glory that should follow. They lost the blessing that might have been theirs. Yet they were assured that all heaven knew of the sin of the Jewish nation in rejecting Christ. They were given a clearer insight into the work of the Redeemer. They were "eyewitnesses of His majesty" (2 Peter 1:16) and realized that Jesus was indeed the Messiah, recognized as such by the heavenly universe.

While they were still gazing upon the scene, a bright cloud overshadowed them: and behold a voice out of the cloud, which said, "This is My beloved Son, in whom I am well pleased; hear ye Him." As they heard the voice of God speak in awful majesty that caused the mountain to tremble, the disciples fell smitten to the earth, their faces hidden, till Jesus came near, dispelling their fears with His well-known voice, "Arise and be not afraid." The heavenly glory had passed away, the forms of Moses and Elijah had disappeared. They were alone with Jesus.

47 / A Battle With Satan's Spirits

As the sun arose, Jesus and His disciples descended to the plain. Absorbed in thought, the disciples were awed and silent. Gladly they would have lingered in that holy place, but there was work to be done.

At the foot of the mountain a large company had gathered. As the Saviour drew near, He charged His three companions to keep silence concerning what they had witnessed, saying, "Tell the vision to no man, until the Son of man be risen again from the dead." To relate the revelation to the multitudes would excite only ridicule or idle wonder. How slow of comprehension even the three favored disciples were, is seen in that they queried among themselves what the rising from the dead should mean. Yet they asked no explanation from Jesus.

As the people on the plain caught sight of Jesus, they ran to greet Him. Yet His quick eye discerned that a circumstance had occurred that had caused the disciples bitter disappointment and humiliation. A father had brought his son to be delivered from a dumb spirit that tormented him. Authority to cast out unclean spirits had been conferred on the disciples when Jesus sent them to preach through Galilee. As they went forth strong in faith, the evil spirits had obeyed their word. Now in the name of Christ they commanded the torturing spirit to leave his victim, but the demon only mocked them. The disciples, unable to account for their defeat, felt they were bringing dishonor on themselves and their Master. And in the crowd were scribes

This chapter is based on Matthew 17:19-21; Mark 9:9-29; Luke 9: 37-45.

Waking suddenly, the disciples were startled to see Jesus, transfigured into His heavenly glory, talking to Moses and Elijah.

seeking to prove that they and their Master were deceivers. Here was an evil spirit that neither the disciples nor Christ Himself could conquer! A feeling of contempt and scorn pervaded the crowd.

But suddenly Jesus and the three disciples were seen approaching. The night of communion with heavenly glory had left on their countenances a light that awed the beholders. The Saviour came to the scene of conflict, and fixing His gaze on the scribes inquired, "What question ye with them?"

But the voices so bold and defiant before were silent. Now the afflicted father made his way through the crowd, and falling at the feet of Jesus, poured out the story of his trouble and disappointment.

"Master," he said, "I have brought unto Thee my son which hath a dumb spirit; and wheresoever he taketh him, he teareth him: . . . and I spake to Thy disciples that they should cast him out; and they could not."

Jesus read the unbelief in every heart, and exclaimed, "O faithless generation, how long shall I be with you? how long shall I suffer you?" Then He bade the distressed father, "Bring thy son hither."

The boy was brought, and the evil spirit cast him to the ground in convulsions of agony. He lay wallowing and foaming, rending the air with unearthly shrieks.

Again the Prince of life and the prince of darkness met on the field of battle—Christ to "preach deliverance to the captives, . . . to set at liberty them that are bruised" (Luke 4:18), Satan seeking to hold his victim under his control. For a moment, Jesus permitted the evil spirit to display his power.

Jesus asked, "How long is it ago since this came unto him?" The father told the story of long years of suffering, and then, as if he could endure no more, exclaimed, "If Thou canst do anything, have compassion on us, and help us." "If Thou canst!" Even now the father questioned the power of Christ.

Jesus answered, "All things are possible to him that

believeth." With a burst of tears, realizing his own weakness, the father cast himself on Christ's mercy: "I believe; help Thou mine unbelief."

Jesus turned to the suffering one and said: "Thou dumb and deaf spirit, I charge thee, come out of him, and enter no more into him." There was a cry, an agonized struggle. Then the boy lay motionless, apparently lifeless. The multitude whispered, "He is dead." But Jesus took him by the hand, and lifting him up, presented him in perfect soundness of mind and body to his father. Father and son praised their Deliverer, while the scribes, defeated and crestfallen, turned sullenly away.

Faith Connects Us With Heaven

"If Thou canst do anything, have compassion on us, and help us." How many a sin-burdened soul has echoed that prayer. And to all the answer is, "All things are possible to him that believeth." In Christ, God has provided means for subduing every sinful trait and resisting every temptation, however strong. But many feel that they lack faith, and therefore they remain away from Christ. Let these souls look not to self, but to Christ. Faith comes by the Word of God. Grasp His promise, "Him that cometh to Me I will in no wise cast out." John 6:37. Cast yourself at His feet with the cry, "I believe; help Thou mine unbelief." You can never perish while you do this—never.

In a brief space of time the favored disciples had seen humanity as transfigured into the image of God, and as debased into the likeness of Satan. They had seen Jesus proclaimed the Son of God, and had seen Him meet the maniac boy gnashing his teeth in agony. This mighty Redeemer, who a few hours before stood glorified, stooped to lift the victim of Satan from the earth, and restore him to his father and home.

It was an object lesson of redemption—the Divine One stooping to save the lost. It represented also the disciples' mission. Not alone on the mountaintop with

Jesus is the life of Christ's servants to be spent. Down in the plain, souls whom Satan has enslaved are waiting for the word of faith and prayer to set them free.

When Jesus was once more alone with the nine disciples, they questioned, "Why could not we cast him out?" Jesus answered, "Because of your unbelief: for verily I say unto you, If ye have faith as a grain of mustard seed, ye shall say unto this mountain, Remove hence to yonder place; and it shall remove; and nothing shall be impossible unto you. Howbeit this kind goeth not out but by prayer and fasting." Their unbelief, that shut them out from deeper sympathy with Christ, and the carelessness with which they regarded the sacred work committed to them had caused their failure. Jealous of the three disciples selected to accompany Jesus to the mountain, they had been dwelling on their discouragements and personal grievances. In this state of darkness they had undertaken the conflict with Satan.

In order to succeed in such a conflict, their faith must be strengthened by fervent prayer, fasting, and humiliation of heart. They must be emptied of self and be filled with the Spirit and power of God. Faith that leads to entire dependence on God and unreserved consecration to His work can alone bring men the Holy Spirit's aid in the battle against wicked spirits.

Lay hold on God's word and all the helpful agencies He has appointed. Thus your faith will strengthen. The obstacles piled by Satan across your path, apparently as insurmountable as the eternal hills, shall disappear before the demand of faith. "Nothing shall be impossible unto you."

48 / Who Is the Greatest?

Returning to Capernaum, Jesus quietly sought the house that was to be His temporary home. During the remainder of His stay in Galilee, it was His object to instruct the disciples rather than labor for the multitudes.

Christ had again told them that He was to be put to death and to rise again. And He added that He was to be betrayed into the hands of His enemies. The disciples did not even now comprehend His words. Although the shadow of a great sorrow fell upon them, they disputed among themselves which should be accounted greatest in the kingdom. This strife they thought to conceal from Jesus. He read their thoughts and longed to counsel them, but for this He awaited a quiet hour when their hearts should be open to receive His words.

Soon after they reached town the collector of the temple revenue questioned Peter, "Doth not your Master pay tribute?" This religious contribution every Jew was required to pay annually. A refusal to pay would be, in the estimation of the rabbis, a grievous sin. Now His enemies saw an opportunity of casting discredit upon Him. In the collector of the tribute they found a ready ally.

Zealous for his Master's honor, Peter hastily answered that Jesus would pay the tribute. But some classes were exempt from payment of the tribute. The priests and Levites, still regarded as especially devoted to the temple, were not required to make the an-

This chapter is based on Matthew 17:22-27; 18:1-20; Mark 9:30-50; Luke 9:46-48.

nual contribution for its support. Prophets also were exempt. In requiring tribute from Jesus, the rabbis were setting aside His claim as a prophet and were dealing with Him as with any commonplace person. A refusal to pay would be represented as disloyalty to the temple; on the other hand, payment would be taken as justifying their rejection of Him as a prophet. By his answer to the collector, Peter virtually sanctioned the false conception to which the priests and rulers were trying to give currency.

When Peter entered the house, the Saviour made no reference to what had taken place, but inquired, "What thinkest thou, Simon? of whom do the kings of the earth take custom or tribute? of their own children, or of strangers?" Peter answered, "Of strangers." And Jesus said, "Then are the children free." While the people are taxed for the maintenance of their king, the monarch's own children are exempt. So Israel, the people of God, were required to maintain His service; but Jesus, the Son of God, was under no such obligation.

If Jesus had paid the tribute without a protest, He would virtually have acknowledged the justice of the claim and thus denied His divinity. But He denied the claim on which it was based. In providing for the payment, He gave evidence of His divine character, and therefore was not under tribute as a mere subject of the kingdom.

"Go thou to the sea," He directed Peter, "and cast an hook, and take up the fish that first cometh up; and when thou hast opened his mouth, thou shalt find a piece of money: that take, and give unto them for Me and thee."

While Jesus made it plain that He was under no obligation to pay the tribute, He entered into no controversy in regard to the matter. Lest He should give offense by withholding the tribute, He did that which He could not justly be required to do. This lesson would be of great value to His disciples. They were not to place themselves needlessly in antagonism to established order. Christians are not to sacrifice one principle of truth, but they should avoid controversy whenever possible.

While Peter was gone to the sea, Jesus called the other disciples to Him, and asked, "What was it that ye disputed among yourselves by the way?" Shame and self-condemnation kept them silent. Jesus had told them that He was to die for their sake, and their selfish ambition was in painful contrast to His unselfish love. But although He had spoken so plainly of what awaited Him, His mention of the fact that He was soon to go to Jerusalem again kindled their hope that the kingdom was about to be set up. This had led to questioning as to who should fill the highest offices. At last one ventured to ask Jesus, "Who is the greatest in the kingdom of heaven?"

Strife for Highest Place

The Saviour said to them, "If any man desire to be first, the same shall be last of all, and servant of all." They did not understand the nature of Christ's kingdom, and this was the apparent cause of their contention. But the real cause lay deeper. Even after they had received the fullest knowledge, any question of precedence might have renewed the trouble. Thus disaster would have been brought to the church after Christ's departure. The strife for the highest place was the outworking of that same spirit which was the beginning of the great controversy in the worlds above which had brought Christ from heaven to die. There rose up before Him a vision of Lucifer, who had said, "I will be like the Most High." Isaiah 14:14. The desire for self-exaltation had brought strife into the heavenly courts. Lucifer desired God's power, but not His character. He sought the highest place, and every being actuated by his spirit will do the same. The kingdom of Satan is a kingdom of force; every individual regards every other as an obstacle in the way of his own advancement, or a steppingstone on which to climb to a higher place.

While Lucifer sought to be equal with God, Christ "made Himself of no reputation, and took upon Him the form of a servant, and was made in the likeness of men: and being found in fashion as a man, He humbled Himself, and became obedient unto death, even the death of the cross." Philippians 2:7, 8. Now the cross was just before Him; and His own disciples were so filled with self-seeking that they could not enter into sympathy with their Lord, or even understand Him as He spoke of His humiliation for them.

Jesus tried to correct the evil. He showed what is the principle that bears sway in the kingdom of heaven, and in what true greatness consists. Those who were actuated by pride and love of distinction were thinking of themselves, and of the rewards they were to have. They would have no place in the kingdom of heaven, for they were identified with the ranks of Satan.

Before honor is humility. To fill a high place before men, Heaven chooses the worker who takes a lowly place before God. The most childlike disciple is the most efficient in labor for God. He who feels his need of divine aid will plead for it. From communion with Christ he will go forth to work, anointed for his mission, and he succeeds where many of the intellectually wise would fail.

But when men exalt themselves, feeling that they are a necessity for the success of God's plan, the Lord causes them to be set aside. The work does not stop, but goes forward with greater power.

It was not enough for the disciples of Jesus to be instructed as to the nature of His kingdom. What they needed was a change of heart. Calling a little child to Him, Jesus set him in the midst of them; then tenderly folding the little one in His arms, He said, "Except ye be converted, and become as little children, ye shall not enter into the kingdom of heaven." The simplicity, the self-forgetfulness, and the confiding love of a little child are the attributes that Heaven values, the characteristics of real greatness. At the feet of Jesus earthly dignity and display are forgotten. Rich and poor, learned and ignorant, meet together as blood-bought souls, with no thought of caste or worldly preeminence.

God places His own signet on men, not by rank, not by wealth, not by intellectual greatness, but by their oneness with Christ. "Thou hast also given me," said David, "the shield of Thy salvation: . . . and Thy gentleness"—as an element in the human character— "hath made me great." Psalm 18:35.

The Saviour's words awakened in the disciples a feeling of self-distrust. John was led to question whether in one case his action had been right. "Master," he said, "we saw one casting out devils in Thy name, . . . and we forbade him, because he followeth not us."

James and John thought that in checking this man they had in view their Lord's honor; they began to see they were jealous for their own. They acknowledged their error, and accepted the reproof of Jesus, "Forbid him not: for there is no man which shall do a miracle in My name, that can lightly speak evil of Me." Many had been deeply moved by the character and work of Christ and whose hearts were opening to Him in faith. The disciples must be careful not to discourage these souls. They must manifest the same far-reaching sympathy they had seen in their Master.

Christ is the Great Teacher; we are to sit at His feet and learn of Him. Every soul whom God has made willing is a channel through which Christ will reveal His pardoning love. How careful we should be lest we discourage one of God's light bearers, and thus intercept the rays He would have shine to the world!

Such an act as that of John in forbidding one to work miracles in Christ's name might result in causing the loss of a soul. Rather than for one to do this, said Jesus, "It is better for him that a millstone were hanged about his neck, and he were cast into the sea."

Why this strong language? Because "the Son of man

is come to save that which was lost." Luke 19:10. Shall His disciples show less regard for the souls of their fellowmen than the Majesty of heaven has shown? How terrible the sin of turning one soul away, so that for him the Saviour's love and agony shall have been in vain.

"Woe to the world for temptations to sin! For it is necessary that temptations come." RSV. The world will surely oppose the followers of Christ, but woe to him who has taken Christ's name and yet is found doing this work. Multitudes are deceived and led into false paths by those who claim to serve Him but misrepresent His character.

Anything That Leads to Sin Must Be Put Away

One sin cherished is sufficient to degrade the character and mislead others. If the foot or the hand would be cut off, or even the eye be plucked out, to save the body from death, how earnest should we be to put away sin that brings death to the soul!

In the ritual service salt was added to every sacrifice. This, like the offering of incense, signified that only the righteousness of Christ could make the service acceptable to God. Referring to this, Jesus said, "Have salt in yourselves, and have peace one with another." All must receive the saving salt, the righteousness of our Saviour. Then they become "the salt of the earth," restraining evil among men, as salt preserves from corruption. Matthew 5:13. But if the salt has lost its savor, the life can exert no saving influence on the world. Jesus says, You must be partakers of My grace, in order to be savor of life unto life. Then there will be no rivalry, no self-seeking, no desire for the highest place.

When we see Jesus, a Man of Sorrows and acquainted with grief, working to save the lost, slighted, scorned, driven from city to city till His mission was accomplished; when we behold Him in Gethsemane, sweating great drops of blood, and on the cross dying in agony—when we see this, self will no longer clamor to be recognized. We shall rejoice to bear the cross after Jesus, to endure trial, shame, or persecution for His sake.

No soul who believes in Christ is to be lightly esteemed. By all that has given us advantage over another—education, refinement, nobility of character, religious experience—we are in debt to those less favored. If we are strong, we are to stay up the hands of the weak. Angels are ever present with those who have the hardest battle with self to fight, who have many objectionable traits of character, and whose surroundings are the most discouraging. And in this ministry Christ's true followers will cooperate.

"What do you think?" said Jesus. "If a man has a hundred sheep, and one of them has gone astray, does he not leave the ninety-nine on the mountains and go in search of the one that went astray? And if he finds it, truly, I say to you, he rejoices over it more than over the ninety-nine that never went astray. So it is not the will of My Father who is in heaven that one of these little ones should perish." RSV.

Need of the Delicate Touch

Do not put the erring one to shame by exposing his fault to others, nor bring dishonor on Christ by making public the sin of one who bears His name. The erring must be led to see his error, that he may reform; but you are not to judge or condemn. In treating the wounds of the soul, there is need of the most delicate touch. Only the love that flows from the Suffering One of Calvary can avail here. If you succeed, you will "save a soul from death," and "hide a multitude of sins." James 5:20.

But even this effort may be unavailing. Then Jesus said, "Take one or two others along with you." RSV. If he will not hear them, then, and not till then, the matter is to be brought before the whole body of believers. Let the members of the church unite in prayer and loving entreaty that the offender may be restored. The

Holy Spirit will speak through His servants, pleading with the wanderer to return to God: "We pray you in Christ's stead, be ye reconciled to God." 2 Corinthians 5:20. He who rejects this united overture has broken the tie that binds him to Christ, and thus has severed himself from the fellowship of the church. Henceforth, said Jesus, "Let him be unto thee as an heathen man and a publican." But let him not be despised or neglected by his former brethren. Treat him with tenderness and compassion.

If one neglects the duty Christ has enjoined, of trying to restore those who are in error and sin, he becomes a partaker in the sin. See Leviticus 19:17. For evils that we might have checked, we are just as responsible as if we were guilty of the acts ourselves.

We are not to make the wrong a matter of comment and criticism among ourselves, nor to repeat it to others. While we seek to correct the errors of a brother, we will shield him as far as possible from the criticism of his own brethren, and how much more from the censure of the unbelieving world. As we wish Christ to deal with us, He bids us deal with one another. "Whatsoever ye shall bind on earth shall be bound in heaven: and whatsoever ye shall loose on earth shall be loosed in heaven." Matthew 16:19. The issues of your work are for eternity!

But we are not to bear this great responsibility alone. Wherever His word is obeyed with a sincere heart, there Christ abides. In the assemblies of the church and wherever disciples, however few, meet in His name, there also He will be. "If two of you shall agree on earth as touching anything that they shall ask, it shall be done for them of My Father which is in heaven." While by His humanity Jesus is a sharer with His disciples in their trials and sympathizes with them in their sufferings, by His divinity He is connected with the throne of the Infinite.

Wonderful assurance! All the power of heaven combines with human ability in drawing souls to Christ.

49 / "If Any Man Thirst, Let Him Come!"

Three times a year the Jews were required to assemble at Jerusalem for religious purposes. The Feast of Tabernacles was the closing gathering of the year. From the valleys and plains of Palestine the harvest had been gathered. The olive berries had been picked. The palm had yielded her store. The purple clusters of the vine had been trodden in the wine press.

The feast continued for seven days, and for its celebration the inhabitants of Palestine, with many from other lands, came to Jerusalem. Old and young, rich and poor, all brought some gift as a tribute of thanksgiving to Him who had crowned the year with His goodness. Everything that could give expression to the universal joy was brought from the woods; the city bore the appearance of a beautiful forest.

The feast was not only the harvest thanksgiving but the memorial of God's care over Israel in the wilderness. In commemoration of their tent life the Israelites during the feast dwelt in tabernacles of green boughs erected in the streets, in the courts of the temple, or on the housetops. The hills and valleys surrounding Jerusalem were dotted with these leafy dwellings. With sacred song and thanksgiving the worshipers celebrated this occasion.

A little before the feast was the Day of Atonement, when the people were declared to be at peace with Heaven. "O give thanks unto the Lord; . . . for His mercy endureth for ever" (Psalm 106:1) rose trium-

This chapter is based on John 7:1-15; 37-39.

phantly, while all kinds of music accompanied the united singing.

The temple was the center of the universal joy. On either side of the white marble steps of the sacred building, the choir of Levites led the service of song. The melody was caught up by voices near and far, till the encircling hills were vocal with praise.

At night the temple blazed with artificial light. The music, the waving of palm branches, the great concourse of people, over whom the light streamed from the hanging lamps, and the majesty of the ceremonies deeply impressed the beholders. But the most impressive ceremony was one commemorating an event in the wilderness sojourn.

At dawn the priests sounded a long blast on their silver trumpets, and the glad shouts of the people from their booths welcomed the festal day. Then the priest dipped from the flowing waters of the Kedron a flagon of water. Lifting it on high, while the trumpets were sounding, he ascended the broad steps of the temple, keeping time with the music with slow and measured tread.

At the altar in the court of the priests were two silver basins. The water was poured into one, and a flagon of wine into the other; and the contents of both flowed into the Kedron and to the Dead Sea. This consecrated water represented the fountain that at the command of God gushed from the rock to quench the thirst of the children of Israel.

As the sons of Joseph made preparation to attend the feast, they saw that Christ made no movement signifying His intention of attending. Since the healing at Bethesda He had not attended the national gatherings. To avoid useless conflict at Jerusalem, He had restricted His labors to Galilee. His apparent neglect of the great religious assemblies and the enmity manifested toward Him by the priests and rabbis, were a cause of perplexity even to His own disciples and His kindred. In His teachings He dwelt upon the blessings of obedience, yet He Himself seemed indifferent to the service which had been divinely established.

His mingling with publicans, His disregard of rabbinical observances, and the freedom with which He set aside traditional requirements concerning the Sabbath, all seemed to place Him in antagonism to the religious authorities. His brothers thought it a mistake to alienate the great and learned men of the nation. They felt that these men must be in the right. But they had witnessed Jesus' blameless life and had been deeply impressed by His works. They still hoped He would lead the Pharisees to sce that He was the Messiah, the Prince of Israel! They cherished this thought with proud satisfaction.

So anxious were they about this that they urged Christ to go to Jerusalem. "Depart hence," they said, "and go unto Judea, that Thy disciples also may see the works that Thou doest. For there is no man that doeth anything in secret, and he himself seeketh to be known openly. If Thou do these things, show Thyself to the world." If He knew He was the Messiah, why this strange reserve? Why not go boldly to Jerusalem and perform the wonderful works reported of Him in Galilee? Do not hide in secluded provinces, they said. Present yourself at the capital, win the support of the priests and rulers, and establish the new kingdom.

Selfish Motives Exposed

These brothers of Jesus reasoned from the selfish motive of those ambitious for display. "Then Jesus said to them, My time is not yet come: but your time is always ready. The world cannot hate you; but Me it hateth because I testify of it, that the works thereof are evil. Go ye up unto this feast: I go not up yet unto this feast; for My time is not yet full come. When He had said these words unto them, He abode still in Galilee." His brothers had spoken to Him in a tone of authority. He cast their rebuke back to them classing them not with His self-denying disciples, but with the world.

The world does not hate those who are like it in spirit; it loves them as its own.

Christ was not to be presumptuous, not to rush into danger, not to hasten a crisis. He knew that He was to receive the world's hatred; He knew that His work would result in His death; but to expose Himself prematurely would not be the will of His Father.

Many from all parts of the world had come to the Feast of Tabernacles in the hope of seeing Christ. The Pharisees and rulers looked for Him, hoping for an opportunity to condemn Him. They anxiously inquired, "Where is He?" but no one knew. None dared acknowledge Him as the Messiah, but everywhere there was quiet, earnest discussion concerning Him. Many defended Him as one sent from God, while others denounced Him as a deceiver.

Meanwhile Jesus quietly arrived at Jerusalem by an unfrequented route. Had he joined the caravans, public attention would have been attracted to Him, and a popular demonstration would have aroused the authorities against Him.

In the midst of the feast, He entered the court of the temple in the presence of the multitude. It had been urged that He dared not place Himself in the power of the priests and rulers. All were surprised at His presence. Every voice was hushed.

Standing thus, the center of attraction to that vast throng, Jesus addressed them as no man had ever done. His words showed a knowledge of the sacrificial service and the teachings of the prophets, far exceeding that of the priests and rabbis. As one who beheld the Unseen, He spoke with positive authority of the earthly and the heavenly. As at Capernaum, the people were astonished at His teaching, "for His word was with power." Luke 4:32. He made every possible effort to bring them to repentance. He would not be rejected and murdered by His own nation if He could save them from the guilt of such a deed.

The question passed from one to another, "How

knoweth this Man letters, having never learned?"
Both Jesus and John the Baptist had been represented
as ignorant because they had not received training in
the rabbinical schools. Those who heard them were astonished at their knowledge of the Scriptures, but the
God of heaven was their teacher. As Jesus spoke in the
temple court, the people were held spellbound. The
men most violent against Him felt powerless to do Him
harm.

Weariness of the Worshipers Recognized

The morning of the last day of the feast found the
people wearied from the long festivity. Suddenly Jesus
lifted up His voice: "If any man thirst, let him come
unto Me, and drink. He that believeth on Me, as the
scripture hath said, out of his belly shall flow rivers of
living water." The people had been engaged in a continued scene of pomp and festivity, their eyes dazzled
with light and color, and their ears regaled with the
richest music; but there had been nothing to meet the
wants of the spirit, nothing to satisfy the thirst of the
soul.

The priest had that morning performed the ceremony which commemorated the smiting of the rock in
the wilderness. That rock was a symbol of Him who by
His death would cause living streams of salvation to
flow. There in the presence of the multitude Christ set
Himself apart to be smitten, that the water of life might
flow to the world. As Jesus spoke, their hearts thrilled
with a strange awe. Many were ready to exclaim, with
the woman of Samaria, "Give me this water, that I
thirst not." John 4:15.

Many who heard Jesus were mourners over disappointed hopes, nourishing a secret grief, or seeking to
satisfy their restless longing with the things of the
world; but amid the glitter of the joyous scene they
stood dissatisfied and sad. That sudden cry, "If any
man thirst," startled them, and as they listened to the
words that followed, their minds kindled with a new

hope. They saw in the symbol before them the offer of the priceless gift of salvation.

The cry of Christ to the thirsty soul is still going forth, and it appeals to us with even greater power than to those who heard it in the temple on the last day of the feast. "Let him that is athirst come. And whosoever will, let him take the water of life freely." Revelation 22:17.

50/Among Snares

All during the feast Jesus was shadowed by spies. Day after day new schemes to silence Him were tried. The priests and rulers were planning to stop Him by violence. On the first day at the feast they demanded by what authority He taught.

"My teaching is not Mine," said Jesus, "but His who sent Me; if any man's will is to do His will, he shall know whether the teaching is from God or whether I am speaking on My own authority." John 7:16, 17, RSV. The perception and appreciation of truth, He said, depends less upon the mind than on the heart. Truth claims the homage of the will. It is to be received through the work of grace in the heart; and its reception depends on the renunciation of every sin that the Spirit of God reveals. There must be a conscientious surrender of every habit and practice opposed to its principles. Those who thus yield themselves to God will be able to distinguish between him who speaks for God and him who speaks merely from himself. The Pharisees were not seeking to know the truth, but to find some excuse for evading it; this was why they did not understand Christ's teaching.

"He who speaks on his own authority seeks his own glory; but he who seeks the glory of Him who sent him is true, and in him there is no falsehood." RSV. The Spirit of self-seeking betrays its origin. But Christ was seeking the glory of God. This was the evidence of His authority as a teacher of the truth.

Jesus gave the rabbis an evidence of His divinity by

This chapter is based on John 7:16-36, 40-53; 8:1-11.

showing that He read their hearts. They had been plotting His death, thus breaking the law which they professed to be defending. "Did not Moses give you the law," He said, "and yet none of you keepeth the law? Why go ye about to kill Me?"

Like a swift flash of light these words revealed the pit of ruin into which they were about to plunge. For an instant they saw that they were in conflict with Infinite Power. But they would not be warned. Their murderous designs must be concealed. Evading the question, they exclaimed, "Thou hast a devil: who goeth about to kill Thee?"

To the insinuation that His wonderful works were instigated by an evil spirit, Christ gave no heed. He went on to show that His work of healing at Bethesda was justified by the interpretation which the Jews themselves put upon the Sabbath law. According to the law, every child must be circumcised on the eighth day. Should the appointed time fall on the Sabbath, the rite must then be performed. How much more must it be in harmony with the spirit of the law to make a man "every whit whole on the Sabbath day." He warned them, "Judge not according to the appearance, but judge righteous judgment." The rulers were silenced.

Erroneous Ideas of the Messiah and His Coming

Many who were dwellers at Jerusalem felt drawn to Christ by an irresistible power. The conviction pressed upon them that He was the Son of God. But Satan was ready to suggest doubt. It was generally believed that Christ would be born at Bethlehem, but that after a time He would disappear, and at His second appearance none would know whence He came. Not a few held that the Messiah would have no natural relationship to humanity.

While many were thus wavering between doubt and faith, Jesus took up their thoughts: "You know Me, and you know where I come from? But I have not come of My own accord; He who sent Me is true, and

Him you do not know." RSV. Christ's words were a repetition of the claim He had made in the presence of the Sanhedrin many months before, when He declared Himself the Son of God.

Among the people many believed on Him and said, "When Christ cometh, will He do more miracles than these which this Man hath done?" The leaders of the Pharisees, watching the course of events, caught the expressions of sympathy among the throng. Hurrying to the chief priests, they laid plans to arrest Him when He was alone, for they dared not seize Him in the presence of the people.

Many who were convinced that Jesus was the Son of God were misled by the false reasoning of the priests and rabbis. These teachers had repeated with great effect the prophecies concerning the Messiah, that He would "reign in Mount Zion, and in Jerusalem, and before His ancients gloriously," that He would "have dominion also from sea to sea, and from the river unto the ends of the earth." Isaiah 24:23; Psalm 72:8. Then they made contemptuous comparisons between the glory here pictured and the humble appearance of Jesus. Had the people studied the Word for themselves, they would not have been misled. Isaiah 61 testifies that Christ was to do the very work He did. Chapter 53 sets forth His rejection; and chapter 59 describes the character of the priests and rabbis.

Power to Discriminate Between Right and Wrong

God does not compel men to give up their unbelief. He designs that men shall decide not from impulse but from weight of evidence, carefully comparing scripture with scripture. Had the Jews compared written prophecy with the facts, they would have perceived a beautiful harmony between the prophecies and their fulfillment in the life and ministry of the lowly Galilean.

Many are deceived today in the same way as were the Jews. Religious teachers read the Bible in the light of their traditions; and the people do not search the

Scriptures for themselves, but yield up their judgment, and commit their souls to their leaders. Whoever will prayerfully study the Bible that he may obey it, will receive divine enlightenment. He will understand the Scriptures. "If any man's will is to do His will, he shall know whether the teaching is from God or whether I am speaking on My own authority." RSV.

On the last day of the feast, the officers who had been sent to arrest Jesus returned without Him. They were angrily questioned, "Why have ye not brought Him?" They answered, "Never man spake like this Man."

Hardened as were their hearts, they were melted by His words. While He was speaking, they had lingered near, to catch something that might be turned against Him. But as they listened, Christ revealed Himself to their souls. They saw that which priests and rulers would not see—humanity flooded with the glory of divinity.

The priests and rulers, on first coming into the presence of Christ, had felt the same conviction. Their hearts were deeply moved and the thought was forced on them, "Never man spake like this Man." But they had stifled the conviction of the Holy Spirit. Now, enraged, they cried, "Are ye also deceived? Have any of the rulers or of the Pharisees believed on Him? But this people, who knoweth not the law are cursed."

Those to whom the message of truth is spoken seldom ask, "Is it true?" but, "By whom is it advocated?" Multitudes estimate it by the numbers who accept it, and the question is still asked, "Have any of the learned men or religious leaders believed?" It is not an argument against the truth that large numbers are not ready to accept it, or that it is not received by the world's great men, or even by the religious leaders.

Again it was urged that if Jesus were left at liberty, He would draw the people away from the established leaders and the only safe course was to silence Him without delay. In the full tide of their discussion, they were suddenly checked. Nicodemus questioned, "Doth our law judge any man, before it hear him, and know what he doeth?" Silence fell on the assembly. They could not condemn a man unheard. But the haughty rulers were startled and chagrined that one of their own number had been so impressed by Jesus as to speak a word in His defense. "Are you from Galilee too? Search and you will see that no prophet is to rise from Galilee." RSV.

Yet because of the protest, the rulers were defeated for the time, and "every man went unto his own house."

Jesus Deals With a Case of Adultery

From the confusion of the city, from eager crowds and treacherous rabbis, Jesus turned to the quiet of the olive groves, where He could be alone with God. But in the early morning He returned to the temple, and the people gathered about Him.

He was soon interrupted. A group of Pharisees and scribes approached, dragging a terror-stricken woman. With hard, eager voices they accused her of having violated the seventh commandment. Having pushed her into the presence of Jesus, they said, "Moses in the law commanded us, that such should be stoned: but what sayest Thou?"

They had seized this opportunity to secure His condemnation, thinking that whatever decision He might make, they would find occasion to accuse Him. Should He acquit the woman, He might be charged with despising the law of Moses. Should He declare her worthy of death, He could be accused to the Romans as assuming authority that belonged only to them.

Jesus looked on the scene—the trembling victim in her shame, the hard-faced dignitaries devoid of pity. He read the heart and knew the character and life history of every one. Giving no sign that He had heard their question, He stooped and began to write in the dust.

Impatient at His delay and apparent indifference, the accusers drew nearer. But as their eyes fell on the pavement at His feet, their countenances changed. There, traced before them, were the guilty secrets of their own lives. The people saw the sudden change of expression, and pressed forward to discover what it was they were regarding with such astonishment and shame.

With all their professions of reverence for the law, these rabbis were disregarding its provisions. It was the husband's duty to take action against the woman; and the guilty parties were to be punished equally. The action of the accusers was unauthorized. Jesus, however, met them on their own ground. The law specified that the witnesses in the case should be the first to cast a stone. Now rising and fixing His eyes on the plotting elders, Jesus said, "He that is without sin among you, let him first cast a stone at her." And He continued writing on the ground.

Now the accusers, defeated, their robe of pretended holiness torn from them, stood guilty and condemned in the presence of Infinite Purity. One by one, with bowed heads and downcast eyes, they stole away, leaving their victim with the pitying Saviour.

Jesus arose, and looking at the woman said, "Woman, where are those thine accusers? hath no man condemned thee? She said, No man, Lord. And Jesus said unto her, Neither do I condemn thee: go, and sin no more."

The woman had stood before Jesus, cowering with fear. His words, "He that is without sin among you, let him first cast a stone," had come to her as a death sentence. Silently she awaited her doom. In astonishment she saw her accusers depart speechless and confounded; then those words of hope fell on her ear, "Neither do I condemn thee: go, and sin no more." Her heart was melted, and sobbing out her grateful love, with bitter tears she confessed her sins.

This was to her the beginning of a life of purity and

peace. In uplifting this fallen soul, Jesus performed a greater miracle than in healing the most grievous physical disease. He cured the spiritual malady which is unto death everlasting. This penitent woman became one of His most steadfast followers.

Jesus does not palliate sin nor lessen the sense of guilt, but He seeks to save. The Sinless One pities the weakness of the sinner and reaches a helping hand. It is not Christ's follower that leaves the erring unhindered to pursue their downward course. Men hate the sinner, while they love the sin. Christ hates the sin, but loves the sinner. This will be the spirit of all who follow Him. Christian love is slow to censure, quick to discern penitence, ready to forgive, to encourage, to set the wanderer in the path of holiness.

51 / "The Light of Life"

"I am the light of the world: he that followeth Me shall not walk in darkness, but shall have the light of life."

It was morning; the sun had just risen above the Mount of Olives, and its rays fell with dazzling brightness on the marble palaces, and lighted up the gold of the temple walls, when Jesus, pointing to it, said, "I am the light of the world." These words were long afterward reechoed by the apostle John in that sublime passage, "In Him was life, and the life was the light of men. The light shines in the darkness, and the darkness has not overcome it." "The true light that enlightens every man was coming into the world." John 1:4, 5, 9, RSV. God is light; and in the words, "I am the light of the world," Christ declared His oneness with God and His relation to the whole human family. It was He who at the beginning had caused the "light to shine out of darkness." 2 Corinthians 4:6. He is the light of sun, moon, and star. As the sunbeams penetrate to the remotest corners of the earth, so does the light of the Sun of Righteousness shine on every soul.

"That was the true light, which lighteth every man that cometh into the world." Men of giant intellect and wonderful research, whose utterances have opened vast fields of knowledge, have been honored as benefactors of their race. But One stands higher than they. "As many as received Him, to them gave He power to become the sons of God." "No man hath seen God at any time; the only-begotten Son, which is in the bosom of the Father, He hath declared Him." John 1:12, 18.

This chapter is based on John 8:12-59; 9.

We can trace the line of the world's great teachers as far back as human records extend; but the Light was before them. As the moon and the stars of the solar system reflect the light of the sun, so, as far as their teaching is true, do the world's great thinkers reflect the rays of the Sun of Righteousness. The true "higher education" is that imparted by Him "in whom are hid all the treasures of wisdom and knowledge." Colossians 2:3. "He that followeth Me shall not walk in darkness, but shall have the light of life."

When Jesus said, "I am the light of the world," the people could not fail to recognize His claim to be the Messiah, the Promised One. To the Pharisees and rulers this claim seemed arrogant. That a man like themselves should make such pretensions they could not tolerate. They demanded, "Who art Thou?" They were bent upon forcing Him to declare Himself the Christ. His wily enemies believed that His appearance and work were so at variance with the expectations of the people that a direct announcement of Himself as the Messiah would cause Him to be rejected as an impostor.

But Jesus replied, "Even what I have told you from the beginning." RSV. He was the embodiment of the truths He taught. "I do nothing on My own authority," He continued, "but speak thus as the Father taught Me. And He who sent Me is with Me." He did not attempt to prove His Messianic claim, but showed His unity with God.

Among His hearers many were drawn to Him in faith, and to them He said, "If ye continue in My word, then are ye My disciples indeed; and ye shall know the truth, and the truth shall make you free."

These words offended the Pharisees. "We be Abraham's seed, and were never in bondage to any man: how sayest Thou, ye shall be made free?" Jesus looked on these men, slaves of malice, and sadly answered, "Verily, verily, I say unto you, Whosoever committeth sin is the servant of sin." They were in the worst kind of bondage—ruled by the spirit of evil.

Every soul that refuses to give himself to God is under the control of another power. He is in the most abject slavery, his mind under the control of Satan. Christ came to break the shackles of sin-slavery from the soul. "If the Son therefore shall make you free, ye shall be free indeed."

In the work of redemption there is no compulsion. Man is left free to choose whom he will serve. When the soul surrenders to Christ, there is the highest sense of freedom. The expulsion of sin is the act of the soul itself. When we desire to be set free from sin, and cry out for a power out of and above ourselves, the powers of the soul are imbued with the energy of the Holy Spirit, and they obey the dictates of the will in fulfilling the will of God.

The only condition on which the freedom of man is possible is that of becoming one with Christ. Sin can triumph only by destroying the liberty of the soul. Subjection to God is restoration to one's self—to the true glory and dignity of man. The divine law, to which we are brought into subjection, is "the law of liberty." James 2:12.

The Pharisees had declared themselves the children of Abraham. The true children would not try to kill One who was speaking the truth given Him from God. A mere lineal descent from Abraham was of no value. Without possessing the same spirit and doing the same works, they were not his children.

The Question of Apostolic Succession

As descent from Abraham was proved, not by name and lineage, but by likeness of character, so apostolic succession rests not on the transmission of ecclesiastical authority, but on spiritual relationship. A life actuated by the apostles' spirit, the belief and teaching of the truth they taught—this is the true evidence of apostolic succession.

Jesus said, "Ye do the deeds of your father." In mockery the Jews answered, "We be not born of forni-

316 / FROM HEAVEN WITH LOVE

cation; we have one Father, even God." These words, in allusion to the circumstances of His birth, were intended as a thrust against Christ in the presence of those who were beginning to believe on Him. Jesus gave no heed to the base insinuation, but said, "If God were your Father, ye would love Me: for I proceeded forth and came from God."

"You are of your father the devil," said Jesus. "Your will is to do your father's desires. He was a murderer from the beginning, and has nothing to do with the truth, because there is no truth in him. . . . If I tell the truth, why do you not believe Me?" RSV. The fact that Jesus spoke the truth with certainty was why He was not received by the Jewish leaders. The truth offended these self-righteous men. The truth exposed the fallacy of error; it condemned their teaching and practice; and it was unwelcome. They did not love truth.

No Sin in Jesus

"Which of you convicts Me of sin? If I tell the truth, why do you not believe Me?" RSV. Day by day for three years Christ's enemies had been trying to find some stain in His character. Satan had been seeking to overcome Him but had found nothing in Him by which to gain an advantage. Even the devils were forced to confess, "Thou art the Holy One of God." Mark 1:24. Jesus lived the law in the sight of heaven, in the sight of unfallen worlds, and in the sight of sinful men. He had spoken, unchallenged, words that from any other lips would have been blasphemy: "I do always those things that please Him."

The Jews did not recognize God's voice in the message of His Son. They thought themselves passing judgment on Christ; but they were pronouncing sentence on themselves. "He that is of God," said Jesus, "heareth God's words: ye therefore hear them not, because ye are not of God."

Many who delight to quibble, to criticize, seeking for

something to question in the Word of God, think that this is evidence of independence of thought and mental acuteness. But hunting for sticks and straws betrays a narrow and earthly nature, a heart that is fast losing its capacity to appreciate God. As a flower turns to the sun, that the bright rays may touch it with tints of beauty, so will the soul turn to the Sun of Righteousness, that heaven's light may beautify the character with the graces of Christ.

Jesus continued: "Your father Abraham rejoiced to see My day: and he saw it, and was glad." Abraham offered up the most earnest prayer that before his death he might behold the Messiah. And a supernatural light was given him. He was given a view of the divine sacrifice for sin. Of this sacrifice he had an illustration in his own experience. The command came to Him, "Take now thy son, thine only son Isaac, whom thou lovest, . . . and offer him . . . for a burnt offering." Genesis 22:2. Upon the altar he laid the son of promise, then with knife upraised to obey God he heard a voice from heaven saying, "Lay not thine hand upon the lad, neither do thou anything unto him: for now I know that thou fearest God, seeing thou hast not withheld thy son, thine only son from Me." Genesis 22:2, 12. This terrible ordeal was imposed on Abraham that he might see the day of Christ and realize the great love of God for the world, so great that He gave His only-begotten Son to raise it from its degradation.

By making an entire surrender, Abraham was shown that in giving His only Son to save sinners from eternal ruin, God was making a greater and more wonderful sacrifice than ever man could make.

In God's provision of a sacrifice instead of Isaac, it was declared that no man could make expiation for himself; the pagan system of sacrifice was wholly unacceptable to God. No father was to offer up his son or daughter for a sin offering. The Son of God alone can bear the guilt of the world.

Christ's words concerning Abraham conveyed to

His hearers no deep significance. The Pharisees saw in them only fresh ground for caviling. They retorted with a sneer, as if they would prove Jesus to be a madman, "Thou art not yet fifty years old, and hast Thou seen Abraham?"

With solemn dignity Jesus answered, "Verily, verily I say unto you, Before Abraham was, I am."

Silence fell on the vast assembly. The name of God, given to Moses to express the idea of the eternal presence, had been claimed by this Galilean Rabbi. He had announced Himself to be the self-existent One, He "whose goings forth have been from of old, from everlasting." Micah 5:2.

Again the priests and rabbis cried out against Jesus as a blasphemer. Because He was, and avowed Himself to be, the Son of God, they were bent on destroying Him. Many of the people, siding with the priests and rabbis, took up stones to cast at Him. "But Jesus hid Himself, and went out of the temple."

The Man Born Blind

"As Jesus passed by, He saw a man which was blind from his birth. And His disciples asked him, saying, Master, who did sin, this man, or his parents, that he was born blind? Jesus answered, Neither hath this man sinned, nor his parents: but that the works of God should be made manifest in him. . . . When He had thus spoken, He spat on the ground, and made clay of the spittle, and He anointed the eyes of the blind man with the clay, and said unto him, Go, wash in the pool of Siloam, (which is by interpretation, Sent). He went his way therefore, and washed, and came seeing."

It was generally believed by the Jews that sin is punished in this life. Satan, the author of sin and its results, had led men to look on disease and death as proceeding from God. One on whom some great affliction had fallen had the burden of being regarded as a great sinner. Thus the way was prepared for the Jews to reject Jesus. He who "hath borne our griefs, and carried our sorrows" was looked upon by the Jews as "stricken, smitten of God, and afflicted," and they hid their faces from Him. Isaiah 53:4, 3.

The belief of the Jews in regard to the relation of sin and suffering was held by Christ's disciples. Having anointed the eyes of the blind man, Jesus sent him to wash in the pool of Siloam, and the man's sight was restored. Thus Jesus answered the question of the disciples in a practical way. The disciples were not to discuss as to who had sinned or had not sinned, but to understand the mercy of God in giving sight to the blind. There was no healing virtue in the clay or in the pool where the blind man was sent to wash; the virtue was in Christ.

A Miracle on the Sabbath

The Pharisees, astonished at the cure, were more than ever filled with hatred, for the miracle had been performed on the Sabbath day.

The neighbors who knew the young man in his blindness looked on him with doubt, for when his eyes were opened, his countenance was changed and brightened, and he appeared like another man. Some said, "This is he"; others, "he is like him." But he settled the question by saying, "I am he." He then told them of Jesus, and by what means he had been healed, and they inquired, "Where is He? He said, I know not."

Before a council of the Pharisees the man was asked how he had received his sight. "He said unto them, He put clay upon mine eyes, and I washed, and do see. Therefore said some of the Pharisees, This man is not of God, because He keepeth not the Sabbath day." The Pharisees appeared wonderfully zealous for the observance of the Sabbath, yet were planning murder on that very day. But many were convicted that He who had opened the eyes of the blind was more than a common man. They said, "How can a man that is a sinner do such miracles?"

Again the rabbis appealed to the blind man. "What

sayest thou of Him, that He hath opened thine eyes? He said, He is a prophet." The Pharisees then asserted that he had not been born blind. They called for his parents and asked them, saying, "Is this your son, who ye say was born blind?"

There was the man himself, declaring he had been blind and had had his sight restored; but the Pharisees would rather deny the evidence of their own senses than admit that they were in error. So powerful is prejudice, so distorting is Pharisaical righteousness.

The Pharisees had one hope left, and that was to intimidate the man's parents. They asked, "How then doth he now see?" It had been declared that whoever should acknowledge Jesus as the Christ should be "put out of the synagogue," that is, excluded for thirty days. The sentence was regarded as a great calamity. The great work wrought for their son had brought conviction to the parents, yet they answered, "We know that this is our son, and that he was born blind: but by what means he now seeth, we know not; or who hath opened his eyes, we know not: he is of age; ask him: he shall speak for himself." Thus they shifted all responsibility to their son.

The Miracle Could Not Be Denied

The Pharisees' questioning and prejudice, their unbelief in the facts of the case, were opening the eyes of the multitude. The question in many minds was, Would God do such mighty works through an impostor, as the Pharisees insisted that Jesus was?

The Pharisees could not deny the miracle. Filled with joy and gratitude, the blind man freely related his experience. Again the Pharisees tried to silence him. "Give God the praise; we know that this Man is a sinner." That is, Do not say again that this Man gave you sight; it is God who has done this.

The blind man answered, "Whether He be a sinner or no, I know not: one thing I know, that, whereas I was blind, now I see."

Jesus reached people's hearts with illustrations from the common things of life. He taught that His relationship to them resembled that of a shepherd to his sheep.

As these hypocrites tried to make him disbelieve, God helped him to show, by the vigor and pointedness of his replies, that he was not to be ensnared. He answered, "I have told you already, and ye did not hear: wherefore would ye hear it again? Will ye also be His disciples? Then they reviled him, and said, Thou art His disciple; but we are Moses' disciples. We know that God spake unto Moses: as for this fellow, we know not from whence He is."

The Lord gave the man grace and utterance so that he became a witness for Christ in words that were a cutting rebuke to his questioners. Here was One performing miracles, and they were confessedly ignorant as to the source of His power. "Why, this is a marvel! You do not know where He comes from, and yet He opened my eyes. We know that God does not listen to sinners, but if any one is a worshiper of God and does His will, God listens to him. Never since the world began has it been heard that any one opened the eyes of a man born blind. If this Man were not from God, He could do nothing." RSV.

The man's reasoning was unanswerable. The Pharisees were spellbound before his pointed, determined words. For a few moments there was silence. Then the frowning priests and rabbis gathered about them their robes, as though they feared contamination from contact with him. "Thou wast altogether born in sins, and dost thou teach us?" And they excommunicated him.

Jesus heard what had been done, and finding him soon after, said, "Dost thou believe on the Son of God?"

For the first time the blind man looked on the face of his Restorer. He had seen his parents troubled and perplexed; he had looked on the frowning faces of the rabbis; now his eyes rested on the loving, peaceful countenance of Jesus. Already, at great cost to himself, he had acknowledged Him as a delegate of divine power; now a higher revelation was granted him.

To the Saviour's question, the blind man replied by

asking, "Who is He, Lord, that I might believe on Him?" And Jesus said, "Thou hast both seen Him, and it is He that talketh with thee." The man cast himself at the Saviour's feet in worship. Christ had been revealed to his soul, and he received Him as the Sent of God.

A group of Pharisees had gathered near, and the sight of them brought to the mind of Jesus the contrast ever manifest in the effect of His words and works. "For judgment I am come into this world, that they which see not might see; and that they which see might be made blind." The people at the Saviour's advent were favored with a fuller manifestation of the divine presence than the world had ever enjoyed before. But in this very revelation, judgment was passing upon men. Their character was tested, their destiny determined.

Some of His hearers, feeling that Christ's words applied to them, inquired, "Are we blind also?" Jesus answered, "If ye were blind, ye should have no sin." If God had made it impossible for you to see the truth, your ignorance would involve no guilt. "But now ye say, We see." You believe yourselves able to see, and reject the means through which alone you could receive sight. The Pharisees refused to come to Christ, hence were left in blindness. Jesus said, "Your sin remaineth."

52 / The Divine Shepherd

"I am the Good Shepherd . . . and I lay down My life for the sheep." John 10:11, 15.

Jesus found access to His hearers by the pathway of their familiar associations. In a beautiful pastoral picture He represents His relation to those that believe on Him. No picture was more familiar to His hearers than this. Recalling the Saviour's lesson, the disciples would see Christ in each faithful shepherd, themselves in each helpless, dependent flock.

The Pharisees had just driven one from the fold because he dared to bear witness to the power of Christ. They had cut off a soul whom the True Shepherd was drawing to Himself. In this they had shown themselves unworthy of their trust as shepherds of the flock. Now Jesus pointed to Himself as the real keeper of the Lord's flock.

"He that entereth not by the door into the sheepfold, but climbeth up some other way, the same is a thief and a robber. But he that entereth in by the door is the shepherd of the sheep." When the Pharisees reasoned in their hearts as to the meaning, Jesus told them plainly, "I am the door: by Me if any man enter in, he shall be saved, and shall go in and out, and find pasture. The thief cometh not, but for to steal, and to kill, and to destroy: I am come that they might have life, and that they might have it more abundantly."

Christ is the door to the fold of God. Through this door all His children from earliest times have found en-

This chapter is based on John 10:1-30.

trance. Shadowed in symbols, manifest in the revelation of the prophets, unveiled in the lessons given to His disciples and in miracles, they have beheld "the Lamb of God, which taketh away the sin of the world." John 1:29. Ceremonies and systems have been devised by which men hope to receive justification and peace with God. But all who interpose something to take the place of Christ, to enter the fold in some other way, are thieves and robbers.

The priests and rulers, the scribes and Pharisees, destroyed the living pastures and defiled the wellsprings of the water of life. Inspiration describes these false shepherds: "The weak you have not strengthened, the sick you have not healed, the crippled you have not bound up, the strayed you have not brought back, the lost you have not sought, and with force and harshness you have ruled them." Ezekiel 34:4, RSV.

Every heathen nation has had its great teachers and religious systems offering some other means of redemption than Christ, turning the eyes away from the Father's face, and filling men's hearts with fear. Millions are bound down under false religions, bereft of hope or joy here, and with only a dull fear of the hereafter. The gospel of the grace of God alone can uplift the soul. The love of God manifested in His Son will stir the heart and arouse the powers of the soul as nothing else can. Whoever turns men away from Christ is turning them away from the source of true development, defrauding them of the hope and glory of life. He is a thief and a robber.

Responsibility of a Faithful Shepherd

In the East the shepherd's care for his flock was untiring and incessant. Marauders or beasts of prey lay in wait to plunder the flocks. The shepherd watched his charge at the peril of his own life. Jacob, who kept the flocks of Laban, said, "By day the heat consumed me, and the cold by night, and my sleep fled from my eyes." Genesis 31:40, RSV. While guarding his father's sheep, the boy David, singlehanded, rescued the stolen lamb from the lion and the bear.

A strong and tender attachment unites the shepherd to the objects of his care. Every sheep has its name and responds at the shepherd's call. So does the divine Shepherd know His flock that are scattered throughout the world. Jesus says, "I have called thee by thy name; thou art Mine." Isaiah 43:1. Jesus knows us individually and is touched with the feeling of our infirmities. He knows the very house in which we live. He has at times given directions to His servants to go to a certain street in a certain city, to such a house, to find one of His sheep.

Every soul is as fully known to Jesus as if he were the only one for whom the Saviour died. The distress of every one touches His heart. He came to draw all men unto Himself. He knows who gladly hear His call, and are ready to come under His pastoral care. He says, "My sheep hear My voice, and I know them, and they follow Me." He cares for each one as if there were not another on the face of the earth.

Why His Sheep Gladly Follow Him

The Eastern shepherd does not drive his sheep. He depends not upon force or fear; but going before, he calls them. So does the Saviour-Shepherd with His sheep. He declares, "I have loved thee with an everlasting love: therefore with loving-kindness have I drawn thee." Jeremiah 31:3.

It is not fear of punishment or hope of everlasting reward that leads the disciples of Christ to follow Him. They behold the Saviour's matchless love revealed from the manger of Bethlehem to Calvary's cross, and the sight of Him attracts, softens, and subdues the soul. Love awakens in the heart. They hear His voice, and they follow Him.

The shepherd goes before his sheep, himself first encountering the perils. So does Jesus with His people. The way to heaven is consecrated by the Saviour's footprints.

Though now He shares the throne of the universe, Jesus has lost none of His compassion. Today the hand that was pierced is reached forth to bless His people in the world. "And they shall never perish, neither shall any man pluck them out of My hand." The soul that has given himself to Christ is more precious in His sight than the whole world. The Saviour would have passed through the agony of Calvary that one might be saved in His kingdom. He will never abandon one for whom He has died. Unless His followers choose to leave Him, He will hold them fast.

Christ Is Still Our Personal Shepherd

Our never-failing Helper does not leave us alone to struggle with temptation and be finally crushed with burdens and sorrow. Though now He is hidden from mortal sight, the ear of faith can hear His voice saying, Fear not; I am with you. I have endured your sorrows, experienced your struggles, encountered your temptations. I know your tears; I also have wept. The griefs that lie too deep to be breathed into any human ear, I know. You are not forsaken. Though your pain touch no responsive chord in any heart on earth, look to Me and live. See Isaiah 54:10.

Because we are the gift of His Father and the reward of His work, Jesus loves us as His children. He loves you. Heaven itself can bestow nothing greater, nothing better. Therefore trust.

Jesus thought about the souls all over the earth who were misled by false shepherds, scattered among wolves, and He said, "I have other sheep that are not of this fold; I must bring them also, and they will heed my voice. So there shall be one flock, one shepherd." RSV.

"Therefore doth My Father love Me, because I lay down My life, that I might take it again. . . . I have power to lay it down, and I have power to take it again." As a member of the human family Jesus was mortal; as God He was the fountain of life for the world. He could have withstood the advances of death, but voluntarily He laid down His life that He might bring life and immortality to light. "He was wounded for our transgressions, He was bruised for our iniquities: the chastisement of our peace was upon Him; and with His stripes we are healed. All we like sheep have gone astray; we have turned every one to his own way; and the Lord hath laid on Him the iniquity of us all." Isaiah 53:5, 6.

53 / The Last Journey From Galilee

As the close of His ministry drew near, there was a change in Christ's manner of labor. Heretofore He had sought to shun publicity, refused the homage of the people, and had commanded that none should declare Him to be the Christ.

At the time of the Feast of Tabernacles He had made His way to Jerusalem unobserved, and entered the city unannounced. But not so with His last journey. He now traveled in the most public manner, preceded by such an announcement of His coming as He had never made before. He was going to the scene of His great sacrifice, and to this the attention of the people must be directed.

"As Moses lifted up the serpent in the wilderness, even so must the Son of man be lifted up." John 3:14. All eyes must be drawn to Christ, the sacrifice that brought salvation to the lost world.

The disciples would have prevented Him from making the journey to Jerusalem. They knew the deadly hostility of the religious leaders. To Christ it was a bitter task to lead His beloved disciples to the anguish and despair that awaited them at Jerusalem. And Satan was at hand to press his temptations. Why should He now go to Jerusalem, to certain death? On every hand were suffering ones waiting for healing. He was full of the vigor of manhood's prime. Why not go to the vast fields of the world with the words of His grace, the touch of His healing power? Why not give light and gladness to those darkened and sorrowing millions?

This chapter is based on Luke 9:51-56; 10:1-24.

Why face death now and leave the work in its infancy? The foe assailed Christ with fierce and subtle temptations. Had Jesus changed His course in the least to save Himself, the world would have been lost.

But Jesus had "steadfastly set His face to go to Jerusalem." The one law of His life was the Father's will. In His boyhood, He had said to Mary, "Wist ye not that I must be about My Father's business?" Luke 2:49. But in God's great plan the hour for the offering of Himself for the sins of men was soon to strike. He would not fail nor falter. His foes had long plotted to take His life; now He would lay it down.

And He "sent messengers before His face: and they went, and entered into a village of the Samaritans, to make ready for Him." But the people refused to receive Him, because He was on His way to Jerusalem. Little did they realize that they were turning from their doors the best gift of heaven. But all was lost to the Samaritans because of their prejudice and bigotry.

James and John, Christ's messengers, were greatly annoyed at the insult; they were filled with indignation because He had been so rudely treated by the Samaritans. They reported to Christ that the people had even refused to give Him a night's lodging. Seeing Mount Carmel in the distance, where Elijah had slain the false prophets, they said, "Wilt Thou that we command fire to come down from heaven, and consume them?" They were surprised at Jesus' rebuke: "Ye know not what manner of spirit ye are of. For the Son of man is not come to destroy men's lives, but to save them." And He went to another village.

It is no part of Christ's mission to compel men to receive Him. He desires only voluntary service, the willing surrender of the heart under the constraint of love. There can be no more conclusive evidence that we possess the spirit of Satan than the disposition to hurt and destroy those who do not appreciate our work, who act contrary to our ideas. Nothing can be more offensive to God than for men, through religious bigotry, to bring suffering on those who are the purchase of the Saviour's blood.

A considerable part of the closing months of Christ's ministry was spent in Perea, the province beyond the Jordan from Judea. See Mark 10:1. Here the multitude thronged His steps, and much of His former teaching was repeated.

As He had sent out the Twelve, so He "appointed seventy others, and sent them on ahead of Him, two by two into every town and place where He Himself was about to come." RSV. For some time these disciples had been in training for their work. They had had the privilege of intimate association with Him and direct personal instruction.

The command to the Twelve—not to enter into any city of the Gentiles or the Samaritans—was not given to the Seventy. Though Christ had been repulsed by the Samaritans, His love toward them was unchanged. In His name the Seventy visited, first of all, the cities of Samaria.

Samaritans Responded to Christ's Love

In His commission to the disciples just before His ascension, Jesus mentioned Samaria with Jerusalem and Judea as the places where they were first to preach the gospel. When they went to Samaria, they found the people ready to receive them. The Samaritans saw that, notwithstanding their rude treatment of Him, Jesus had only thoughts of love toward them, and their hearts were won. After His ascension the disciples gathered a precious harvest from among those who had once been their bitterest enemies. "A bruised reed shall He not break, and the dimly burning flax shall He not quench: He shall bring forth judgment unto truth." Isaiah 42:3, margin.

In sending out the Seventy, Jesus bade them not to urge their presence where they were unwelcome. "Into whatsoever city ye enter, and they receive you not," He said, "go your ways out into the streets of the same, and say, Even the very dust of your city, which cleaveth on us, we do wipe off against you: notwithstanding be ye sure of this, that the kingdom of God is come nigh unto you." They were not to do this from resentment or wounded dignity, but to show how grievous it is to refuse the Lord's message. To reject the Lord's servants is to reject Christ Himself.

Religious Leaders Turned Many Against Christ

"I say unto you," Jesus added, "it shall be more tolerable in that day for Sodom, than for that city." Then His mind reverted to the Galilean towns where so much of His ministry had been spent. Day after day the Prince of life had gone in and out among them. The glory of God had shone upon the multitudes that thronged the Saviour's steps. Yet they had refused the heavenly Gift.

The rabbis had warned against receiving the doctrines taught by this new teacher. In place of seeking to understand the Word of God for themselves, the people honored the priests and rulers, rejected the truth, and kept their traditions. Many had been almost persuaded, but they did not act on their convictions. Thus many rejected the truth that would have proved the saving of the soul.

The True Witness says, "Behold, I stand at the door, and knock." Revelation 3:20. Every entreaty in the Word or through God's messengers is a knock at the door of the heart. It is the voice of Jesus asking entrance. With every knock unheeded, the disposition to open becomes weaker. The impressions of the Holy Spirit, if disregarded today, will not be as strong tomorrow. The heart becomes less impressible, and lapses into a perilous unconsciousness of the shortness of life and of eternity beyond. Condemnation in the judgment will not result from the fact that we have been in error, but from the fact that we have neglected heaven-sent opportunities for learning what is truth.

When their work was completed, the Seventy returned with joy, saying, "Lord, even the devils are subject unto us through Thy name." Jesus answered, "I beheld Satan as lightning fall from heaven." Beyond the cross of Calvary, with its agony and shame, Jesus looked forward to the great final day when Satan will meet his destruction in the earth so long marred by his rebellion.

Henceforth Christ's followers were to look on Satan as a conquered foe. Upon the cross, Jesus was to gain the victory for them; that victory He desired them to accept as their own. "Behold," He said, "I have given unto you power to tread on serpents and scorpions, and over all the power of the enemy: and nothing shall by any means hurt you."

The omnipotent power of the Holy Spirit is the defense of every contrite soul. Not one that in penitence and faith has claimed His protection will Christ permit to pass under the enemy's power. When temptations and trials come, look to Jesus, your helper. Thank God, we have a mighty Saviour, who cast out the evil one from heaven. Why not talk of Him? God will never forsake His people in their struggle with evil.

Secret of Personal Power

Jesus added, "Notwithstanding in this rejoice not, that the spirits are subject to you; but rather rejoice, because your names are written in heaven." Be careful lest self-sufficiency come in, and you work in your own strength. Self is ever ready to take the credit if any success attends the work. When we realize our weakness, we learn to depend on a power not inherent. See 2 Corinthians 12:10. Nothing reaches so fully down to the deepest motives of conduct as a sense of the pardoning love of Christ. We are to come in touch with God; then we shall be imbued with His Holy Spirit that enables us to come in touch with our fellowmen. The more closely you connect yourself with the Source of light and power, the greater power will be yours to work for God.

As the Seventy listened to Christ, the Holy Spirit was writing truth on the soul. Though multitudes surrounded them, they were as though shut in with God.

Knowing that they had caught the inspiration of the hour, Jesus "rejoiced in spirit, and said, I thank Thee, O Father, Lord of heaven and earth, that Thou hast hid these things from the wise and prudent, and hast revealed them unto babes: even so, Father; for so it seemed good in Thy sight."

The honored of the world, the so-called great and wise men, could not comprehend the character of Christ. But to fishermen and publicans it had been given to see the Invisible. From time to time, as they surrendered to the Holy Spirit's power, the disciples' minds were illuminated. They realized that the mighty God, clad in the garb of humanity, was among them. Often as He had presented the Old Testament Scriptures, and showed their application to Himself, they had been lifted into a heavenly atmosphere. They had a clearer understanding than the original writers themselves. Hereafter they would read the Old Testament Scriptures as a new revelation from God. They beheld Him "whom the world cannot receive, because it seeth Him not, neither knoweth Him." John 14:17.

The only way in which we can gain a more perfect apprehension of truth is by keeping the heart tender and subdued by the Spirit of Christ. Human science is too limited to comprehend the plan of redemption. Philosophy cannot explain it. But the science of salvation can be known by experience. Only he who sees his own sinfulness can discern the preciousness of the Saviour.

Full of instruction were the lessons Christ taught as He slowly made His way toward Jerusalem. In Perea the people were less under the control of Jewish bigotry than in Judea, and His teaching found a response in their hearts.

During the last months, many of Christ's parables were spoken. The priests and rabbis could not mistake

His meaning, yet they could find nothing on which to ground an accusation against Him. The beautiful parable of the lost sheep Christ repeated. And He carried its lesson still farther, as He told of the lost piece of silver and the prodigal son. After the outpouring of the Holy Spirit, as the disciples went out in their Master's name facing reproach, poverty, and persecution, they often strengthened their hearts by repeating His injunction spoken on this last journey: "Fear not, little flock; for it is your Father's good pleasure to give you the kingdom. Sell that ye have, and give alms; provide yourselves bags which wax not old, a treasure in the heavens that faileth not, where no thief approacheth, neither moth corrupteth. For where your treasure is, there will your heart be also." Luke 12:32-34.

54 / The Good Samaritan

As Christ was teaching the people, "a certain lawyer stood up, and tempted him, saying, Master, what shall I do to inherit eternal life?" The priests and rabbis had thought to entangle Christ by having the lawyer ask this question. But the Saviour entered into no controversy. "What is written in the law?" He said. "How readest thou?" He turned the question of salvation on the keeping of God's commandments.

The lawyer said, "Thou shalt love the Lord thy God with all thy heart, and with all thy soul, and with all thy strength, and with all thy mind; and thy neighbor as thyself." Jesus said, "Thou hast answered right: this do, and thou shalt live."

The lawyer had been studying the Scriptures to learn their real meaning. In his answer as to the requirements of the law, he claimed no value for the mass of ceremonial and ritualistic precepts, but presented the two great principles on which hang all the law and the prophets. This answer, being commended by Christ, placed the Saviour on vantage ground with the rabbis.

"This do, and thou shalt live," Jesus said. He presented the law as a divine unity. It is not possible to keep one precept, and break another; the same principle runs through them all. Supreme love to God and impartial love to man are the principles to be wrought out in the life.

The lawyer was convicted under Christ's searching words. He had not manifested love toward his fellow-

This chapter is based on Luke 10:25-37.

man. But instead of repenting, he tried to justify himself, saying, "Who is my neighbor?"

Among the Jews this question caused endless dispute. The heathen and Samaritans were strangers and enemies, but where should the distinction be made among people of their own nation and different classes of society? Were they to regard the ignorant and careless multitude, the "unclean," as neighbors?

Dispel Darkness by Admitting Light

Jesus did not denounce the bigotry of those watching to condemn Him. But by a simple story He held up such a picture of the outflowing of heaven-born love as touched all hearts, and drew from the lawyer a confession of the truth. The best way to deal with error is to present truth. "A man," said Jesus, "was going down from Jerusalem to Jericho; and he fell among robbers, who stripped him and beat him, and departed, leaving him half dead. Now by chance a priest was going down that road; and when he saw him he passed by on the other side. So likewise a Levite, when he came to the place and saw him, passed by on the other side." RSV. This was an actual occurrence, known to be exactly as represented. The priest and Levite were in the company that listened to Christ's words.

From Jerusalem to Jericho the road led down a wild, rocky ravine infested by robbers, often the scene of violence. Here the traveler was attacked and left half dead. The priest merely glanced toward the wounded man. The Levite was convicted of what he ought to do, but persuaded himself that the case was no concern of his.

Both these men were of the class specially chosen to be representatives of God to the people. They were to "have compassion on the ignorant, and on them that are out of the way." Hebrews 5:2.

Angels of heaven look upon the distress of God's family on earth, and are prepared to cooperate with men in relieving oppression and suffering. All heaven watched to see if the priest and the Levite would be touched with pity for human woe. The Saviour had instructed the Hebrews in the wilderness, and had taught a very different lesson from that which the people were now receiving from their priests and teachers. The message had been given through Moses that the Lord their God "doth execute the judgment of the fatherless and widow, and loveth the stranger." "Love ye therefore the stranger." "Thou shalt love him as thyself." Deuteronomy 10:18, 19; Leviticus 19:34.

But, trained in the school of national bigotry, the priest and Levite had become selfish, narrow, and exclusive. When they looked upon the wounded man they could not tell whether he was of their nation. They thought he might be a Samaritan, and they turned away.

But now a Samaritan came where the sufferer was and had compassion on him. The Samaritan well knew that, were their conditions reversed, the stranger, a Jew, would pass him by with contempt. He himself might be in danger of violence by tarrying in the place. It was enough that there was before him a human being in need and suffering. He took off his own garment to cover him. The oil and wine provided for his own journey he used to heal and refresh the wounded man. He lifted him on his own beast and moved slowly along with even pace, so that the stranger might not be jarred and suffer increased pain. He brought him to an inn and cared for him through the night, watching him tenderly.

In the morning, the Samaritan, before going on his way, placed him in the care of the innkeeper, paid the charge, and left a deposit for his benefit. Not satisfied even with this, he made provision for any further need, saying, "Take care of him; and whatsoever thou spendest more, when I come again, I will repay thee."

The story ended, Jesus fixed His eyes on the lawyer and said, "Which of these three, do *you* think, proved neighbor to the man who fell among the robbers?" RSV. The lawyer answered, "He that showed mercy on him." Jesus said, "Go, and do *thou* likewise."

Thus the question, "Who is my neighbor?" is forever answered. Our neighbor is every person who needs our help, every soul wounded and bruised by the adversary, everyone who is the property of God.

In the story of the good Samaritan, Jesus gave a picture of Himself and His mission. Man had been bruised, robbed, and left to perish by Satan. But the Saviour left His glory to come to our rescue. He healed our wounds. He covered us with His robe of righteousness. He made complete provision for us at His own charges. Pointing to His own example, He says to His followers, "As I have loved you, . . . love one another." John 13:34.

The Samaritan had obeyed the dictates of a kind and loving heart and in this had proved himself a doer of the law. Christ bade the lawyer, "Go, and do thou likewise."

The lesson is no less needed today. Selfishness and cold formality have well-nigh extinguished the fire of love and dispelled the graces that should make fragrant the character. Many who profess His name have forgotten that Christians are to represent Christ. Unless there is practical self-sacrifice for the good of others wherever we may be, whatever our profession, we are not Christians.

Christ asks us to be one with Him for the saving of humanity. "Freely ye have received," He says, "freely give." Matthew 10:8. Many err and feel their shame and folly. They are hungry for encouragement. They look on their mistakes until they are driven almost to desperation. If we are Christians, when we see human beings in distress, whether through affliction, or through sin, we shall never say, This does not concern me.

The story of the good Samaritan and the character of Jesus reveal the true significance of the law and what is meant by loving our neighbor as ourselves. And when the children of God manifest love toward all men, they also are witnessing to the character of the statutes of heaven. "If we love one another, God dwelleth in us, and His love is perfected in us." 1 John 4:12.

55 / Not With Outward Show

More than three years had passed since John the Baptist gave the message, "The kingdom of heaven is at hand." Matthew 3:2. Many of those who rejected John and at every step had opposed Jesus were insinuating that His mission had failed.

Jesus answered, "The kingdom of God cometh not with outward show ["signs to be observed," RSV]: neither shall they say, Lo here! or, lo there! for, behold, the kingdom of God is within you." The kingdom of God begins in the heart. Look not for earthly power to mark its coming.

"The days will come," Jesus said, turning to His disciples, "when ye shall desire to see one of the days of the Son of man, and ye shall not see it." You do not realize how great is your present privilege in having among you Him who is the life and light of men. You will look back with longing on the opportunities you now enjoy to walk and talk with the Son of God.

Not until after Christ's ascension and the outpouring of the Holy Spirit, did the disciples fully appreciate the Saviour's character and mission. They began to realize they had been in the very presence of the Lord of glory. See John 1:14. Their minds were opened to comprehend the prophecies and to understand the miracles He had wrought. They were as men awakened from a dream. The disciples never wearied of rehearsing Christ's words and works. His lessons now came as a fresh revelation. The Scriptures became to them a new book.

This chapter is based on Luke 17:20-22.

As the disciples searched the prophecies that testified of Christ, they were brought into fellowship with the Deity, and learned of Him who had ascended to heaven to complete the work He had begun on earth. With amazement they reread the prophetic delineations of His character and work. How dimly had they comprehended the prophetic scriptures! Looking upon Him as He walked, a man among men, they had not understood the mystery of His incarnation. They did not fully recognize divinity in humanity. But after they were illuminated by the Holy Spirit, how they longed to see Him again, and wished they might have Him explain the scriptures which they could not comprehend. What had Christ meant when He said, "I have yet many things to say unto you, but ye cannot bear them now"? John 16:12. They grieved that their faith had been so feeble, that they had so failed of comprehending the reality.

The wonderful personage whom John had announced had been among them for more than thirty years, and they had not really known Him as the One sent from God. The disciples had allowed the prevailing unbelief to becloud their understanding. They often repeated His conversations and said, Why did we allow the opposition of the priests and rabbis to confuse our senses, so that we did not comprehend that a greater than Moses was among us, that One wiser than Solomon was instructing us? How dull were our ears!

As they were brought before councils and thrust into prison, the followers of Christ rejoiced "that they were counted worthy to suffer shame for His name." Acts 5:41. They recognized the glory of Christ, and chose to follow Him at the loss of all things.

The kingdom of God comes not with outward show. The gospel, with its spirit of self-abnegation, can never be in harmony with the spirit of the world. But today multitudes desire to make our Lord the ruler of the kingdoms of this world, the ruler in its courts, legislative halls, palaces, and marketplaces. They expect Him to rule through legal enactments, enforced by human authority. Since Christ is not now here in person, they themselves will act in His stead. Such a kingdom is what the Jews desired in the days of Christ. But He said, "My kingdom is not of this world." John 18:36.

The government under which Jesus lived was corrupt and oppressive. On every hand were crying abuses—extortion, intolerance, and grinding cruelty. Yet the Saviour attempted no civil reforms, attacked no national abuses, nor condemned the national enemies. He did not interfere with the authority of those in power. He who was our example kept aloof from earthly governments; not because He was indifferent to the woes of men, but because the remedy did not lie in merely human and external measures. The cure must regenerate the heart.

Not by courts, councils, or legislative assemblies is the kingdom of Christ established, but by implanting Christ's nature in humanity through the work of the Holy Spirit. Here is the only power that can uplift mankind. And the human agency for the accomplishment of this work is the teaching and practicing of the Word of God.

Now, as in Christ's day, the work of God's kingdom lies not with those who clamor for recognition and support by earthly rulers and human laws, but with those who declare to the people in His name those spiritual truths that work in the receivers the experience of Paul: "I am crucified with Christ: nevertheless I live; yet not I, but Christ liveth in me." Galatians 2:20.

56 / Jesus' Love for Children

Jesus was a lover of children. He accepted their childish sympathy and open, unaffected love. The grateful praise from their lips refreshed His spirit when oppressed by contact with crafty and hypocritical men. Wherever He went, His gentle, kindly manner won the love and confidence of children.

It was customary for children to be brought to some rabbi, that he might lay his hands on them in blessing. But when the mothers came to Jesus with their little ones, the disciples looked on them with disfavor. They thought these children too young to be benefited by a visit to Jesus, and concluded that He would be displeased. But it was the disciples with whom He was displeased. The Saviour understood the burden of the mothers who were seeking to train their children. He Himself had drawn them into His presence.

Several mothers came together, with their little ones, to have Jesus bless their children. Jesus heard with sympathy their timid, tearful request. But He waited to see how the disciples would treat them. When He saw them send the mothers away, He showed them their error, saying, "Suffer the little children to come unto Me, and forbid them not: for of such is the kingdom of heaven." He took the children in His arms and gave them the blessing for which they came.

The mothers were strengthened by the words of Christ, and were encouraged to take up their burden with new cheerfulness. The mothers of today are to receive His words with the same faith. Christ is a per-

This chapter is based on Matthew 19:13-15; Mark 10:13-16; Luke 18:15-17.

sonal Saviour, and is as verily the helper of mothers today as when He gathered the little ones in His arms in Judea.

Jesus knows the burden of every mother's heart. He made a long journey to relieve the anxious heart of a Canaanite woman. He gave back to the widow of Nain her only son, and in His agony on the cross He remembered His own mother. He is touched today by the mother's sorrow. In every grief and need He will give comfort and help.

He who said, "Suffer the little children to come unto Me, and forbid them not," still invites mothers to lead their little ones to be blessed by Him. Even the babe in its mother's arms may dwell as under the shadow of the Almighty through the faith of the praying mother. John the Baptist was filled with the Holy Spirit from his birth. If we will live in communion with God, we too may expect the divine Spirit to mold our little ones, even from their earliest moments.

Jesus saw that some of the children who were brought in contact with Him would become martyrs for His sake. These children would accept Him as their Redeemer far more readily than many grown-up people. The Majesty of heaven answered their questions and simplified His important lessons to meet their childish understanding.

An Example to Mothers and Fathers

Children are still the most susceptible to the teachings of the gospel; their hearts are strong to retain the lessons received. Little children may be Christians, in accordance with their years.

Fathers and mothers should look on their children as younger members of the Lord's family, committed to them to educate for heaven. The Christian home becomes a school, with the parents as underteachers and Christ Himself the chief instructor. We should teach our children to bring their sins to Jesus, asking forgiveness and believing that He pardons them as He received the children when He was personally on earth.

As the mother teaches her children to obey her because they love her, she is teaching them the first lesson in the Christian life. The mother's love represents to the child the love of Christ, and the little ones who trust and obey their mother are learning to trust and obey the Saviour.

Jesus was also the father's example. His word was with power; yet even with rude and violent men He did not use one unkind or discourteous expression. The grace of Christ in the heart will soften whatever is harsh and subdue all that is coarse and unkind. It will lead fathers and mothers to treat their children as they themselves would like to be treated.

Parents, in training your children, study the lessons God has given in nature. If you would train a rose or lily, how would you do it? Ask the gardener how he makes every branch and leaf to develop in symmetry and loveliness. He will tell you: it was by no rude touch, no violent effort; this would only break the delicate stems. It was by little attentions, often repeated. He moistened the soil and protected the growing plants from the fierce blasts and scorching sun, and God caused them to blossom into loveliness. By gentle touches, seek to fashion the characters of your children after the pattern of the character of Christ.

Encourage the expression of love toward God and toward one another. The reason why there are so many hardhearted men and women in the world is that true affection has been discouraged and repressed. The better nature of these persons was stifled in childhood; and unless divine love shall melt away their cold selfishness, their happiness will be forever ruined. If we wish our children to possess the tender spirit of Jesus, we must encourage the generous, loving impulses of childhood.

Teach the children to see Christ in nature. Take them out into the open air, under the noble trees, into the garden. In all the wonderful works of creation teach them to see His love. He made the laws which govern all living things, and He has made laws for our happiness and joy. Do not weary them with long prayers and tedious exhortations, but through nature's object lessons teach them obedience to the law of God.

As you try to make plain the truths of salvation, point the children to Christ as a personal Saviour. Angels will be by your side. The Lord will give to fathers and mothers grace to interest their little ones in the precious story of the Babe in Bethlehem.

Do not keep the little ones away from Jesus by coldness and harshness. Never give them cause to feel that heaven will not be a pleasant place if you are there. Do not speak of religion as something that children cannot understand. Do not give the false impression that the religion of Christ is a religion of gloom and that in coming to the Saviour they must give up all that makes life joyful.

As the Holy Spirit moves upon the hearts of the children, cooperate with His work. The Saviour is calling them. Nothing can give Him greater joy than for them to give themselves to Him in the bloom and freshness of their years. His heart is drawn out, not only to the best-behaved children, but to those who have by inheritance objectionable traits of character. Many parents have not the tenderness and wisdom to deal with the erring children whom they have made what they are. But Jesus looks upon these children with pity.

Be Christ's agent in drawing these children to the Saviour. By wisdom and tact give them courage and hope. Through the grace of Christ they may be transformed in character, so that of them it may be said, "Of such is the kingdom of God."

57 / The Rich Young Ruler Lacked One Thing

"And when He was gone forth into the way, there came one running, and kneeled to Him, and asked Him, Good Master, what shall I do that I may inherit eternal life?"

This young man, a ruler, had great possessions and a position of responsibility. He saw the love Christ manifested toward the children, and his heart kindled with love for the Saviour. He was so deeply moved that He ran after Christ and, kneeling at His feet, asked with sincerity and earnestness the question so important to his soul and to every human being.

"Why callest thou Me good?" said Christ, "there is none good but One, that is, God." Jesus desired to draw from him the way in which he regarded Him as good. Did he realize that the One to whom he was speaking was the Son of God? What was the true sentiment of his heart?

This ruler had a high estimate of his own righteousness, yet he felt the want of something he did not possess. Could Jesus bless him and satisfy his soul want?

In reply, Jesus told him that obedience to the commandments of God was necessary if he would obtain eternal life. The ruler's answer was positive: "All these things have I kept from my youth up: what lack I yet?"

Christ looked into the face of the young man, as if reading his life and searching his character. He loved him and hungered to give him peace and joy. "One thing thou lackest: go sell whatsoever thou hast, and

This chapter is based on Matthew 19:16-22; Mark 10:17-22; Luke 18:18-23.

give to the poor, and thou shalt have treasure in heaven: and come, take up the cross, and follow Me.''

Christ was drawn to this young man. The Redeemer longed to create in him that discernment to see the necessity of heart devotion. He longed to see in him a humble and contrite heart, hiding its lack in the perfection of Christ.

Jesus saw in this ruler just the help He needed in the work of salvation. If he would place himself under Christ's guidance, he would be a power for good. Christ, seeing into his character, loved him. Love for Christ was awakening in the ruler's heart, for love begets love. Jesus longed to see him a coworker with Him. He longed to develop the excellence of his character, and sanctify it to the Master's use. If the ruler had then given himself to Christ, how different would have been his future!

"One thing thou lackest," Jesus said. "Go and sell that thou hast, and give to the poor, and thou shalt have treasure in heaven: and come and follow Me." Christ read the ruler's heart. Only one thing he lacked, but that was a vital principle. He needed the love of God in the soul. This lack, unless supplied, would prove fatal. His whole nature would become corrupted. That he might receive the love of God, his supreme love of self must be surrendered.

Christ called upon him to choose between heavenly treasure and worldly greatness. Self must yield; his will must be given into Christ's control. The young ruler had the privilege of becoming a coheir with Christ to the heavenly treasure. But he must take up the cross and follow the Saviour in the path of self-denial.

The choice was left with him. Jesus had shown him the plague spot in his character. If he decided to follow Christ, he must turn from his ambitious projects. With earnest, anxious longing, the Saviour looked at the young man, hoping he would yield to the invitation of the Spirit of God.

Christ's words were words of wisdom, though they

appeared severe. In accepting and obeying them was the ruler's only hope of salvation. His position and possessions were exerting a subtle influence for evil on his character. If cherished, they would supplant God in his affections.

Did Jesus Demand Too Much?

The ruler, quick to discern all that Christ's words involved, became sad. He was a member of the honored council of the Jews, and Satan was tempting him with flattering prospects of the future. He wanted the heavenly treasure, but he wanted also the advantages his riches would bring. He desired eternal life, but the sacrifice seemed too great; and he went away sorrowful, "for he had great possessions."

His claim that he had kept the law of God was a deception. He showed that riches were his idol. He loved the gifts of God more than he loved the Giver. Christ had offered the young man fellowship with Himself. "Follow Me," He said. But the Saviour was not so much to him as his own name among men or his possessions. To give up the seen for the unseen was too great a risk. He refused the offer of eternal life, and went away. Ever after the world was to receive his worship. Thousands pass through this ordeal, weighing Christ against the world; and many choose the world.

Christ's dealing with the young man is presented as an object lesson. God has given us the rule of conduct which His servants must follow. It is obedience to His law, not merely a legal obedience, but an obedience which enters into the life and is exemplified in the character. Only those who will say, Lord, all I have and all I am is Thine, will be acknowledged as sons and daughters of God. Think of what it means to say No to Christ. The Saviour offers to share with us the work God has given us to do. Only in this way can He save us.

God entrusts men with means, talents, and opportunities, that they may be His agents in helping the poor and the suffering. He who uses his entrusted gifts as God designs becomes a coworker with the Saviour.

To those who, like the young ruler, are in high positions and have great possessions, it may seem too great a sacrifice to give up all in order to follow Christ. But nothing short of obedience can be accepted. Self-surrender is the substance of the teachings of Christ. There is no other way to save man than to cut away those things which, if entertained, will demoralize the whole being.

When Christ's followers give back to the Lord His own, they are accumulating treasure which will be given to them when they hear the words, "Well done, good and faithful servant; . . . enter thou into the joy of thy Lord." Matthew 25:23. The joy of seeing souls eternally saved is the reward of all who put their feet in the footprints of Him who said, "Follow Me."

58 / The Raising of Lazarus

Among the most steadfast of Christ's disciples was Lazarus of Bethany, and he was greatly loved by the Saviour. For Lazarus the greatest of Christ's miracles was performed. The Saviour loves all the human family, but to some He is bound by peculiarly tender associations.

At the home of Lazarus, Jesus often found rest. The Saviour had no home of His own. When weary, thirsting for human fellowship, He had been glad to escape to this peaceful household. Here He found a sincere welcome and pure, holy friendship.

As the multitudes followed Christ through the open fields, He unfolded to them the beauties of the natural world. But the multitudes were slow of hearing, and in the home at Bethany Christ found rest from the weary conflict of public life. Here He needed not to speak in parables.

As Christ gave His wonderful lessons, Mary sat at His feet, a reverent and devoted listener. On one occasion, Christ's first visit to Bethany, Martha, preparing the meal, went to Him, saying, "Lord, dost Thou not care that my sister hath left me to serve alone? Bid her therefore that she help me." Jesus answered her with mild and patient words, "Martha, Martha, thou art careful and troubled about many things: but one thing is needful: and Mary hath chosen that good part, which shall not be taken away from her." Mary was storing her mind with words from the Saviour's lips, words more precious to her than earth's most costly jewels.

Martha needed less anxiety for the things which pass

This chapter is based on Luke 10:38-42; John 11:1-44.

away, and more for those things which endure forever. The cause of Christ needs Marthas, with their zeal in active religious work; but let them first sit with Mary at the feet of Jesus. Let diligence and energy be sanctified by the grace of Christ.

Sorrow entered the peaceful home where Jesus had rested. Lazarus was stricken with sudden illness, and his sisters sent to the Saviour, saying, "Lord, behold, he whom Thou lovest is sick." They saw the violence of the disease that had seized their brother, but they knew that Christ had shown Himself able to heal all manner of diseases. They made no urgent demand for His immediate presence but thought He would be with them as soon as He could reach Bethany.

Anxiously they waited. As long as the spark of life was in their brother, they prayed and watched for Jesus to come. But the messenger returned without Him. Yet he brought the message, "This sickness is not unto death," and they clung to the hope that Lazarus would live. When the sufferer died they were bitterly disappointed, but they felt the sustaining grace of Christ.

When Christ heard the message, He did not manifest the sorrow the disciples expected Him to show. He said, "This sickness is not unto death, but for the glory of God, that the Son of God might be glorified thereby." For two days Jesus remained in the place where He was. This delay was a mystery to the disciples, for His strong affection for the family at Bethany was well known.

During the two days, Christ seemed to have dismissed the message from His mind. The disciples thought of John the Baptist. With the power to perform miracles, why had Jesus permitted John to languish in prison and die a violent death? The Pharisees presented this question as an unanswerable argument against Christ's claim to be the Son of God. The Saviour had warned His disciples of trials, losses, and persecution. Would He forsake them in trial? All were deeply troubled.

After waiting two days, Jesus said, "Let us go into Judea again." The disciples questioned why, if Jesus were going to Judea, He had waited two days. But anxiety for Christ and for themselves was now uppermost in their minds. They could see nothing but danger in the course He was about to pursue. "Master," they said, "the Jews of late sought to stone Thee; and goest Thou thither again? Jesus answered, Are there not twelve hours in the day?" I am under the guidance of My Father; as long as I do His will, My life is safe. I have entered upon the last remnant of My day; but while any of this remains, I am safe.

"If any man walk in the day, he stumbleth not, because he seeth the light of this world." The light of God's guiding Spirit gives him a clear perception of his duty and leads him till the close of his work. "But if any man walk in the night, he stumbleth, because there is no light in him." He who walks in a path of his own choosing will stumble. Wherever he may be, he is not secure.

"These things said He; and after that He saith unto them, Our friend Lazarus sleepeth; but I go, that I may awake him out of sleep." In the thought of the peril their Master was about to incur by going to Jerusalem, the disciples had almost forgotten the bereaved family at Bethany. But not so Christ. The disciples had been tempted to think Jesus had not the tender love for Lazarus and his sisters that they thought He had. But the words, "Our friend Lazarus sleepeth," awakened right feelings in their minds. Christ had not forgotten His suffering friends.

"Then said His disciples, Lord, if he sleep, he shall do well. Howbeit Jesus spake of his death: but they thought that He had spoken of taking of rest in sleep." Christ represents death as a sleep to His believing children. Their life is hid with Christ in God, and until the last trump shall sound those who die will sleep in Him. See 1 Corinthians 15:51-54.

"Then said Jesus unto them plainly, Lazarus is

The stone rolled from the entrance to the tomb, Jesus raised Lazarus from the dead in the presence of an astonished crowd.

dead. And I am glad for your sakes that I was not there, to the intent ye may believe; nevertheless let us go unto him.''

The disciples marveled at Christ's words when He said, ''Lazarus is dead. And I am glad . . . that I was not there.'' Did the Saviour by His own choice avoid the home of His suffering friends? But Christ beheld the whole scene, and the bereaved sisters were upheld by His grace. Jesus witnessed the sorrow of their rent hearts as their brother wrestled with death. But Christ had not only the loved ones at Bethany to think of; He had the training of His disciples to consider. They were to be His representatives to the world. For their sake He permitted Lazarus to die. Had He restored him from illness to health, the miracle that is the most positive evidence of His divine character would not have been performed.

Had Christ been in the sickroom, death could not have aimed his dart at Lazarus. Therefore Christ remained away. He permitted the suffering sisters to see their brother laid in the grave. He suffered every pang of sorrow that they endured. He loved them no less because He tarried, but He knew that for them, for Lazarus, for Himself, and for His disciples, a victory was to be gained.

To all who are reaching out to feel the guiding hand of God, the moment of greatest discouragement is the time when divine help is nearest. They will look back with thankfulness on the darkest part of their way. From every temptation and trial He will bring them forth with firmer faith and a richer experience.

Christ had tarried so that by raising Lazarus from the dead He might give to His stubborn, unbelieving people another evidence that He was indeed ''the resurrection and the life.'' He was loath to give up all hope of the people of Israel, and He purposed to give them one more evidence that He was the One who alone could bring life and immortality to light. This was the reason of His delay in going to Bethany.

On reaching Bethany Jesus sent a messenger to the sisters with the tidings of His arrival, but He remained in a quiet place by the wayside. The great outward display observed by the Jews at the death of friends or relatives was not in harmony with the spirit of Christ. He heard the sound of wailing from the hired mourners, and did not wish to meet the sisters in the scene of confusion. Among the mourning friends were some of Christ's bitterest enemies. Christ knew their purposes, and therefore did not at once make His presence known.

The message was given to Martha so quietly that others, even Mary, did not hear. Martha went out to meet her Lord, but Mary sat still in her sorrow, making no outcry.

Martha's heart was agitated by conflicting emotions. In Christ's expressive face she read the same tenderness and love that had always been there, but she thought of her dearly loved brother. With grief surging in her heart because Christ had not come before, she said, "Lord, if Thou hadst been here, my brother had not died." Over and over again the sisters had repeated these words.

Martha had no inclination to recount the past, but looking into the face of love, she added, "I know, that even now, whatsoever Thou wilt ask of God, God will give it Thee."

Jesus encouraged her, saying, "Thy brother shall rise again." His answer fixed Martha's thoughts on the resurrection of the just, that she might see in the resurrection of Lazarus a pledge of the resurrection of all the righteous dead.

Martha answered, "I know that he shall rise again in the resurrection at the last day." Seeking to give a true direction to her faith, Jesus declared, "I am the resurrection and the life." In Christ is life, original, unborrowed, underived. "He that hath the Son hath life." 1 John 5:12. Said Jesus, "He that believeth in Me, though he were dead, yet shall he live: and whosoever liveth and believeth in Me shall never die. Believest thou this?" Christ here looked forward to the time of His second coming. At the time of His second coming, the righteous dead shall be raised incorruptible, and the living righteous shall be translated to heaven without seeing death. The raising of Lazarus would represent the resurrection of all the righteous dead. By His word and His works Jesus asserted His right and power to give eternal life.

To the Saviour's words, "Believest thou?" Martha responded, "Yea, Lord: I believe that Thou art the Christ, the Son of God, which should come into the world." She confessed her faith in His divinity, and her confidence that He was able to perform whatever it pleased Him to do.

"When she had so said, she went her way, and called Mary her sister secretly, saying, The Master is come, and calleth for thee." She delivered her message as quietly as possible; for the priests and rulers were prepared to arrest Jesus when opportunity offered. The cries of the mourners prevented her words from being heard.

On hearing the message, Mary rose hastily and left the room. Thinking that she had gone to the grave to weep, the mourners followed her. When she reached the place where Jesus was waiting, she said with quivering lips, "Lord, if Thou hadst been here, my brother had not died." The cries of the mourners were painful to her, for she longed for a few quiet words alone with Jesus.

"When Jesus therefore saw her weeping, and the Jews also weeping which came with her, He groaned in the spirit, and was troubled." He saw that with many, what passed as grief was only pretense. Some now manifesting hypocritical sorrow would plan the death, not only of the mighty miracle worker, but of the one to be raised from the dead. "Where have ye laid him?" He asked. "Lord, come and see." Together they proceeded to the grave. Lazarus had been much loved, and his sisters wept with breaking hearts, while his friends mingled their tears with those of the bereaved sisters. In view of this human distress, and of the fact that the afflicted friends could mourn while the Saviour of the world stood by, "Jesus wept." The Son of God had taken human nature upon Him, and was moved by human sorrow. His tender, pitying heart is ever awakened to sympathy by suffering.

But it was not only because of sympathy with Mary and Martha that Jesus wept. Christ wept because the weight of the grief of ages was upon Him. He saw the terrible effects of the transgression of God's law. He saw that the conflict between good and evil had been unceasing. He saw the suffering and sorrow, tears and death, that were to be the lot of the human family of all ages in all lands. Woes of the sinful race were heavy upon His soul, and the fountain of His tears was broken up as He longed to relieve all their distress.

Lazarus had been laid in a cave, and a massive stone had been placed before the entrance. "Take ye away the stone," Christ said. Thinking He only wished to look upon the dead, Martha objected, saying that the body had been buried four days, and corruption had already begun its work. This statement, made before the raising of Lazarus, left no room for Christ's enemies to say that a deception had been practiced. When Christ raised the daughter of Jairus, He had said, "The damsel is not dead, but sleepeth." Mark 5:39. As she had been raised immediately after her death, the Pharisees declared that the child had not been dead, that Christ Himself said she was only asleep. They had tried to make it appear that there was foul play about His miracles. But in this case, none could deny that Lazarus was dead.

When the Lord is about to do a work, Satan moves upon someone to object. Martha was unwilling that the decomposing body should be brought to view. Her faith had not grasped the true meaning of His promise. Christ reproved Martha with the utmost gentleness:

"Said I not unto thee, that, if thou wouldest believe, thou shouldest see the glory of God?" You have My word. Natural impossibilities cannot prevent the work of the Omnipotent One. Unbelief is not humility. Implicit belief in Christ's word is true humility, true self-surrender.

"Take *ye* away the stone." Christ could have bidden the angels close by His side to remove the stone. But Christ would show that humanity is to cooperate with divinity. What human power can do divine power is not summoned to do.

The command was obeyed. The stone was rolled away. Everything was done openly and deliberately. All saw that no deception was practiced. There lay the body of Lazarus, cold and silent in death. Surprised and expectant, the company stood around the sepulcher, waiting to see what was to follow.

A sacred solemnity rested upon all present. Christ stepped closer to the sepulcher. Lifting His eyes to heaven, He said, "Father, I thank Thee that Thou hast heard Me." Christ's enemies had accused Him of blasphemy because He claimed to be the Son of God. But here, with perfect confidence, Christ declared He was the Son of God.

Christ was careful to make it evident that He did not work independently of His Father; it was by faith and prayer that He wrought His miracles. Christ desired all to know His relationship with His Father. "Father," He said, "I thank Thee that Thou hast heard Me. And I knew that Thou hearest Me always: but because of the people which stand by I said it, that they may believe that thou hast sent Me." Here the disciples and the people were to be shown that Christ's claim was not a deception.

"And when He thus had spoken, He cried with a loud voice, Lazarus, come forth." Divinity flashed through humanity. In His face, which was lighted up by the glory of God, the people saw the assurance of His power. Every eye was fastened on the cave, every ear bent to catch the slightest sound. With intense interest all waited for the evidence that was to substantiate Christ's claim to be the Son of God, or to extinguish the hope forever.

There was a stir in the silent tomb; then he who was dead stood at the door of the sepulcher. His movements were impeded by the graveclothes, so Christ said to the astonished spectators, "Loose him, and let him go." Again they were shown that humanity is to work for humanity. Lazarus was set free and stood before the company, not as one emaciated from disease but as a man in the prime of life. His eyes beamed with intelligence and love for His Saviour. In adoration he cast himself at the feet of Jesus.

The beholders were at first speechless with amazement; then there followed inexpressible rejoicing. The sisters received their brother back to life as the gift of God, and with joyful tears they brokenly expressed their thanks to the Saviour. But while all were rejoicing in this reunion, Jesus withdrew from the scene. When they looked for the Life-giver, He was not to be found.

59 / Priests and Rulers Continue Plotting

News of the raising of Lazarus was soon carried to Jerusalem. Through spies the Jewish rulers were speedily in possession of the facts. A meeting of the Sanhedrin was called at once to decide what should be done. That mighty miracle was the crowning evidence offered by God that He had sent His Son into the world for their salvation. It was a demonstration of divine power sufficient to convince every mind that was under the control of reason and enlightened conscience.

But the priests were only enraged at this new miracle. The dead had been raised in the full light of day, and before a crowd of witnesses. No artifice could explain away such evidence. For this reason the priests were more than ever determined to put a stop to Christ's work.

The Sadducees had not been so full of malignity toward Christ as were the Pharisees, but now they were thoroughly alarmed. They did not believe in a resurrection of the dead, reasoning that it would be impossible for a dead body to be brought to life. But by a few words from Christ, they were shown to be ignorant both of the Scriptures and of the power of God. How could men be turned away from Him who had prevailed to rob the grave of its dead? The miracle could not be denied, and how to counteract its effect they knew not. After the resurrection of Lazarus the Sadducees decided that only by His death could His fearless denunciations against them be stopped.

The Pharisees believed in the resurrection, and they

This chapter is based on John 11:47-54.

could not but see that this miracle was an evidence that the Messiah was among them. But from the first they had hated Him because He had torn aside the cloak under which their moral deformity was hidden. The pure religion that He taught had condemned their hollow professions of piety. They thirsted to be revenged for His pointed rebukes. Several times they had attempted to stone Him, but He had quietly withdrawn.

To excite the Romans against Him, the Pharisees had represented Him as trying to subvert their authority. They had tried every pretext to cut Him off from influencing the people. But their attempts had been foiled. The multitudes who witnessed His works and heard His pure teachings knew that these were not the deeds and words of a Sabbathbreaker or blasphemer. In desperation the Jews had finally passed an edict that anyone who professed faith in Jesus should be cast out of the synagogue.

So, Pharisees and Sadducees were more nearly united than ever before. They became one in their opposition to Christ.

The Sanhedrin was not at this time a legal assembly. It existed only by tolerance. Some of its members questioned the wisdom of putting Christ to death. They feared that this would excite an insurrection. The Sadducees, united with the priests in hatred of Christ, were inclined to be cautious, fearing that the Romans would deprive them of their high standing.

How the Holy Spirit Tried to Help Them

In this council, assembled to plan the death of Christ, the Witness who heard the boastful words of Nebuchadnezzar and witnessed the idolatrous feast of Belshazzar, was now impressing the rulers with the work they were doing. Events in the life of Christ rose up before them with a distinctness that alarmed them. They remembered when Jesus, a child of twelve, stood before the learned doctors of the law, asking questions at which they wondered. The miracle just performed bore witness that Jesus was none other than the Son of God. Perplexed and troubled, the rulers asked, "What do we?" There was a division in the council.

While the council was at the height of its perplexity, Caiaphas the high priest arose. Proud and cruel, overbearing and intolerant, he spoke with great authority and assurance: "Ye know nothing at all, nor consider that it is expedient for us, that one man should die for the people, and that the whole nation perish not." Even if Jesus were innocent, He must be put out of the way. He was lessening the authority of the rulers, and if the people were to lose confidence in their rulers, the national power would be destroyed. After this miracle, the followers of Jesus would likely rise in revolt. The Romans would then come, he said, close our temple, and destroy us as a nation. What is the life of this Galilean in comparison with the nation? Is it not doing God a service to remove Him? Better that one man perish than that the whole nation be destroyed.

The policy Caiaphas advocated was based on a principle borrowed from heathenism. The dim consciousness that one was to die for the human race had led to the offering of human sacrifices. So Caiaphas proposed by the sacrifice of Jesus to save the guilty nation, not from transgression, but in transgression, that they might continue in sin.

At this council Christ's enemies had been deeply convicted. The Holy Spirit had impressed their minds. But Satan urged upon their notice the grievances they had suffered on account of Christ. How little He had honored their righteousness. Taking no notice of their forms and ceremonies, He had encouraged sinners to go directly to God as a merciful Father, and make known their wants. He had refused to acknowledge the theology of the rabbinical schools, and, by exposing the evil practices of the priests, had irreparably hurt their influence.

With the exception of a few who dared not speak their minds, the Sanhedrin received the words of Caiaphas as the words of God. Relief came to the council; the discord ceased. They resolved to put Christ to death at the first favorable opportunity. These priests and rulers had come wholly under the sway of Satan, yet such was their deception that they were well pleased with themselves. They regarded themselves as patriots seeking the nation's salvation.

Lest the people should become incensed and the violence meditated toward Jesus should fall on themselves, the council delayed to execute the sentence they had pronounced. The Saviour knew that their purpose would soon be accomplished, but it was not His place to hasten the crisis, and He withdrew from that region, taking the disciples with Him.

Jesus had now given three years of public labor to the world. His self-denial, disinterested benevolence, purity, and devotion were known to all. Yet this short period was as long as the world could endure the presence of its Redeemer. He who was ever touched by human woe, who healed the sick, fed the hungry, and comforted the sorrowful, was driven from the people He had labored to save. He who broke the slumbers of the dead and held thousands entranced by His words of wisdom was unable to reach the hearts of those who were blinded by prejudice and hatred, and who stubbornly rejected light.

60 / What Is the Highest Position?

Passover was drawing near, and again Jesus turned toward Jerusalem. In His heart was the peace of perfect oneness with the Father's will, and with eager steps He pressed on toward the place of sacrifice. But a sense of mystery, of doubt and fear, fell upon the disciples. The Saviour "went before them: and they were amazed; and as they followed, they were afraid."

Again Christ opened to the Twelve His betrayal and sufferings: "Behold, we go up to Jerusalem, and all things that are written by the prophets concerning the Son of man shall be accomplished. For He shall be delivered unto the Gentiles, and shall be mocked, and spitefully entreated, and spitted on: and they shall scourge Him, and put Him to death: and the third day He shall rise again. And they understood none of these things: and this saying was hid from them, neither knew they the things which were spoken."

Had they not just before proclaimed everywhere, "The kingdom of heaven is at hand"? Had not Christ Himself given to the Twelve the special promise of positions of high honor in His kingdom? And had not the prophets foretold the glory of the Messiah's reign? In the light of these thoughts, His words in regard to betrayal, persecution, and death seemed vague and shadowy. Whatever difficulties might intervene, they believed that the kingdom was soon to be established.

John and his brother James had been among the first group who had forsaken home and friends to be with Him. Their hearts seemed linked with His, and in the

This chapter is based on Matthew 20:20-28; Mark 10:32-45; Luke 18:31-34.

363

ardor of their love they longed to be nearest to Him in His kingdom. At every opportunity, John took his place next to the Saviour, and James longed to be honored with as close connection with Him.

Their mother had ministered to Christ freely of her substance. With a mother's love and ambition for her sons, she coveted for them the most honored place in the new kingdom. Together mother and sons came to Jesus.

"What would ye that I should do for you?" He questioned.

"Grant that these my two sons may sit, the one on Thy right hand, and the other on the left, in Thy kingdom."

Jesus read their hearts. He knew the depth of their attachment to Him. Their love, though defiled by the earthliness of its human channel, was an outflowing from the fountain of His own redeeming love.

"Are ye able to drink of the cup that I shall drink of, and to be baptized with the baptism that I am baptized with?" They recalled His mysterious words, pointing to trial and suffering, yet answered confidently, "We are able."

"Ye shall drink indeed of My cup, and be baptized with the baptism that I am baptized with," He said. John and James were to share with their Master in suffering; the one, first of the brethren to perish with the sword; the other, longest of all to endure toil and persecution.

"But to sit on My right hand, and on My left, is not Mine to give, but it shall be given to them for whom it is prepared of My Father." In the kingdom of God, position is not gained through favoritism, nor received through arbitrary bestowal. It is the result of character. The crown and the throne are tokens of a condition attained through our Lord Jesus Christ. The one who stands nearest to Christ will be he who on earth has drunk most deeply of the spirit of His self-sacrificing love—love that moves the disciple to give all, to live and labor and sacrifice, even unto death, for the saving of humanity.

The ten were much displeased. The highest place in the kingdom was just what every one of them was seeking for himself, and they were angry that the two disciples had gained a seeming advantage over them.

Jesus said to the indignant disciples, "Ye know that they which are accounted to rule over the Gentiles exercise lordship over them; and their great ones exercise authority upon them. But so shall it not be among you."

In the kingdoms of the world, position means self-aggrandizement. The people existed for the benefit of the ruling classes. Wealth and education were means of gaining control of the masses. The higher classes were to think, decide, and rule; the lower, to obey and serve. Religion, like all things else, was a matter of authority.

A Kingdom of Different Principles

Christ was establishing a kingdom on different principles. He called men, not to authority, but to service, the strong to bear the infirmities of the weak. Power, position, talent, education, placed their possessor under greater obligation to serve.

"The Son of man came not to be ministered unto, but to minister, and to give His life a ransom for many." The principle on which Christ acted is to actuate the members of the church, His body. In the kingdom of Christ those are greatest who follow the example He has given.

The words of Paul reveal the true dignity and honor of the Christian life: "Though I be free from all men, yet have I made myself servant unto all," "not seeking mine own profit, but the profit of many, that they may be saved." 1 Corinthians 9:19; 10:33.

In matters of conscience, no one is to control another's mind or prescribe his duty. God gives to every soul freedom to think, and to follow his own convictions. In matters where principle is involved, "let every man be fully persuaded in his own mind." Romans 14:5. The angels of heaven do not come to earth to rule and to exact homage, but to cooperate with men in uplifting humanity.

The principles and words of the Saviour's teaching dwelt in the memory of the beloved disciple to his latest days. The burden of John's testimony was, "This is the message that ye heard from the beginning, that we should love one another." "Hereby perceive we the love of God, because He laid down His life for us: and we ought to lay down our lives for the brethren." 1 John 3:11, 16.

This spirit pervaded the early church. After the outpouring of the Holy Spirit, "the multitude of them that believed were of one heart and of one soul." "And with great power gave the apostles witness of the resurrection of the Lord Jesus." Acts 4:32, 33.

61 / The Little Man Who Became Important

The city of Jericho lay in the midst of tropic verdure and luxuriance. Watered by living springs, it gleamed like an emerald in the setting of limestone hills and desolate ravines. The city was a great center of traffic, and Roman officials and soldiers, with strangers from different quarters, were found there, while the collection of customs made it the home of many publicans.

The "chief tax collector," Zacchaeus, was a Jew, and detested by his countrymen. His rank and wealth were the reward of a calling which they regarded as another name for injustice and extortion. Yet the wealthy customs officer was not altogether the hardened man that he seemed. Zacchaeus had heard of Jesus. The report of His kindness and courtesy toward the proscribed classes had spread far and wide. John the Baptist had preached at the Jordan, and Zacchaeus had heard of the call to repentance. Now, hearing the words reported to have come from the Great Teacher, he felt that he was a sinner in the sight of God. Yet what he had heard of Jesus kindled hope in his heart. Repentance, reformation of life, was possible, even to him. Was not one of the new Teacher's most trusted disciples a publican? Zacchaeus began at once to follow the conviction that had taken hold upon him and to make restitution to those whom he had wronged.

When the news sounded through Jericho that Jesus was entering the town, Zacchaeus determined to see Him. The tax collector longed to look on the face of Him whose words had brought hope to his heart.

This chapter is based on Luke 19:1-10.

The streets were crowded, and Zacchaeus, who was small, could see nothing over the heads of the people. So, running a little in advance of the multitude to a wide-branching fig tree, he climbed to a seat among the boughs. As the procession passed below, Zacchaeus scanned with eager eyes to discern the one figure he longed to see.

Suddenly, just beneath the fig tree, the company came to a standstill, and One looked upward whose glance seemed to read the soul. Almost doubting his senses, the man in the tree heard the words, "Zacchaeus, make haste, and come down; for today I must abide at thy house."

Zacchaeus, walking as in a dream, led the way toward his own home. But the rabbis, with scowling faces, murmured in scorn that "He was gone to be guest with a man that is a sinner."

Zacchaeus had been overwhelmed at the condescension of Christ in stooping to him, so unworthy. Now love to his new-found Master unsealed his lips. He would make public his repentance. In the presence of the multitude, "Zacchaeus stood, and said unto the Lord; Behold, Lord, the half of my goods I give to the poor; and if I have taken anything from any man by false accusation, I restore him fourfold. And Jesus said unto him, This day is salvation come to this house, forsomuch as he also is a son of Abraham."

Now the disciples had a demonstration of the truth of Christ's words, "The things which are impossible with men are possible with God." Luke 18:27. They saw how, through the grace of God, a rich man could enter into the kingdom.

Before Zacchaeus had looked upon the face of Christ, he had confessed his sin. He had begun to carry out the teaching written for ancient Israel as well as for ourselves: "If your brother becomes poor, and cannot maintain himself with you, you shall maintain him; as a stranger and a sojourner he shall live with you. Take no interest from him or increase, but fear your God."

"You shall not wrong one another, but you shall fear your God, for I am the Lord your God." Leviticus 25:35, 36, 17, RSV. The very first response of Zacchaeus to the love of Christ was to manifest compassion toward the poor and suffering.

Among the publicans there was a confederacy so that they could oppress the people, and sustain one another in their fraudulent practices. But no sooner did Zacchaeus yield to the Holy Spirit than he cast aside every practice contrary to integrity.

No repentance is genuine that does not work reformation. The righteousness of Christ is not a cloak to cover unconfessed and unforsaken sin. It is a principle of life that transforms the character and controls the conduct. Holiness is wholeness for God, entire surrender of heart and life to the indwelling of the principles of heaven.

The Christian in his business life is to represent to the world the manner in which our Lord would conduct business. In every transaction he is to make it manifest that God is his teacher. "Holiness unto the Lord" is to be written on ledgers, deeds, receipts, and bills of exchange. Every converted soul will signal the entrance of Christ into his heart by abandonment of unrighteous practices. Like Zacchaeus he will give proof of his sincerity by making restitution. "If the wicked restore the pledge, give again that he had robbed, walk in the statutes of life, without committing iniquity, he shall surely live." Ezekiel 33:15.

If we have injured others, overreached in trade, or defrauded any man, even though it be within the pale of the law, we should confess our wrong, and make restitution as far as lies in our power. It is right to restore not only that which we have taken, but all that it would have accumulated if put to a wise use during the time it has been in our possession.

To Zacchaeus the Saviour said, "This day is salvation come to this house." Christ went to his home to give him lessons of truth, and to instruct his household in the things of the kingdom. Shut out from the synagogues by the contempt of rabbis and worshipers, now they gathered in their own home about the divine Teacher and heard the words of life.

When Christ is received as a personal Saviour, salvation comes to the soul. Zacchaeus had received Jesus, not merely as a passing guest, but as One to abide in the soul temple. The scribes and Pharisees accused him as a sinner, but the Lord recognized him as a son of Abraham. See Galatians 3:7, 29.

62 / Mary Anoints Jesus

Simon of Bethany was one of the few Pharisees who had openly joined Christ's followers. He hoped that Jesus might be the Messiah, but had not accepted Him as a Saviour. His character was not transformed; his principles were unchanged.

Simon had been healed of leprosy, and he desired to show his gratitude. At Christ's last visit to Bethany he made a feast for the Saviour and His disciples. This feast brought together many of the Jews who closely watched His movements, some with unfriendly eyes.

According to His custom the Saviour had sought rest at the home of Lazarus. Many of the people flocked to Bethany, some out of sympathy with Jesus, and others from curiosity to see one who had been raised from the dead. With assurance and power, Lazarus declared that Jesus was the Son of God.

The people were eager to see whether Lazarus would accompany Jesus to Jerusalem and whether the prophet would be crowned king at the Passover. The priests and rulers could hardly wait for the opportunity of removing Him forever from their way. They remembered how often He had baffled their murderous designs, and were fearful that He would remain away. They questioned among themselves, "What think ye, that He will not come to the feast?"

A council was called. Since the raising of Lazarus the sympathies of the people were so fully with Christ that it would be dangerous to seize Him openly. So the authorities determined to take Him secretly and carry

This chapter is based on Matthew 26:6-13; Mark 14:3-11; Luke 7:36-50; John 11:55-57; 12:1-11.

on the trial as quietly as possible. They hoped that when His condemnation became known, the fickle tide of public opinion would set in their favor.

But so long as Lazarus lived, the priests and rabbis knew they were not secure. The existence of a man who had been four days in the grave and had been restored by a word from Jesus would cause a reaction. The people would be avenged on their leaders for taking the life of One who could perform such a miracle. The Sanhedrin therefore decided that Lazarus also must die.

While this plotting was going on at Jerusalem, Jesus and His friends were invited to Simon's feast. At the table Simon sat on one side of the Saviour, and Lazarus, on the other. Martha served, but Mary was earnestly listening to every word from the lips of Jesus. In His mercy, Jesus had pardoned her sins and called forth her brother from the grave, and Mary's heart was filled with gratitude. She had heard Jesus speak of His approaching death, and she had longed to show Him honor.

At great personal sacrifice she had purchased an alabaster box of "ointment of spikenard, very costly," with which to anoint His body. But now many were declaring that He was about to be crowned king. Her grief was turned to joy, and she was eager to be first in honoring her Lord. Breaking her box of ointment, she poured its contents on the head and feet of Jesus; then, as she knelt weeping, moistening them with her tears, she wiped His feet with her long, flowing hair. Her movements might have passed unnoticed, but the ointment filled the room with its fragrance and published her act to all present.

Why Judas Was Annoyed

Judas looked upon this act with great displeasure. He began to whisper his complaints to those near him, throwing reproach on Christ for suffering such waste. Judas, treasurer for the disciples, had secretly drawn from their little store for his own use, thus narrowing their resources to a pittance. He was eager to put into the bag all he could obtain. When something that he did not think essential was bought, he would say, Why was not the cost of this put into the bag that I carry for the poor?

The act of Mary was in such marked contrast to his selfishness that he was put to shame. He sought to assign a worthy motive for his objection to her gift: "Why was not this ointment sold for three hundred pence, and given to the poor? This he said, not that he cared for the poor; but because he was a thief." Had Mary's ointment been sold and the proceeds fallen into his possession, the poor would have received no benefit.

As a financier Judas thought himself greatly superior to his fellow disciples, and he had gained a strong influence over them. His professed sympathy for the poor deceived them. The murmur passed round the table, "To what purpose is this waste? For this ointment might have been sold for much, and given to the poor."

Mary heard the criticism. Her heart trembled within her. She feared that her sister would reproach her for extravagance. The Master, too, might think her improvident. She was about to shrink away, when the voice of her Lord was heard, "Let her alone; why trouble ye her?" He knew that in this act she had expressed her gratitude for the forgiveness of her sins. Lifting His voice above the murmur of criticism, He said, "She has wrought a good work on Me. For ye have the poor with you always, and whensoever ye will ye may do them good: but Me ye have not always. She hath done what she could: she is come aforehand to anoint My body to the burying."

The fragrant gift which Mary had thought to lavish upon the dead body of the Saviour she poured upon His living form. At the burial its sweetness could only have pervaded the tomb; now it gladdened His heart. Pouring out her love while the Saviour was conscious of her devotion, she was anointing Him for the burial. As He went down into the darkness of His great trial, He carried with Him the memory of that deed, an earnest of the love that would be His from His redeemed ones forever.

Mary Had Obeyed the Holy Spirit's Promptings

Mary knew not the full significance of her deed of love. She could not explain why she had chosen that occasion for anointing Jesus. The Holy Spirit had planned for her, and she had obeyed His promptings. Inspiration stoops to give no reason. An unseen presence, it moves the heart to action. It is its own justification.

Christ told Mary the meaning of her act: "In that she hath poured this ointment on My body, she did it for My burial." As the alabaster box was broken and filled the house with fragrance, so Christ's body was to be broken; but He was to rise from the tomb, and the fragrance of His life was to fill the earth. "Christ hath loved us, and hath given Himself for us, an offering and a sacrifice to God for a sweet-smelling savor." Ephesians 5:2.

"Verily I say unto you," Christ declared, "Wheresoever this gospel shall be preached throughout the whole world, this also that she hath done shall be spoken of for a memorial of her." The Saviour spoke with certainty concerning His gospel that was to be preached throughout the world. And as far as the gospel extended, Mary's gift would shed its fragrance, and hearts would be blessed through her unstudied act. Kingdoms would rise and fall, the names of conquerors would be forgotten, but this woman's deed would be immortalized on the pages of sacred history. Until time should be no more, that broken alabaster box would tell the story of the abundant love of God for a fallen race.

What a sharp lesson Christ might have given Judas! He who reads the motives of every heart might have opened before those at the feast dark chapters in the experience of Judas. Instead of sympathizing with the poor, he was robbing them of the money intended for their relief. But had Christ unmasked Judas, this would have been urged as a reason for the betrayal. Judas would have gained sympathy, even among the disciples. The Saviour avoided giving him an excuse for his treachery.

Judas Goes From the Feast to Negotiate Jesus' Betrayal

But the look which Jesus cast on Judas convinced him that the Saviour penetrated his hypocrisy and read his contemptible character. And in commending Mary's action, Christ rebuked Judas. The reproof rankled in his heart, and he went directly to the palace of the high priest and offered to betray Jesus into their hands.

The leaders of Israel had been given the privilege of receiving Christ as their Saviour, without money and without price. But they refused the precious gift and bought their Lord for thirty pieces of silver.

Judas grudged Mary's gift of costly ointment to Jesus. His heart burned with envy that the Saviour should be the recipient of a gift suitable for the monarchs of the earth. For far less than the ointment cost, he betrayed his Lord.

The disciples were not like Judas. They loved the Saviour but did not rightly appreciate His character. The wise men from the East, who knew so little of Jesus, had shown a truer appreciation of the honor due Him.

Christ values acts of heartfelt courtesy. He did not refuse the simplest flower plucked by the hand of a child and offered to Him in love. He accepted the offerings of children, and blessed the givers. In the Scriptures, Mary's anointing of Jesus is mentioned as distinguishing her from the other Marys. Acts of love and reverence for Jesus are an evidence of faith in Him as the Son of God.

Christ accepted Mary's wealth of pure affection which His disciples did not, would not, understand. It was the love of Christ that constrained her. That ointment was a symbol of the heart of the giver, the outward demonstration of a love fed by heavenly streams until it overflowed.

The loneliness of Christ, living the life of humanity, was never appreciated by the disciples as it should have been. He was often grieved. He knew that if they were under the influence of the heavenly angels that accompanied Him, they too would think no offering of sufficient value to declare the heart's affection.

Jesus Never Really Appreciated

When Jesus was no longer with them and they felt as sheep without a shepherd, they began to see how they might have brought gladness to His heart. They no longer cast blame on Mary, but on themselves. Oh, if they could have taken back their censure, presenting the poor as more worthy of the gift than Christ! They felt the reproof keenly as they took from the cross the bruised body of their Lord.

Today, few appreciate all that Christ is to them. If they did, the great love of Mary would be expressed. Nothing would be thought too costly to give for Christ, no self-denial or self-sacrifice too great to be endured for His sake.

The words spoken in indignation, "To what purpose is this waste?" brought vividly before Christ the greatest sacrifice ever made—the gift of Himself as the propitiation for a lost world. From a human point of view, the plan of salvation is a wanton waste of mercies and resources. Well may the heavenly host look with amazement on the human family who refuse to be enriched with the boundless love expressed in Christ. Well may they exclaim, Why this great waste?

But the atonement for a lost world was to be full, abundant, and complete. Christ's offering was exceedingly abundant to reach every soul. Not all are saved; yet the plan of redemption is not a waste because it does not accomplish all that its liberality has provided for. There must be enough and to spare.

Simon the host was surprised at the conduct of Jesus, and he said in his heart: "This Man, if He were a prophet, would have known who and what manner of woman this is that toucheth Him: for she is a sinner."

Because Christ allowed this woman to approach Him, because He did not indignantly spurn her as one whose sins were too great to be forgiven, because He did not show that He realized she had fallen, Simon was tempted to think that Christ was not a prophet. But it was Simon's ignorance of God and of Christ that led him to think as he did.

How God Really Acts

He did not realize that God's Son must act in God's way, with compassion, tenderness, and mercy. Simon's way was to take no notice of Mary's penitent service. Mary's act of kissing Christ's feet and anointing them with ointment was exasperating to his hardheartedness. He thought that Christ should recognize sinners and rebuke them.

To this unspoken thought the Saviour answered: "Simon, I have somewhat to say unto thee. . . . There was a certain creditor which had two debtors: the one owed five hundred pence, and the other fifty. And when they had nothing to pay, he frankly forgave them both. Tell me therefore, which of them will love him most? Simon answered and said, I suppose that he, to whom he forgave most. And he said unto him, Thou hast rightly judged."

As did Nathan with David (2 Samuel 12:1-7), Christ threw upon His host the burden of pronouncing sentence on himself. Simon had led into sin the woman he now despised. She had been deeply wronged by him. By the two debtors of the parable, Simon and the woman were represented. Jesus did not design to teach that different degrees of obligation should be felt by the two persons, for each owed a debt of gratitude that never could be repaid. But Jesus desired to show Simon that his sin was as much greater than hers as a debt of five hundred pence exceeds a debt of fifty pence.

Simon now began to see himself in a new light. He saw how Mary was regarded by One who was more than a prophet. Shame seized upon him, and he realized that he was in the presence of One superior to himself.

"I entered into thine house," Christ continued, "thou gavest Me no water for My feet," but with tears of repentance Mary has washed My feet and wiped them with the hair of her head. "Thou gavest Me no kiss: but this woman," whom you despise, "since the time I came in hath not ceased to kiss My feet." Christ recounted the opportunities Simon had had to show his appreciation of what his Lord had done for him.

The Heart Searcher read the motive that led to Mary's action; He saw also the spirit that prompted Simon's words. "Seest thou this woman?" He said to him. "I say unto thee, Her sins, which are many, are forgiven; for she loved much: but to whom little is forgiven, the same loveth little."

Simon had thought he honored Jesus by inviting Him to his house. But he now saw himself as he really was. He saw that his religion had been a robe of Pharisaism. He had despised the compassion of Jesus. He had not recognized Him as the representative of God. Mary was a sinner pardoned; he was a sinner unpardoned.

How Simon's Pride Was Humbled

Simon was touched by the kindness of Jesus in not openly rebuking him before the guests. He had not been treated as he desired Mary to be treated. He saw that Jesus sought by pitying kindness to subdue his heart. Stern denunciation would have hardened him against repentance, but patient admonition convinced him of his error. He saw the magnitude of the debt he owed his Lord. He repented, and the proud Pharisee became a lowly, self-sacrificing disciple.

Christ knew the circumstances that had shaped Mary's life. He might have extinguished every spark of hope in her soul, but He did not. He had lifted her from despair and ruin. Seven times she had heard Him rebuke the demons that controlled her heart and mind. She had heard His strong cries to the Father in her behalf. She knew how offensive is sin to His unsullied purity, and in His strength she had overcome.

When to human eyes her case seemed hopeless, Christ saw in Mary capabilities for good. The plan of redemption has invested humanity with great possibilities, and in Mary these were to be realized. Through His grace she became a partaker of the divine nature. The one who had fallen, whose mind had been a habitation of demons, was brought near to the Saviour in fellowship and ministry. Mary sat at His feet and learned of Him; Mary poured on His head the precious anointing oil and bathed His feet with her tears; Mary stood beside the cross and followed Him to the sepulcher; Mary was first at the tomb after His resurrection; Mary first proclaimed a risen Saviour.

Jesus knows the circumstances of every soul. You may say, I am sinful, very sinful. You may be; but the worse you are, the more you need Jesus. He turns no weeping, contrite one away. He freely pardons all who come to Him for forgiveness and restoration.

The souls that turn to Him for refuge, Christ unites to His own divine-human nature. No man or evil angel can impeach them. They stand beside the great Sin Bearer in the light proceeding from the throne of God. "Who shall lay anything to the charge of God's elect? It is God that justifieth. Who is he that condemneth? It is Christ that died, yea rather, that is risen again, who is even at the right hand of God, who also maketh intercession for us." Romans 8:33, 34.

63 / Jesus Acclaimed as Israel's King

Five hundred years before the birth of Christ, the prophet Zechariah foretold the coming of the King to Israel: "Rejoice greatly, O daughter of Zion; shout, O daughter of Jerusalem: behold, thy King cometh unto thee: He is just, and having salvation; lowly and riding upon an ass, and upon a colt the foal of an ass." Zechariah 9:9. He who had so long refused royal honors now came to Jerusalem as the promised heir to David's throne.

On the first day of the week Christ made His triumphal entry. Multitudes who had flocked to see Him at Bethany accompanied Him. Many on their way to keep the Passover joined the multitude. All nature seemed to rejoice. The trees were clothed with verdure, and their blossoms shed a delicate fragrance. The hope of the new kingdom was again springing up.

Jesus had sent two disciples to bring Him an ass and its colt. Although "the cattle on a thousand hills" (Psalm 50:10) are His, He was dependent on a stranger's kindness for an animal on which to enter Jerusalem as its King. But again His divinity was revealed, even in the minute directions given. As He foretold, the plea, "The Lord hath need of them," was readily granted. The disciples spread their garments on the beast and seated their Master on it. Jesus had always traveled on foot, and the disciples wondered that He should now choose to ride. But hope brightened in their hearts with the thought that He was about to enter the capital, proclaim Himself King, and assert His

This chapter is based on Matthew 21:1-11; Mark 11:1-10; Luke 19:29-44; John 12:12-19.

royal power. Excitement spread far and near, raising the expectations of the people to the highest pitch.

Christ was following the Jewish custom for a royal entry. Prophecy had foretold that thus the Messiah should come to His kingdom. No sooner was He seated on the colt than the multitude hailed Him as Messiah, their King. The disciples and the multitude in imagination saw the Roman armies driven from Jerusalem and Israel once more an independent nation. All vied with one another in paying Him homage. Unable to present Him with costly gifts, they spread their outer garments as a carpet in the path and strewed the leafy branches of the olive and the palm in the way. With no royal standards to wave, they cut down the spreading palm boughs, Nature's emblem of victory, and waved them aloft.

Spectators mingling with the throng asked, Who is this? What does all this commotion signify? They knew that Jesus had discouraged all effort to place Him on the throne, and were astonished to learn that this was He. What wrought this change in Him who had declared that His kingdom was not of this world?

From the multitudes gathered to attend the Passover, thousands greeted Him with the waving of palm branches and a burst of sacred song. The priests at the temple sounded the trumpet for evening service, but few responded, and the rulers said to one another in alarm, "The world has gone after Him."

Why Jesus Permitted This Demonstration

Never before had Jesus permitted such a demonstration. He clearly foresaw the result. It would bring Him to the cross. But He desired to call attention to the sacrifice that was to crown His mission to a fallen world. He, the antitypical Lamb, by a voluntary act set Himself apart as an oblation. His church in all succeeding ages must make His death a subject of deep thought and study. Every fact connected with it should be verified beyond a doubt. The events which preceded His great sacrifice must call attention to the sacrifice itself. After such a demonstration as that attending His entry into Jerusalem, all eyes would follow His rapid progress to the final scene. This triumphal ride would be the talk of every tongue and bring Jesus before every mind. After His crucifixion, many would recall these events and be led to search the prophecies. They would be convinced that Jesus was the Messiah.

This day, which seemed to the disciples the crowning day of their lives, would have been shadowed with clouds had they known it was but a prelude to the death of their Master. He had repeatedly told them of His sacrifice, yet in the glad triumph they had forgotten His sorrowful words.

With few exceptions, all who joined the procession caught the inspiration of the hour. The shouts went up continually, "Hosanna to the Son of David: Blessed is He that cometh in the name of the Lord; Hosanna in the highest!"

No Train of Mourning in This Triumph

Never had the world seen such a triumphal procession. About the Saviour were the glorious trophies of His labors of love for sinful man. These were the captives rescued from Satan's power. The blind He had restored to sight led the way. The dumb whose tongues He had loosed shouted the loudest hosannas. Cripples whom He had healed bounded with joy. Lepers He had cleansed spread their untainted garments in His path. Awakened from the sleep of death, Lazarus led the beast on which the Saviour rode.

Many Pharisees, burning with envy, tried to silence the people, but their appeals and threats only increased the enthusiasm. As a last resort they accosted the Saviour with reproving and threatening words: "Master, rebuke Thy disciples." They declared that such noisy demonstrations were unlawful. But they were silenced by the reply of Jesus, "I tell you that, if these should hold their peace, the stones would immediately cry out." That scene of triumph had been foretold by the prophet. Had men failed to carry out the plan, God would have given voice to inanimate stones, and they would have hailed His Son with praise. As the silenced Pharisees drew back, the words of Zechariah were taken up by hundreds of voices: "Rejoice greatly, O daughter of Zion; shout, O daughter of Jerusalem: behold, thy King cometh unto thee: He is just, and having salvation; lowly, and riding upon an ass, upon a colt the foal of an ass."

When the procession reached the brow of the hill, Jesus and all the multitude halted. Before them lay Jerusalem in its glory, bathed in the light of the declining sun. In stately grandeur the temple towered above all else, long the pride and glory of the Jewish nation. The Romans also prided themselves in its magnificence. Its strength and richness had made it one of the wonders of the world.

While the westering sun was gilding the heavens, its resplendent glory lighted up the pure white marble of the temple walls and sparkled on its gold-capped pillars. From the hill where Jesus stood, it had the appearance of a massive structure of snow, set with golden pinnacles, shining as if with glory borrowed from heaven.

Jesus Breaks Down in Tears

Jesus gazed upon the scene, and the multitude hushed their shouts, spellbound by the sudden vision of beauty. All eyes turned upon the Saviour. They were surprised and disappointed to see His eyes fill with tears and His body rock to and fro like a tree before the tempest. A wail of anguish burst from His quivering lips, as if from a broken heart. What a sight for angels to behold! What a sight for the glad throng that were escorting Him to the glorious city, where they hoped He was about to reign! This sudden sorrow was like a note of wailing in a grand triumphal chorus. Israel's King was in tears; not silent tears of gladness, but of insuppressible agony. The multitude were struck with a sudden gloom. Many wept in sympathy with a grief they could not comprehend.

Just before Jesus was Gethsemane, where soon the horror of a great darkness would overshadow Him. The sheepgate also was in sight, through which for centuries the beasts for sacrificial offerings had been led. This gate was soon to open for Him, the great Antitype, toward whose sacrifice all these offerings had pointed. Nearby was Calvary, the scene of His approaching agony. Yet His was no selfish sorrow. The thought of His own agony did not intimidate that noble, self-sacrificing soul. It was the sight of Jerusalem that pierced the heart of Jesus—Jerusalem that had rejected the Son of God, scorned His love, and was about to take His life. He saw what she might have been had she accepted Him who alone could heal her wound. How could He give her up?

Israel had been a favored people; God had made their temple His habitation; it was "beautiful for situation, the joy of the whole earth." Psalm 48:2. In it Jehovah had manifested His glory, the priests had officiated, and the pomp of symbol and ceremony had gone on for ages. But all this must have an end. Jesus waved His hand toward the doomed city, and in grief exclaimed, "If thou hadst known, even thou, at least in this thy day, the things which belong unto thy peace!" The Saviour left unsaid what might have been the condition of Jerusalem had she accepted the help that God desired to give her—the gift of His Son. Jerusalem might have stood forth in the pride of prosperity, the queen of kingdoms, free in the strength of her God-given power, no Roman banners waving from her walls. The Son of God saw that she might have been liberated from bondage and established as the mighty metropolis of the earth. From her walls the dove of peace would have gone forth to all nations. She would have been the world's diadem of glory.

But the Saviour realized she now was under the Ro-

At Christ's time, kings commonly rode donkeys, especially at their coronation—a fact that the crowd quickly recognized when He entered Jerusalem on a donkey.

man yoke, doomed to God's retributive judgment: "But now they are hid from thine eyes. For the days shall come upon thee, that thine enemies shall cast a trench about thee, and compass thee round, and keep thee in on every side, and shall lay thee even with the ground, and thy children within thee; and they shall not leave in thee one stone upon another; because thou knewest not the time of thy visitation."

Jesus saw the doomed city encompassed with armies, the besieged inhabitants driven to starvation and death, mothers feeding on the dead bodies of their children, and parents and children snatching the last morsel of food from one another—natural affection destroyed by the gnawing pangs of hunger. He saw that the stubbornness of the Jews would lead them to refuse submission to the invading armies. He beheld Calvary set with crosses as thickly as forest trees. He saw the beautiful palaces destroyed, the temple in ruins, and of its massive walls not one stone left on another, while the city was plowed like a field.

As a tender father mourns over a wayward son, so Jesus wept over the beloved city. How can I give thee up? How can I see thee devoted to destruction? When the westering sun should pass from sight, Jerusalem's day of grace would be ended. While the procession was halting on Olivet, it was not yet too late for Jerusalem to repent. While the last rays of the setting sun were lingering on temple, tower, and pinnacle, would not some good angel lead her to the Saviour's love? Beautiful, unholy city, that had stoned the prophets and rejected the Son of God—her day of mercy was almost spent!

Yet again the Spirit of God would speak to Jerusalem. Before the day was done, another testimony would be borne to Christ. If Jerusalem would receive the Saviour entering her gates, she might yet be saved!

But the rulers in Jerusalem had no welcome for the Son of God. As the procession was about to descend the Mount of Olives, they intercepted it, inquiring the cause of the tumultuous rejoicing. As they questioned, "Who is this?" the disciples, filled with the spirit of inspiration, repeated the prophecies concerning Christ:

Adam will tell you: It is the seed of the woman that shall bruise the serpent's head. See Genesis 3:15.

Abraham will tell you: It is Melchizedek, King of Salem, King of Peace. See Genesis 14:18.

Jacob will tell you, He is Shiloh of the tribe of Judah.

Isaiah will tell you: "Immanuel," "Wonderful, Counselor, The mighty God, The everlasting Father, The Prince of Peace." Isaiah 7:14; 9:6.

Jeremiah will tell you: The Branch of David, "the Lord our Righteousness." Jeremiah 23:6.

Daniel will tell you: He is the Messiah ("the Anointed One"). See Daniel 9:24-27.

John the Baptist will tell you: He is "the Lamb of God, which taketh away the sin of the world." John 1:29.

The great Jehovah has proclaimed: "This is My beloved Son." Matthew 3:17.

We, His disciples, declare: This is Jesus, the Messiah, the Prince of life, the Redeemer of the world.

And the prince of the powers of darkness acknowledges Him: "I know Thee who Thou art, the Holy One of God." Mark 1:24.

64 / A Doomed People

The last appeal to Jerusalem had been in vain. The priests and rulers had heard the prophetic voice echoed by the multitude in answer to the question, "Who is this?" but they did not accept it as the voice of Inspiration. In anger they tried to silence the people. To Roman officers in the throng, His enemies denounced Jesus as the leader of a rebellion. They represented that He was about to take possession of the temple, and reign as king in Jerusalem.

But in a calm voice Jesus again declared that He had not come to establish a temporal rule; He would soon ascend to His Father, and His accusers would see Him no more until He should come again in glory. Then, too late, they would acknowledge Him.

These words Jesus spoke with sadness and with singular power. The Roman officers were silenced and subdued. Their hearts were moved as they had never been moved before. In the solemn face of Jesus they read love and quiet dignity. Stirred by a sympathy they could not understand, they were inclined to pay Him homage. Turning on the priests and rulers, they charged them with creating the disturbance.

Meanwhile Jesus passed unnoticed to the temple. All was quiet there, for the scene on Olivet had called away the people. For a short time Jesus remained, looking on the temple with sorrow. Then He returned to Bethany. When the people sought Him to place Him on the throne, He was not to be found.

The entire night Jesus spent in prayer, and in the

This chapter is based on Matthew 21:17-19; Mark 11:11-14, 20, 21.

morning came again to the temple. On the way He was hungry, "and seeing a fig tree afar off having leaves, He came, if haply He might find anything thereon; and when He came to it, He found nothing but leaves; for the time of figs was not yet."

On the highlands about Jerusalem it might truly be said, "The time of figs was not yet." But in the orchard to which Jesus came, one tree appeared to be in advance of all the others. It was already covered with leaves, giving promise of well-developed fruit. But its appearance was deceptive. Jesus found "nothing but leaves." It was a mass of pretentious foliage, nothing more.

Christ uttered against it a withering curse. "May no one ever eat fruit from you again," He said. RSV. Next morning, as the Saviour and His disciples were again on their way to the city, the blasted branches and drooping leaves attracted their attention. "Master," said Peter, "behold, the fig tree which Thou cursedst is withered away."

Christ's act in cursing the fig tree seemed to the disciples unlike His ways. They remembered His words, "The Son of man is not come to destroy men's lives, but to save them." Luke 9:56. His works had been done to restore, never to destroy. This act stood alone. What was its purpose? they questioned.

"As I live, saith the Lord God, I have no pleasure in the death of the wicked." Ezekiel 33:11. To Him the work of destruction and the denunciation of judgment is a "strange work." Isaiah 28:21. But in mercy and love He lifts the veil from the future and reveals the results of a course of sin.

The barren fig tree, flaunting its pretentious foliage in the face of Christ, was a symbol of the Jewish nation. The Saviour desired to make plain the cause and the certainty of Israel's doom. For this purpose He made the tree the expositor of divine truth. The Jews laid claim to righteousness above every other people. But they were corrupted by the love of the world and the greed of gain. They spread their pretentious branches aloft, luxuriant in appearance and beautiful to the eye, but they yielded "nothing but leaves." The Jewish religion, with its magnificent temple and impressive ceremonies, was indeed fair in outward appearance, but humility, love, and benevolence were lacking.

Why This One Tree Was Cursed

The leafless trees raised no expectation and caused no disappointment. These represented the Gentiles, who were as destitute as the Jews of godliness; but they made no boastful pretentions to goodness. With them "the time of figs" was not yet. They were still waiting for light and hope. The Jews, who had received greater blessings from God, were held accountable for their abuse of these gifts. The privileges of which they boasted only increased their guilt.

Jesus had come to Israel, hungering to find in them the fruits of righteousness. Every privilege had been granted them, and in return He longed to see in them self-sacrifice, compassion, and a deep yearning for the salvation of their fellowmen. But love to God and man was eclipsed by pride and self-sufficiency. The treasures of truth which God had committed to them, they did not give to the world. In the barren tree they might read both their sin and its punishment. Withered, dried up by the roots, the fig tree showed what the Jewish people would be when the grace of God was removed from them. Refusing to impart blessing, they would no longer receive it. "O Israel," the Lord says, "thou hast destroyed thyself." Hosea 13:9.

Christ's act in cursing the tree which His own power had created stands as a warning to all churches and all Christians. There are many who do not live out Christ's merciful, unselfish life. Time is of value to them only as they can gather for themselves. In all the affairs of life this is their object. God designed them to help their fellowmen in every possible way. But self is so large that they cannot see anything else. Those who thus live for self are like the fig tree. They observe the forms of worship without repentance or faith. In profession they honor the law of God, but obedience is lacking. In the sentence pronounced on the fig tree Christ declares that the open sinner is less guilty than he who professes to serve God but bears no fruit to His glory.

The parable of the fig tree, spoken before Christ's visit to Jerusalem, had a direct connection with the lesson He taught in cursing the fruitless tree. For the barren tree of the parable the gardener pleaded, "Let it alone, sir, this year also, till I dig about it and put on manure. And if it bears fruit next year, well and good; but if not, you can cut it down." Luke 13: 8, 9, RSV. It was to have every advantage. In the parable, the result of the gardener's work was not foretold: it depended on that people to whom Christ's words were spoken, represented by the fruitless tree. It rested with them to decide their own destiny. Every advantage was given them, but they did not profit by their increased blessings. By Christ's act in cursing the barren fig tree, the result was shown. They had determined their own destruction.

For more than a thousand years the Jewish nation had rejected God's warnings and slain His prophets. For these sins the people of Christ's day made themselves responsible by following the same course. The fetters which the nations had for centuries been forging, the people of Christ's day were fastening on themselves.

There comes a time when mercy makes her last plea. Then the sweet, winning voice of the Spirit entreats the sinner no longer.

That day had come to Jerusalem. Jesus wept in anguish over the doomed city, but could not deliver her. He had exhausted every resource. In rejecting the warnings of God's Spirit, Israel had rejected the only means of help.

The Jewish nation was a symbol of the people of all

ages who scorn the pleadings of Infinite Love. The tears of Christ when He wept over Jerusalem were for the sins of all time.

In this generation many are treading the same ground as the unbelieving Jews. The Holy Spirit has spoken to their hearts, but they are not willing to confess their errors. They reject God's message and His messenger.

Today Bible truth, the religion of Christ, struggles against a strong current of moral impurity. Prejudice is stronger now than in Christ's day. The truth of God's Word does not harmonize with men's natural inclination, and thousands reject its light and choose their independent judgment. But they do it at the peril of their souls.

Those who caviled at the words of Christ found ever-increasing cause for cavil, until they turned from the Truth and the Life. God does not propose to remove every objection which the carnal heart may bring against His truth. To those who refuse light which would illuminate the darkness, the mysteries of God's Word remain such forever. From them the truth is hidden.

Christ's words are applicable to every soul who slights the pleadings of divine mercy. Christ is shedding bitter tears for you, who have no tears to shed for yourself. And every evidence of the grace of God, every ray of divine light, is either melting and subduing the soul, or confirming it in hopeless impenitence.

Christ foresaw that Jerusalem would remain impenitent, yet all the guilt lay at her own door. Thus it will be with every soul who follows the same course. The Lord declares: "O Israel, thou hast destroyed thyself." "Hear, O earth: behold, I will bring evil upon this people, even the fruit of their thoughts, because they have not hearkened unto My words, nor to My law, but rejected it." Hosea 13:9; Jeremiah 6:19.

65 / The Temple Cleansed Again

At the beginning of His ministry, Christ had driven from the temple those who defiled it by their unholy traffic. His stern and godlike demeanor had struck terror to the scheming traders.

At the close of His mission He came again to the temple and found it still desecrated as before—with the cries of animals, the sharp chinking of coin, and the sound of angry altercation. The dignitaries of the temple were themselves buying and selling. So completely were they controlled by greed of gain that in the sight of God they were no better than thieves.

At every Passover and Feast of Tabernacles, thousands of animals were slain, their blood caught by the priests and poured on the altar. The Jews had almost lost sight of the fact that sin made necessary all this shedding of blood. They did not discern that it prefigured the blood of God's dear Son, to be shed for the life of the world.

Jesus saw how the Jews had made these great convocations scenes of bloodshed and cruelty. They had multiplied the sacrifice of beasts, as if God could be honored by a heartless service. The priests and rulers had made the symbols pointing to the Lamb of God a means of getting gain. Thus the sacredness of the sacrificial service had been in a great measure destroyed. Jesus knew that His blood, so soon to be shed for the sins of the world, would be as little appreciated by the priests and elders as was the blood of beasts!

Against these practices Christ had spoken through

This chapter is based on Matthew 21:12-16, 23-46; Mark 11:15-19, 27-33; 12:1-12; Luke 19:45-48; 20:1-19.

the prophets. Isaiah, seeing in prophetic vision the apostasy of the Jews, addressed them: "What to Me is the multitude of your sacrifices? says the Lord; I have had enough of burnt offerings of rams and the fat of fed beasts; I do not delight in the blood of bulls, or of lambs, or of he-goats." "Wash yourselves; make yourselves clean; remove the evil of your doings from before My eyes." Isaiah 1:11, 16, RSV.

He who had Himself given these prophecies now for the last time repeated the warning. In fulfillment of prophecy the people had proclaimed Jesus king of Israel. He had received their homage and accepted the office of king. In this character He must act. He knew His efforts to reform a corrupt priesthood would be in vain; nevertheless, to an unbelieving people the evidence of His divine mission must be given.

Again the piercing look of Jesus swept over the desecrated court of the temple. All eyes were turned toward Him. Divinity flashed through humanity, investing Christ with a dignity and glory He had never manifested before. Those nearest Him drew as far away as the crowd would permit. Except for a few of His disciples, the Saviour stood alone. The deep silence seemed unbearable. Christ spoke with a power that swayed the people like a mighty tempest: "It is written, My house is the house of prayer; but ye have made it a den of thieves." His voice sounded like a trumpet through the temple. "Take these things hence." John 2:16.

Three years before, the rulers of the temple had been ashamed of their flight before the command of Jesus. They had felt it impossible for their undignified surrender to be repeated. Yet they were now more terrified than before, and in greater haste to obey His command. Priests and traders fled, driving their cattle before them.

On the way from the temple they were met by a throng who came with their sick inquiring for the Great Healer. The report given by the fleeing people caused some of these to turn back, but a large number pressed through the crowd, eager to reach Him. Again the temple court was filled by the sick and the dying, and once more Jesus ministered to them.

After a season the priests and rulers ventured back to the temple. They expected Jesus to take the throne of David. Upon entering the temple, they stood transfixed. They saw the sick healed, the blind restored to sight, the deaf receive their hearing, and the crippled leap for joy. Children were foremost in the rejoicing. Jesus had healed their maladies; He had clasped them in His arms. Now with glad voices the children sounded His praise. They repeated the hosannas of the day before and waved palm branches triumphantly before the Saviour.

The sound of these happy, unrestrained voices was an offense to the rulers of the temple. They represented to the people that the house of God was desecrated by the feet of the children and the shouts of rejoicing. The rulers appealed to Christ: "Hearest Thou what these say? And Jesus said to them, Yes, have ye never read, Out of the mouth of babes and sucklings Thou hast perfected praise?" Prophecy had foretold that Christ should be proclaimed as king, and God moved upon the children to be His witnesses. Had the voices of the children been silent, the very pillars of the temple would have sounded the Saviour's praise.

The Pharisees were utterly disconcerted. Never before had Jesus assumed such kingly authority. He had done marvelous works, but never before in a manner so solemn and impressive. Though enraged and confounded, the priests and rulers were unable to accomplish anything further that day. The next morning the Sanhedrin again considered what course to pursue toward Jesus. For three years the rulers had evidences of His Messiahship. They now decided to demand no sign of His authority, but to draw out some admission or declaration by which He might be condemned.

In the temple they proceeded to question Him: "By

what authority doest Thou these things? and who gave Thee this authority?'' Jesus met them with a question apparently pertaining to another subject, and He made His reply conditional on their answering this question: ''The baptism of John, whence was it? from heaven, or of men?''

The priests saw they were in a dilemma from which no sophistry could extricate them. If they said that John's baptism was from heaven, Christ would say, Why have ye not then believed on him? John had testified of Christ, ''Behold, the Lamb of God, which taketh away the sin of the world.'' John 1:29. If the priests believed John's testimony, how could they deny the Messiahship of Christ?

If they declared their real belief, that John's ministry was of men, they would bring on themselves a storm of indignation, for the people believed John to be a prophet. The multitude knew that the priests had professed to accept John, and they expected them to acknowledge that he was sent from God. But after conferring secretly together, the priests decided not to commit themselves. Hypocritically professing ignorance, they said, ''We cannot tell.'' ''Neither tell I you,'' said Christ, ''by what authority I do these things.''

Priests and Rulers Silenced

Baffled and disappointed, scribes, priests, and rulers all stood with lowering brows, not daring to press further questions on Christ. The people stood by, amused to see these proud, self-righteous men defeated.

All these sayings and doings of Christ were important, and their influence was to be felt in an ever-increasing degree after His crucifixion and ascension. Many were finally to become His disciples, first drawn by His words on that eventful day. The contrast between Jesus and the high priest as they talked together was marked. The proud dignitary of the temple was clothed in rich and costly garments. Upon his head was a glittering tiara, his bearing majestic, his hair and beard silvered by age. Before this august person stood the Majesty of heaven, without adornment or display, His garments travel-stained, His face pale, expressing a patient sadness. Yet written there were dignity and benevolence. Many who witnessed the words and deeds of Jesus in the temple from that time enshrined Him in their hearts as a prophet of God. But as the popular feeling turned in His favor, the hatred of the priests toward Jesus increased.

It was not Christ's purpose to humiliate His opponents. He had an important lesson to teach. The acknowledged ignorance of His enemies in regard to John's baptism gave Him opportunity to speak, presenting before them their real position, and adding another warning to the many already given:

"What think ye?" He said. "A certain man had two sons; and he came to the first, and said, Son, go work today in my vineyard. He answered and said, I will not: but afterward he repented, and went. And he came to the second, and said likewise. And he answered and said, I go, sir: and went not. Whither of them twain did the will of his father?"

This abrupt question threw His hearers off their guard. They immediately answered, "The first." Fixing His steady eye on them, Jesus responded in stern and solemn tones: "Verily I say unto you, that the publicans and the harlots go into the kingdom of God before you. For John came unto you in the way of righteousness, and ye believed him not: but the publicans and the harlots believed him: and ye, when ye had seen it, repented not afterward, that ye might believe him."

The priests and rulers could not but give a correct answer to Christ's question, and thus He obtained their opinion in favor of the first son, who represented the publicans. When John came, preaching repentance and baptism, the publicans received his message and were baptized.

The second son represented the leading men of the

Jewish nation who would not acknowledge that John came from God. They "rejected the counsel of God against themselves, being not baptized of him." Luke 7:30. Like the second son, the priests and rulers professed obedience, but acted disobedience.

The priests and rulers remained silent. But Christ said: "Hear another parable. There was a certain householder, which planted a vineyard, and hedged it round about, and digged a wine press in it, and built a tower, and let it out to husbandmen, and went into a far country: and when the time of the fruit drew near, he sent his servants to the husbandmen, that they might receive the fruits of it. And the husbandmen took his servants, and beat one, and killed another, and stoned another. Again, he sent other servants more than the first: and they did unto them likewise. But last of all he sent unto them his son, saying, They will reverence my son. But when the husbandmen saw the son, they said among themselves, This is the heir; come, let us kill him, and let us seize on his inheritance. And they caught him, and cast him out of the vineyard, and slew him. When the lord therefore of the vineyard cometh, what will he do unto those husbandmen?"

The priests and rulers answered, "He will miserably destroy those wicked men, and will let out his vineyard unto other husbandmen, which shall render him the fruits in their seasons." The speakers now saw that they had pronounced their own condemnation. As the husbandmen were to return to the lord a due proportion of the fruits of the vineyard, so God's people were to honor Him by a life corresponding to their sacred privileges. But as the husbandmen had killed the servants whom the master sent to them for fruit, so the Jews had put to death the prophets whom God sent to call them to repentance.

Thus far the application of the parable could not be questioned, and in what followed it was no less evident. In the beloved son whom the lord of the vineyard finally sent to his disobedient servants, and whom they seized and slew, the priests and rulers saw a distinct picture of Jesus and His impending fate. In the retribution inflicted on the ungrateful husbandmen was portrayed the doom of those who should put Christ to death.

The Strange Stone That Prefigured Christ

Looking with pity on them, the Saviour continued, "Did ye never read in the scriptures, The stone which the builders rejected, the same is become the head of the corner: this is the Lord's doing, and it is marvellous in our eyes? Therefore say I unto you, The kingdom of God shall be taken from you, and given to a nation bringing forth the fruits thereof. And whosoever shall fall on this stone shall be broken: but on whomsoever it shall fall, it will grind him to powder."

This prophecy the Jews had often repeated in the synagogues, applying it to the coming Messiah. Christ was the Cornerstone of the Jewish economy, and of the whole plan of salvation. This foundation stone the Jewish builders were now rejecting. By every means in His power the Saviour sought to make plain the nature of the deed they were about to do. His warnings, failing to arouse them to repentance, would seal their doom, and He designed to show them the justice of God in the withdrawal of their national privileges, which would end not only in the destruction of their temple and their city, but in the dispersion of the nation.

The hearers recognized the warning, but notwithstanding the sentence they themselves had pronounced, the priests and rulers were ready to fill out the picture by saying, "This is the heir; come, let us kill him." "But when they sought to lay hands on Him, they feared the multitudes," for the public sentiment was in Christ's favor.

In quoting the prophecy of the rejected stone, Christ referred to an actual incident connected with the building of the first temple. It had a special lesson at Christ's first advent, but it also has a lesson for us. When the temple of Solomon was erected, the immense stones were entirely prepared at the quarry. After they were brought to the place of building, the workmen had only to place them in position. For the foundation, one stone of unusual size and peculiar shape had been brought, but the workmen could find no place for it. It was an annoyance as it lay unused in their way. Long it remained a rejected stone.

But when the builders came to laying the corner, they searched for a long time to find a stone of sufficient size and strength, and of the proper shape, to bear the great weight which would rest on it. Should they make an unwise choice, the safety of the entire building would be endangered. Several stones had been chosen, but under the pressure of immense weights they had crumbled to pieces.

But at last attention was called to the stone so long rejected. It had been exposed to sun and storm without revealing the slightest crack. It had borne every test but one—the test of severe pressure. The trial was made. The stone was accepted, brought to its assigned position, and found to be an exact fit. This stone was a symbol of Christ. Isaiah says:

"He shall be for a sanctuary; but for a stone of stumbling and for a rock of offense to both the houses of Israel. . . . And many among them shall stumble, and fall, and be broken, and be snared, and be taken." Christ was to bear trials and tests of which the chief cornerstone in the temple of Solomon was symbolic. "Behold, I lay in Zion for a foundation a stone, a tried stone, a precious cornerstone, a sure foundation: he that believeth shall not make haste." Isaiah 8:14, 15; 28:16.

God chose the foundation stone and called it "a sure foundation." The entire world may lay upon it their burdens and griefs. With perfect safety they may build upon it. Those who trust in Him, He never disappoints. He has borne every test. He has borne the burdens cast upon Him by every repenting sinner. All who make Him their dependence rest in perfect security.

Christ is both "a sure foundation" and "a stone of stumbling." "Unto you therefore which believe He is precious: but unto them which be disobedient, the stone which the builders disallowed, the same is made the head of the corner, and a stone of stumbling, and a rock of offense, even to them which stumble at the word, being disobedient." 1 Peter 2:7, 8.

How to Be Built-up by Being Broken

To those who believe, Christ is the sure foundation. They fall on the Rock and are "broken." To fall on the Rock and be broken is to give up our self-righteousness, to go to Christ with the humility of a child, repenting of our transgressions, and believing in His forgiving love. So also by faith and obedience we build on Christ as our foundation.

Upon this living stone, Jews and Gentiles alike may build. It is broad enough for all, and strong enough to sustain the weight and burden of the whole world. By connection with Christ all who build on this foundation become living stones. See 1 Peter 2:5.

"To them which stumble at the word, being disobedient," Christ is a Rock of offense. Like the rejected stone, Christ had borne neglect and abuse. He was "despised and rejected of men; a man of sorrows, and acquainted with grief. . . . He was despised, and we esteemed Him not." Isaiah 53:3. But by the resurrection from the dead He would be declared the "Son of God with power." Romans 1:4. At His second coming He would be revealed as Lord of heaven and earth. Before the universe the rejected stone would become the head of the corner.

And on "whomsoever it shall fall, it will grind him to powder." The people who rejected Christ were soon to see their city and nation destroyed, their glory scattered as the dust before the wind. And what was it that destroyed the Jews? The rock which, had they built on it, would have been their security. It was the goodness of God despised, mercy slighted. Men set themselves in opposition to God, and all that would have been their salvation was turned to their destruction.

In the Jews' crucifixion of Christ was involved the destruction of Jerusalem. The blood shed on Calvary was the weight that sank them to ruin.

So in the great final day, when judgment shall fall on the rejecters of God's grace. Christ will then appear as an avenging mountain. The glory of His countenance, which to the righteous is life, will be to the wicked a consuming fire. Because of love rejected, grace despised, the sinner will be destroyed. The desecrated temple, the disobedient son, the false husbandmen, the contemptuous builders have their counterpart in the experience of every sinner. Unless he repents, the doom which they foreshadowed will be his.

66 / Christ Confounds His Enemies

The priests and rulers could not refute Christ's charges. But they were only the more determined to entrap Him. They sent spies, "who pretended to be sincere, that they might take hold of what He said, so as to deliver Him up to the authority and jurisdiction of the governor." RSV. These young men, ardent and zealous, were accompanied by Herodians who were to hear Christ's words, that they might testify against Him at His trial.

The Pharisees had ever chafed under the exaction of tribute by the Romans, holding that it was contrary to the law of God. Now the spies came to Jesus as though desiring to know their duty: "Master, we know that Thou sayest and teachest rightly, neither acceptest Thou the person of any, but teachest the way of God truly: is it lawful for us to give tribute unto Caesar, or no?"

Those who put the question to Jesus thought they had disguised their purpose, but Jesus read their hearts as an open book. "Why tempt ye Me?" He said, showing that He read their hidden purpose. They were still more confused when He added, "Show me a penny." They brought it, and He asked them, "Whose image and superscription hath it? They answered and said, Caesar's." Pointing to the coin, Jesus said, "Render therefore unto Caesar the things which are Caesar's; and unto God the things that are God's."

The spies felt baffled and defeated. The summary manner in which their question had been settled left

This chapter is based on Matthew 22:15-46; Mark 12:13-40; Luke 20:20-47.

them nothing further to say. Christ's reply was no evasion, but a candid answer to the question. Holding in His hand the Roman coin, He declared that since they were living under the protection of the Roman power, they should render to that power the support it claimed. But, while peaceably subject to the laws of the land, they should at all times give their first allegiance to God.

Had the Jews faithfully fulfilled their obligations to God, they would not have become subject to a foreign power. No Roman ensign would have waved over Jerusalem, no Roman governor would have ruled within her walls.

The Pharisees marveled at Christ's answer. He had not only rebuked their hypocrisy but had stated a great principle that clearly defines the limits of man's duty to the civil government and his duty to God. And although many went away dissatisfied, they saw that the principle underlying the question had been clearly set forth, and they marveled at Christ's far-seeing discernment.

No sooner were the Pharisees silenced than the Sadducees came forward with artful questions. As a class they were bigoted, yet among them were persons of genuine piety, who accepted Christ's teachings. The Sadducees professed to believe the greater portion of the Scriptures, but practically they were skeptics and materialists.

The Resurrection, a Subject of Controversy

Between the Pharisees and Sadducees the resurrection was especially a subject of controversy. The Pharisees had been firm believers in the resurrection, but their views in regard to the future state became confused. Death became an inexplicable mystery. The discussions between the two parties usually resulted in angry disputes.

The Sadducees had not so strong a hold on the common people, but many had the influence which wealth imparts. From among them the high priest was usually chosen. The fact that they were eligible to such office gave influence to their errors.

The Sadducees rejected the teaching of Jesus; His teaching in regard to the future life contradicted their theories. It was their belief that, having created man, God had left him to himself, independent of a higher influence. They held that he was free to control his own life and to shape the events of the world; his destiny was in his own hands.

Ideas of God Mold Character

Their ideas of God molded their own character. As in their view He had no interest in man, so they had little regard for one another. Refusing to acknowledge the influence of the Holy Spirit, they lacked His power in their lives. They boasted of their birthright as children of Abraham, but of the faith and benevolence of Abraham they were destitute. Their hearts were not touched by the wants and sufferings of others. They lived for themselves.

By His words and works, Christ testified to a divine power that produces supernatural results, to a future life, to God as a Father of the children of men, ever watchful of their true interests. He taught that God moves upon the heart by the Holy Spirit. He showed the error of trusting to human power for that transformation of character which can be wrought only by the Spirit of God.

In seeking a controversy with Jesus, the Sadducees felt confident of bringing Him into disrepute, if not condemnation. The resurrection was the subject on which they chose to question Him. Should He agree with them, He would give offense to the Pharisees. Should He differ with them, they designed to hold His teaching up to ridicule. The Sadducees reasoned that if the body is to be composed of the same particles of matter in its immortal as in its mortal state, then it must have flesh and blood and resume in the eternal world the life interrupted on earth. Husband and wife would be reunited, marriages consummated, and all things go on the same as before death.

In answer to their questions, Jesus lifted the veil from the future life. "In the resurrection," He said, "they neither marry, nor are given in marriage, but are as the angels of God in heaven." The Sadducees were wrong. "Ye do err," He added, "not knowing the Scriptures, nor the power of God." He did not charge them with hypocrisy, but with error of belief.

Their ignorance of the Scriptures and the power of God He declared to be the cause of their confusion of faith and darkness of mind. Christ called on them to open their minds to those sacred truths that would broaden the understanding. Thousands become infidels because they cannot comprehend the mysteries of God. The only key to the mysteries that surround us is to acknowledge in them the presence and power of God. Men need to recognize God as the Creator of the universe, One who commands and executes all things.

Christ declared to His hearers that if there were no resurrection of the dead, the Scriptures which they professed to believe would be of no avail. He said, "But as touching the resurrection of the dead, have ye not read that which was spoken unto you by God, saying, I am the God of Abraham, and the God of Isaac, and the God of Jacob? God is not the God of the dead, but of the living." God sees the result of His work as though it were now accomplished. The precious dead will hear the voice of the Son of God and come forth from the grave to immortal life. There will be a close and tender relationship between God and the risen saints. This condition He beholds as if it were already existing. The dead live unto Him.

The Sadducees were put to silence. Not a word had been spoken of which the least advantage could be taken for His condemnation.

The Pharisees, however, did not yet despair. They

prevailed on a certain learned scribe to question Jesus as to which of the ten precepts of the law was of the greatest importance. They had exalted the first four commandments, which point out the duty of man to his Maker, as of far greater consequence than the other six, which define man's duty to his fellowman. Jesus had been charged with exalting the last six commandments above the first four.

The lawyer approached Jesus with a direct question, "Which is the first commandment of all?" The answer of Christ was direct: "The first of all the commandments is . . . Thou shalt love the Lord thy God with all thy heart, and with all thy soul, and with all thy mind, and with all thy strength." The second is like the first, said Christ, for it flows out of it: "Thou shalt love thy neighbor as thyself. There is none other commandment greater than these." "On these two commandments hang all the law and the prophets."

Both these commandments are an expression of the principle of love. The first cannot be kept and the second broken, nor can the second be kept while the first is broken. Only as we love God supremely is it possible to love our neighbor impartially.

Christ taught His hearers that the law of God is a divine whole, not so many separate precepts, some of great importance, others of small importance. Love to God will be shown by obedience to all His commandments.

The scribe who had questioned Jesus was astonished. Before the assembled priests and rulers he honestly acknowledged that Christ had given the right interpretation to the law.

The scribe had some sense of the worthlessness of mere ceremonial offerings and the faithless shedding of blood for expiation of sin. Love and obedience to God, and unselfish regard for man, appeared to him of more value than all these rites. His decided and prompt response before the people manifested a spirit entirely different from that of the priests and rulers. The heart of Jesus went out in pity to the honest scribe who had dared to speak the convictions of his heart. "And when Jesus saw that he answered discreetly, He said unto him, Thou art not far from the kingdom of God."

The Pharisees had gathered close about Jesus as He answered the scribe. Now He put a question to them: "What think ye of Christ? whose son is He?" This question was designed to show whether they regarded Him simply as a man or as the Son of God. A chorus of voices answered, "The Son of David." When Jesus revealed His divinity by His mighty miracles, when He healed the sick and raised the dead, the people had inquired among themselves, "Is not this the Son of David?" But many who called Jesus the Son of David did not recognize His divinity. The Son of David was also the Son of God.

In reply, Jesus said, "How then doth David in spirit [the Spirit of Inspiration from God] call Him Lord, saying, The Lord said unto my Lord, Sit Thou on My right hand, till I make Thine enemies Thy footstool? If David then call Him Lord, how is He his son? And no man was able to answer Him a word, neither durst any man from that day forth ask Him any more questions."

67 / Jesus' Last Visit to the Temple

It was the last day of Christ's teaching in the temple. There stood the young Galilean, bearing no earthly honor or royal badge. Surrounding Him were priests in rich apparel, rulers with robes and badges, and scribes with scrolls in their hands, to which they made frequent reference. Jesus stood calmly, as one invested with the authority of heaven. He looked unflinchingly upon His adversaries who thirsted for His life. Their schemes to ensnare Him had been in vain. Challenge after challenge He had met, presenting pure, bright truth in contrast to the darkness and errors of the priests and Pharisees. The warning had been faithfully given. Yet another work remained for Christ to do.

The people were charmed with His teaching, but they were greatly perplexed. They had respected the priests and rabbis, yet they now saw these men trying to cast discredit on Jesus, whose virtue and knowledge shone brighter from every assault. They marveled that the rulers would not believe on Jesus, when His teachings were so plain and simple. They themselves knew not what course to take.

In the parables it was Christ's purpose to warn the rulers and instruct the people. But there was need to speak yet more plainly. Through their blind faith in a corrupt priesthood, the people were enslaved. These chains Christ must break. "The scribes and the Pharisees," He said, "sit in Moses' seat: all therefore whatsoever they bid you observe, that observe and do; but do not ye after their works: for they say, and do not."

This chapter is based on Matthew 23; Mark 12:41-44; Luke 20:45-47; 21:1-4.

The scribes and Pharisees assumed to take Moses' place as expounders of the law, but they did not practice their own teaching. And they taught much that was contrary to the Scriptures: "They bind heavy burdens and grievous to be borne, and lay them on men's shoulders; but they themselves will not move them with one of their fingers." Certain portions of the law they so explained as to impose upon the people observances which they themselves secretly ignored or from which they actually claimed exemption.

"They do all their deeds to be seen by men; for they make their phylacteries broad and their fringes long, and they love the place of honor at feasts and the best seats in the synagogues, and salutations in the market places, and being called rabbi by men. But you are not to be called rabbi, for you have one Teacher, and you are all brethren. And call no man your father on earth, for you have one Father, who is in heaven. Neither be called masters, for you have one Master, the Christ." RSV.

In such plain words the Saviour revealed the selfish ambition that was ever reaching for place and power, displaying a mock humility, while the heart was filled with avarice and envy. The Pharisees were ever scheming to secure the first attention and special favors. This practice Jesus rebuked.

He also reproved the vanity shown in coveting the title of rabbi, or master. Priests, scribes, and rulers were all brethren, children of one Father. The people were to give no man a title of honor indicating his control of their conscience or their faith.

If Christ were on earth today, surrounded by those who bear the title of "Reverend" or "Right Reverend," would He not repeat His saying, "Neither be called masters, for you have one Master, the Christ"? The Scripture declares of God, "Holy and reverend is His name." Psalm 111:9. How many who assume this title misrepresent the name and character of God. How often have worldly ambition and the basest sins been hidden under the broidered garments of a high and holy office!

The Saviour continued: "He that is greatest among you shall be your servant. And whosoever shall exalt himself shall be abased; and he that shall humble himself will be exalted." Again and again Christ had taught that true greatness is measured by moral worth. In the estimation of heaven, greatness of character consists in living for the welfare of our fellowmen. Christ the King of glory was a servant to fallen man.

"You shut the kingdom of heaven against men; for you neither enter yourselves, nor allow those who would enter to go in." RSV. By perverting the Scriptures, the priests and lawyers blinded the minds of those who would otherwise have received a knowledge of Christ's kingdom.

You "devour widows' houses, and for a pretense make long prayer: therefore ye shall receive the greater damnation." The Pharisees gained the confidence of pious widows, and then represented it as a duty for them to devote their property to religious purposes. Having secured control of their money, the wily schemers used it for their own benefit. To cover their dishonesty, they offered long prayers in public, and made a great show of piety. The same rebuke falls on many in our day. Their lives are stained by selfishness and avarice, yet they throw over it all a garment of seeming piety.

The Priceless Gift of the Poor Widow

Christ unsparingly condemned abuses, but He was careful not to lessen obligation. Man's abuse of the gift could not turn God's blessing from the giver.

Jesus was in the court and watched those who came to deposit their gifts. Many of the rich brought large sums with great ostentation. Jesus looked upon them sadly, but made no comment on their liberal offerings. Presently His countenance lighted as He saw a poor widow approach hesitatingly, as though fearful of being observed. She looked at the gift in her hand. It was very small in comparison with the gifts of those around her, yet it was her all. She hurriedly threw in her two mites ("copper coins," RSV) and turned to hasten away. But in doing this she caught the eye of Jesus fastened earnestly upon her.

The Saviour bade His disciples mark the widow's poverty. Then His words of commendation fell on her ear: "Of a truth I say unto you, that this poor widow hath cast in more than they all." Tears of joy filled her eyes as she felt that her act was appreciated. Many would have advised her to keep her pittance for her own use; it would be lost sight of among the many costly gifts brought to the treasury. But she believed the service of the temple to be of God's appointment, and she was anxious to do her utmost to sustain it. She did what she could, and her act was to be a monument to her memory through all time, and her joy in eternity.

She "hath cast in more than they all." The large donations of the rich had required no sacrifice, and could not be compared in value with the widow's mite.

Motive gives character to our acts, stamping them with ignominy or with high moral worth. Little duties cheerfully done, little gifts which make no show, often stand highest in God's sight. The poor widow deprived herself of food in order to give those two mites to the cause she loved. And she did it in faith, believing that her heavenly Father would not overlook her need. This unselfish spirit and childlike faith won the Saviour's commendation.

Many among the poor long to show their gratitude to God for His grace and truth. Let them lay up their mites in the bank of heaven. If given from a heart filled with love for God, these seeming trifles become priceless offerings which God smiles on and blesses.

When Jesus said of the widow, She "hath cast in more than they all," His words were true, not only of the motive, but of the results of her gift. The "two copper coins, which make a penny" (RSV) have brought to God's treasury an amount of money far greater than the contributions of those rich Jews. That little gift has been like a stream, widening and deepening through the ages. In a thousand ways it has contributed to the relief of the poor and the spread of the gospel. Her example of self-sacrifice has acted and reacted on thousands of hearts in every land and in every age. God's blessing upon the widow's mite has made it the source of great results. So with every gift bestowed with a sincere desire for God's glory. Its results for good no man can measure.

"Woe unto you, scribes and Pharisees, hypocrites! for ye pay tithe of mint and anise and cummin, and have omitted the weightier matters of the law, justice, mercy, and faith: these ought ye to have done, and not to leave the other undone." The obligation itself, Christ did not set aside. The tithing system was ordained by God, observed from earliest times. Abraham paid tithes of all that he possessed. As God gave it, the system was just and reasonable, but the priests and rabbis had made it a wearisome burden.

The Pharisees were very exact in tithing garden herbs, such as mint, anise, and rue; this cost little and gave them a reputation for exactness and sanctity. At the same time, the weightier matters of the law, justice, mercy, and truth were neglected. "These," Christ said, "ought ye to have done, and not to leave the other undone."

Other laws had been perverted by the rabbis in like manner. In the directions given through Moses, the use of swine's flesh and of certain other animals was prohibited, as likely to fill the blood with impurities and to shorten life. But the Pharisees went to unwarranted extremes. The people were required to strain all the water used, lest it should contain the smallest insect, which might be classed with the unclean animals. Contrasting these trivial exactions with the magnitude of actual sins, Jesus said to the Pharisees, "Ye blind guides, which strain at a gnat, and swallow a camel."

"You are like whitewashed tombs, which outwardly appear beautiful, but within they are full of dead men's bones and all uncleanness." RSV. The whited and beautifully decorated tomb concealed the putrefying remains within. So the outward holiness of the priests and rulers concealed iniquity.

Jesus continued: "You build the tombs of the prophets and adorn the monuments of the righteous, saying, 'If we had lived in the days of our fathers, we would not have taken part with them in shedding the blood of the prophets.' Thus you witness against yourselves, that you are sons of those who murdered the prophets." RSV.

A superstitious regard was cherished for the resting places of the dead, and vast sums of money were lavished on their decoration. In the sight of God this was idolatry. It showed that they did not love God supremely, nor their neighbor as themselves. Today many neglect the widow and the fatherless, the sick and the poor, in order to build expensive monuments for the dead. Duties to the living—duties which Christ has plainly enjoined—are left undone.

The Pharisees said one to another, If we had lived in the days of our fathers, we would not have united with them in shedding the blood of God's servants. At the same time they were planning to take the life of His Son. This should open our eyes to the power of Satan to deceive the mind that turns from the light of truth. Many wonder at the blindness of the Jews in rejecting Christ. Had we lived in His day, they declare, we would never have been partakers in the guilt of those who rejected the Saviour. But when obedience to God requires self-denial and humiliation, these very persons refuse obedience. They manifest the same spirit as did the Pharisees.

Little did the Jews realize the terrible responsibility involved in rejecting Christ. In every age prophets had lifted up their voices against the sins of kings, rulers, and people, obeying God's will at the peril of their lives. There had been heaping up a terrible punishment for the rejecters of light and truth. By their rejection of the Saviour, the priests and rulers were making themselves responsible for the blood of all the righteous slain from Abel to Christ. They were about to fill to overflowing their cup of iniquity. And soon it was to be poured on their heads in retributive justice. Of this, Jesus warned them:

"That upon you may come all the righteous blood shed upon the earth, from the blood of righteous Abel unto the blood of Zacharias son of Barachias, whom ye slew between the temple and the altar. Verily I say unto you, All these things shall come upon this generation."

The scribes and Pharisees knew how the prophet Zacharias had been slain. While words of warning from God were on his lips, a satanic fury seized the apostate king, and at his command the prophet was put to death. See 2 Chronicles 24:18-22. His blood had imprinted itself on the very stones of the temple court, and remained to bear testimony against apostate Israel. As long as the temple should stand, there would be the stain of that righteous blood, crying to God to be avenged. As Jesus referred to these fearful sins, a thrill of horror ran through the multitude.

Looking forward, Jesus declared that the impenitence of the Jews would be the same in the future as it had been in the past:

"Wherefore, behold, I send unto you prophets, and wise men, and scribes: and some of them ye shall kill and crucify; and some of them ye shall scourge in your synagogues, and persecute them from city to city."

With hand uplifted to heaven and a divine light enshrouding His person, Christ spoke as a judge, in rebuke and condemnation. The listeners shuddered. Never was the impression made by His words and His look to be effaced.

Christ's indignation was directed against the gross sins by which men were destroying their own souls, deceiving the people, and dishonoring God. But He spoke no words of retaliation. He manifested no irritated temper. Divine pity marked the countenance of the Son of God as He cast one lingering look on the temple and then on His hearers. In a voice choked by anguish and bitter tears He exclaimed, "O Jerusalem, Jerusalem, thou that killest the prophets, and stonest them which are sent unto thee, how often would I have gathered thy children together, even as a hen gathereth her chickens under her wings, and ye would not!" In the lamentation of Christ the very heart of God poured forth. It was the mysterious farewell of the long-suffering love of the Deity.

Pharisees and Sadducees were alike silenced. Jesus summoned His disciples and prepared to leave the temple, not as one defeated, but as one whose work was accomplished. He retired a victor from the contest.

On that eventful day, in many hearts new thoughts started into life, and a new history began. After the crucifixion and resurrection, these persons came to the front with wisdom and zeal. They bore a message that appealed to hearts. Before their testimony human theories and philosophies became as idle fables.

But Israel as a nation had divorced herself from God. Looking for the last time on the interior of the temple, Jesus said with mournful pathos, "Behold, your house is left unto you desolate. For I say unto you, ye shall not see Me henceforth, till ye shall say, Blessed is He that cometh in the name of the Lord." As the Son of God should pass out from those walls, God's presence would be withdrawn forever from the temple built to His glory. Its ceremonies would be meaningless, its services a mockery.

68 / When the Greeks Wished to "See Jesus"

"Among those who went up to worship at the feast were some Greeks. So these came to Philip, . . . and said to him, Sir, we wish to see Jesus. . . . Andrew went with Philip and they told Jesus." RSV.

At this time Christ's work bore the appearance of cruel defeat. He had been victor in the controversy with the priests and Pharisees, but it was evident that He would never be received by them as the Messiah. The final separation had come. The case seemed hopeless. But the great event which concerned the whole world was about to take place. When Christ heard the eager request, "We wish to see Jesus," echoing the hungering cry of the world, His countenance lighted up, and He said, "The hour is come, that the Son of man should be glorified."

These men came from the West to find the Saviour at the close of His life. The wise men had come from the East at the beginning. These Greeks represented the nations, tribes, and peoples of the world. People of all lands and all ages would be drawn by the Saviour's cross.

The Greeks longed to know the truth in regard to Christ's mission. When they said, "We wish to see Jesus," He was in that part of the temple from which all except Jews were excluded, but He went out to the Greeks in the outer court and had a personal interview with them.

The inquiry of the Greeks showed Christ that the

This chapter is based on John 12:20-43.

Jesus looked past the wealthy with their expensive gifts, commending instead a poor widow who gave her last coins and tried to slip away unnoticed.

sacrifice He was about to make would bring many sons and daughters to God. He knew that the Greeks would soon see Him in a position they did not then dream of. They would see Him placed beside Barabbas, a robber and a murderer. To the question, "What shall I do . . . with Jesus?" the answer would be given, "Let Him be crucified." Matthew 27:22. By making this propitiation for sin Christ knew that His kingdom would be perfected and would extend throughout the world. He would work as the Restorer, and His Spirit would prevail.

For a moment He heard voices proclaiming in all parts of the earth, "Behold, the Lamb of God, which taketh away the sin of the world." John 1:29. In these strangers He saw the pledge of a great harvest. The anticipation of this, the consummation of His hopes, was expressed in His words, "The hour is come, that the Son of man should be glorified." But the way in which this glorification must take place was never absent from Christ's mind. Only by His death could the world be saved. Like a grain of wheat, the Son of man must be cast into the ground and die, and be buried out of sight; but He was to live again.

"Verily, verily, I say unto you, Except a corn of wheat fall into the ground and die, it abideth alone: but if it die, it bringeth forth much fruit." When the grain of wheat falls into the ground and dies, it springs up, and bears fruit. So the death of Christ would result in fruit for the kingdom of God. In accordance with the law of the vegetable kingdom, life was to be the result of His death.

Year by year man preserves his supply of grain by apparently throwing away the choicest part. For a time it must be hidden under the furrow, to be watched over by the Lord. Then appears the blade, then the ear, and then the corn in the ear.

The seed buried in the ground produces fruit, and in turn this is planted. Thus the harvest is multiplied. So the death of Christ on the cross will bear fruit unto eternal life. Contemplation of this sacrifice will be the glory of those who, as the fruit of it, live through eternal ages.

Christ could, if He chose, save Himself from death. But should He do this, He must "abide alone." Only by falling into the ground to die could He become the seed of that vast harvest—the great multitude redeemed to God.

This lesson of self-sacrifice all should learn: "He that loveth his life shall lose it; and he that hateth his life in this world shall keep it unto life eternal." The life must be cast into the furrow of the world's need. Self-love, self-interest, must perish. And the law of self-sacrifice is the law of self-preservation. To give is to live. The life that will be preserved is the life freely given in service to God and man.

The life spent on self is like the grain that is eaten. There is no increase. A man may gather all he can; he may live, think, and plan for self; but his life passes away, and he has nothing. The law of self-serving is the law of self-destruction.

"If any man serve Me," said Jesus, "let him follow Me; and where I am, there shall also My servant be: if any man serve Me, him will My Father honor." All who have borne with Jesus the cross of sacrifice will be sharers with Him of His glory. They are workers together with Christ, and the Father will honor them as He honors His Son.

The message of the Greeks brought to the mind of Jesus the work of redemption from the time when in heaven the plan was laid, to the death now so near at hand. A mysterious cloud seemed to enshroud the Son of God. He sat rapt in thought. At last the silence was broken by His mournful voice, "Now is My soul troubled; and what shall I say? Father, save Me from this hour." Christ's humanity shrank from the hour of abandonment, when all would see Him stricken, smitten of God, and afflicted. He shrank from being treated as the worst of criminals, from a shameful, dishonored death. A sense of the awful burden of human transgression and the Father's wrath because of sin caused the spirit of Jesus to faint, and the pallor of death to overspread His countenance.

Voice of God Heard

Then came divine submission to His Father's will. "For this cause," He said, "came I unto this hour. Father, glorify Thy name." Only through the death of Christ could Satan's kingdom be overthrown, man be redeemed, and God be glorified. Jesus accepted the sacrifice; He consented to suffer as the Sin Bearer. A response came from the cloud which hovered above His head: "I have both glorified it, and will glorify it again." In the coming trial Christ's divine-human sufferings would indeed glorify His Father's name.

As the voice was heard, a light encircled Christ, as if the arms of Infinite Power were thrown about Him like a wall of fire. No one dared to speak. All stood with eyes fixed on Jesus. The testimony of the Father having been given, the cloud lifted, and scattered in the heavens.

The inquiring Greeks saw the cloud, heard the voice, comprehended its meaning, and discerned Christ indeed; to them He was revealed as the Sent of God. The voice of God had been heard at the baptism of Jesus and again at His transfiguration. Now it was heard for the third time by a larger number of persons. Jesus had just made His last appeal and pronounced the doom of the Jews. Now God again recognized the One whom Israel had rejected. "This voice came not because of Me," said Jesus, "but for your sakes." It was the signal from the Father that Jesus had spoken the truth, and was the Son of God.

"Now is the judgment of this world," Christ continued; "now shall the prince of this world be cast out. And I, if I be lifted up from the earth, will draw all men unto Me. This He said, signifying what death He should die." If I become the propitiation for the sins of men, the world will be lighted up. Satan's hold upon men will be broken. The defaced image of God will be restored in humanity, and a family of believing saints will finally inherit the heavenly home. The Saviour saw the cross, the cruel, ignominious cross, with all its attending horrors, blazing with glory.

But human redemption is not all that is accomplished by the cross. The love of God is manifested to the universe. The reproach Satan has cast on heaven is forever removed. Angels as well as men are drawn to the Redeemer. "I, if I be lifted up from the earth," He said, "will draw all men unto Me."

Many people were round about Christ as He spoke these words. But "though He had done so many miracles before them, yet they believed not on Him." Innumerable signs had been given, but they had closed their eyes and hardened their hearts. Now that the Father Himself had spoken, and they could ask for no further sign, they still refused to believe.

"Nevertheless among the chief rulers also many believed on Him; but because of the Pharisees they did not confess Him, lest they should be put out of the synagogue." To save themselves from reproach and shame, they denied Christ, and rejected the offer of eternal life.

Alas for those who knew not the time of their visitation! Slowly and regretfully Christ left forever the precincts of the temple.

69 / Signs of the Second Coming of Christ

Christ's words to the priests and rulers, "Behold, your house is left unto you desolate" (Matthew 23:38), had struck terror to their hearts. The question kept rising in their minds as to the import of these words. Could it be that the magnificent temple, the nation's glory, was soon to be a heap of ruins?

The foreboding of evil was shared by the disciples. As they passed with Him out of the temple, they called His attention to its strength and beauty. The stones of the temple were of the purest marble, some of almost fabulous size. A portion of the wall had withstood the siege by Nebuchadnezzar's army. In its perfect masonry it appeared like one solid stone dug entire from the quarry.

The view before Christ was indeed beautiful, but He said with sadness, I see it all. You point to these walls as apparently indestructible; but listen: The day will come when "there shall not be left one stone upon another, that shall not be thrown down."

When He was alone, Peter, John, James, and Andrew came to Him. "Tell us, when shall these things be? and what shall be the sign of Thy coming, and of the end of the world?" Matthew 24:3. Jesus did not answer by taking up separately the destruction of Jerusalem and the great day of His coming. He mingled the description of these two events. Had He opened to His disciples future events as He beheld them, they would have been unable to endure the sight. In mercy He blended the description of the two great crises, leaving

This chapter is based on Matthew 24; Mark 13; Luke 21:5-38.

421

the disciples to study out the meaning for themselves. When He referred to the destruction of Jerusalem, His prophetic words reached beyond that event to that day when the Lord shall rise out of His place to punish the world for their iniquity. This entire discourse was given, not for the disciples only, but for those who should live in the last scenes of this earth's history.

Christ said, "Take heed that no man deceive you. For many shall come in My name, saying, I am Christ; and shall deceive many." Many false messiahs will appear, declaring that the time of the deliverance of the Jewish nation has come. These will mislead many. Christ's words were fulfilled. Between His death and the siege of Jerusalem many false messiahs appeared. The same deceptions will be practiced again.

"And ye shall hear of wars and rumors of wars: see that ye be not troubled: for all these things must come to pass, but the end [of the Jewish nation as a nation] is not yet. For nation shall rise against nation, and kingdom against kingdom: and there will be famines, and pestilences, and earthquakes, in divers places. All these are the beginning of sorrows." The rabbis will declare that these signs are the token of the advent of the Messiah. Be not deceived; the signs that they represent as tokens of their release from bondage are signs of their destruction.

"Then shall they deliver you up to be afflicted, and shall kill you: and ye shall be hated of all nations for My name's sake. And then shall many be offended, and shall betray one another, and shall hate one another." All this the Christians suffered. Fathers and mothers betrayed their children, children their parents. Friends delivered friends up to the Sanhedrin. The persecutors killed Stephen, James, and other Christians.

Through His servants, God gave the Jewish people a last opportunity to repent. He manifested Himself through His witnesses in their arrest and trial, yet their judges pronounced on them the death sentence. By killing them, the Jews crucified afresh the Son of God.

So it will be again. The authorities will make laws to restrict religious liberty. They will think they can force the conscience, which God alone should control. This work they will continue till they reach a boundary over which they cannot step. God will interpose in behalf of His loyal, commandment-keeping people.

When persecution takes place, many stumble and fall, apostatizing from the faith they once advocated. Those who apostatize in time of trial will, to secure their own safety, bear false witness and betray their brethren. Christ has warned us of this, that we may not be surprised at the unnatural, cruel course of those who reject the light.

Christ told His disciples how to escape the ruin to come on Jerusalem: "When ye shall see Jerusalem compassed with armies, then know that the desolation thereof is nigh. Then let them which are in Judea flee to the mountains; and let them which are in the midst of it depart out; and let not them that are in the countries enter thereinto." This warning was given to be heeded forty years after, at the destruction of Jerusalem. The Christians obeyed the warning, and not one perished in the fall of the city.

"Pray ye that your flight be not in the winter, neither on the Sabbath day," Christ said. He who made the Sabbath did not abolish it. The Sabbath was not rendered null and void by His death. Forty years after His crucifixion it was still to be held sacred.

Dark Centuries of Persecution

From the destruction of Jerusalem, Christ passed on rapidly to the last link in the chain of this earth's history—the coming of the Son of God in majesty and glory. Between these two events, there lay open to Christ's view long centuries of darkness, centuries for His church marked with blood, tears, and agony. Jesus passed these scenes by with a brief mention. "Then shall be great tribulation," He said, "such as was not since the beginning of the world to this time, no, nor ever shall be. And except those days should be shortened, there should no flesh be saved: but for the elect's sake those days shall be shortened."

For more than a thousand years, persecution such as the world had never before known was to come upon Christ's followers. Millions of His faithful witnesses were to be slain. Had not God's hand been stretched out to preserve His people, all would have perished.

Now, in unmistakable language, our Lord speaks of His second coming: "If any man shall say unto you, Lo, here is Christ, or there; believe it not. For there shall arise false Christs, and false prophets, and shall show great signs and wonders; insomuch that, if it were possible, they shall deceive the very elect. . . . If they shall say unto you, Behold, He is in the desert; go not forth: behold, He is in the secret chambers; believe it not. For as the lightning cometh out of the east and shineth even unto the west; so shall also the coming of the Son of man be." From thousands of gatherings where men profess to hold communion with departed spirits is not the call now heard, "Behold, He is in the secret chambers"? This is the claim that spiritism puts forth. But what says Christ? "Believe it not."

Signs in the Heavens

The Saviour gives signs of His coming and fixes the time when the first of these signs shall appear: "Immediately after the tribulation of those days shall the sun be darkened, and the moon shall not give her light, and the stars shall fall from heaven, and the powers of the heavens shall be shaken: and then shall appear the sign of the Son of man in heaven: and then shall all the tribes of the earth mourn, and they shall see the Son of man coming in the clouds of heaven with power and great glory. And He shall send His angels with a great sound of a trumpet, and they shall gather together His elect from the four winds, from one end of heaven to the other."

At the close of the great papal persecution, Christ

declared, the sun should be darkened, and the moon should not give her light. Next, the stars should fall from heaven. And He says, "When ye shall see all these things, know that He is near, even at the doors." Matthew 24:33, margin. Christ says of those who see these signs, "This generation shall not pass, till all these things be fulfilled." These signs have appeared. Now we know of a surety that the Lord's coming is at hand.

Christ is coming with great glory. A multitude of shining angels will attend Him. He will come to raise the dead and to change the living saints; to honor those who have loved Him and kept His commandments, and to take them to Himself. When we look on our dead, we may think of the morning when "the dead shall be raised incorruptible, and we shall be changed." 1 Corinthians 15:52. The King will wipe all tears from our eyes, and present us "faultless before the presence of His glory with exceeding joy." Jude 24. "When these things begin to come to pass, then look up, and lift up your heads; for your redemption draweth nigh."

But Christ stated plainly that He Himself could not make known the day or the hour of His second appearing. The exact time of the second coming is God's mystery.

The Overwhelming Wickedness of the Last Days

Christ continues: "As the days of Noah were, so shall also the coming of the Son of man be. For as in the days that were before the Flood they were eating and drinking, marrying and giving in marriage, until the day that Noah entered into the ark, and knew not until the Flood came, and took them all away; so shall also the coming of the Son of man be."

How was it in Noah's day? "God saw that the wickedness of man was great in the earth, and that every imagination of the thoughts of his heart was only evil continually." Genesis 6:5. The inhabitants of the antediluvian world followed their own unholy imagination and perverted ideas. Because of their wickedness they were destroyed. Today the world is following the same way. The transgressors of God's law are filling the earth with wickedness. Their gambling, dissipation, lustful practices, and untamable passions are fast filling the world with violence.

Christ said, "Because iniquity shall abound, the love of many shall wax cold. But he that shall endure unto the end, the same shall be saved. And this gospel of the kingdom shall be preached in all the world for a witness unto all nations; and then shall the end come." Before the fall of Jerusalem, Paul declared that the gospel was preached to "every creature which is under heaven." Colossians 1:23. So now, the everlasting gospel is to be preached "to every nation, and kindred, and tongue, and people." Revelation 14:6. Christ does not say that all the world will be converted, but that "this gospel of the kingdom shall be preached in all the world for a witness unto all nations; and then shall the end come." By giving the gospel to the world it is in our power to hasten our Lord's return. We are not only to look for but to hasten the coming of the day of God. See 2 Peter 3:12. Had the church done her appointed work as the Lord ordained, the whole world would before this have been warned, and Jesus would have come.

Something to Live For!

Because we know not the exact time of His coming, we are commanded to watch. See Luke 12:37. Those who watch for the Lord's coming are not waiting in idle expectancy. They are purifying their souls by obedience to the truth. With vigilant watching they combine earnest working. Their zeal is quickened to cooperate with divine intelligences in working for the salvation of souls. They are declaring the truth that is now specially applicable. As Enoch, Noah, Abraham, and Moses each declared the truth for his time, so will Christ's servants now give the special warning for their generation.

But Christ brings to view another class: "If that evil servant shall say in his heart, My lord delayeth his coming; and shall begin to smite his fellow servants, and to eat and drink with the drunken; the lord of that servant shall come in a day when he looketh not for him."

The evil servant does not say that Christ will not come. But by his actions and words he declares that the Lord's coming is *delayed*. He banishes from the minds of others the conviction that the Lord is coming quickly. His influence confirms men in their worldliness and stupor. Earthly passions, corrupt thoughts take possession of the mind. The evil servant smites his fellow servants, accusing and condemning those who are faithful to their Master. He mingles with the world, and with the world he is taken in the snare. "The lord of that servant shall come . . . in an hour that he is not aware of, and shall cut him asunder, and appoint him his portion with the hypocrites."

The advent of Christ will surprise false teachers. Upon all who make this world their home, the day of God will come as a snare, as a prowling thief. Full of rioting, full of godless pleasure, the world is asleep in carnal security. Men laugh at warnings. "Tomorrow shall be as this day, and much more abundant." Isaiah 56:12. We will go deeper into pleasure loving. But Christ says, "I come as a thief." Revelation 16:15. When the scorner has become presumptuous, when the routine of money-making is carried on without regard to principle, when the student is eagerly seeking knowledge of everything but his Bible, Christ comes as a thief.

Everything in the world is in agitation. The signs of the times are ominous. The Spirit of God is withdrawing from the earth, and calamity follows calamity by sea and by land. There are tempests, earthquakes, fires, floods, murders of every grade. Who can read the future? Where is security? There is assurance in nothing that is human or earthly.

There are those who are waiting, watching, and working for our Lord's appearing. Another class are falling into line under the generalship of the first great apostate.

The crisis is stealing gradually upon us. The sun shines in the heavens, passing over its usual round. Men are still eating and drinking, planting and building. Merchants are still buying and selling. Men are contending for the highest place. Pleasure lovers are crowding to theaters, horse races, gambling hells. The highest excitement prevails, yet probation's hour is fast closing, and every case is about to be eternally decided. Satan has set all his agencies at work that men may be deceived, occupied, and entranced until the door of mercy is forever shut.

"Watch ye therefore, and pray always, that ye may be accounted worthy to escape all these things that shall come to pass, and to stand before the Son of man."

70 / Christ Identifies With the Poor and Suffering

"When the Son of man shall come, . . . then shall He sit upon the throne of His glory: and before Him shall be gathered all nations: and He shall separate them one from another." Thus Christ pictured the scene of the great judgment day. When the nations are gathered before Him, there will be but two classes, and their eternal destiny will be determined by what they have done or have neglected to do for Him in the person of the poor and suffering.

In that day Christ does not present before men the great work He has done for them in giving His life; He presents the faithful work they have done for Him. "Come, ye blessed of My Father, inherit the kingdom prepared for you from the foundation of the world: for I was an hungered, and ye gave Me meat: I was thirsty, and ye gave Me drink: I was a stranger, and ye took Me in: naked, and ye clothed Me: I was sick, and ye visited Me: I was in prison, and ye came unto Me." But those whom Christ commends know not that they have been ministering to Him. To their perplexed inquiries He answers, "Inasmuch as ye have done it unto one of the least of these My brethren, ye have done it unto Me."

In all who suffer for My name, said Jesus, you are to recognize Me. As you would minister to Me, so you are to minister to them. All who have been born into the heavenly family are in a special sense the brethren of our Lord. The love of Christ binds together the members of His family. "Everyone that loveth is born of God, and knoweth God." 1 John 4:7.

This chapter is based on Matthew 25:31-46.

Those whom Christ commends in the judgment may have known little of theology, but they have cherished His principles. Even among the heathen are those who have cherished the spirit of kindness. Before the words of life had fallen on their ears, they befriended missionaries, even at the peril of their own lives. Those who worship God ignorantly, those to whom the light is never brought by human instrumentality, will not perish. Though ignorant of the written law of God, they have done the things that the law required. Their works are evidence that the Holy Spirit has touched their hearts; and they are recognized as the children of God.

How surprised will be the lowly among the nations to hear from the lips of the Saviour, "Inasmuch as ye have done it unto one of the least of these My brethren, ye have done it unto Me"!

But not to any class is Christ's love restricted. He is the Son of man, and thus a brother to every son and daughter of Adam. His followers are not to feel detached from the perishing world around them. They are a part of the great web of humanity, brothers to sinners as well as to saints. The fallen and the sinful, Christ's love embraces; and every kindness done to uplift a fallen soul is accepted as done to Him.

Angels of heaven are sent forth to minister to those who shall be heirs of salvation. It is not yet made manifest who shall share the inheritance of the saints in light; but angels are passing throughout the earth seeking to comfort the sorrowing, protect the imperiled, and win men to Christ. Not one is passed by. God is no respecter of persons.

As you open your door to Christ's needy, suffering ones, you are welcoming unseen angels. They bring a sacred atmosphere of joy and peace. Every deed of mercy makes music in heaven. The Father from His throne numbers unselfish workers among His most precious treasures.

Those on the left hand of Christ, those who had neglected Him in the person of the poor and suffering were unconscious of their guilt. They had been self-absorbed, and cared not for others' needs.

To the rich, God has given wealth that they may relieve His suffering children, but too often they are indifferent to the wants of others. They do not understand the temptations and struggles of the poor, and mercy dies out of their hearts. The means that God has given to bless the needy is spent in pampering pride and selfishness. The poor are robbed of the education they should have concerning the tender mercies of God, for He has made ample provision that they should be comforted with the necessities of life. They feel the poverty that narrows life, and are often tempted to become envious and full of evil surmisings.

How to Ignore Christ

But Christ sees it all, and He says, It was I who was hungry and thirsty. It was I who was a stranger. While you were feasting at your bountifully spread table, I was famishing in the hovel. While you were at ease in your luxurious home, I had nowhere to lay My head. While you pursued your pleasures, I languished in prison. When you doled out the pittance of bread to the starving poor, when you gave those flimsy garments to shield them from the biting frost, did you remember that you were giving them to the Lord of glory? All the days of your life I was near you in the person of these afflicted ones, but you did not seek Me. You would not enter into fellowship with Me. I know you not.

Many visit the scenes of Christ's life on earth, to look on the lake beside which He loved to teach, and the hills and valleys on which His eyes rested. But we need not go to Nazareth or to Bethany in order to walk in the steps of Jesus. We shall find His footprints beside the sickbed, in hovels of poverty, in every place where there are human hearts in need of consolation.

All may find something to do. Millions of human souls bound in ignorance and sin have never so much as heard of Christ's love for them. Christ's rule of life, by which every one of us must stand or fall in the judgment, is, "Whatsoever ye would that men should do to you, do ye even so to them." Matthew 7:12.

The Saviour has given His life to establish a church capable of caring for tempted souls. Believers may be poor, uneducated, and unknown, yet in Christ they may do a work in the neighborhood and even in "the regions beyond" whose results shall be as far-reaching as eternity. Because this work is neglected, many young disciples never advance beyond the mere alphabet of Christian experience. The restless energy that is so often a source of danger might be directed into streams of blessing. Self would be forgotten in earnest work to do others good. Those who minister to others will not be longing for exciting amusements, or for some change in their lives. The great topic of interest will be how to save souls ready to perish.

To make us children of one family, the King of glory became one with us. "Love one another, as I have loved you." John 15:12. When we love the world as He has loved it, then for us His mission is accomplished. We are fitted for heaven, for we have heaven in our hearts. In the great judgment day, those who have not worked for Christ, who have drifted along thinking of themselves, will be placed by the Judge of the whole earth with those who did evil.

To every soul a trust is given. Of everyone the Chief Shepherd will demand, "Where is the flock that was given thee, thy beautiful flock?" Jeremiah 13:20.

71 / A Servant of Servants

Christ with His disciples had gathered to celebrate the Passover. The Saviour knew that His hour was come; He Himself was the true paschal lamb, and on the day the Passover was eaten He was to be sacrificed. A few quiet hours yet remained to Him to be spent for the benefit of His disciples.

The life of Christ had been one of unselfish service. "Not to be ministered unto, but to minister" (Matthew 20:28) had been the lesson of His every act. But not yet had the disciples learned the lesson. At this last Passover Jesus was troubled. A shadow rested upon His countenance. The disciples perceived that something weighed heavily on His mind.

As they were gathered about the table, He said, "With desire I have desired to eat this passover with you before I suffer: for I say unto you, I will not anymore eat thereof until it be fulfilled in the kingdom of God. And He took the cup, and gave thanks, and said, Take this, and divide it among yourselves: for I say unto you, I will not drink of the fruit of the vine, until the kingdom of God shall come."

Christ was now in the shadow of the cross, and the pain was torturing His heart. He knew He would be deserted; He knew that by the most humiliating process to which criminals were subjected He would be put to death. He knew the ingratitude and cruelty of those He had come to save. He knew that for many the sacrifice He must make would be in vain. Knowing all that was before Him, He might naturally have been

This chapter is based on Luke 22:7-18, 24; John 13:1-17.

overwhelmed with the thought of His own humiliation and suffering. But He did not think of Himself. His care for His disciples was uppermost in His mind.

On this last evening, Jesus had much to tell them. But He saw that they could not bear what He had to say. As He looked into their faces, the words were stayed on His lips. Moments passed in silence. The disciples were ill at ease. The glances they cast on each other told of jealousy and contention.

There was "a strife among them, which of them should be accounted the greatest." This contention grieved and wounded Jesus. Each still longed for the highest place in the kingdom. That James and John should presume to ask for the highest position so stirred the ten that alienation threatened. Judas was the most severe on James and John.

When the disciples entered the supper room, Judas pressed next to Christ on the left side; John was on the right. If there was a highest place, Judas was determined to have it.

Another cause of dissension had arisen. It was customary for a servant to wash the feet of the guests. On this occasion the pitcher, the basin, and the towel were in readiness; but no servant was present, and it was the disciples' part to perform it. But each determined not to act the part of a servant. All manifested a stoical unconcern. By their silence they refused to humble themselves.

How was Christ to bring these poor souls where Satan would not gain over them a decided victory? How could He show that a mere profession of discipleship did not make them disciples? How was He to kindle love in their hearts and enable them to comprehend what He longed to tell them?

Jesus waited for a time to see what they would do. Then He, the divine Teacher, rose from the table. Laying aside the outer garment that would have impeded His movements, He took a towel. In silence the disciples waited to see what was to follow. "After that He poureth water into a basin, and began to wash the disciples' feet, and to wipe them with the towel wherewith He was girded." This action opened the eyes of the disciples. Bitter shame filled their hearts, and they saw themselves in a new light.

Christ gave them an example they would never forget. His love for them was not easily disturbed. He had full consciousness of His divinity; but He had laid aside His royal crown, and had taken the form of a servant. One of the last acts of His life on earth was to gird Himself as a servant, and perform a servant's part.

Before the Passover Judas had closed the contract to deliver Jesus into the hands of the priests and scribes. The disciples knew nothing of the purpose of Judas. Jesus alone could read his secret, yet He did not expose him. He felt for him such a burden as for Jerusalem when He wept over the doomed city.

The constraining power of that love was felt by Judas. When the Saviour's hands were bathing those soiled feet and wiping them with the towel, the heart of Judas thrilled with the impulse to confess his sin. But he would not humble himself. He hardened his heart against repentance, and the old impulses again controlled him. Judas was now offended at Christ's act in washing the feet of His disciples. If Jesus could so humble Himself, he thought, He could not be Israel's king. He was satisfied that there was nothing to be gained by following Christ. He was confirmed in his purpose to disown Him and confess himself deceived. Possessed by a demon, he resolved to complete the work he had agreed to do in betraying his Lord.

The Great Miracle of Changed Hearts

Judas, in choosing his position at table, had tried to place himself first, and Christ as a Servant served him first. John was left till last. But John did not take this as a rebuke or slight. When Peter's turn came He exclaimed with astonishment, "Lord, dost thou wash my feet?" Christ's condescension broke his heart. He was filled with shame to think that one of the disciples was not performing this service. "What I do," Christ said, "thou knowest not now; but thou shalt know hereafter." Peter could not bear to see his Lord, the Son of God, acting the part of a servant. His whole soul rose up against this humiliation. With great emphasis he exclaimed, "Thou shalt never wash my feet."

Christ said, "If I wash thee not, thou hast no part with Me." Christ had come to wash the heart from the stain of sin. Peter was refusing the higher cleansing included in the lower. He was really rejecting his Lord. It is not humiliating to the Master to allow Him to work for our purification.

Peter surrendered his pride. Separation from Christ would have been death to him. "Not my feet only," he said, "but also my hands and my head. Jesus saith to him, He that is washed needeth not save to wash his feet, but is clean every whit."

These words mean more than bodily cleanliness. Christ is speaking of the higher cleansing as illustrated by the lower. He who came from the bath was clean, but the sandaled feet soon again needed to be washed. So Peter and his brethren had been washed in the great fountain opened for sin and uncleanness. But temptation had led them into evil, and they still needed Christ's cleansing grace.

Jesus desired to wash the alienation, jealousy, and pride from their hearts. This was of far more consequence than washing their dusty feet. With the spirit they had, not one was prepared for communion with Christ. Until brought into a state of humility and love, they were not prepared to share in the memorial service Christ was about to institute. Pride and self-seeking create dissension, but all this Jesus washed away in washing their feet. A change of feeling was brought about. Jesus could say, "Ye are clean." Now there was union of heart, love for one another. Except Judas, each was ready to concede to another the highest place. Now they could receive Christ's words.

We too have been washed in the blood of Christ, yet often the heart's purity is soiled. We must come to Christ for cleansing grace. How often we bring our sinful, polluted hearts in contact with the heart of Christ! How grievous to Him is our evil temper, our vanity, our pride! Yet all our infirmity and defilement we must bring to Him. He alone can wash us clean.

Why Christ Instituted This Religious Service

After Christ had washed the disciples' feet, He said: "Know ye what I have done to you? Ye call Me Master and Lord: and ye say well; for so I am. If I then, your Lord and Master, have washed your feet; ye also ought to wash one another's feet. For I have given you an example, that ye should do as I have done to you. Verily, verily, I say unto you, The servant is not greater than his lord; neither he that is sent greater than he that sent him."

That His people might not be misled by the selfishness which dwells in the natural heart, Christ Himself set the example of humility. He Himself, equal with God, acted as servant to His disciples. He to whom every knee shall bow, bowed down to wash the feet of those who called Him Lord. He washed the feet of His betrayer.

God does not live for Himself. He is constantly ministering for others. Jesus was given to stand at the head of humanity, that by His example He might teach what it means to minister. He served all, ministered to all. Thus He lived the law of God, and by His example showed how we are to obey it.

Having washed the disciples' feet, Jesus said, "I have given you an example, that ye should do as I have done to you." In these words Christ was instituting a religious service. By the act of our Lord this humiliating ceremony was made a consecrated ordinance. It was to be observed by the disciples, that they might ever keep in mind His lessons of humility and service.

This ordinance is Christ's appointed preparation for

the sacramental service. While pride, variance, and strife for supremacy are cherished, we are not prepared to receive the communion of His body and His blood. Therefore Jesus appointed the memorial of His humiliation to be first observed.

There is in man a disposition to esteem himself more highly than his brother, to work for self, to seek the highest place; and often this results in evil surmisings and bitterness. The ordinance preceding the Lord's Supper is to bring man out of his selfishness, down from self-exaltation, to the humility of heart that will lead him to serve his brother. The holy Watcher from heaven is present to make this season one of soul searching, conviction of sin, and the assurance of sins forgiven. Christ is there to change the current of thoughts that have been running in selfish channels.

As the Saviour's humiliation for us is remembered, a chain of memories is called up, memories of God's goodness and of the favor and tenderness of earthly friends. Blessings forgotten, kindnesses slighted are called to mind. Defects of character, neglect of duties, ingratitude, coldness are called to remembrance. The mind is energized to break down every barrier that has caused alienation. Sins are confessed; they are forgiven. The subduing grace of Christ draws hearts together. The desire is kindled for a higher spiritual life. The soul will be uplifted. We can partake of the Communion with the sunshine of Christ's righteousness filling the soul temple.

To those who receive the spirit of this service, it can never become merely ceremonial. Whenever this ordinance is rightly celebrated, the children of God covenant that the life shall be given to unselfish ministry for one another. The world is full of those who need our ministry. Those who have communed with Christ in the upper chamber will go forth to minister as He did.

"If you know these things, happy are ye if ye do them."

72 / The Lord's Supper Instituted

"The Lord Jesus the same night in which He was betrayed took bread: and when He had given thanks, He brake it, and said, Take, eat: this is My body, which is broken for you: this do in remembrance of Me. After the same manner also He took the cup, when He had supped, saying, This cup is the new testament in My blood: this do ye, as oft as ye drink it, in remembrance of Me. For as often as ye eat this bread, and drink this cup, ye do show the Lord's death till He come." 1 Corinthians 11:23-26.

Christ, the Lamb of God, was about to bring to an end the system of types and ceremonies that for 4000 years had pointed to His death. The Passover, the national festival of the Jews, was to pass away forever. The service which Christ established was to be observed by His followers in all lands and through all ages.

The Passover was ordained as a commemoration of the deliverance of Israel from Egyptian bondage. The Lord's Supper was given to commemorate the great deliverance wrought out as the result of the death of Christ. This ordinance is the means by which His great work for us is to be kept fresh in our minds.

In Christ's time, the people partook of the Passover supper in a reclining position. The guests lay on couches placed about the table, the right hand free for use in eating. In this position a guest could lay his head on the breast of the one who sat next above him. And the feet, at the outer edge of the couch, could be

This chapter is based on Matthew 26:20-29; Mark 14:17-25; Luke 22:14-23; John 13:18-30.

washed by one passing around the outside of the circle.

Christ was still at the table on which the paschal supper had been spread. The unleavened cakes were before Him. The Passover wine, untouched by fermentation, was on the table. These emblems Christ employed to represent His own unblemished sacrifice. See 1 Peter 1:19.

"And as they were eating, Jesus took bread, and blessed it, and brake it, and gave it to the disciples, and said, Take, eat; this is My body. And He took the cup, and gave thanks, and gave it to them, saying, Drink ye all of it; for this is My blood of the new testament, which is shed for many for the remission of sins. But I say unto you, I will not drink henceforth of this fruit of the vine, until that day when I drink it new with you in My Father's kingdom."

Judas the betrayer received from Jesus the emblems of His broken body and spilled blood. Sitting in the very presence of the Lamb of God, the betrayer brooded on his dark purposes, and cherished his revengeful thoughts.

At the feet washing, Christ had given convincing proof that He understood the character of Judas. "Ye are not all clean," He said. John 13:11. Now Christ spoke out more plainly: "I speak not of you all: I know whom I have chosen: but that the scripture may be fulfilled, He that eateth bread with Me hath lifted up his heel against Me."

Even now the disciples did not suspect Judas. But a cloud settled over them, a premonition of some dreadful calamity. As they ate in silence, Jesus said, "Verily, I say unto you, that one of you shall betray Me." Consternation seized them. How could any one of them deal treacherously with their divine Teacher? Betray Him? To whom? Surely not one of the favored Twelve!

As they remembered how true His sayings were, fear and self-distrust seized them. With painful emotion, one after another inquired, "Lord, is it I?" But

Judas sat silent. John at last inquired, "Lord, who is it?" And Jesus answered, "He that dippeth his hand with Me in the dish, the same shall betray Me." The silence of Judas drew all eyes to him. Amid the confusion of questions and astonishment, Judas had not heard the words of Jesus in answer to John's question. But now, to escape the scrutiny of the disciples, he asked as they had done, "Master, is it I?" Jesus solemnly replied, "Thou hast said."

In surprise and confusion at the exposure of his purpose, Judas rose hastily to leave the room. Then said Jesus, "That thou doest, do quickly. . . . He then having received the sop went immediately out: and it was night." Night it was as the traitor turned from Christ into outer darkness.

Until this step, Judas had not passed the possibility of repentance. But when he left his Lord and his fellow disciples, he had passed the boundary line. Nothing that could be done to save Judas had been left undone. After he had twice covenanted to betray his Lord, Jesus still gave him opportunity for repentance. By reading the secret purpose of the traitor's heart, Christ gave to Judas the final, convincing evidence of His divinity. This was the last call to repentance. From the sacramental supper Judas went out to complete the work of betrayal.

In pronouncing the woe on Judas, Christ also had a purpose of mercy toward His disciples. "I tell you before it come," He said, "that, when it is come to pass, ye may believe that I am." Had Jesus remained silent, the disciples might have thought that their Master had not divine foresight, and had been surprised. A year before, Jesus had told the disciples that He had chosen twelve, and that one was a devil. Now His words to Judas would strengthen the faith of Christ's true followers during His humiliation. When Judas should come to his dreadful end, they would remember the woe that Jesus had pronounced on the betrayer.

And the Saviour had still another purpose. The disciples had something to consider as to the patience and mercy of God toward the most grievously erring. The betrayer was privileged to unite with Christ in partaking of the sacrament. This example is for us. When we suppose one to be in error and sin, we are not to divorce ourselves from him, to leave him a prey to temptation, or drive him on Satan's battleground. It was because the disciples were erring and faulty that Christ washed their feet, and all but one were thus brought to repentance.

Christ's Example Forbids Exclusiveness

It is true that open sin excludes the guilty at the Lord's Supper. See 1 Corinthians 5:11. But beyond this none are to judge. Who can read the heart or distinguish tares from wheat? "Let a man examine himself, and so let him eat of that bread, and drink of that cup." "Whosoever shall eat this bread, and drink this cup of the Lord, unworthily, shall be guilty of the body and blood of the Lord." "He that eateth and drinketh unworthily, eateth and drinketh damnation to himself, not discerning the Lord's body." 1 Corinthians 11:28, 27, 29.

When believers assemble to celebrate the ordinances, there may be a Judas in the company; and if so, messengers from the prince of darkness are there, for they attend all who refuse to be controlled by the Holy Spirit. Heavenly angels also are present. There may come into the company persons who are not servants of truth and holiness, but who wish to take part in the service. They should not be forbidden. There are witnesses present who were present when Jesus washed the feet of the disciples.

Christ by the Holy Spirit is there to convict and soften the heart. Not a thought of contrition escapes His notice. For the repentant, brokenhearted one He is waiting. He who washed the feet of Judas longs to wash every heart from the stain of sin.

None should exclude themselves from Communion because some who are unworthy may be present. At these, His own appointments, Christ meets His people and energizes them by His presence. Hearts and hands that are unworthy may even administer the ordinance, yet all who come with their faith fixed on Christ will be greatly blessed. All who neglect these seasons will suffer loss. The administration of the Sacrament was to keep before the disciples the infinite sacrifice made for each of them individually as part of the great whole of fallen humanity.

The Reasons for Celebrating the Lord's Supper

But the Communion service was not to be a season of sorrowing. As the Lord's disciples gather about His table, they are not to lament their shortcomings. They are not to recall differences between them and their brethren. The preparatory service has embraced all this. Now they come to meet with Christ. They are not to stand in the shadow of the cross, but in its saving light. They are to open the soul to the bright beams of the Sun of Righteousness. They are to hear His words, "Peace I leave with you, My peace I give unto you: not as the world giveth, give I unto you." John 14:27.

Our Lord says, When oppressed and afflicted for My sake and the gospel's, remember My love, so great that for you I gave My life. When your duties appear severe, your burdens too heavy to bear, remember that for your sake I endured the cross, despising the shame. Your Redeemer liveth to make intercession for you.

The Communion service points to Christ's second coming. It was designed to keep this hope vivid in the mind. "As often as ye eat this bread, and drink this cup, ye do show the Lord's death till He come." 1 Corinthians 11:26.

Christ instituted this service that it may speak to our senses of the love of God. There can be no union between our souls and God except through Christ. And nothing less than the death of Christ could make His love efficacious for us. Only because of His death can we look with joy to His second coming. Our senses

need to be quickened to lay hold of the mystery of godliness, to comprehend, far more than we do, the expia-
tory sufferings of Christ.

Our Lord has said, "Except ye eat the flesh of the
Son of man, and drink His blood, ye have no life in
you. . . . For My flesh is meat indeed, and My blood is
drink indeed." John 6:53-55. To the death of Christ we
owe even this earthly life. The bread we eat is the purchase of His broken body; the water we drink, of His
spilled blood. Never one, saint or sinner, eats his daily
food, but he is nourished by the body and blood of
Christ. The cross of Calvary is stamped on every loaf;
it is reflected in every water spring. The light shining
from that Communion service makes sacred the provisions for our daily life. The family board becomes as
the table of the Lord, and every meal a sacrament.

Of our spiritual nature Jesus declares, "Whoso eateth
My flesh, and drinketh My blood, hath eternal life." By
receiving His word, by doing those things which He has
commanded, we become one with Him. "He that eateth
My flesh," He says, "and drinketh My blood, dwelleth
in Me, and I in him. As the living Father hath sent Me,
and I live by the Father: so he that eateth Me, even he
shall live by Me." John 6:56, 57. As faith contemplates
our Lord's great sacrifice, the soul assimilates the spiritual life of Christ. Every Communion service forms a
living connection by which the believer is bound up
with Christ, and thus with the Father.

As we receive the bread and wine symbolizing
Christ's broken body and spilled blood, we in imagination witness the struggle by which our reconciliation
with God was obtained. Christ is set forth crucified
among us. The thought of Calvary awakens living and
sacred emotions in our hearts. Pride and self-worship
cannot flourish in the soul that keeps fresh in memory
the scenes of Calvary. He who beholds the Saviour's
matchless love will be transformed in character. He
will go forth to be a light to the world, to reflect in some
degree this mysterious love.

73 / "Let Not Your Heart Be Troubled"

Judas had left the upper chamber, and Christ was alone with the eleven. He was about to speak of His approaching separation from them; but before this He pointed to the great object of His mission. He kept ever before Him His joy that all His humiliation and suffering would glorify the Father's name. To this He first directed the thoughts of His disciples.

Their Master and Lord, their beloved Teacher and Friend, was dearer to them than life. Now He was to leave them. Dark were the forebodings that filled their hearts.

But the Saviour's words were full of hope. He knew that Satan's craft is most successful against those who are depressed by difficulties. Therefore He turned their thoughts to the heavenly home: "Let not your heart be troubled. . . . In My Father's house are many mansions: if it were not so, I would have told you. I go to prepare a place for you. And if I go and prepare a place for you, I will come again, and receive you unto Myself; that where I am, there ye may be also." When I go away, I shall still work earnestly for you. I go to the Father to cooperate with Him in your behalf.

Christ's departure was the opposite of what the disciples feared—it did not mean a final separation. He was going to prepare a place for them, that He might receive them to Himself. While He was building mansions for them, they were to build characters after the divine similitude.

This chapter is based on John 13:31-38; 14-17.

Thomas, troubled by doubts, said, "Lord, we know not whither Thou goest; and how can we know the way? Jesus saith unto him, I am the way, the truth, and the life: no man cometh unto the Father, but by Me. If ye had known Me, ye should have known My Father also: and from henceforth ye know Him, and have seen Him."

There are not many ways to heaven. Each may not choose his own way. Christ was the way by which patriarchs and prophets were saved. He is the way by which alone we can have access to God.

But not yet did the disciples understand. "Lord, show us the Father, and it sufficeth us," exclaimed Philip. Christ asked with pained surprise, "Have I been so long time with you, and yet hast thou not known Me, Philip?" Is it possible that you do not see the Father in the works He does through Me? "How sayest thou, Show us the Father?" "He that hath seen Me hath seen the Father." Christ had not ceased to be God when He became man; the Godhead was still His own. Christ's work testified to His divinity. Through Him the Father had been revealed.

If the disciples believed this vital connection between the Father and the Son, their faith would not forsake them when they saw Christ's suffering and death. How perseveringly our Saviour sought to prepare His disciples for the storm of temptation soon to beat upon them. All present felt a sacred awe as they listened with rapt attention to His words. And as their hearts were drawn to Christ in greater love, they were drawn to one another. They felt that heaven was very near.

The Saviour was anxious for His disciples to understand why His divinity was united to humanity. He came to the world to display the glory of God, that man might be uplifted by its restoring power. Jesus revealed no qualities, and exercised no powers, that men may not have through faith in Him. His perfect humanity is that which all His followers may possess, if they will be in subjection to God as He was.

"Greater works than these shall he do; because I go unto My Father." By this Christ meant that the disciples' work would have greater extent under the working of the Holy Spirit. After the Lord's ascension, the disciples realized the fulfillment of His promise. They knew that the divine Teacher was all that He had claimed to be. As they exalted the love of God, men's hearts were subdued, and multitudes believed on Jesus.

The Wonderful Privilege of Prayer

The Saviour explained that the secret of their success would be in asking for strength and grace in His name. The prayer of the humble suppliant He presents before the Father as His own desire in that soul's behalf. Sincere prayer may not be fluently expressed, but it will ascend to the sanctuary where Jesus ministers. He will present it to the Father without one awkward, stammering word, fragrant with the incense of His own perfection.

The path of sincerity and integrity is not free from obstruction, but in every difficulty we are to see a call to prayer. "Whatsoever ye shall ask in My name," said Jesus, "that will I do, that the Father may be glorified in the Son. If ye shall ask anything in My name, I will do it."

In Christ's name His followers are to stand before God. Because of the imputed righteousness of Christ they are accounted precious. The Lord does not see in them the vileness of the sinner. He recognizes in them the likeness of His Son, in whom they believe.

The Lord is disappointed when His people place a low estimate on themselves. God wanted them, else He would not have sent His Son on such an expensive errand to redeem them. He is well pleased when they make the very highest demands on Him, that they may glorify His name. They may expect large things if they have faith in His promises.

But to pray in Christ's name means that we are to

accept His character, manifest His spirit, and work His works. The Saviour saves men, not in sin, but from sin; and those who love Him show their love by obedience.

All true obedience comes from the heart. It was heart work with Christ. And if we consent, He will so blend our hearts and minds into conformity to His will, that when obeying Him we shall be but carrying out our own impulses. When we know God as it is our privilege to know Him, our life will be a life of continual obedience. Through communion with God, sin will become hateful to us.

As Christ lived the law in humanity, so we may do if we will take hold of the Strong for strength. But we cannot depend for counsel on humanity. The Lord will teach us our duty just as willingly as He will teach somebody else. If we come to Him in faith, He will speak His mysteries to us personally. Those who decide to do nothing in any line that will displease God, will know, after presenting their case before Him, just what course to pursue. And they will receive not only wisdom, but strength. Power for obedience, for service, will be imparted to them, as Christ has promised.

How the Holy Spirit Makes Christ's Work for Us Effective

Before offering Himself as the sacrificial victim Christ sought for the most essential gift to bestow on His followers. "I will pray the Father," He said, "and He shall give you another Comforter, that He may abide with you forever; even the Spirit of truth; whom the world cannot receive, because it seeth Him not, neither knoweth Him: but ye know Him; for He dwelleth with you, and shall be in you. I will not leave you orphans: I will come to you." John 14:16-18, margin. While Christ was on earth, the disciples had desired no other helper. Not until deprived of His presence would they feel their need of the Spirit, and then He would come.

The Holy Spirit is Christ's representative, but divested of the personality of humanity, and independent

Looking to the future, Jesus saw His disciples persecuted for their faith, and He promised that through the Spirit He would be with them in every trial. That promise is still ours today.

thereof. Cumbered with humanity, Christ could not be in every place personally. It was for their interest that He should go, and send the Spirit to be His successor on earth. No one could then have any advantage because of his location. By the Spirit the Saviour would be accessible to all.

Jesus read the future of His disciples. He saw one brought to the scaffold, one to the cross, one to exile among the lonely rocks of the sea, others to persecution and death. But in every trial He would be with them. When for the truth's sake the believer stands at the bar of unrighteous tribunals, Christ stands by his side. The reproaches that fall on him, fall on Christ. When one is incarcerated in prison walls, Christ ravishes the heart with His love.

At all times and in all places, when we feel helpless and alone, the Comforter will be sent in answer to the prayer of faith. Circumstances may separate us from every earthly friend, but no circumstance can separate us from the heavenly Comforter. He is always at our right hand to sustain and cheer.

The disciples still failed to understand Christ's words, and again He explained: By the Spirit He would manifest Himself to them. "The Comforter, which is the Holy Ghost, whom the Father will send in My name, He shall teach you all things." No more will you say, I cannot comprehend.

Through the disciples Christ was to speak to all the people on the face of the earth. But in the death of Christ they were to suffer great disappointment. That after this experience their word might be accurate, Jesus promised that the Comforter should "bring all things to your remembrance, whatsoever I have said unto you." "When He, the Spirit of truth is come, He will guide you into all truth: for He shall not speak of Himself; but whatsoever He shall hear, that shall He speak: and He will show you things to come. He shall glorify Me: for He shall receive of Mine, and shall show it unto you."

Jesus' disciples had been educated to accept the teaching of the rabbis as the voice of God, and it still held a power over their minds. They did not understand the spiritual nature of Christ's kingdom. Many of His lessons seemed almost lost on them. Jesus promised that the Holy Spirit should recall these sayings to their minds.

The Comforter is called "the Spirit of truth." His work is to define and maintain truth. He first dwells in the heart as the Spirit of truth, and thus He becomes the Comforter. There is comfort in truth, but no real comfort in falsehood. Through false traditions Satan gains his power over the mind. False standards misshape the character. The Holy Spirit exposes error and expels it from the soul. By the Spirit of truth, working through the Word of God, Christ subdues His chosen people to Himself.

The Chief Purpose of the Spirit

Jesus sought to inspire His disciples with the joy and hope that inspired His own heart. He rejoiced because the Holy Spirit was the highest of all gifts He could solicit from His Father for His people. The Spirit was to be given as a regenerating agent, and without this the sacrifice of Christ would have been of no avail. The power of evil had been strengthening for centuries, and the submission of men to satanic captivity was amazing. Sin could be resisted and overcome only through the mighty agency of the Third Person of the Godhead, who would come in the fullness of divine power. The Spirit makes effectual what has been wrought out by the world's Redeemer. By the Spirit the heart is made pure. Christ has given His Spirit to overcome all hereditary and cultivated tendencies to evil, and to impress His own character on His church. The very image of God is to be reproduced in humanity. The honor of God, the honor of Christ, is involved in the perfection of the character of His people.

"When He [the Spirit of truth] is come, He will reprove the world of sin, and of righteousness, and of judgment." The preaching of the Word will be of no avail without the presence of the Holy Spirit. Only when truth is accompanied to the heart by the Spirit will it quicken the conscience or transform the life. Unless the Holy Spirit sets home the truth, no souls will fall on the Rock and be broken. No amount of education, no advantages, however great, can make one a channel of light without the cooperation of the Spirit of God.

Christ has promised the gift of the Holy Spirit to His church, and the promise belongs to us as much as to the first disciples. But like every other promise, it is given on conditions. Many who profess to claim the Lord's promise talk *about* Christ and *about* the Holy Spirit, yet receive no benefit. They do not surrender the soul to be guided by the divine agencies. We cannot use the Holy Spirit. The Spirit is to use us. But many want to manage themselves. Only to those who wait humbly upon God is the Spirit given. This promised blessing, claimed by faith, brings all other blessings in its train.

Before leaving the upper chamber, the Saviour led His disciples in a song of praise. His voice was heard, not in the strains of some mournful lament, but in the joyful notes of the Passover hallel:

O praise the Lord, all ye nations:
Praise Him, all ye people.
For His merciful kindness is great toward us:
And the truth of the Lord endureth forever.
Praise ye the Lord.
Psalm 117

After the hymn they made their way out of the city gate toward the Mount of Olives. Slowly they proceeded, each busy with his own thoughts. As they began to descend toward the mount, Jesus said, "All ye shall be offended because of Me this night: for it is written, I will smite the shepherd, and the sheep of the flock will be scattered abroad." Matthew 26:31. In the upper chamber Jesus said that one of the twelve would betray Him and that Peter would deny Him. But now His words included them all.

Peter's Buried Sin

Now Peter's voice was heard, protesting, "Although all shall be offended, yet will not I." Jesus had warned him that he would that very night deny his Saviour. Now He repeated the warning: "Verily I say unto thee, that this day, even in this night, before the cock crow twice, thou shalt deny Me thrice." But Peter only "spake the more vehemently, If I should die with Thee, I will not deny Thee in any wise. Likewise also said they all." Mark 14:29-31.

When Peter said he would follow his Lord to prison and to death, he meant every word of it, but he did not know himself. Hidden in his heart were elements of evil that circumstances would fan into life. Unless he was made conscious of his danger, these would prove his eternal ruin. The Saviour saw in him a self-love that would overbear even his love for Christ. Peter needed to distrust himself and to have a deeper faith in Christ. When on the Sea of Galilee he was about to sink, he cried, "Lord, save me." So now if he had cried, Save me from myself, he would have been kept. But Peter thought it cruel that he was distrusted, and he became more persistent in his self-confidence.

Jesus could not save His disciples from the trial, but He did not leave them comfortless. Before the denial, they had the assurance of forgiveness. After His death and resurrection, they knew they were forgiven and were dear to the heart of Christ.

Jesus and the disciples were on the way to Gethsemane, at the foot of Mount Olivet. The moon was shining brightly and revealed to Him a flourishing grapevine. Drawing the attention of His disciples to it, Jesus said, "I am the true vine." The vine with its clinging tendrils represents Himself. The palm tree, the cedar, and the oak stand alone; they require no support. But the vine entwines about the trellis, and thus climbs heavenward. So Christ in His humanity was dependent upon divine power. "I can of Mine own self do nothing." John 5:30.

"I am the true vine, and My Father is the husbandman." On the hills of Palestine our heavenly Father had planted this goodly Vine. Many were attracted by the beauty of this Vine, and declared its heavenly origin. But the leaders in Israel trampled the plant under their unholy feet. After men thought they had killed it, the heavenly Husbandman took it and replanted it on the other side of the wall. The vine stock was to be no longer visible. It was hidden from the rude assaults of men. But the branches of the Vine hung over the wall, and through them grafts might still be united to the Vine.

The connection of the branch with the vine, Jesus said, represents the relation His followers are to sustain to Him. The scion is engrafted into the living vine, and fiber by fiber, vein by vein, it grows into the vine stock. So the soul receives life through connection with Christ. The sinner unites His weakness to Christ's strength, his emptiness to Christ's fullness. Then he has the mind of Christ. The humanity of Christ has touched our humanity, and our humanity has touched divinity.

This union must be maintained. Christ said, "Abide in Me, and I in you. As the branch cannot bear fruit of itself, except it abide in the vine; no more can ye, except ye abide in Me." This is no off-and-on connection. The branch becomes a part of the living vine. The life you have received from Me, said Jesus, can be preserved only by continual communion. Without Me you cannot overcome sin or resist temptation. We are to cling to Jesus and receive from Him by faith the perfection of His own character.

The root sends its nourishment through the branch to the outermost twig. "He that abideth in Me," said

Jesus, "and I in him, the same bringeth forth much fruit: for without Me ye can do nothing." When we live by faith on the Son of God, the fruits of the Spirit will be seen in our lives; not one will be missing.

"My Father is the husbandman. Every branch in Me that beareth not fruit He taketh away." There may be an apparent connection with Christ without a real union with Him by faith. A profession of religion places men in the church, but the character shows whether they are in connection with Christ. If they bear no fruit, they are false branches. "If a man abide not in Me," said Christ, "he is cast forth as a branch, and is withered; and men gather them, and cast them into the fire, and they are burned."

"And every branch that beareth fruit, He purgeth [pruneth] it, that it may bring forth more fruit." From the Twelve who had followed Jesus, one as a withered branch was about to be taken away; the rest were to pass under the pruning knife of bitter trial. The pruning will cause pain, but it is the Father who applies the knife. He works with no wanton hand. Excessive foliage that draws away the life current from the fruit must be pruned off. Overgrowth must be cut out to give room for the healing beams of the Sun of Righteousness. The husbandman prunes away the harmful growth, that the fruit may be more abundant.

"Herein is My Father glorified," said Jesus, "that ye bear much fruit." God desires to manifest through you the holiness, benevolence, and compassion of His own character. Yet the Saviour does not bid the disciples labor to bear fruit. He tells them to abide in Him. Through the Word Christ abides in His followers. The life of Christ in you produces the same fruits as in Him. Living in Christ, adhering to Christ, supported by Christ, drawing nourishment from Christ, you bear fruit after the similitude of Christ.

Jesus' very first injunction when alone with His disciples in the upper chamber was, "A new commandment I give unto you, That ye love one another; as I have loved you, that ye also love one another." To the disciples this commandment was new, for they had not loved one another as Christ had loved them. But through His life and death they were to receive a new conception of love. The command to love one another had a new meaning in the light of His self-sacrifice.

When men are bound together, not by force or self-interest, but by love, they show the working of an influence that is above every human influence. It is evidence that the image of God is being restored in humanity. This love, manifested in the church, will surely stir the wrath of Satan. "If the world hate you," He said, "ye know that it hated Me before it hated you. If ye were of the world, the world would love his own: but because ye are not of the world, but I have chosen you out of the world, therefore the world hateth you. Remember the word that I said unto you, The servant is not greater than his lord. If they have persecuted Me, they will also persecute you; if they have kept My saying, they will keep yours also. But all these things will they do unto you for My name's sake, because they know not Him that sent Me." The gospel is to be carried forward in the midst of opposition, peril, loss, and suffering.

As the world's Redeemer, Christ was constantly confronted with apparent failure. He seemed to do little of the work He longed to do. Satanic influences were constantly working to oppose His way. But He would not be discouraged. Through Isaiah He declares, "I have labored in vain, I have spent My strength for nought, and in vain: yet surely My judgment is with the Lord, and My work with My God." Isaiah 49:4.

Upon this word Jesus rested, and He gave Satan no advantage. When the deepest sorrow was closing about His soul, He said to His disciples, "The prince of this world cometh, and hath nothing in Me." "The prince of this world is judged." Now shall he be cast out. John 14:30; 16:11; 12:31.

Christ knew that when He should exclaim, "It is finished," all heaven would triumph. His ear caught the distant music and the shouts of victory in the heavenly courts. He knew that the name of Christ would be heralded from world to world throughout the universe. He knew that truth, armed with the Holy Spirit, would conquer in the contest with evil. He knew that the life of His trusting disciples would be like His, a series of uninterrupted victories, not seen to be such here, but recognized as such in the great hereafter.

Christ did not fail, neither was He discouraged, and His followers are to manifest a faith of the same enduring nature. They are to live as He lived and work as He worked. Instead of deploring difficulties, they are to surmount them, to despair of nothing.

Christ designs that heaven's order and divine harmony shall be represented in His church and on earth. Thus through His people He may receive a large revenue of glory. The church, endowed with the righteousness of Christ, is His depositary, in which the riches of His grace and love are to appear in full display. Christ looks on His people in their purity and perfection as the reward of His humiliation and the supplement of His glory.

With strong, hopeful words the Saviour ended His instruction. He had finished the work given Him to do. He had manifested the Father's name and gathered out those who were to continue His work among men.

As a consecrated high priest Christ interceded for His people: "Holy Father, keep through Thine own name those whom Thou hast given Me, that they may be one, even as We are." "Neither pray I for these alone, but for them also which shall believe on Me through their word; that they all may be one; . . . that the world may know that Thou hast sent Me, and hast loved them, as Thou hast loved Me."

Christ gave His elect church into the Father's arms. For Him there waited the last battle with Satan, and He went forth to meet it.

74 / The Awesome Struggle in Gethsemane

With His disciples the Saviour made His way to the garden of Gethsemane. The Passover moon shone from a cloudless sky. As He neared Gethsemane, He became strangely silent. Throughout His life on earth He had walked in the light of God's presence. But now He was numbered with the transgressors. The guilt of fallen humanity He must bear. So great was its weight that He was tempted to fear it would shut Him out forever from His Father's love. He exclaimed, "My soul is exceeding sorrowful, even unto death."

Never before had the disciples seen their Master so utterly sad. His form swayed as if He were about to fall. On reaching the garden, the disciples looked anxiously for His usual place of retirement, that their Master might rest. Twice His companions supported Him, or He would have fallen.

Near the entrance, Jesus left all but three of the disciples, bidding them pray for themselves and for Him. With Peter, James, and John, He entered its secluded recesses. In His great struggle, Christ desired their presence near Him. Often they had passed the night with Him in this retreat. After a season of prayer, they would sleep undisturbed until He awoke them in the morning to go forth anew to labor. Now He desired them to spend the night with Him in prayer, yet could not bear that even they should witness the agony He was to endure.

"Tarry ye here," Jesus said, "and watch with Me."

This chapter is based on Matthew 26:36-56; Mark 14:32-50; Luke 22:39-53; John 18:1-12.

He went a little distance—not so far but that they could both see and hear Him—and fell prostrate on the ground. He felt that by sin He was being separated from His Father. The gulf was so broad, so black, so deep, that His spirit shuddered before it. This agony He must not exert His divine power to escape. As man He must suffer the consequences of man's sin. As man He must endure the wrath of God against transgression.

The Terrible Temptation

Christ was now standing in a different attitude from that in which He had ever stood before. As the substitute for man, Christ was suffering under divine justice. Hitherto He had been an intercessor for others; now He longed to have an intercessor for Himself.

As Christ felt His unity with the Father broken up, He feared that in His human nature He would be unable to endure the conflict. The tempter had come for the last fearful struggle; if he failed here, the kingdoms of the world would finally become Christ's, and he himself would be overthrown. But if Christ could be overcome, the earth would become Satan's kingdom, and the human race would be forever in his power.

Satan told Christ that if He became the surety for a sinful world, He would be identified with Satan's kingdom and nevermore be one with God. And what was to be gained by this sacrifice? Satan pressed the situation on the Redeemer: The people who claim to be above all others in spiritual advantages are seeking to destroy You. One of Your own disciples will betray You. One of Your most zealous followers will deny You. All will forsake You. That those whom He loved so much should unite in the plots of Satan, pierced Christ's soul. The conflict was terrible. The sins of men weighed heavily on Christ, and the sense of God's wrath against sin was crushing out His life.

In His agony He clung to the cold ground, as if to prevent Himself from being drawn farther from God.

From His pale lips came the bitter cry, "O My Father, if it be possible, let this cup pass from Me." Yet even now He added, "Nevertheless not as I will, but as Thou wilt."

Jesus Hungered for Human Sympathy

The human heart longs for sympathy in suffering. This longing Christ felt to the very depths of His being. He came to His disciples yearning to hear some words of comfort. He longed to know that they were praying for Him and for themselves. How dark seemed the malignity of sin! Terrible was the temptation to let the human race bear its own guilt, while He stood innocent before God. If He could only know that His disciples appreciated this, He would be strengthened.

But He "findeth them asleep." Had He found them seeking refuge in God, that satanic agencies might not prevail over them, He would have been comforted. But they had not heeded the warning, "Watch and pray." They had not intended to forsake their Lord, but they seemed paralyzed by a stupor which they might have shaken off if they had continued pleading with God. When the Saviour was most in need of their prayers, they were asleep.

The disciples awakened at the voice of Jesus, but they hardly knew Him, His face was so changed by anguish. Addressing Peter, Jesus said, "Simon, sleepest thou? couldest thou not watch one hour? Watch ye and pray, lest ye enter into temptation. The spirit truly is ready, but the flesh is weak." Jesus feared they would not be able to endure the test of His betrayal and death.

Again the Son of God was seized with superhuman agony, and, fainting and exhausted, He staggered back to the place of His former struggle. His suffering was even greater than before. "His sweat was as it were great drops of bood falling down to the ground." The cypress and palm trees were the silent witnesses of His anguish. From their leafy branches dropped heavy dew on His stricken form, as if nature wept over its Author wrestling alone with the powers of darkness.

A short time before, Jesus had stood like a mighty cedar, withstanding the storm of opposition that spent its fury on Him. Now He was like a reed beaten and bent by the angry storm. As one already glorified, He had claimed oneness with God. Now His voice was heard on the still evening air, full of human anguish, "O My Father, if this cup may not pass away from Me, except I drink it, Thy will be done."

Again Jesus felt a longing for some words from His disciples which would break the spell of darkness that well-nigh overpowered Him. But their eyes were heavy; "neither wist they what to answer Him." They saw His face marked with the bloody sweat of agony, but His anguish of mind they could not understand. "His visage was so marred more than any man, and His form more than the sons of men." Isaiah 52:14.

When the World's Fate Trembled in the Balance

Turning away, Jesus sought again His retreat, and fell prostrate. The humanity of the Son of God trembled in that trying hour. The awful moment to decide the destiny of the world had come. The fate of humanity trembled in the balance. Christ might even now refuse to drink the cup apportioned to guilty man. He might wipe the bloody sweat from His brow and leave man to perish in his iniquity. He might say, Let the transgressor receive the penalty of his sin, and I will go back to My Father. Will the innocent suffer the consequences of the curse of sin, to save the guilty? "O My Father, if this cup may not pass away from Me, except I drink it, Thy will be done."

Three times has He shrunk from the last, crowning sacrifice. But now He sees that the human race is helpless. He sees the power of sin. The woes of a doomed world rise before Him. He beholds its impending fate, and His decision is made. He will save man at any cost to Himself. He has left the courts of heaven to save the one world that has fallen by transgression. And He will not turn from His mission.

Having made the decision, He fell dying to the ground. Where now were His disciples, to place their hands beneath the head of their fainting Master? The Saviour trod the winepress alone, and of the people there was none with Him. See Isaiah 63:3.

But God suffered with His Son. Angels beheld the Saviour's agony. There was silence in heaven. No harp was touched. The angelic host in silent grief watched the Father separating His beams of light, love, and glory from His beloved Son.

Satan and his confederacy of evil watched intently. What answer would come to Christ's thrice-repeated prayer? In this awful crisis, when the mysterious cup trembled in the hand of the sufferer, the mighty angel who stands in God's presence came to the side of Christ. The angel came not to take the cup from Christ's hand, but to strengthen Him with the assurance of His Father's love. He assured Him that His death would result in the utter discomfiture of Satan, and that the kingdom of this world would be given to the saints of the Most High. He told Him that He would see a multitude of the human race saved, eternally saved.

How Christ's Prayer Was Answered

Christ's agony did not cease, but His depression and discouragement left Him. The storm had not abated, but He was strengthened to meet its fury. A heavenly peace rested on His bloodstained face. He had borne that which no human being could ever bear; for He had tasted the sufferings of death for every man.

The sleeping disciples, suddenly awakened, saw the angel. They heard his voice speaking words of comfort and hope to the Saviour. Now they had no further fear for their Master; He was under the care of God. Again the disciples yielded to the strange stupor that overpowered them, and again Jesus found them sleeping.

Looking sorrowfully on them Jesus said, "Sleep on now, and take your rest: behold, the hour is at hand, and the Son of man is betrayed into the hands of sinners." Even as He spoke, He heard the footsteps of the mob in search of Him, and said, "Rise, let us be going: behold, he is at hand that doth betray Me."

No traces of His recent agony were visible as Jesus stepped forth to meet His betrayer. "Whom seek ye?"

They answered, "Jesus of Nazareth."

Jesus replied, "I am He." As these words were spoken, the angel who had ministered to Jesus moved between Him and the mob. A divine light illuminated the Saviour's face. In the presence of this divine glory, the murderous throng staggered back. Even Judas fell to the ground.

The angel withdrew, and the light faded away. Jesus had opportunity to escape, but He remained in the midst of that hardened band, now prostrate and helpless at His feet.

But quickly the scene changed. The Roman soldiers, the priests, and Judas gathered about Christ, fearful that He would escape. They had had evidence that He who stood before them was the Son of God, but they would not be convinced. To the question, "Whom seek ye?" again they answered, "Jesus of Nazareth." The Saviour then said, "I have told you that I am He; if therefore ye seek Me, let these go their way"—pointing to the disciples. For them He was ready to sacrifice Himself.

Judas the betrayer did not forget the part he was to act. To the pursuers of Jesus he had given a sign, saying, "Whomsoever I shall kiss, that same is He: hold Him fast." Now, coming close to Jesus, he took His hand as a familiar friend. With the words, "Hail, Master," he kissed Him repeatedly, and appeared to weep as if in sympathy with Him in His peril.

Jesus said, "Friend, wherefore art thou come?" His voice trembling with sorrow, He added, "Judas, betrayest thou the Son of man with a kiss?" This appeal should have aroused the conscience of the betrayer, but honor and human tenderness had forsaken him. He had given himself up to Satan and had no power to resist him. Jesus did not refuse the traitor's kiss.

The mob now laid hold of Jesus, and proceeded to bind those hands that had ever been employed in doing good.

The disciples were disappointed and indignant as they saw the cords brought forward to bind the hands of Him whom they loved. Peter in anger drew his sword and cut off an ear of the high priest's servant. When Jesus saw what was done, He released His hands, though held firmly by the Roman soldiers, and saying, "Suffer ye thus far," He touched the wounded ear, and it was instantly made whole.

He then said to Peter, "Put up again thy sword into his place: for all they that take the sword shall perish with the sword. Thinkest thou that I cannot now pray to My Father, and He shall presently give Me more than twelve legions of angels?"—a legion in place of each disciple. Oh, why, the disciples thought, does He not save Himself and us? Answering their unspoken thought, He added, "But how then shall the scriptures be fulfilled, that thus it must be?" "The cup which My Father hath given Me, shall I not drink it?"

The wily priests and elders had joined the temple police and rabble in following Judas to Gethsemane. What a company for those dignitaries to unite with—a mob armed with all kinds of implements, as if in pursuit of a wild beast!

Turning to the priests and elders, Christ spoke words they would never forget: You come out against Me with swords and staves as you would against a thief or a robber. Day by day I sat teaching in the temple. You had every opportunity of laying hands on Me, and you did nothing. The night is better suited to your work. "This is your hour, and the power of darkness."

The disciples were terrified as they saw Jesus permit

Himself to be taken and bound. They were offended that He should suffer this humiliation to Himself and them. They could not understand His conduct, and they blamed Him for submitting. In their indignation and fear, Peter proposed that they save themselves. Following this suggestion, "they all forsook Him, and fled."

75 / The Illegal Trial of Jesus

Through the hushed streets of the sleeping city they hurried Jesus. It was past midnight. Bound and closely guarded, the Saviour moved painfully to the palace of Annas, the ex-high priest. Annas was the head of the officiating priestly family, and in deference to his age he was recognized by the people as high priest. His counsel was sought as the voice of God. He must be present at the examination of the prisoner, for fear that the less-experienced Caiaphas might fail of securing the object for which they were working. His cunning and subtlety must be used, for Christ's condemnation must be secured.

Christ was to be tried formally before the Sanhedrin, but before Annas in a preliminary trial. Under Roman rule the Sanhedrin could only examine a prisoner and pass judgment, to be ratified by the Roman authorities. It was therefore necessary to bring against Christ charges regarded as criminal by the Romans and also in the eyes of the Jews. Not a few priests and rulers had been convicted by Christ's teaching. Joseph of Arimathea and Nicodemus were not now to be summoned, but others might dare to speak in favor of justice. The trial must unite the Sanhedrin against Christ. Two charges the priests desired to maintain. If Jesus could be proved a blasphemer, He would be condemned by the Jews. If convicted of sedition, it would secure His condemnation by the Romans.

The second charge Annas tried first to establish. He questioned Jesus, hoping the prisoner would say some-

This chapter is based on Matthew 26:57-75; 27:1; Mark 14:53-72; 15:1; Luke 22:54-71; John 18:13-27.

thing to prove that He was seeking to establish a secret society, with the purpose of setting up a new kingdom. Then the priests could deliver Him to the Romans as a creator of insurrection.

As if reading the inmost soul of His questioner, Christ denied that He gathered His followers secretly and in the darkness to conceal His designs. "I spake openly to the world," He answered. "I ever taught in the synagogue, and in the temple, whither the Jews always resort; and in secret have I said nothing."

The Saviour contrasted His manner of work with the methods of His accusers. They had hunted Him, to bring Him before a secret tribunal, where they might obtain by perjury what it was impossible to gain by fair means. The midnight seizure by a mob, the mockery and abuse before He was even accused, was their manner of work, not His. Their action was in violation of the law. Their own rules declared that every man should be treated as innocent until proved guilty.

Turning upon His questioner, Jesus said, "Why askest thou Me?" Had not spies been present at every gathering of the people and carried to the priests information of all His sayings and doings? "Ask them which heard Me, what I have said unto them; behold, they know what I said."

Annas was silenced. One of his officers, filled with wrath, struck Jesus on the face, saying, "Answerest Thou the high priest so?" Christ calmly replied, "If I have spoken evil, bear witness of the evil: but if well, why smitest thou Me?" His calm answer came from a heart sinless, patient, and gentle, that would not be provoked.

At the hands of the beings for whom He was making an infinite sacrifice, Christ received every indignity. And He suffered in proportion to His holiness and hatred of sin. His trial by men who acted as fiends was to Him a perpetual sacrifice. To be surrounded by human beings under the control of Satan was revolting. And He knew that by flashing forth His divine power, He could lay His cruel tormentors in the dust. This made the trial harder to bear.

The Jews expected a Messiah, by one flash of overmastering will, to change the current of men's thoughts and force an acknowledgment of His supremacy. Thus when Christ was treated with contempt, there came to Him a strong temptation to manifest His divine character, to compel His persecutors to confess that He was Lord above kings and rulers, priests and temple. It was difficult to keep the position He had chosen as one with humanity.

Angels Would Gladly Have Delivered Christ

The angels of heaven longed to deliver Christ. How easily could they, beholding the shameful scene, have consumed the adversaries of God! But they were commanded not to. It was part of His mission to bear in His humanity all the abuse that men could heap upon Him.

Christ had said nothing that could give His accusers an advantage, yet He was bound, to signify that He was condemned. There must, however, be the form of a legal trial. This the authorities were determined to hasten. They knew the regard in which Jesus was held by the people, and feared a rescue would be attempted. Again, if the execution were not brought about at once, there would be a week's delay on account of the Passover. This might defeat their plans. Should there be a week's delay, a reaction would likely set in. The better part of the people would come forward with testimony in His vindication, bringing to light the mighty works He had done. The Sanhedrin's proceedings would be condemned, and Jesus would be set free. The priests and rulers therefore determined that before their purpose could become known, Jesus should be delivered into the hands of the Romans.

But first, an accusation was to be found. They had gained nothing as yet. Annas ordered Jesus to be taken to Caiaphas. Though wanting in force of character, Caiaphas was fully as heartless and unscrupulous as

Annas. It was now early morning, and dark. By torches and lanterns the armed band with their prisoner proceeded to the high priest's palace. While the Sanhedrin were coming together, Annas and Caiaphas again questioned Jesus, but without success.

In the judgment hall Caiaphas took his seat as presiding officer. On either side were the judges and those specially interested in the trial. Roman soldiers were on the platform below the throne. At the foot of the throne stood Jesus. The excitement was intense. Of all the throng He alone was calm and serene.

Caiaphas had regarded Jesus as his rival. The eagerness of the people to hear the Saviour had aroused the bitter jealousy of the high priest. But as Caiaphas now looked upon the prisoner, he was struck with admiration for His noble, dignified bearing. A conviction came over him that this man was akin to God. The next instant he banished the thought, in haughty tones demanding that Jesus work one of His mighty miracles. But his words fell on the Saviour's ears as though He heard them not. In the minds of that hardened multitude arose the question, Is this man of godlike presence to be condemned as a criminal?

The enemies of Jesus were in perplexity. How to accomplish His condemnation they knew not. Caiaphas wished to avoid stirring up a contention. There were plenty of witnesses to prove that Christ had called the priests and scribes hypocrites and murderers, but this was not expedient to bring forward. Such testimony would have no weight with the Romans. There was abundant evidence that Jesus had spoken irreverently of many of the ordinances of the Jews. This evidence also would have no weight with the Romans. Christ's enemies dared not accuse Him of Sabbathbreaking, lest an examination bring to light His miracles of healing.

False witnesses had been bribed to accuse Jesus of seeking to establish a separate government. But their testimony proved to be vague and contradictory. Under examination they falsified their own statements.

Early in His ministry Christ had said, "Destroy this temple, and in three days I will raise it up." He had thus foretold His own death and resurrection. "He spake of the temple of His body." John 2:19, 21. Of all that Christ had said, the priests could find nothing to use against Him save this. The Romans had engaged in rebuilding and embellishing the temple, and they took great pride in it; any contempt shown it would excite their indignation. Here Romans and Jews could meet; for all held the temple in great veneration.

One witness who had been bribed to accuse Jesus, declared, "This fellow said, I am able to destroy the temple of God, and to build it in three days." If Christ's words had been reported exactly as He spoke them, they would not have secured His condemnation even by the Sanhedrin. His declaration would only have indicated an unreasonable, boastful spirit, but not blasphemy. Even as misrepresented by false witnesses, His words contained nothing regarded by the Romans as a crime worthy of death.

At last Jesus' accusers were entangled, confused, and maddened. It seemed that their plottings were to fail. Caiaphas was desperate. One last resort remained: Christ must be forced to condemn Himself. The high priest started from the judgment seat, his face contorted with passion: "Answerest Thou nothing?" he exclaimed; "what is it which these witness against Thee?"

Jesus held His peace. "He was oppressed, and He was afflicted, yet He opened not His mouth: He is brought as a lamb to the slaughter, and as a sheep before her shearers is dumb, so He openeth not His mouth." Isaiah 53:7.

At last, Caiaphas addressed Jesus in the form of a solemn oath: "I adjure Thee by the living God, that Thou tell us whether Thou be the Christ, the Son of God."

To this appeal Christ could not remain silent. He

knew that to answer now would make His death certain. But the appeal was made by the highest acknowledged authority of the nation, and in the name of the Most High. He must plainly declare His character and mission. Jesus had said to His disciples, "Whosoever therefore shall confess Me before men, him will I confess also before My Father which is in heaven." Matthew 10:32. Now by His own example He repeated the lesson.

Every eye was fixed on Jesus' face as He answered, "Thou hast said." A heavenly light seemed to illuminate His pale countenance as He addcd, "Nevertheless I say unto you, Hereafter shall ye see the Son of man sitting on the right hand of power, and coming in the clouds of heaven." For a moment the high priest quailed before the penetrating eyes of the Saviour. Never in afterlife did he forget that searching glance of the persecuted Son of God.

Caiaphas Almost Convinced

The thought that all would stand at the bar of God, to be rewarded according to their works, was a thought of terror to Caiaphas. There rushed before his mind the scenes of the final judgment. For a moment he saw the graves giving up their dead, with the secrets he had hoped were forever hidden. He felt as if the eternal Judge was reading his soul, bringing to light mysteries supposed to be hidden with the dead.

Caiaphas had denied the resurrection, the judgment, and a future life. Now he was maddened by satanic fury. Rending his robe, he demanded that the prisoner be condemned for blasphemy. "What further need have we of witnesses?" he said; "behold, now ye have heard His blasphemy. What think ye?" And they all condemned Him.

Caiaphas was furious with himself for believing Christ's words, and instead of rending his heart and confessing that Jesus was the Messiah, he rent his priestly robes in determined resistance. This act was deeply significant. Done to secure Christ's condemnation, the high priest had condemned himself. By the law of God he was disqualified for the priesthood. He had pronounced on himself the death sentence.

A high priest was not to rend his garments. By the Levitical law, under no circumstances was the priest to rend his robe. Express command had been given by Christ to Moses concerning this. See Leviticus 10:6. Finite man might rend his own heart by showing a contrite and humble spirit. But no rent must be made in the priestly robes, for this would mar the representation of heavenly things. The high priest who dared to engage in the service of the sanctuary with a rent robe was looked on as having severed himself from God. This action exhibited by Caiaphas showed human passion, human imperfection.

By rending his garments, Caiaphas made of no effect the law of God, to follow the traditions of men. A manmade law provided that in case of blasphemy a priest might rend his garments in horror at the sin, and be guiltless. Thus the law of God was made void by the laws of men. But in this act, he himself was committing blasphemy.

When Caiaphas rent his garment, his act was significant of the place the Jewish nation would thereafter occupy toward God. The Jewish people had rejected Him who was the antitype of all their types, the substance of all their shadows. Israel was divorced from God. Well might the high priest rend his robes in horror for himself and for the nation.

The Injustice of Christ's Trial

The Sanhedrin had pronounced Jesus worthy of death, but it was contrary to Jewish law to try a prisoner by night. In legal condemnation nothing could be done except in the light of day and before a full session of the council. Notwithstanding this, the Saviour was now treated as a condemned criminal, to be abused by the lowest of humankind. Through the open court Jesus was taken to the guardroom, on every side meeting with mockery of His claim to be the Son of God. His own words, "coming in the clouds of heaven," were jeeringly repeated. While in the guardroom awaiting His legal trial, Jesus was not protected, and the ignorant rabble took license to manifest all the satanic elements of their nature. Christ's godlike bearing goaded them to madness. Mercy and justice were trampled upon. Never was a criminal treated in so inhuman a manner as was the Son of God.

But the blow that inflicted the deepest pain no enemy's hand could have dealt. While He was undergoing the examination before Caiaphas, Christ had been denied by one of His own disciples.

Peter and John had ventured to follow at a distance the mob that had Jesus in charge. The priests recognized John and admitted him to the hall, hoping that as he witnessed the humiliation of his Leader, he would scorn the idea of such a one being the Son of God. John spoke in favor of Peter, and gained an entrance for him also.

In the court a fire had been kindled, for it was cold, being just before dawn. A company drew about the fire, and Peter presumptuously took his place with them. By mingling with the crowd, he hoped to be taken for one of those who had brought Jesus to the hall.

Peter Fails

But the woman who kept the door cast a searching glance on him. She marked the dejection on his face, and thought he might be a disciple of Jesus. Curious to know, she asked, "Art not thou also one of His disciples?" Peter was startled and confused; he pretended not to understand. But she was persistent. Peter felt compelled to answer, and said angrily, "Woman, I know Him not." This was the first denial, and immediately the cock crowed. In assuming an air of indifference, Peter had become an easy prey to temptation.

Attention was called to him the second time, and he was charged with being a follower of Jesus. Peter now declared with an oath, "I do not know the man." Another hour passed, when a near kinsman of the man whose ear Peter had cut off, asked him, "Did not I see thee in the garden with Him?" "Surely thou art one of them: for thou art a Galilean." At this Peter flew into a rage. In order fully to deceive his questioners and justify his assumed character, Peter now denied his Master with cursing and swearing. Again the cock crowed. Peter heard it, and remembered the words of Jesus, "Before the cock crow twice, thou shalt deny Me thrice." Mark 14:30.

While the degrading oaths were fresh upon Peter's lips, and the shrill crowing of the cock was ringing in his ears, the Saviour turned and looked full upon His poor disciple. At the same time Peter's eyes were drawn to his Master. In that gentle countenance he read deep pity and sorrow, but no anger.

The sight of that suffering face, those quivering lips, pierced his heart like an arrow. Peter called to mind his promise of a few short hours before, when the Saviour told him he would deny his Lord thrice that same night. Peter now realized how accurately his Lord had read his heart, the falseness of which was unknown to himself.

A tide of memories rushed over him. The Saviour's long-suffering, His patience—all was remembered. He reflected with horror on his own falsehood, his perjury. Once more he saw a sacrilegious hand raised to smite his Master in the face. Unable longer to endure the scene, he rushed, heartbroken, from the hall.

He pressed on in solitude and darkness, he knew not and cared not whither. At last he found himself in Gethsemane. He remembered with bitter remorse that Jesus had agonized in prayer alone. He remembered His solemn charge, "Watch and pray, that ye enter not into temptation." Matthew 26:41. It was torture to his bleeding heart to know that he had added the heaviest burden to the Saviour's humiliation and grief. Peter fell on his face and wished that he might die.

Had those hours in the garden been spent in watching and prayer, Peter would not have been left to depend on his own feeble strength. He would not have denied his Lord. Had the disciples watched with Christ in His agony, they would have been prepared to behold His suffering on the cross. Amid the gloom of the most trying hour, hope would have lighted up the darkness and sustained their faith.

Determined Efforts to Condemn Jesus

As soon as it was day, the Sanhedrin again assembled, and again Jesus was brought into the council room. He had declared Himself the Son of God, but they could not condemn Him on this, for many had not been present at the night session and had not heard His words. And they knew that the Roman tribunal would find in them nothing worthy of death. But if from His own lips they could all hear His claim to the Messiahship, they might construe this into a seditious political claim.

"Art Thou the Christ?" they said, "tell us." But Christ remained silent. They continued to ply Him with questions. At last He answered, "If I tell you, ye will not believe: and if I also ask you, ye will not answer Me, nor let Me go." But He added the solemn warning, "Hereafter shall the Son of man sit on the right hand of the power of God."

"Art Thou then the Son of God?" they asked. He said unto them, "Ye say that I am." They cried out, "What need we any further witness? for we ourselves have heard of His own mouth."

And Jesus was to die. All that was now necessary was for the Romans to ratify this condemnation.

Then came the third scene of abuse, worse even than that received from the ignorant rabble. In the very presence of the priests and rulers, with their sanction this took place. When the condemnation of Jesus was pronounced by the judges, a satanic fury took possession of the people. The crowd made a rush toward Jesus. Had it not been for the Roman soldiers, He would not have lived to be nailed to the cross of Calvary. He would have been torn in pieces. Roman authority interposed, and by force of arms restrained the violence of the mob.

Heathen men were angry at the brutal treatment of One against whom nothing had been proved. The Roman officers declared that it was against Jewish law to condemn a man to death on his own testimony. This brought a momentary lull in the proceedings; but the Jewish leaders were dead alike to pity and to shame.

Priests and rulers forgot the dignity of their office, and abused the Son of God with foul epithets. They taunted Him with His parentage. They declared His proclaiming Himself the Messiah made Him deserving of the most ignominious death. An old garment was thrown over His head, and His persecutors struck Him in the face, saying, "Prophesy unto us, thou Christ, Who is he that smote Thee?" One poor wretch spat in His face.

Angels faithfully recorded every insulting look, word, and act against their beloved Commander. One day the base men who scorned the calm, pale face of Christ will look upon it in its glory, shining brighter than the sun.

76 / How Judas Lost His Soul

The history of Judas presents the sad ending of a life that might have been honored of God. Had Judas died before his last journey to Jerusalem, he would have been regarded as worthy of a place among the Twelve, one who would be greatly missed. The abhorrence which has followed him through the centuries would not have existed. But his character was laid open to the world as a warning to all who should betray sacred trusts.

Since the feast at the house of Simon, Judas had had opportunity to reflect on the deed he had covenanted to perform, but his purpose was unchanged. For the price of a slave he sold the Lord of glory.

Judas had naturally a strong love for money, but he had not always been corrupt enough to do such a deed as this. He had fostered the spirit of avarice until it had overbalanced his love for Christ. Through one vice he gave himself to Satan, to be driven to any lengths in sin.

Judas had joined the disciples when multitudes were following Christ. He witnessed the Saviour's mighty works in healing the sick, casting out devils, and raising the dead. He recognized the teaching of Jesus as superior to all that he had ever heard. He felt a desire to be changed in character, and hoped to experience this through connecting himself with Jesus.

The Saviour did not repulse Judas. He gave him a place among the Twelve and endowed him with power to heal the sick and cast out devils. But Judas did not surrender himself fully to Christ. He did not give up his worldly ambition or his love of money. He did not bring himself under the divine molding, but cultivated a disposition to criticize and accuse.

Judas had great influence over the disciples. He had a high opinion of his own qualifications and looked on his brethren as greatly inferior to him. Judas flattered himself that the church would often be brought into embarrassment if it were not for his ability as a manager. In his own estimation he was an honor to the cause, and as such always represented himself.

Christ placed him where he would have an opportunity to see and correct his weakness of character, but Judas indulged his covetous disposition. The small sums that came into his hands were a continual temptation. When he did a little service for Christ, he paid himself out of this meager fund. In his own eyes these pretexts served to excuse his action; but in God's sight he was a thief.

Judas had marked out a line on which he expected Christ to work. He had planned that John the Baptist should be delivered from prison. But John was left to be beheaded. And Jesus, instead of avenging the death of John, retired into a country place. Judas wanted more aggressive warfare. He thought that if Jesus would not prevent the disciples from carrying out their schemes, the work would be more successful. He saw the Jewish leaders' challenge unheeded when they demanded from Christ a sign from heaven. His heart was open to disbelief, and the enemy supplied thoughts of rebellion. Why did Jesus predict trial and persecution for Himself and His disciples? Were his hopes for a high place in the kingdom to be disappointed?

Working Against Christ

Judas was continually advancing the idea that Christ would reign as king in Jerusalem. At the miracle of the loaves it was he who set on foot the project to take Christ by force and make Him king. His hopes were high, his disappointment, bitter.

Christ's discourse concerning the bread of life was the turning point. He saw Christ offering spiritual rather than worldly good. He thought he could see that Jesus would have no honor, and could bestow no high position on His followers. He determined not to unite himself so closely to Christ but that he could draw away. He would watch. And he did watch.

From that time he expressed doubts that confused the disciples. He introduced controversies and texts of Scripture that had no connection with the truths Christ was presenting. These texts, separated from their connection, perplexed the disciples and increased the discouragement pressing upon them. Yet Judas appeared conscientious. Thus in a very religious, and apparently wise, way he was attaching to Jesus' words a meaning He had not conveyed. His suggestions were constantly exciting ambitious desire for temporal preferment. The dissension as to which should be greatest was generally excited by Judas.

When Jesus presented to the rich young ruler the condition of discipleship, Judas thought that a mistake had been made. Such men as this ruler would help sustain Christ's cause. Judas thought that he personally could suggest many plans for the advantage of the little church. In these things, he thought himself wiser than Christ.

Judas's Last Opportunity to Repent

In all that Christ said to His disciples, there was something with which, in heart, Judas disagreed. Under his influence the leaven of disaffection was doing its work. Jesus saw that Satan was opening up a channel through which to influence the other disciples. Yet Judas made no outward murmur until the feast in Simon's house. When Mary anointed the Saviour's feet, Judas manifested his covetous disposition. At the reproof from Jesus, wounded pride and desire for revenge broke down the barriers. This will be the experience of everyone who persists in tampering with sin.

But Judas was not yet wholly hardened. Even after he had twice pledged to betray the Saviour, there was opportunity for repentance. At the Passover supper Jesus tenderly included Judas in the ministry to the disciples. But the last appeal of love was unheeded. The feet that Jesus had washed went forth to the betrayer's work.

Judas reasoned that if Jesus was to be crucified, the event must come to pass. His act would not change the result. If Jesus was not to die, it would only force Him to deliver Himself. He counted that he had made a sharp bargain in betraying his Lord.

Judas did not, however, believe Christ would permit Himself to be arrested. In betraying Him, it was his purpose to teach Him a lesson. He intended to make the Saviour careful thenceforth to treat him with due respect. Often when the scribes and Pharisees had taken up stones to cast at Him, He had made His escape. Since He had escaped so many snares, He certainly would not now allow Himself to be taken.

Judas decided to put the matter to the test. If Jesus really was the Messiah, the people would proclaim Him king. Judas would have the credit of having placed the king on David's throne, and this would secure to him the first position, next to Christ, in the new kingdom.

In the garden, Judas said to the leaders of the mob, "Hold Him fast." Matthew 26:48. He fully believed Christ would escape. Then if they blamed him, he could say, Did I not tell you to hold Him fast?

In amazement Judas saw the Saviour suffer Himself to be led away. At every movement he looked for Him to surprise His enemies, by appearing before them as the Son of God. But as hour after hour went by, a terrible fear came to the traitor that he had sold his Master to His death.

As the trial drew to a close, Judas could endure his guilty conscience no longer. Suddenly a hoarse voice rang through the hall: He is innocent; spare Him, O

Caiaphas! The tall form of Judas was seen pressing through the startled throng. His face was pale, and sweat stood on his forehead. Rushing to the throne of judgment, he threw down before the high priest the pieces of silver that had been the price of his Lord's betrayal. Grasping the robe of Caiaphas, he implored him to release Jesus. Caiaphas angrily shook him off, but knew not what to say. The perfidy of the priests was revealed. They had bribed the disciple to betray his Master.

"I have sinned in that I have betrayed the innocent blood." But the high priest, regaining his self-possession, answered, "What is that to us? see thou to that." Matthew 27:4. The priests had been willing to make Judas their tool, but they despised his baseness.

Judas's Agony of Remorse

Judas now cast himself at the feet of Jesus, acknowledging Him to be the Son of God and entreating Him to deliver Himself. The Saviour knew that Judas felt no deep, heartbreaking grief that he had betrayed the spotless Son of God. Yet He spoke no word of condemnation. He looked pityingly upon Judas, and said, For this hour came I into the world.

With amazement the assembly beheld the forbearance of Christ toward His betrayer. This Man was more than mortal! But why did He not free Himself and triumph over His accusers?

His entreaties in vain, Judas rushed from the hall exclaiming, It is too late! It is too late! He felt he could not live to see Jesus crucified, and in despair went out and hanged himself.

Later that day, the throng who were leading Jesus to the place of crucifixion saw the body of Judas at the foot of a lifeless tree. His weight had broken the cord by which he had hanged himself. Dogs were now devouring his mangled body. Retribution seemed already visiting those who were guilty of the blood of Jesus.

When Mary anointed Jesus' feet with expensive perfume, Judas criticized her act of love as an example of waste. Little did he realize that this was his last opportunity to repent.

77 / Christ's Trial Before the Roman Governor

In the judgment hall of Pilate, the Roman governor, Christ stood bound as a prisoner, about Him the guard of soldiers. The hall was fast filling with spectators. Just outside were the judges of the Sanhedrin, priests, rulers, and the mob.

After condemning Jesus, the Sanhedrin had come to Pilate to have the sentence confirmed and executed. But these Jewish officials would not enter the Roman judgment hall. According to their ceremonial law they would be defiled thereby and prevented from taking part in the Passover. They did not see that murderous hatred had defiled their hearts. They did not see that since they had rejected Christ, the real Passover Lamb, the great feast had for them lost its significance.

Pilate looked on the Saviour with no friendly eyes. Called from his bedroom in haste, he determined to do his work as quickly as possible. Assuming his severest expression, he turned to see what kind of man he had to examine.

His gaze rested searchingly on Jesus. He had to deal with all kinds of criminals, but never had a man of such goodness and nobility been brought before him. On His face he saw no sign of guilt, no fear, no boldness or defiance. He saw a man whose countenance bore the signature of heaven.

Pilate's better nature was roused. His wife had told him something of the wonderful deeds performed by the Galilean prophet, who cured the sick and raised the dead. He recalled rumors that he had heard from sev-

This chapter is based on Matthew 27:2, 11-31; Mark 15:1-20; Luke 23:1-25; John 18:28-40; 19:1-16.

eral sources. He demanded of the Jews their charges
against the prisoner. Who is this Man, and why have
you brought Him? They answered that He was a deceiver called Jesus of Nazareth.

Again Pilate asked, "What accusation bring ye
against this Man?" The priests did not answer his
question, but in irritation said, "If He were not a malefactor, we would not have delivered Him up unto
thee." When the Sanhedrin brings to you a man it
deems worthy of death, is there need to ask for an accusation against him? They hoped to lead Pilate to ac-
cede to their request without going through many pre-
liminaries.

Before this, Pilate had hastily condemned to death
men not worthy of death. In his estimation, whether a
prisoner was innocent or guilty was of no special consequence. The priests hoped that Pilate would now in-
flict the death penalty on Jesus without giving Him a
hearing.

But something in the prisoner held Pilate back. He
dared not do it. He remembered how Jesus had raised
Lazarus, a man that had been dead four days; and he
determined to know the charges against Him and
whether they could be proved.

If your judgment is sufficient, he said, why bring the
prisoner to me? "Take ye Him, and judge Him according to your law." The priests said they had already
passed sentence on Him, but they must have Pilate's
sentence to render their condemnation valid. What is
your sentence? Pilate asked. Death, they answered.
They asked Pilate to enforce their sentence; they
would take the responsibility of the result. Weak
though he was in moral power, Pilate refused to condemn Jesus until a charge had been brought against
Him.

The priests were in a dilemma. They must not allow
it to appear that Christ had been arrested on religious
grounds, for this would have no weight with Pilate.
They must make it appear that Jesus was a political of-

fender. The Romans were constantly on the watch to repress everything that could lead to an outbreak.

In their extremity the priests called false witnesses. "And they began to accuse Him, saying, We found this fellow perverting the nation, and forbidding to give tribute to Caesar, saying that He Himself is Christ a King." Three charges, each without foundation. The priests knew this but were willing to commit perjury.

Pilate Convinced of a Plot

Pilate did not believe that the prisoner had plotted against the government. He was convinced that a deep plot had been laid to destroy an innocent man. Turning to Jesus he asked, "Art Thou the King of the Jews?" The Saviour answered, "Thou sayest it." And as He spoke, His countenance lighted up as if a sunbeam were shining on it.

When they heard His answer, Caiaphas called Pilate to witness that Jesus had admitted the crime with which He was charged. Pilate said, "Answerest Thou nothing? behold how many things they witness against Thee. But Jesus yet answered nothing."

Standing behind Pilate, in view of all in the court Christ heard the abuse; but to all the false charges He answered not a word. He stood unmoved by the fury of the waves that beat about Him. It was as if the heavy surges of wrath, rising like the waves of the ocean, broke about Him but did not touch Him. His silence was as a light shining from the inner to the outer man.

Pilate was astonished. Does this Man not care to save His life? As he looked at Jesus, he felt that He could not be as unrighteous as were the clamoring priests. To escape the tumult of the crowd, Pilate took Jesus aside and again questioned, "Art Thou the King of the Jews?"

Jesus did not directly answer. The Holy Spirit was striving with Pilate, and He gave him opportunity to acknowledge his conviction. "Sayest thou this thing of thyself," He asked, "or did others tell it thee of Me?"

Pilate understood Christ's meaning, but he would not acknowledge the conviction that pressed upon him. "Am I a Jew?" he said. "Thine own nation and the chief priests have delivered Thee unto me; what hast Thou done?"

Jesus Tries to Save Pilate

Jesus did not leave Pilate without further light. He gave him to understand that He was not seeking an earthly throne.

"My kingdom is not of this world," He said; "if My kingdom were of this world, then would My servants fight, that I should not be delivered to the Jews: but now is My kingdom not from hence. Pilate therefore said unto Him, Art Thou a king then? Jesus answered, Thou sayest that I am a king. To this end was I born, and for this cause came I into the world, that I should bear witness unto the truth. Everyone that is of the truth heareth My voice." Christ desired Pilate to understand that only by receiving and appropriating truth could his ruined nature be reconstructed.

Pilate's mind was confused. His heart was stirred with a great longing to know what the truth really was and how he could obtain it. "What is truth?" he inquired. But he did not wait for an answer. The priests were clamorous for immediate action. Going out to the Jews, he declared emphatically, "I find in Him no fault at all."

As the priests and elders heard this from Pilate, their disappointment and rage knew no bounds. As they saw the prospect of the release of Jesus, they seemed ready to tear Him in pieces. They loudly denounced Pilate, and threatened him with the censure of the Roman government. They accused him of refusing to condemn Jesus who, they affirmed, had set Himself up against Caesar. Angry voices declared that the seditious influence of Jesus was well known throughout the country. "He stirreth up the people, teaching throughout all Jewry, beginning from Galilee to this place."

Pilate at this time had no thought of condemning Jesus. He knew that the Jews had accused Him through hatred and prejudice. Justice demanded that Christ should be released. But should he refuse to give Jesus into the hands of the people, a tumult would be raised, and this he feared to meet. When he heard that Christ was from Galilee, he decided to send Him to Herod, the ruler of that province, who was then in Jerusalem. By this course, Pilate thought to shift the responsibility to Herod. He also thought this a good opportunity to heal an old quarrel between himself and Herod. And so it proved. The two magistrates made friends over the trial of the Saviour.

Amid the insults of the mob Jesus was hurried to Herod. "When Herod saw Jesus, he was exceeding glad." He had "heard many things of Him; and he hoped to have seen some miracle done by Him." This Herod was he whose hands were stained with the blood of John the Baptist. When Herod first heard of Jesus, he was terror-stricken, and said, "It is John . . . risen from the dead." Yet he desired to see Jesus. Now there was opportunity to save the life of this prophet, and the king hoped to banish forever from his mind the memory of that bloody head brought to him in a charger. He also desired to have his curiosity satisfied and thought that if Christ were given a prospect of release, He would do anything that was asked of Him.

When the Saviour was brought in, the priests and elders excitedly urged their accusations against Him. But Herod commanded silence. He ordered that the fetters of Christ should be unloosed, at the same time charging His enemies with roughly treating Him. He as well as Pilate was satisfied that Christ had been accused through malice and envy.

Herod questioned Christ in many words, but the Saviour maintained a profound silence. At the command of the king, the decrepit and maimed were then called in, and Christ was ordered to prove His claim by working a miracle. Jesus did not respond, and Herod continued to urge: Show us a sign that Thou hast the power with which rumor has credited Thee. But the Son of God had taken upon Himself man's nature, and He must do as man must do in like circumstances. Therefore, He would not work a miracle to save Himself the pain and humiliation that man must endure in a similar position.

Herod promised that if Christ would perform some miracle, He should be released. Fear seized Christ's accusers lest He should now work a miracle. Such a manifestation would prove a deathblow to their plans and would perhaps cost them their lives. Raising their voices, the priests and rulers declared, He is a traitor, a blasphemer; He works His miracles through the powers of the prince of the devils!

Herod's conscience was now far less sensitive than when he had trembled with horror at the request of Herodias for the head of John the Baptist. His moral perceptions had become more and more degraded by his licentious life. He could even boast of the punishment he had inflicted on John for daring to reprove him. And he now threatened Jesus, declaring that he had power to condemn Him. But no sign from Jesus gave evidence that He heard a word.

Herod was irritated by this silence. It seemed to indicate utter indifference to his authority. Again he angrily threatened Jesus, who still remained unmoved and silent.

The mission of Christ was not to gratify idle curiosity. Could He have spoken any word to heal sin-sick souls, He would not have kept silent. But He had no words for those who trample truth under their unholy feet. Herod had rejected the truth spoken to him by the greatest of the prophets, and no other message was he to receive. Not a word had the Majesty of heaven for him. Those lips were closed to the haughty king who felt no need of a Saviour.

Herod's face grew dark with passion. He angrily denounced Jesus as an impostor. Then to Christ he said, If You will give no evidence of Your claim, I will deliver You up to the soldiers and the people. If You are an impostor, death is what You merit; if You are the Son of God, save Yourself by working a miracle.

No sooner were these words spoken than, like wild beasts, the crowd darted upon their prey. Jesus was dragged this way and that, Herod joining the mob in seeking to humiliate the Son of God. Had not the Roman soldiers interposed, the Saviour would have been torn in pieces.

"Herod with his men of war set Him at nought, and mocked Him, and arrayed Him in a gorgeous robe." The Roman soldiers joined in this abuse. All that these corrupt soldiers and the Jewish dignitaries could instigate was heaped upon the Saviour. Yet His patience failed not.

Some Trembled Before Jesus

But there were some who trembled in Christ's presence. Some who came forward for mockery turned back, afraid and silenced. Herod was convicted. The last rays of merciful light were shining on his sin-hardened heart. Divinity had flashed through humanity. Herod felt that he was beholding a God upon His throne. Hardened as he was, he dared not ratify the condemnation of Christ. He sent Jesus back to the Roman judgment hall.

Pilate was disappointed when the Jews returned with their prisoner. He reminded them that he had already examined Jesus and found no fault in Him. They had not been able to prove a single charge. And Herod, one of their own nation, also had found in Him nothing worthy of death. "I will therefore chastise Him and release Him."

Here Pilate showed his weakness. Jesus was innocent, yet he was willing to sacrifice justice in order to pacify His accusers. This placed him at a disadvantage. The crowd presumed upon his indecision. If at first Pilate had stood firm, refusing to condemn a man whom he found guiltless, he would have broken the fatal chain that was to bind him in remorse as long as he lived. Christ would have been put to death, but the guilt would not have rested on Pilate. But Pilate had taken step after step in violation of his conscience, and he now found himself almost helpless in the hands of the priests and rulers.

Pilate's Last Chance

Even now Pilate was not left to act blindly. His wife had been visited by an angel and in a dream had conversed with the Saviour. Pilate's wife was not a Jew, but as she looked on Jesus in her dream, she knew Him to be the Prince of God. She saw Pilate give Jesus to the scourging, after he had declared, "I find no fault in Him." She saw him give Christ up to His murderers. She saw the cross uplifted, the earth wrapped in darkness, and heard the mysterious cry, "It is finished."

Still another scene met her gaze. She saw Christ seated on the great white cloud and His murderers fleeing from the presence of His glory. With a cry of horror she awoke and at once wrote to Pilate words of warning.

A messenger pressed through the crowd and handed him the letter from his wife, which read: "Have thou nothing to do with that just Man: for I have suffered many things this day in a dream because of Him."

Pilate's face grew pale. He was confused by his own conflicting emotions. While he had been delaying to act, the priests and rulers were inflaming the minds of the people. He now thought of a custom which might serve to secure Christ's release. It was customary at this feast to release one prisoner whom the people might choose. There was not a shadow of justice in this custom, but it was greatly prized by the Jews. The Roman authorities at this time held a prisoner named Barabbas, who was under sentence of death. This man claimed authority to establish a different order of things. Whatever he could obtain by theft and robbery was his own. He had gained a following among the people and had excited sedition against the Roman government. Under cover of religious enthusiasm he was a hardened villain, bent on rebellion and cruelty.

By giving the people a choice between this man and the innocent Saviour, Pilate thought to arouse them to a sense of justice.

"Whom will ye that I release unto you? Barabbas, or Jesus which is called Christ?" Like the bellowing of wild beasts came the answer, "Release unto us Barabbas!" Thinking that the people had not understood his question, Pilate asked, "Will ye that I release unto you the King of the Jews?" But they cried out again, "Away with this Man, and release unto us Barabbas!" "What shall I do then with Jesus which is called Christ?" Demons in human form were in the crowd, and what could be expected but the answer, "Let Him be crucified."

Pilate Did Not Foresee the Consequences

Pilate had not thought it would come to that. He shrank from delivering an innocent man to the most cruel death that could be inflicted. "Why, what evil hath He done?" But the case had gone too far for argument.

Still Pilate endeavored to save Christ. "He said unto them the third time, Why, what evil hath He done?" But the very mention of His release stirred the people to frenzy. Louder and louder they cried, "Crucify Him, crucify Him!"

Faint and covered with wounds, Jesus was scourged, "and the soldiers led Him away into the hall, called Praetorium; and they call together the whole band. And they clothed Him with purple, and platted a crown of thorns, and put it about His head, and began to salute Him, Hail, King of the Jews! And they . . . did spit upon Him, and bowing their knees worshiped Him. And . . . they . . . mocked Him." Occasionally some wicked hand struck the crown, forcing the thorns into His temples, and sending the blood trickling down His face.

A maddened throng enclosed the Saviour of the world. Mocking and jeering were mingled with oaths of blasphemy. Satan led the mob. It was his purpose to provoke the Saviour to retaliation if possible, or to drive Him to perform a miracle to release Himself. One stain upon His human life, and the Lamb of God would have been an imperfect offering, and the redemption of man a failure. But He submitted with perfect calmness to the coarsest insult and outrage.

Christ's enemies had demanded a miracle as evidence of His divinity. They had evidence far greater than any they had sought. His meekness and patience proved His kinship to God. The blood drops that flowed from His wounded temples were the pledge of His anointing with "the oil of gladness" as our great High Priest. See Hebrews 1:9. Satan's rage was great as he saw that the Saviour had departed in no particular from the will of His Father.

Compromise Leads to Ruin

When Pilate gave Jesus up to be scourged, he hoped the multitude would decide that this was sufficient punishment. But with keen perception the Jews saw the weakness of punishing a man who had been declared innocent. They were determined that Jesus should not be released.

Pilate now sent for Barabbas to be brought into the court, the two prisoners side by side. Pointing to the Saviour he said, "Behold the Man!" There stood the Son of God, stripped to the waist, His back showing the long stripes from which blood flowed freely. His face was stained and bore the marks of pain, but never had it appeared more beautiful than now. Every feature expressed the tenderest pity for His cruel foes. In His manner there was the strength and dignity of long-suffering.

In striking contrast was the prisoner at His side. Every line of the countenance of Barabbas proclaimed him a hardened ruffian. The contrast spoke to every beholder. As some looked on Jesus they wept, their hearts full of sympathy. The priests and rulers were convicted that He was all that He claimed to be.

The Roman soldiers that surrounded Christ were not all hardened. They looked at the divine Sufferer with feelings of pity, His silent submission stamped upon their minds. The scene was never to be effaced until they either acknowledged Him as the Christ, or by rejecting Him decided their own destiny.

Pilate did not doubt that the sight of this Man in contrast with Barabbas would move the Jews to sympathy. But he did not understand the fanatical hatred of the priests. Again priests, rulers, and people raised that awful cry, "Crucify Him, crucify Him." At last, losing all patience with their unreasoning cruelty, Pilate cried out despairingly, "Take ye Him, and crucify Him: for I find no fault in Him."

The Roman governor, though familiar with cruel scenes, was moved with sympathy for the suffering prisoner. But the priests declared, "We have a law, and by our law He ought to die, because He made Himself the Son of God."

Jesus' Kindness to Pilate

Pilate was startled; it might be a divine being that stood before him! Again he said to Jesus "Whence art Thou?" But Jesus gave no answer. The Saviour had spoken freely to Pilate, explaining His mission. Pilate had disregarded the light. He had abused the high office of judge by yielding to the demands of the mob. Jesus had no further light for him. Vexed at His silence, Pilate said haughtily: "Speakest Thou not unto me? knowest Thou not that I have power to crucify Thee, and have power to release Thee?"

Jesus answered, "Thou couldest have no power at all against Me, except it were given thee from above:

therefore he that delivered Me unto thee hath the greater sin." Christ meant Caiaphas, who represented the Jewish nation. They had light in the prophecies that testified of Christ, and unmistakable evidence of the divinity of Him whom they condemned to death. The heaviest responsibility belonged to those who stood in the highest places in the nation. Pilate, Herod, and the Roman soldiers were comparatively ignorant of Jesus. They had not the light which the Jewish nation had so abundantly received. Had the light been given to the soldiers, they would not have treated Christ as they did.

Again Pilate proposed to release the Saviour. "But the Jews cried out, saying, If thou let this man go, thou art not Caesar's friend." Of all the opponents of Roman rule, the Jews were most bitter; but to accomplish the destruction of Christ, they would profess loyalty to the foreign rule which they hated.

"Whosoever maketh himself a king," they continued, "speaketh against Caesar." Pilate was under suspicion by the Roman government and knew that such a report would ruin him. He knew the Jews would leave nothing undone to accomplish their revenge.

Pilate again presented Jesus to the people, saying, "Behold your King!" Again the mad cry was heard, "Away with Him, crucify Him." In a voice that was heard far and near, Pilate asked, "Shall I crucify your King?" But from profane, blasphemous lips went forth the words, "We have no king but Caesar."

Thus by choosing a heathen ruler, the Jewish nation rejected God as their king. Henceforth they had no king but Caesar. To this the priests and teachers had led the people. For this, with the fearful results that followed, they were responsible. A nation's sin and a nation's ruin were due to the religious leaders.

"When Pilate saw that he could prevail nothing, but that rather a tumult was made, he took water, and washed his hands before the multitude, saying, I am innocent of the blood of this just Person: see ye to it."

Pilate looked upon the Saviour, and said in his heart, He is a God. Turning to the multitude he declared, I am clear of His blood. Crucify Him, but I pronounce Him a just man. May He whom He claims as His Father judge you and not me for this day's work. Then to Jesus he said, Forgive me for this act; I cannot save You. And when he had again scourged Jesus, He delivered Him to be crucified.

Pilate longed to deliver Jesus, but he saw that he could not do this and yet retain his own position. Rather than lose his worldly power, he chose to sacrifice an innocent life. How many in like manner sacrifice principle. Conscience and duty point one way, and self-interest another. The current sets in the wrong direction, and he who compromises with evil is swept away into the thick darkness of guilt.

But in spite of his precautions, the very thing Pilate dreaded came upon him. He was cast down from his high office, and, stung by remorse and wounded pride, not long after the crucifixion he ended his own life.

When Pilate declared himself innocent of the blood of Christ, Caiaphas answered defiantly, "His blood be on us, and on our children." The awful words were echoed by the crowd in an inhuman roar of voices. The whole multitude said, "His blood be on us, and on our children."

The people of Israel had made their choice—Barabbas, the robber and murderer, the representative of Satan. Christ, the representative of God, had been rejected. In making this choice they accepted him who from the beginning was a liar and a murderer. Satan was their leader. His rule they must endure.

The Jews had cried, "His blood be on us, and on our children." That prayer was heard. The blood of the Son of God was on their children and their children's children. Terribly was it realized in the destruction of Jerusalem and in the condition of the Jewish nation for nearly two thousand years—a branch severed from the vine, dead. From land to land throughout the world, from century to century, dead in trespasses and sins!

Terribly will that prayer be fulfilled in the great judgment day. Christ will come in glory. Thousands and thousands of angels, the beautiful and triumphant sons of God, will escort Him on His way. Before Him shall be gathered all nations. In the place of thorns, He will wear a crown of glory. On His vesture and on His thigh a name will be written, "King of kings, and Lord of lords." Revelation 19:16.

The priests and rulers will behold again the scene in the judgment hall. Every circumstance will appear as if written in letters of fire. Then those who prayed, "His blood be on us, and on our children," will receive the answer to their prayer. In awful agony and horror they will cry to the rocks and mountains, Fall on us. See Revelation 6:16, 17.

78 / Jesus Dies on Calvary

"And when they were come to the place, which is called Calvary, there they crucified Him."

The news of Christ's condemnation had spread, and people of all classes and ranks flocked toward the place of crucifixion. The priests and rulers had been bound by a promise not to molest Christ's followers if He Himself were delivered to them, and the disciples and believers joined the throng.

The cross which had been prepared for Barabbas was laid on Jesus' bleeding shoulders. Two companions of Barabbas were to suffer death at the same time, and on them also crosses were placed. Since the Passover supper with His disciples, Jesus had taken neither food nor drink. He had endured the anguish of betrayal and had seen His disciples forsake Him. He had been taken to Annas, to Caiaphas, to Pilate, to Herod, then again to Pilate. All that night there had been scene after scene to try the soul of man to the uttermost. Christ had not failed. He had borne Himself with dignity. But when after the second scourging the cross was laid on Him, human nature could bear no more. He fell fainting beneath the burden.

The crowd manifested no compassion. They taunted Him because He could not carry the heavy cross. Again the burden was laid on Him, and again He fell. His persecutors saw that it was impossible for Him to carry His burden further. Who would bear the humiliating load? The Jews could not, because the defilement would prevent them from keeping the Passover.

This chapter is based on Matthew 27:31-53; Mark 15:20-38; Luke 23:26-46; John 19:16-30.

At this time a stranger, Simon a Cyrenian, coming in from the country, met the throng. He stopped in astonishment at the scene, and as he expressed compassion, they seized him and placed the cross on his shoulders.

Simon's sons were believers in the Saviour, but he himself was not. Bearing the cross to Calvary was a blessing to Simon. It led him to take the cross of Christ from choice and ever cheerfully stand beneath its burden.

Not a few women were in the crowd that followed the Uncondemned to His cruel death. Some had carried to Him their sick and suffering ones. Some had themselves been healed. They wondered at the hatred of the crowd toward Him. And notwithstanding the angry words of priests and rulers, as Jesus fell beneath the cross these women broke forth into wailing. This attracted Christ's attention. He knew that they were not lamenting Him as one sent from God, but He did not despise their sympathy. It awakened in His heart a deeper sympathy for them. "Daughters of Jerusalem," He said, "weep not for Me, but weep for yourselves, and for your children." Christ looked forward to the time of Jerusalem's destruction when many who were now weeping for Him were to perish with their children.

A Wider Judgment

From the fall of Jerusalem the thoughts of Jesus passed to a wider judgment. In the destruction of the impenitent city He saw a symbol of the final destruction to come on the world: "Then shall they begin to say to the mountains, Fall on us; and to the hills, Cover us. For if they do these things in a green tree, what shall be done in the dry?" The green tree represented Himself, the innocent Redeemer. God's wrath against transgression fell on His beloved Son. What suffering, then, would the sinner bear who continued in sin? The impenitent would know a sorrow that language would fail to express.

Of the multitude that followed the Saviour to Calvary, many had attended Him with hosannas and palm branches as He rode triumphantly into Jerusalem. Not a few who then shouted His praise because it was popular, now swelled the cry, "Crucify Him!" When Christ rode into Jerusalem, the disciples pressed close about Him, feeling that it was a high honor to be connected with Him. Now in His humiliation they followed Him at a distance.

The Agony of Christ's Mother

At the place of execution, the two thieves wrestled in the hands of those who placed them on the cross; but Jesus made no resistance. The mother of Jesus, supported by John, had followed the steps of her Son to Calvary. She had longed to place a supporting hand beneath His wounded head. But she was not permitted this mournful privilege. She still cherished the hope that Jesus would deliver Himself from His enemies. Again her heart would sink, as she recalled He had foretold the scenes then taking place.

As the thieves were bound to the cross, she looked on with agonizing suspense. Would He who had given life to the dead suffer Himself to be crucified? Must she give up her faith that He was the Messiah? She saw His hands stretched on the cross; the hammer and nails were brought, and as the spikes were driven through the tender flesh, the disciples bore away from the cruel scene the fainting form of the mother of Jesus.

The Saviour made no complaint, but great drops of sweat stood on His brow. There was no pitying hand to wipe the death dew from His face; no words of sympathy and fidelity to stay His human heart. While the soldiers were doing their fearful work, Jesus prayed, "Father, forgive them; for they know not what they do." His mind passed from His own suffering to the terrible retribution that would be theirs. No curses were called down on the soldiers who were handling Him so roughly, no vengeance invoked on the priests and rul-

ers. He breathed only a plea for their forgiveness—
"they know not what they do."

But their ignorance did not remove their guilt, for it
was their privilege to know and accept Jesus as their
Saviour. Some would yet see their sin, and repent, and
be converted. Some by impenitence would make it impossible for the prayer of Christ to be answered for
them. Yet, just the same, God's purpose was reaching
its fulfillment. Jesus was earning the right to become
the advocate of men in the Father's presence.

That prayer of Christ for His enemies took in every
sinner from the beginning of the world to the end of
time. Upon all rests the guilt of crucifying the Son of
God. To all, forgiveness is freely offered.

As soon as Jesus was nailed to the cross, it was lifted
by strong men and with violence thrust into the place
prepared for it. This caused intense agony. Pilate then
wrote an inscription in Hebrew, Greek, and Latin, and
placed it on the cross above the head of Jesus. It read,
"Jesus of Nazareth, the King of the Jews." This irritated the Jews. They had cried, "We have no king but
Caesar." But Pilate wrote what they had expressed.
No offense was mentioned, except that Jesus was the
King of the Jews, a virtual acknowledgment of the allegiance of the Jews to Rome. It declared that whoever
might claim to be the King of Israel would be judged by
them worthy of death. In order to destroy Christ, the
priests had been ready to sacrifice even their national
existence.

The priests asked Pilate to change the inscription.
"Write not, The King of the Jews; but that He said, I
am King of the Jews." But Pilate, angry with himself,
replied coldly, "What I have written I have written."

In the providence of God that inscription was to
awaken investigation of the Scriptures. People from all
lands were then at Jerusalem, and the inscription declaring Jesus the Messiah would come to their notice.
It was transcribed by a hand that God had guided.

In the sufferings of Christ on the cross, prophecy

was fulfilled. "The assembly of the wicked have enclosed Me: they pierced My hands and My feet. . . . They part My garments among them, and cast lots upon My vesture." Psalm 2:16-18. His clothing was given to the soldiers. His tunic was woven without seam, and they said, "Let us not rend it, but cast lots for it, whose it shall be."

In another prophecy the Saviour declared, "I looked for some to take pity, but there was none; and for comforters, but I found none. They gave Me also gall for my meat; and in My thirst they gave Me vinegar to drink." Psalm 69:20, 21. To those who suffered death by the cross, it was permitted to give a stupefying drug to deaden the pain. But when Jesus had tasted it, He refused it. His faith must keep hold on God, His only strength. To becloud His senses would give Satan an advantage.

Priests, rulers, and scribes joined the mob in mocking the dying Saviour. The Father's voice from heaven, witnessing to Christ's divinity, was silent. No testimony in His favor was heard. Alone He suffered.

"If Thou be the Son of God," they said, "come down from the cross." "Let Him save himself, if He be Christ, the chosen of God." Satan and his angels in human form, were present at the cross, cooperating with the priests and rulers, confederated in a satanic frenzy.

Jesus heard the priests declare, "He saved others; Himself he cannot save. Let Christ the King of Israel descend now from the cross, that we may see and believe." Christ could have come down from the cross. But because He would not save Himself, the sinner has hope of pardon and favor with God.

One Crucified Thief Believes

To Jesus on the cross there came one gleam of comfort—the prayer of the penitent thief. Both men crucified with Jesus at first railed on Him; and one under his suffering only became more desperate and defiant. But his companion was not a hardened criminal; he was less guilty than many who stood beside the cross reviling the Saviour. He had seen and heard Jesus, but had been turned away from Him by the priests and rulers. Seeking to stifle conviction, he had plunged into sin, until he was arrested and condemned.

On the cross he saw the great religionists ridicule Jesus. He heard the upbraiding speech taken up by his companion in guilt: "If Thou be Christ, save Thyself and us." Among the passersby he heard many repeating Jesus' words, and telling of His works. The conviction came back that this was the Christ. Turning to his fellow criminal he said, "Dost thou not fear God, seeing thou art in the same condemnation?" The dying thieves no longer had anything to fear from man. But on one of them pressed the conviction that there is a God to fear, a future to cause him to tremble. And now, his life history was about to close. "And we indeed justly; for we receive the due reward of our deeds; but this Man hath done nothing amiss."

When condemned for his crime, the thief had become despairing, but strange, tender thoughts now sprang up. The Holy Spirit illuminated his mind and little by little the chain of evidence joined together. In Jesus, mocked and hanging on the cross, he saw the Lamb of God. Hope mingled with anguish in his voice as the dying soul cast himself on a dying Saviour. "Lord, remember me when Thou comest into Thy kingdom."

Quickly the answer came, soft and melodious the tone, full of love and power the words: Verily I say unto thee today, Thou shalt be with Me in paradise.* With longing heart Jesus had listened for some expression of faith from His disciples. He had heard only the mournful words, "We trusted that it had been He which should have redeemed Israel." How grateful then to the Saviour was the utterance of faith and love from

---

*The comma in Luke 23:43 is often misplaced in English translations. No comma existed in the Greek text.

the dying thief! While even the disciples doubted, the poor thief called Jesus "Lord." No one acknowledged Him on the cross save the penitent thief, saved at the eleventh hour.

The tone of the repentant man arrested the attention of bystanders. Those who had been quarreling over Christ's garments stopped to listen and waited for the response from Christ's dying lips.

As He spoke the words of promise, the dark cloud that seemed to enshroud the cross was pierced by a living light. Christ in His humiliation was glorified. He who in all other eyes appeared conquered, was Conqueror. He was acknowledged as the Sin Bearer. They could strip from Him His raiment, but they could not rob Him of His power to forgive sins. It is His royal right to save all who come to God by Him!

I say unto thee today, Thou shalt be with Me in Paradise. Christ did not promise that the thief should be with Him in Paradise that day. He Himself did not go that day to Paradise. He slept in the tomb, and on the morning of the resurrection He said, "I am not yet ascended to My Father." John 20:17. But on the day of apparent defeat the promise was given. "Today" while dying on the cross as a malefactor, Christ assured the sinner, "You will be with Me in Paradise."

Christ's position "in the midst" between the thieves was done by direction of the priests and rulers to indicate that He was the greatest criminal of the three. But as Jesus was placed "in the midst," so His cross was placed in the midst of a dying world lying in sin. And the words of pardon spoken to the penitent thief kindled a light that will shine to earth's remotest bounds. In His humiliation, Jesus as a prophet had addressed the daughters of Jerusalem; as priest and advocate He had pleaded with the Father to forgive His murderers; as Saviour He had forgiven the sins of the penitent thief.

At the foot of the cross stood His mother, supported by John. She could not endure to remain away from her Son, and John, knowing that the end was near, had brought her again. Looking into her grief-stricken face, He said to her, "Woman, behold thy son!" then to John, "Behold, thy mother!" John understood and accepted the trust. From that hour he cared for Mary tenderly. The Saviour had no money with which to provide for His mother, but He provided that which she most needed—the tender sympathy of one who loved her because she loved Jesus. And John received a great blessing—she was a constant reminder of his beloved Master.

For nearly thirty years Jesus by His daily toil had helped bear the burdens of the home. And now, even in His last agony, He provided for His sorrowing, widowed mother. Those who follow Christ will respect and provide for their parents. From the heart where His love is cherished, father and mother will never fail of receiving thoughtful care and tender sympathy. And now the Lord of glory was dying. All was oppressive gloom. Not the dread of death, not the pain of the cross, caused Christ's agony. His suffering was from a sense of the malignity of sin. Christ saw how few would be willing to break from its power. Without help from God, humanity must perish, and He saw multitudes perishing within reach of help.

The Terrible Weight That Christ Bore

Upon Christ as our substitute and surety was laid the iniquity of us all. The guilt of every descendant of Adam was pressing on His heart. All His life Christ had been publishing the good news of the Father's pardoning love, but now with the terrible weight of guilt upon Him He could not see the Father's reconciling face. This pierced His heart with a sorrow that can never be fully understood by man. So great was this agony that His physical pain was hardly felt.

Satan with fierce temptations wrung the heart of Jesus. Hope did not present to Him His coming forth from the grave a conqueror or tell Him of the Father's acceptance. Christ felt the anguish the sinner will feel when mercy shall no longer plead for the guilty race. It was the sense of sin, bringing the Father's wrath on Him as man's substitute, that broke the heart of the Son of God.

The hosts of heaven veiled their faces from the fearful sight. The sun refused to look on the awful scene. Its full, bright rays were illuminating the earth at midday, when suddenly it seemed to be blotted out. Complete darkness enveloped the cross. "There was darkness over all the land until the ninth hour." There was no natural cause for this darkness, which was as deep as midnight without moon or stars. It was a miraculous testimony given by God that the faith of after generations might be confirmed.

In that thick darkness God's presence was hidden. God and holy angels were beside the cross. The Father was with His Son. Yet His presence was not revealed. In that dreadful hour Christ was not to be comforted with the Father's presence.

In the thick darkness God veiled the last human agony of His Son. All who had seen Christ in His suffering had been convicted of His divinity. Through long hours of agony He had been gazed on by the jeering multitude. Now He was mercifully hidden by the mantle of God.

A nameless terror held the throng gathered about the cross. Cursing and reviling ceased. Vivid lightnings occasionally flashed from the cloud and revealed the crucified Redeemer. Priests, rulers, executioners, the mob, all thought their time of retribution had come. Some whispered that Jesus would now come down from the cross.

At the ninth hour the darkness lifted from the people, but still enveloped the Saviour. No eye could penetrate the deep gloom that enshrouded the suffering soul of Christ. Then "Jesus cried with a loud voice, saying, Eloi, Eloi, lama sabachthani?" that is, "My God, My God, why hast Thou forsaken Me?" Many voices exclaimed: The vengeance of heaven is upon Him because He claimed to be the Son of God! Many who believed on Him heard His despairing cry. Hope left them. If God had forsaken Jesus, in what could His followers trust?

Last Chance to Show Human Pity

When the darkness lifted, Christ revived to a sense of physical suffering, and said, "I thirst." One of the Roman soldiers, touched with pity, took a sponge and dipping it in vinegar, offered it to Him. But the priests mocked His agony. His words, "Eloi, Eloi, lama sabachthani?" they misinterpreted. They said, "This man calleth for Elijah." The last opportunity to relieve His sufferings they refused. "Let be," they said, "let us see whether Elias will come to save Him."

The spotless Son of God hung upon the cross, His flesh lacerated with stripes; those hands so often reached out in blessing, nailed to the wooden bars; those feet so tireless on ministries of love, spiked to the tree; that royal head pierced by the crown of thorns; those quivering lips shaped to the cry of woe. And all that He endured—the blood drops that flowed from His head, His hands, His feet, the agony that racked His frame, and the unutterable anguish that filled His soul at the hiding of His Father's face—speaks to each child of humanity, declaring, For you the Son of God consents to bear this burden of guilt; for you He spoils the domain of death; for you He opens the gates of Paradise; for you He offers Himself as a sacrifice—from love to you.

Christ Dies Triumphant

Suddenly the gloom lifted from the cross. In trumpetlike tones that seemed to resound throughout creation, Jesus cried, "It is finished." "Father, into Thy hands I commend My spirit." A light encircled the cross, and the face of the Saviour shone with a glory like the sun. He then bowed His head and died.

Amid the awful darkness, Christ had drained the dregs in the cup of human woe. In those dreadful hours He had relied on the evidence of His Father's acceptance heretofore given Him. Acquainted with the character of His Father, by faith He rested in Him whom it had ever been His joy to obey. And as He committed Himself to God, the sense of the loss of His Father's favor was withdrawn. By faith, Christ was victor.

Again darkness settled on the earth, and there was a violent earthquake. Wild confusion ensued. In the surrounding mountains, rocks were rent asunder, and went crashing into the plains. Sepulchers were broken open, and the dead were cast out. Priests, soldiers, executioners, and people, lay prostrate on the ground.

When the loud cry, "It is finished," came from the lips of Christ, it was the hour of the evening sacrifice. The lamb representing Christ had been brought to be slain. The priest stood with lifted knife, the people looking on. But the earth trembled, for the Lord Himself drew near. With a rending noise the inner veil of the temple was torn from top to bottom by an unseen hand, throwing open to the gaze of the multitude a place once filled with the presence of God. The most holy place of the earthly sanctuary was no longer sacred.

All was terror and confusion. The priest was about to slay the victim; but the knife dropped from his nerveless hand, and the lamb escaped. Type had met antitype. The great sacrifice had been made. A new and living way was prepared for all. Henceforth the Saviour was to officiate as priest and advocate in the heaven of heavens. "By His own blood He entered in once into the holy place, having obtained eternal redemption for us." Hebrews 9:12.

79 / How Christ's Death Defeated Satan

Christ had accomplished the work He came to do, , and with His parting breath He exclaimed, "It is finished." John 19:30. The battle had been won. All heaven triumphed in the Saviour's victory. Satan knew his kingdom was lost. It was for the angels and unfallen worlds as well as for us that the great work of redemption had been accomplished. Until the death of Christ, Satan had so clothed himself with deception that even holy beings had not understood his principles nor clearly seen the nature of his rebellion.

Lucifer had been the covering cherub, the highest of all created beings. He had been foremost in revealing God's purposes to the universe. After he had sinned, his power to deceive was the more deceptive, and unveiling his character was more difficult because of the exalted position he had held with the Father.

God could have destroyed Satan and his sympathizers, but He did not do this. Force, compelling power, are found only under Satan's government. The Lord's authority rests on goodness, mercy, and love, and these principles are the means to be used. God's government is moral, and truth and love are to be the prevailing power.

In the councils of heaven it was decided that time must be given for Satan to develop the principles of his government. He had claimed that these were superior to God's. Time was given for the working of Satan's principles, that they might be seen by the heavenly universe. For 4000 years, Christ was working for man's uplifting, and Satan for his ruin. And the heavenly universe beheld it all.

From the time when Jesus appeared as a babe in Bethlehem, Satan worked to bring about His destruction. He sought to prevent Him from developing a perfect childhood, a faultless manhood, a holy ministry, and an unblemished sacrifice. But he was defeated. He could not lead Jesus into sin. All the efforts of Satan to overcome Him only brought out in a purer light His spotless character.

With intense interest heaven and the unfallen worlds followed the closing scenes of the conflict. They heard His bitter cry, "Father, if it be possible, let this cup pass from Me." Matthew 26:39. They saw Him sorrowful with a bitterness exceeding that of the last great struggle with death. The bloody sweat was forced from His pores, and thrice the prayer for deliverance was wrung from His lips. Heaven could no longer endure the sight, and a messenger of comfort was sent to the Son of God.

Earth the Stage, Heaven the Audience

Heaven beheld the Victim betrayed and with violence hurried from one tribunal to another. It heard the sneers of His persecutors and the denial with cursing by one of His disciples. It saw the Saviour dragged to and fro from palace to judgment hall, arraigned twice before the priests, twice before the Sanhedrin, twice before Pilate, and once before Herod, mocked, scourged, condemned, and led out to be crucified.

Heaven viewed with amazement Christ hanging on the cross, blood flowing from His wounded temples, His hands, His feet. The wounds gaped as the weight of His body dragged on His hands. His soul panted under the burden of the sins of the world. All heaven was filled with wonder when Christ prayed in the midst of His terrible suffering, "Father, forgive them; for they know not what they do." Luke 23:34.

The powers of darkness around the cross cast the

hellish shadow of unbelief into the hearts of men. Satanic agencies led the people to believe Christ the chief of sinners and to make Him the object of detestation. Those who mocked Christ were imbued with the spirit of the first great rebel. He inspired their taunts. But by all this he gained nothing.

Had Christ in one particular yielded to Satan to escape the terrible torture, the enemy would have triumphed. Christ bowed His head and died, but He held fast His faith. "And I heard a loud voice saying in heaven, Now is come salvation, and strength, and the kingdom of our God, and the power of His Christ: for the accuser of our brethren is cast down, which accused them before our God day and night." Revelation 12:10.

Satan saw that his disguise was torn away. He had revealed himself as a murderer. By shedding the blood of the Son of God, he had uprooted himself from the sympathies of the heavenly beings. Henceforth he could no longer await the angels as they came from the heavenly courts, and before them accuse Christ's brethren of being clothed with the defilement of sin. The last link of sympathy between Satan and the heavenly world was broken.

Yet the angels did not even then understand all that was involved in the great controversy. The principles at stake were to be more fully revealed. Man as well as angels must see the contrast between the Prince of light and the prince of darkness. He must choose whom he will serve.

In the opening of the great controversy, Satan had declared that the law of God could not be obeyed, that justice was inconsistent with mercy, and that, should the law be broken, it would be impossible for the sinner to be pardoned. If God should remit the punishment of sin, urged Satan, He would not be a God of justice. When men broke the law of God, Satan declared it was proved that the law could not be obeyed; man could not be forgiven. Because he, after his rebellion, had been banished from heaven, Satan claimed that the human race must be forever shut out from God's favor. God could not be just, he urged, and yet show mercy to the sinner.

But man was in a different position from that of Satan. Lucifer had sinned in the light of God's glory. Understanding the character of God, Satan chose to follow his own selfish will. There was no more that God could do to save him. But man was deceived, his mind darkened by Satan's sophistry. The height and depth of the love of God he did not know. By beholding His character he might be drawn back to God.

How Justice Is Blended With Mercy

Through Jesus, God's mercy was manifested to men; but mercy does not set aside justice. The law could not be changed, but God sacrificed Himself in Christ for man's redemption. "God was in Christ, reconciling the world unto Himself." 2 Corinthians 5:19.

The law requires a righteous life, a perfect character, and this man has not to give. But Christ, as man, lived a holy life and developed a perfect character. These He offers as a free gift to all who will receive Him. His life stands for the life of men. Thus they have remission of sins that are past. More than this, Christ imbues men with the attributes of God. He builds up the human character after the similitude of the divine character. Thus "the righteousness of the law" is fulfilled in the believer in Christ. God can "be just, and the justifier of him which believeth in Jesus." Romans 3:26.

It had been Satan's purpose to divorce mercy from truth and justice. But Christ showed that in God's plan they are joined together; the one cannot exist without the other. "Righteousness and peace have kissed each other." Psalm 85:10.

By His life and His death, Christ proved that God's justice did not destroy His mercy, but that sin could be forgiven, and that the law is righteous, and can be perfectly obeyed. Satan's charges were refuted.

Another deception was now to be brought forward. Satan declared that the death of Christ abrogated the Father's law. Had it been possible for the law to be changed or abrogated, then Christ need not have died. But to abrogate the law would be to immortalize transgression and place the world under Satan's control. Because the law was changeless, Jesus was lifted up on the cross. Yet the means by which Christ established the law Satan represented as destroying it. Here will come the last conflict of the great controversy between Christ and Satan.

Satan's "New Model" Lie

That some specification of the law spoken by God's own voice has been set aside is the claim which Satan now puts forward. He need not assail the whole law; if he can lead men to disregard one precept, his purpose is gained. For "whosoever shall keep the whole law, and yet offend in one point, he is guilty of all." James 2:10. By consenting to break one precept, men are brought under Satan's power. Prophecy declares of the great apostate power, the representative of Satan: "He shall speak great words against the Most High, and shall wear out the saints of the Most High, and think to change times and laws: and they shall be given into his hand." Daniel 7:25. Men will set up laws to counterwork the laws of God, and in their zeal to enforce these laws they will oppress their fellow men.

The warfare against God's law will continue until the end of time. All will be called to choose between the law of God and the laws of men. There will be but two classes. Every character will be fully developed. All will show whether they have chosen the side of loyalty or that of rebellion.

Then the end will come. God will vindicate His law and deliver His people. Satan and all who join him in rebellion will be cut off. Sin and sinners will perish, root and branch. See Malachi 4:1.

This is not an arbitrary act on the part of God. The

rejecters of His mercy reap that which they have sown. God is the fountain of life, and when one chooses sin, he cuts himself off from life. Christ says, "All they that hate Me love death." Proverbs 8:36. God gives them existence for a time that they may develop their character and reveal their principles. This accomplished, they receive the results of their own choice. Satan and all who unite with him place themselves so out of harmony with God that the very presence of Him who is love will destroy them.

At the beginning of the great controversy, the angels did not understand this. Had Satan and his host then perished, a doubt of God's goodness would have remained in their minds as evil seed to produce its deadly fruit of sin.

But not so when the great controversy shall be ended. Then, the plan of redemption having been completed, the character of God is revealed to all created intelligences. The precepts of His law are seen to be perfect and immutable. Sin has made manifest its nature, Satan his character. The extermination of sin will vindicate God's love and establish His honor before the universe.

Well, then, might the angels rejoice as they looked on the Saviour's cross; for though they did not then understand all, they knew that the destruction of Satan was made certain, the redemption of man was assured, and the universe was made eternally secure.

Christ Himself fully comprehended the results of the sacrifice made on Calvary. To all these He looked forward when upon the cross He cried out, "It is finished."

80 / Jesus Rests in Joseph's Tomb

At last the long day of shame and torture was ended. As the setting sun ushered in the Sabbath, the Son of God rested in Joseph's tomb, His work completed.

In the beginning the Father and the Son had rested on the Sabbath after their work of creation. See Genesis 2:1. All heavenly beings rejoiced in contemplation of the glorious scene. Now Jesus rested from the work of redemption; and though there was grief among those who loved Him on earth, there was joy in heaven. God and angels saw a redeemed race that, having conquered sin, could never fall—this, the result to flow from Christ's completed work.

When there shall be a "restitution of all things" (Acts 3:21), the creation Sabbath, the day on which Jesus lay at rest in Joseph's tomb, will still be a day of rest and rejoicing. "From one Sabbath to another" (Isaiah 66:23) the nations of the saved shall bow in joyful worship to God and the Lamb.

In the closing events of the crucifixion day, new witness was borne to Christ's divinity. When the Saviour's dying cry had been uttered, another voice was heard, saying, "Truly this was the Son of God." Matthew 27:54.

These words were said in no whispered tones. Who had spoken? It was the centurion, the Roman soldier. The divine patience of the Saviour, His sudden death, the cry of victory on His lips, had impressed this heathen. In the broken body hanging on the cross, the centurion recognized the Son of God. On the very day of

Jesus' friends stood by amazed as two wealthy leaders in Israel removed His body from the cross, wrapped Him in grave clothes, and carried Him to an expensive tomb for burial.

the Redeemer's death, three men had declared their faith—he who commanded the Roman guard, he who bore His cross, and he who died at His side.

As evening drew on, an unearthly stillness hung over Calvary. Many had flocked to the crucifixion from curiosity, not from hatred toward Christ. Still they looked on Christ as a malefactor. Under unnatural excitement they had united in railing against Him. But when the earth was wrapped in blackness, they felt guilty of a great wrong. When it was lifted, they made their way home in solemn silence, convinced that the charges of the priests were false, that Jesus was no pretender. A few weeks later, when Peter preached on the day of Pentecost, they were among the thousands who became converts to Christ.

But the Jewish leaders were unchanged; their hatred had not abated. The darkness at the crucifixion was not more dense than that which still enveloped their minds. Inanimate nature had known Christ and borne witness to His divinity. But the priests and rulers of Israel knew not the Son of God. They had put Christ to death; but even in the hour of their apparent triumph, they were harassed with doubts. What would next take place? They had heard the cry, "It is finished." John 19:30. They had felt the mighty earthquake, and they were uneasy. They dreaded the dead Christ far more than they had feared the living Christ. They dreaded any further attention to the events attending His crucifixion. Not on any account would they have His body remain on the cross during the Sabbath. It would be a violation of its sanctity for the bodies to hang on the cross. So, using this as a pretext, leading Jews requested Pilate that the death of the victims might be hastened, and their bodies be removed before the setting of the sun.

His consent obtained, the legs of the two thieves were broken to hasten their death; but Jesus was already dead. The rude soldiers, softened by what they had heard and seen of Christ, were restrained from breaking His limbs. Thus was fulfilled the law of the Passover, "They shall leave none of it until the morning, nor break any bone of it." Numbers 9:12.

The priests and rulers were amazed to find that Christ was dead. It was unheard of for one to die within six hours of crucifixion. The priests wished to make sure of the death of Jesus, and at their suggestion a soldier thrust a spear into the Saviour's side. From the wound flowed two distinct streams, one of blood, the other of water.

John states: "One of the soldiers with a spear pierced His side, and forthwith there came out blood and water. And he that saw it bare record, and his record is true. . . . These things were done, that the scripture should be fulfilled, A bone of Him shall not be broken. And again another scripture saith, They shall look on Him whom they pierced." John 19:34-37.

After the resurrection the priests circulated the report that Christ did not die on the cross, that He merely fainted and was afterward revived. The action of the Roman soldiers proves He was already dead. Had not life been already extinct, this wound would have caused instant death.

But it was not the spear thrust nor the pain of the cross that caused the death of Jesus. That cry, uttered "with a loud voice" (Matthew 27:50; Luke 23:46), at the moment of death and the stream of blood and water declared that He died of a broken heart—broken by mental anguish, slain by the sin of the world.

The Disciples Discouraged

With the death of Christ the hopes of His disciples perished. Until the last they had not believed He would die; they could hardly believe that He was dead. Overwhelmed with sorrow, nothing that He had said now gave them comfort. Their faith in Jesus had perished, but never had they loved their Lord as now, never had they so felt their need of His presence.

Christ's disciples longed to give Him an honored

burial, but knew not how to accomplish this. Persons put to death for treason against the Roman government were consigned to a burial ground for criminals. John with the women from Galilee could not leave the body of their Lord to be handled by unfeeling soldiers and buried in a dishonored grave. Yet they could obtain no favors from the Jewish authorities and had no influence with Pilate.

In this emergency, Joseph of Arimathea and Nicodemus came to the help of the disciples. Both were members of the Sanhedrin, both were men of wealth and influence, both were acquainted with Pilate. They were determined that the body of Jesus should have an honorable burial.

Help From an Unexpected Place

Joseph went boldly to Pilate and begged from him the body of Jesus. For the first time, Pilate learned that Jesus was dead. The knowledge of Christ's death had been purposely kept from him. Upon hearing Joseph's request, he sent for the centurion who had charge at the cross and drew from him an account of the scenes of Calvary, confirming the testimony of Joseph.

Joseph returned with Pilate's order for the body of Christ, and Nicodemus came bringing a costly mixture of myrrh and aloes of about a hundred pounds' weight for His embalming. The most honored in all Jerusalem could not have been shown more respect in death. The disciples were astonished.

Neither Joseph nor Nicodemus had openly accepted the Saviour while He was living. Such a step would exclude them from the Sanhedrin, and they hoped to protect Him by their influence in its councils. But the wily priests had thwarted their plans. In their absence Jesus had been condemned. Now Joseph and Nicodemus no longer concealed their attachment to Him. They came boldly to the aid of the poor disciples.

Gently and reverently with their own hands they removed the body of Jesus from the cross. Tears of sympathy fell as they looked on His bruised and lacerated form. Joseph owned a new tomb, hewn in rock, reserved for himself. But it was near Calvary, and he now prepared it for Jesus. There the three disciples straightened the mangled limbs and folded the bruised hands on the pulseless breast. The heavy stone was rolled against the entrance of the tomb, and the Saviour was left at rest.

While the evening shadows were gathering, Mary Magdalene and the other Marys lingered about the resting place of their Lord, shedding tears of sorrow. "And they returned, . . . and rested the Sabbath day according to the commandment." Luke 23:56.

That was a never-to-be-forgotten Sabbath to the disciples, the priests, rulers, scribes, and people. The Passover was observed as it had been for centuries, while He to whom it pointed lay in Joseph's tomb. The courts of the temple were filled with worshipers. The high priest was there, splendidly robed. Priests, full of activity, performed their duties.

But some present were not at rest as the blood of bulls and goats was offered for sin. They were not conscious that type had met antitype, that an infinite sacrifice had been made for the sins of the world. But never before had that service been witnessed with such conflicting feelings. A sense of strangeness pervaded everything. The most holy place had been sacredly guarded from intrusion, but now, the heavy veil rent from top to bottom, it was open to all eyes—a place no longer recognized by the Lord. The uncovering of the most holy place filled the priests with dread of coming calamity.

Many Turn to Bible Study

From the crucifixion to the resurrection many sleepless eyes were searching the prophecies, some to find evidence that Jesus was not what He claimed to be, and others searching for proofs that He was the true Messiah. Though searching with different objects in view, all were convicted of the same truth—prophecy had been fulfilled; the Crucified One was the world's Redeemer. Many never again took part in the paschal rites. Many even of the priests searched the prophecies and after His resurrection acknowledged Him as the Son of God.

Nicodemus remembered Jesus' words spoken by night in the Mount of Olives: "As Moses lifted up the serpent in the wilderness, even so must the Son of man be lifted up: that whosoever believeth in Him should not perish, but have eternal life." John 3:14, 15. The words Jesus had spoken to him were no longer mysterious. He felt that he had lost much by not connecting himself with the Saviour during His life. The prayer of Christ for His murderers and His answer to the dying thief spoke to the heart of the learned councilor. Again he heard that last cry, "It is finished," spoken like the words of a conqueror. His faith was forever established. The event that destroyed the hopes of the disciples convinced Joseph and Nicodemus of the divinity of Jesus.

Never had Christ attracted the attention of the multitude as now that He was in the tomb. People brought their sick to the temple courts. On every side was heard the cry, We want Christ the Healer! The friendly hands of Jesus that never refused to touch with healing the loathsome leper, were folded on His breast. The lips that had answered his petition, "I will; be thou clean" (Matthew 8:3) were now silent. Many were determined to have the living Christ among them again. With persistent earnestness they asked for Him. But they were driven from the temple courts, and soldiers were stationed to keep back the multitude with their sick and dying.

The sufferers sank under their disappointment. The sick were dying for want of the healing touch of Jesus. Physicians were consulted in vain; there was no skill like that of Him who lay in Joseph's tomb.

To thousands of minds came the conviction that a

great light had gone out of the world. Without Christ, the earth was darkness. Many whose voices had swelled the cry, "Crucify Him, crucify Him," now realized the calamity that had fallen upon them.

When the people learned that Jesus had been put to death by the priests, inquiries were made. The particulars of His trial were kept as private as possible, but reports of the inhumanity of the priests and rulers were circulated everywhere. Men of intellect called on these priests and rulers to explain the prophecies concerning the Messiah. While trying to frame some falsehood in reply, they became like men insane. The prophecies that pointed to Christ's sufferings and death they could not explain.

The priests knew they were meeting the severe censure of the people. The ones they had influenced against Jesus were now horrified by their own shameful work. These priests trembled for fear that Christ would Himself rise from the dead and again appear before them. They remembered that He had said, "Destroy this temple, and in three days I will raise it up." John 2:19. Judas had told them the words spoken by Jesus on the last journey to Jerusalem: "The Son of man shall be betrayed unto the chief priests and unto the scribes, and they will condemn Him to death, and shall deliver Him to the Gentiles . . . to crucify Him: and the third day He shall rise again." Matthew 20:18, 19. They remembered that Christ's predictions had so far been fulfilled. Who could say that this also would not come to pass?

They longed to shut out these thoughts, but they could not. The image of Christ would intrude on their minds, serene and uncomplaining before His enemies, suffering without a murmur their taunts and abuse. An overpowering conviction came to them that He was the Son of God. He might at any time stand before them, the accused to become the accuser, the slain to demand justice in the death of His murderers.

Though they would not step over a Gentile's threshold for fear of defilement, on the Sabbath they held a council concerning the body of Christ. "The chief priests and the Pharisees came together unto Pilate, saying, Sir, we remember that that deceiver said, while He was yet alive, After three days I will rise again. Command therefore that the sepulcher be made sure until the third day, lest His disciples come by night, and steal Him away, and say unto the people, He is risen from the dead: so the last error will be worse than the first. Pilate said unto them, ye have a watch: go your way, make it as sure as ye can." Matthew 27: 62-65.

The priests gave directions for securing the sepulcher. A great stone had been placed before the opening. Across this stone they placed cords, sealing them with the Roman seal. A guard of one hundred soldiers was then stationed around the sepulcher to prevent it from being tampered with. Jesus was sealed as securely in His tomb as if He were to remain there through all time.

But the efforts made to prevent Christ's resurrection are the most convincing arguments in its proof. The greater the number of soldiers placed around the tomb, the stronger would be the testimony that He had risen. Roman arms were powerless to confine the Lord of life within the tomb. The hour of His release was near.

81 / "The Lord Is Risen"

The night of the first day of the week had worn slowly away. Christ was still a prisoner in His tomb. The Roman seal was unbroken; the Roman guards were keeping their watch. Had it been possible, the prince of darkness would have kept forever sealed the tomb that held the Son of God. But heavenly angels that excel in strength were waiting to welcome the Prince of life.

"And, behold, there was a great earthquake: for the angel of the Lord descended from heaven." The bright beams of God's glory illuminated his pathway. "His countenance was like lightning, and his raiment white as snow: And for fear of him the keepers did shake, and became as dead men."

This messenger was he who fills the position from which Satan fell. As he rolled away the stone, heaven seemed to come down to earth. The soldiers saw him removing the stone as he would a pebble, and heard him cry, Son of God, come forth; Thy Father calls Thee. They saw Jesus come forth from the grave and heard Him proclaim over the rent sepulcher, "I am the resurrection, and the life." As He came forth in majesty and glory, the angel host welcomed Him with songs of praise.

At sight of the angels and the glorified Saviour, the Roman guard had fainted and become as dead men. When the heavenly train was hidden from their view, they arose and, staggering like drunken men, hurried to the city, telling those whom they met the wonderful

This chapter is based on Matthew 28:2-4, 11-15.

news. They were making their way to Pilate, but the priests and rulers sent for them to be brought first into their presence. Trembling with fear, their faces colorless, the soldiers told all, just as they had seen it. They said, It was the Son of God who was crucified; we have heard an angel proclaiming Him as the Majesty of heaven, the King of glory.

Caiaphas Urges Deceit

Caiaphas tried to speak. His lips moved, but they uttered no sound. The soldiers were about to leave when Caiaphas at last found speech. Wait, wait, he said. Tell no one the things you have seen.

"Say ye," said the priests, "His disciples came by night, and stole Him away while we slept." Here the priests overreached themselves. If they were asleep, how could they know? And if the disciples had been proved guilty of stealing Christ's body, would not the priests have been first to condemn them? Or if the sentinels had slept, would not the priests have been foremost in accusing them to Pilate?

The soldiers were horrified. Sleeping at their post was an offense punishable with death. Should they bear false witness and place their own lives in peril? How could they stand the trial, even for the sake of money, if they perjured themselves?

The priests promised to secure the safety of the guard, saying that Pilate would not desire to have such a report circulated any more than they did. The Roman soldiers sold their integrity for money. They came before the priests burdened with a startling message of truth; they went out with a burden of money, and on their tongues a lying report.

Meanwhile the report of Christ's resurrection had been carried to Pilate. Though he had condemned the Saviour unwillingly, he had felt no real compunction until now. In terror he now shut himself within his house, determined to see no one. But the priests made their way into his presence and urged him to overlook the sentinels' neglect of duty. He himself privately questioned the guard. They dared not conceal anything, and Pilate drew from them an account of all that had taken place. He did not prosecute the matter further, but from that time there was no peace for him.

The priests, in putting Christ to death, had made themselves the tools of Satan. Now they were entirely in his power, entangled in a snare from which they saw no escape but in continuing their warfare against Christ. The only hope for them was to prove Christ an impostor by denying that He had risen. They bribed the soldiers and secured Pilate's silence.

But there were witnesses whom they could not silence. Many had heard of the soldiers' testimony to Christ's resurrection. And certain of the dead who came forth with Christ appeared to many and declared that He had risen. The priests and rulers were in continual dread, lest in walking the streets or within the privacy of their own homes, they should come face to face with Christ. Bolts and bars were but poor protection against the Son of God. By day and by night that awful scene when they had cried, "His blood be on us, and on our children," was before them. Matthew 27:25.

The Guarantee of Our Resurrection

When the voice of the mighty angel was heard at Christ's tomb, saying, Thy Father calls Thee, the Saviour came forth from the grave by the life that was in Himself. Christ had proclaimed in triumph, "I am the resurrection and the life." These words could be spoken only by the Deity. All created beings are dependent recipients of the life of God. Only He who is one with God could say, I have power to lay down My life, and I have power to take it again. See John 10:18.

Christ arose from the dead as the first fruits of those that slept, and His resurrection took place on the very day when the wave sheaf was to be presented before the Lord. For more than a thousand years when the people went up to Jerusalem to the Passover, the sheaf of first fruits was waved as a thank offering before the Lord. Not until this was presented could the sickle be put to the grain. The sheaf dedicated to God represented the harvest. So Christ's resurrection is the type and pledge of the resurrection of all the righteous dead. "For if we believe that Jesus died and rose again, even so them also which sleep in Jesus will God bring with Him." 1 Thessalonians 4:14.

Many Resurrected With Jesus

As Christ arose, He brought from the grave a multitude of captives. See Matthew 27:52. They were those who at the cost of their lives had borne testimony to the truth. Now they were to be witnesses for Him who had raised them from the dead.

During His ministry, Jesus had raised the dead to life. But these resurrected ones were not clothed with immortality. But those who came forth from the grave at Christ's resurrection were raised to everlasting life. They ascended with Him as trophies of His victory over death and the grave. They went into the city and appeared unto many, declaring, Christ has risen from the dead, and we be risen with Him. Risen saints bore witness to the truth of the words, "Thy dead men shall live, together with My dead body shall they arise." Isaiah 26:19.

In our Saviour, the life that was lost through sin is restored. He is invested with the right to give immortality. "I am come," He said, "that they might have life, and that they might have it more abundantly." John 10:10. "Whoso eateth My flesh, and drinketh My blood, hath eternal life; and I will raise him up at the last day." John 6:54. To the Christian, death is but a sleep, a moment of silence and darkness. "When Christ, who is our life shall appear, then shall ye also appear with Him in glory." Colossians 3:4.

The voice that cried from the cross, "It is finished," will penetrate the graves and unbar the tombs, and the dead in Christ shall arise. At the Saviour's resurrection a few graves were opened, but at His second coming all the precious dead shall hear His voice and come forth to glorious immortal life. The same power that raised Christ from the dead will raise His church above all powers, not only in this world, but also in the world to come.

82 / "Woman, Why Weepest Thou?"

On the first day of the week, very early, the women who had stood by the cross made their way to the tomb to anoint the Saviour's body. They did not think about His rising from the dead. The sun of their hope had set. They remembered not His words, "I will see you again." John 16:22.

Ignorant of what was even then taking place, they drew near the garden, saying, "Who shall roll us away the stone from the door of the sepulcher?" And lo, the heavens were suddenly alight with glory. The earth trembled. The great stone was rolled away. The grave was empty!

Mary Magdalene was the first to reach the place, and seeing the stone was removed, she hurried to tell the disciples. Meanwhile the other women came. A light was shining about the tomb, but the body of Jesus was not there.

As they lingered, suddenly they saw they were not alone. A young man in shining garments was sitting by the tomb. It was the angel who had rolled away the stone. He had taken the guise of humanity that he might not alarm these friends of Jesus. Yet about him the light of the heavenly glory was still shining, and the women were afraid. "Do not be afraid," the angel said, "for I know that ye seek Jesus, which was crucified. He is not here: for He is risen, as He said. Come, see the place where the Lord lay. And go quickly, and tell His disciples that He is risen from the dead."

They looked into the tomb, and another angel in hu-

This chapter is based on Matthew 28:1, 5-8; Mark 16:1-8; Luke 24:1-12; John 20:1-18.

man form said, "Why seek ye the living among the dead? He is not here, but is risen: remember how He spake unto you when He was yet in Galilee, saying, The Son of man must be delivered into the hands of sinful men, and be crucified, and the third day rise again."

The women remembered now—He said He would rise again! What a day is this to the world! Quickly they departed "with fear and great joy; and did run to bring His disciples word."

Mary had not heard the good news. She went to Peter and John with the sorrowful message, "They have taken away the Lord out of the sepulcher, and we know not where they have laid Him." The disciples hurried to the tomb and saw the shroud and the napkin, but did not find their Lord. Yet even here was testimony that He had risen. The graveclothes were not thrown heedlessly aside, but carefully folded, each in a place by itself. John "saw, and believed." He now remembered the Saviour's words foretelling His resurrection.

Christ Himself placed those graveclothes with such care. As the mighty angel from heaven rolled away the stone, another entered the tomb and unbound the wrappings from the body of Jesus. But it was the Saviour's hand that folded each, and laid it in its place. In His sight who guides alike the star and the atom, nothing is unimportant.

Mary had followed John and Peter to the tomb; when they returned to Jerusalem, she remained. Grief filled her heart. Looking into the empty tomb, she saw the two angels, one at the head and the other at the foot where Jesus had lain. "Woman, why weepest thou?" they asked her. "Because they have taken away my Lord," she answered, "and I know not where they have laid Him."

Then she turned away, thinking that she must find someone who could tell her what had been done with the body. Another voice addressed her: "Woman, why weepest thou? whom seekest thou?" Through tear-dimmed eyes, Mary saw a man, and thinking it was the gardener, said, "Sir, if Thou have borne Him hence, tell me where thou hast laid Him, and I will take Him away." If this rich man's tomb was thought too honorable for Jesus, she herself would provide a place for Him. There was a grave that Christ's own voice had made vacant, the grave where Lazarus had lain.

But now in His own familiar voice, Jesus said to her, "Mary." Turning, she saw before her the living Christ! Springing toward Him as if to embrace His feet, she said, "Rabboni." But Christ raised His hand, saying, Detain Me not; "for I have not yet ascended to My Father: but go to My brethren, and say unto them, I ascend unto My Father, and your Father; and to My God, and your God." Mary went her way with the joyful message.

Jesus refused the homage of His people until He ascended to the heavenly courts and from God Himself heard the assurance that His atonement for the sins of men had been ample, that through His blood all might attain eternal life. The Father ratified the covenant made with Christ, that He would receive repentant and obedient men and would love them even as He loves His Son. All power in heaven and on earth was given to the Prince of life, that He might impart of His power and glory to His followers.

While the Saviour was in God's presence, receiving gifts for His church, the disciples mourned and wept. The day of rejoicing to all heaven was to them a day of confusion and perplexity. Their unbelief in the testimony of the women gives evidence of how low their faith had sunk. They could not believe the news. It was too good to be true, they thought. They had heard so much of the so-called scientific theories of the Sadducees that they scarcely knew what the resurrection from the dead could mean.

"Go your way," the angels had said to the women, "tell His disciples and Peter that He goeth before you into Galilee: there shall ye see Him, as He said unto you." The message of these angels to the disciples should have convinced them of its truth. Such words could have come only from the messengers of their risen Lord.

Since the death of Christ, Peter had been bowed down with remorse. His shameful denial of the Lord was ever before him. Of all the disciples, he had suffered most bitterly. To him the assurance was given that his repentance was accepted. He was mentioned by name.

When Mary Magdalene had told the disciples she had seen the Lord, she repeated the call to the meeting in Galilee. And a third time the message was sent to them. After He ascended to the Father, Jesus appeared to the other women, saying, "Go tell My brethren that they go into Galilee, and there shall they see Me."

Christ's first work after His resurrection was to convince His disciples of His undiminished love and tender regard for them. He would draw the bonds of love still closer around them. Go tell My brethren, He said, that they meet Me in Galilee.

But even now the disciples could not cast off their doubt and perplexity. Even when the women declared that they had seen the Lord, they thought them under an illusion.

Trouble seemed crowding on trouble. They had seen their Master die; they found themselves deprived of His body; and they were accused of having stolen it for the sake of deceiving the people. They despaired of ever correcting the false impressions gaining ground. They feared the enmity of the priests and the wrath of the people. They longed for the presence of Jesus.

Often they repeated the words, "We trusted that it had been He which should have redeemed Israel." Luke 24:21. Lonely and sick at heart, they met together in the upper chamber, and closed and fastened the doors, knowing that the fate of their beloved Teacher might at any time be theirs.

And all the time they might have been rejoicing in the knowledge of a risen Saviour. Many are still doing what these disciples did. The Saviour is close beside them, but their tear-blinded eyes do not discern Him. He speaks to them, but they do not understand.

"Go quickly, and tell His disciples that He is risen." Look not to the empty sepulcher. From grateful hearts, from lips touched with holy fire, let the glad song ring out, Christ is risen! He lives to make intercession for us.

83 / The Walk to Emmaus

Late in the afternoon of the day of the resurrection, two disciples were on their way to Emmaus, a little town eight miles from Jerusalem. These disciples had come to keep the Passover and were greatly perplexed by the events that had taken place. They had heard the news in regard to the removal of Christ's body and also the report of the women who had seen the angels and had met Jesus. Now returning home, they were talking over the scenes of the trial and crucifixion. Never had they been so utterly disheartened.

On their journey they were joined by a stranger, but were so absorbed in their gloom that they did not observe him closely. They continued expressing the thoughts of their hearts, reasoning in regard to the lessons Christ had given, which they seemed unable to comprehend. Jesus longed to comfort them. He understood the conflicting, perplexing ideas that brought to their minds the thought, Can this Man, who suffered Himself to be so humiliated, be the Christ? They wept. Jesus longed to wipe away their tears, and fill them with joy and gladness. But He must first give them lessons they would never forget.

"He said unto them, What manner of communications are these that ye have one to another, as ye walk, and are sad? And the one of them whose name was Cleopas, answering said unto Him, Art thou only a stranger in Jerusalem, and hast not known the things which are come to pass there in these days?" They told Him of their disappointment in regard to their Master,

This chapter is based on Luke 24:13-33.

530

"which was a prophet mighty in deed and word before God and all the people," but "the chief priests and our rulers delivered Him to be condemned to death, and have crucified Him." With quivering lips they added, "We trusted that it had been He which should have redeemed Israel: and beside all this, today is the third day since these things were done."

Strange that they did not remember Christ's words, and that He had foretold that the third day He would rise again. The priests and rulers did not forget!

Incognito, Jesus Explains the Scriptures

"Then He said unto them, O fools, and slow of heart to believe all that the prophets have spoken: ought not Christ to have suffered these things, and to enter into His glory?" Who could this be, that He should speak with such earnestness and sympathy? For the first time, they began to feel hopeful. Often they looked earnestly at their companion, and thought that His words were just the words that Christ would have spoken.

Beginning at Moses, the Alpha of Bible history, Christ expounded in all the Scriptures the things concerning Himself. Had He first made Himself known to them, they would have hungered for nothing more. But it was necessary for them to understand the types and prophecies of the Old Testament. On these their faith must be established. Christ performed no miracle to convince them; it was His first work to explain the Scriptures. He showed from the prophets that His death was the strongest evidence for their faith.

Jesus showed the importance of the Old Testament as a witness to His mission. The Saviour is revealed in the Old Testament as clearly as in the New. Light from the prophetic past brings out the life of Christ and the teachings of the New Testament with clearness and beauty. Stronger proof than the miracles of Christ is found in comparing the prophecies of the Old Testament with the history of the New.

The disciples' expectation of a Messiah who was to

take His throne and kingly power in accordance with the desires of men had been misleading. His disciples must understand in regard to the cup of suffering that had been apportioned Him. He showed them that the awful conflict was the fulfillment of the covenant made before the foundation of the world. Christ must die, as every transgressor of the law must die if he continues in sin. All this was to be, but it was not to end in defeat, but in glorious victory. Jesus told them that every effort must be made to save the world from sin. His followers must live as He lived, and work as He worked, with persevering effort.

Thus Christ discoursed to His disciples, that they might understand the Scriptures. As He told them of the overthrow of Jerusalem, they looked on the doomed city with weeping. But little did they suspect yet who their traveling companion was, for Christ referred to Himself as though He were another person. He walked as carefully as they over the rough stones, now and then halting with them for a little rest.

Their Hearts Were Drawn to the Stranger

During their journey the sun had gone down and the laborers in the fields had left their work. As the disciples were about to enter their home, the stranger appeared as though He would continue His journey. But the disciples hungered to hear more from Him. "Abide with us," they urged. He did not seem to accept the invitation, but they pressed Him. "It is toward evening, and the day is far spent." Christ yielded to this entreaty and "went in to tarry with them."

Had the disciples failed to press their invitation, they would not have known that their traveling companion was the risen Lord. Christ never forces His company on anyone. Gladly will He enter the humblest home, but if men are too indifferent to ask Him to stay with them, He passes on.

The simple evening meal was soon prepared and placed before the Guest, who had taken His seat at the head of the table. Now He put forth His hands to bless the food in exactly the same way as their Master used to do. The disciples started back in astonishment. They looked again and saw in His hands the print of nails. Both exclaimed, It is the Lord Jesus!

They rose to cast themselves at His feet, but He had vanished. They looked at the place occupied by One whose body had lately lain in the grave, and said to each other, "Did not our hearts burn within us, while He talked with us by the way, and while He opened to us the Scriptures?"

With this great news to communicate, their weariness and hunger were gone. They left their meal untasted and hurried on the same path by which they had come, to tell the disciples in the city. They climbed over steep places, slipping on smooth rocks, desiring to go faster than they dared. They lost the track, but found it again. Sometimes running, sometimes stumbling, they pressed forward, their unseen Companion beside them all the way.

The night was dark, but the Sun of Righteousness was shining upon them. They seemed to be in a new world. Christ is risen—over and over they repeated it. They must tell the sorrowing ones the wonderful story of the walk to Emmaus. They must tell who joined them by the way. They carried the greatest message ever given—glad tidings on which the hopes of the human family for time and eternity depend.

84 / The Resurrected Christ Appears

On reaching Jerusalem the two disciples entered at the eastern gate, made their way through the narrow streets by the light of the rising moon, and went to the upper chamber where Jesus had spent the last evening before His death. Here they knew their brethren were to be found. The door was securely barred. They knocked for admission, but no answer came. All was still. Then they gave their names. The door was carefully unbarred, they entered, and Another, unseen, entered with them. Then the door was again fastened, to keep out spies.

The travelers found all in surprised excitement. Voices in the room said, "The Lord has risen indeed, and hath appeared to Simon!" Then the two, panting with haste, told how Jesus had appeared to them. Some were saying they could not believe it, for it was too good to be true, when another Person stood before them. No stranger had knocked for entrance, no footstep had been heard. The disciples were startled. Then they heard the voice of their Master, clear and distinct, "Peace be unto you."

"But they were terrified and affrighted, and supposed that they had seen a spirit. And He said unto them, Why are ye troubled? and why do thoughts arise in your hearts? See My hands and My feet, that it is I Myself: handle Me, and see; for a spirit hath not flesh and bones, as ye see Me have. And when He had thus spoken, He showed them His hands and His feet."

"And while they yet believed not for joy, and won-

This chapter is based on Luke 24:33-48; John 20:19-29.

dered, He said unto them, Have ye here any meat? And they gave Him a piece of a broiled fish, and of an honeycomb. And He took it, and did eat before them.'' ''Then were the disciples glad, when they saw the Lord.'' Faith took the place of unbelief, and they acknowledged their risen Saviour.

We Shall Recognize Our Loved Ones

The countenance of the risen Saviour, His manner, His speech, were all familiar to His disciples. As Jesus arose from the dead, so those who sleep in Him are to rise again. We shall know our friends, as the disciples knew Jesus. In the glorified body their identity will be perfectly preserved. We shall recognize those we love.

Jesus reminded His disciples of the words He had spoken before His death. ''Then opened He their understanding, that they might understand the Scriptures, and said unto them, Thus it is written, and thus it behooved Christ to suffer, and to rise from the dead the third day: and that repentance and remission of sins should be preached in His name among all nations, beginning at Jerusalem. And ye are witnesses of these things.'' Christ's life, His death and resurrection, the prophecies that pointed to these events, the sacredness of the law of God, the mysteries of the plan of salvation, the power of Jesus for the remission of sins—all these they were to make known to the world.

''And when He had said this, He breathed on them, and saith unto them, Receive ye the Holy Ghost: Whosesoever sins ye remit, they are remitted unto them; and whosesoever sins ye retain, they are retained.'' The more abundant impartation of the Holy Spirit did not take place until after Christ's ascension. But Christ breathed His Spirit upon them to impress them with the fact that without the Holy Spirit they could not fulfill their official duties in connection with the church.

The impartation of the Spirit is the impartation of the life of Christ. It imbues the receiver with the attributes of Christ. Only those who possess the inward working of the Spirit, and in whose life the Christ-life is manifested, are to minister in behalf of the church.

"Whosoever sins ye remit," said Christ, "they are remitted; . . . and whosoever sins ye retain, they are retained." Christ here gives no liberty for any man to pass judgment on others. This is the prerogative of God. But on the church in its organized capacity He places a responsibility for the individual members. Toward those who fall into sin, the church has a duty to warn, to instruct, and if possible to restore. Deal faithfully with wrongdoing. Call sin by its right name. Declare what God has said in regard to lying, Sabbath-breaking, stealing, and every other evil. If they persist in sin, the judgment you have declared from God's Word is pronounced on them in heaven. The church must show that she does not sanction their deeds, or she herself dishonors her Lord. She must deal with sin as God directs, and her action is ratified in heaven.

But there is a brighter side. "Whosoever sins ye remit, they are remitted." Let this thought be uppermost. Let the shepherds speak to the erring of the forgiving mercy of the Saviour. Let them encourage the sinner to repent and believe in Him who can pardon. "If we confess our sins, He is faithful and just to forgive us our sins, and to cleanse us from all unrighteousness." 1 John 1:9. Let the trembling hand of the repenting one be placed in the loving hand of Jesus. Such a remission is ratified in heaven.

Only God Can Forgive

Only in this sense has the church power to absolve the sinner. Remission of sins can be obtained only through the merits of Christ. To no man, to no body of men, is given power to free the soul from guilt. The name of Jesus is the only "name under heaven given among men, whereby we must be saved." Acts 4:12.

When Jesus first met the disciples in the upper chamber, Thomas was not with them. He heard the reports of the others that Jesus had risen, but gloom and unbelief filled his heart. If Jesus had really risen, there could be no hope of a literal earthly kingdom. And it wounded his vanity to think that his Master should reveal Himself to all except him. He was determined not to believe, and for a whole week he brooded over his wretchedness.

He repeatedly declared, "Except I shall see in His hands the print of the nails, and put my finger into the print of the nails, and thrust my hand into His side, I will not believe." He would not exercise faith which was dependent on the testimony of his brethren. He loved his Lord, but he had allowed jealousy and unbelief to take possession of his heart.

One evening Thomas determined to meet with the others in the familiar upper room. He had a faint hope that the good news was true. Taking their evening meal, the disciples talked of the evidences Christ had given in the prophecies. "Then came Jesus, the doors being shut, and stood in the midst, and said, Peace be unto you."

Turning to Thomas He said, "Reach hither thy finger, and behold My hands; and reach hither thy hand, and thrust it into My side: and be not faithless, but believing." The doubting disciple knew that none of his companions could have told the Master of his unbelief. He had no desire for further proof. His heart leaped for joy, and he cast himself at the feet of Jesus crying, "My Lord and my God!"

Jesus accepted his acknowledgment, but gently reproved his unbelief: "Thomas, because thou hast seen Me, thou hast believed: blessed are they that have not seen, and yet have believed." Should the world now follow the example of Thomas, no one would believe, for all who receive Christ must do so through the testimony of others. Many who, like Thomas, wait for all cause of doubt to be removed, will never realize their desire. They gradually become confirmed in unbelief. They are sowing seeds of doubt, and will have a harvest of doubt to reap. When faith and confidence are most essential, many will thus find themselves powerless to hope and believe.

Jesus' treatment of Thomas shows how we should treat those who make their doubts prominent. Thomas had been most unreasonable in dictating the conditions of his faith, but Jesus, by His generous consideration, broke down all the barriers. Unbelief is seldom overcome by controversy. But let Jesus, in His love and mercy, be revealed as the crucified Saviour, and from many once unwilling lips will be heard the acknowledgment of Thomas, "My Lord and my God."

85 / By the Sea Once More

Jesus had appointed to meet His disciples in Galilee. Their absence from Jerusalem during Passover week would have been interpreted as disaffection and heresy. But this over, they gladly turned homeward to meet the Saviour as He had directed.

Seven of the disciples were in company. They were poor in worldly goods, but rich in the knowledge of the truth. For three years they had been taught by the greatest Educator the world has ever known. They had become intelligent and refined, agents through whom men might be led to a knowledge of the truth.

The disciples gathered in a place where they were not likely to be disturbed. Within sight was the beach where above ten thousand persons had been fed from a few small loaves and fishes. Not far distant was Capernaum, the scene of many miracles.

Peter, who still had much of his old love for boats and fishing, proposed that they go out on the sea and cast their nets. They were in need of food and clothing, which the proceeds of a successful night's fishing would supply. So they went out; but all night they toiled without success. Through weary hours they talked of their absent Lord. They questioned as to their own future, and grew sad at the prospect before them.

At length morning dawned. The boat was but a little way from shore, and the disciples saw a stranger standing on the beach, who accosted them with the question, "Children, have ye any meat?" When they answered, No, "He said unto them, Cast the net on the

This chapter is based on John 21:1-22.

right side of the ship, and ye shall find. They cast therefore, and now they were not able to draw it for the multitude of fishes."

John recognized the stranger, and exclaimed to Peter, "It is the Lord." Peter was so glad that he cast himself into the water and was soon standing by the side of his Master. The other disciples came in their boat, dragging the net with fishes. "As soon as they were come to land, they saw a fire of coals there, and fish laid thereon, and bread."

"Jesus saith unto them, Bring of the fish which ye have now caught." Peter rushed for the net, which he had dropped, and helped drag it to shore. After the work was done, Jesus divided the food among them and was known and acknowledged by all the seven. But a mysterious awe was on them, and in silence they gazed on the risen Saviour.

Vividly they recalled the scene beside the sea when Jesus had bidden them follow Him. He had called them to leave their fishing boats and had promised to make them fishers of men. To bring this scene to their minds and to deepen its impression, He had again performed the miracle as a renewal of the commission to the disciples. The death of their Master had not lessened their obligation to do the work He had assigned them. Though deprived of support by their former employment, the risen Saviour would provide for their needs. If they labored in connection with Him, they could not fail of success.

Peter Is Restored to Confidence

Another lesson Christ had to give. Peter's denial of his Lord had been in shameful contrast to his former professions of loyalty. He had dishonored Christ, and his brethren thought he would not be allowed to take his former position among them. He himself felt he had forfeited his trust. He must before them all give evidence of his repentance. Without this, his sin might destroy his influence as a minister of Christ. The Saviour gave him opportunity to regain the confidence of his brethren, and, so far as possible, to remove the reproach he had brought on the gospel.

Here is a lesson for all Christ's followers. Secret sins are to be confessed in secret to God; but, for open sin, open confession is required. The disciple's sin causes Satan to triumph and wavering souls to stumble. By giving proof of repentance the disciple is to remove this reproach.

While Christ and the disciples were eating together, the Saviour said to Peter, "Simon, son of Jonas, lovest thou Me more than these?" referring to his brethren. "Yea, Lord," he said, "Thou knowest that I love Thee." Jesus bade him, "Feed My lambs." There was no vehement assurance that his love was greater than that of his brethren.

Again Jesus applied the test: "Simon, son of Jonas, lovest thou Me?" The second response was like the first, free from extravagant assurance: "Yea, Lord; thou knowest that I love Thee." Jesus said to him: "Feed My sheep."

Once more the Saviour put the trying question: "Simon, son of Jonas, lovest thou Me?" Peter was grieved. He knew that his Lord had cause to distrust him, and with an aching heart he answered, "Lord, Thou knowest all things; Thou knowest that I love Thee." Again Jesus said, "Feed My sheep."

Three times Peter had openly denied his Lord, and three times Jesus pressed home that pointed question like a barbed arrow to his wounded heart. Before the assembled disciples Jesus revealed the depth of Peter's repentance and showed how thoroughly humbled was the once boasting disciple.

Just before Peter's fall, Jesus had said to him, "I have prayed for thee that thy faith fail not: and when thou art converted, strengthen thy brethren." Luke 22:32. The transformation in Peter was evident. Because of his humiliation and repentance, Peter was better prepared than before to act as shepherd to the flock.

The first work Christ entrusted to Peter was to feed the "lambs"—to minister to those who were young in the faith, to teach the ignorant, to open the Scriptures to them and educate them for usefulness in Christ's service. For this work his own suffering and repentance had prepared him.

Before his fall, Peter was always ready to correct others and to express his mind. But the converted Peter was very different. He retained his former fervor, but the grace of Christ regulated his zeal. He could then feed the lambs as well as the sheep of Christ's flock.

The Saviour's manner of dealing with Peter taught the disciples to meet the transgressor with patience, sympathy, and forgiving love. Remembering his own weakness, Peter was to deal with his flock as tenderly as Christ had dealt with him.

Christ Tells How Peter Will Die

Before His death, Jesus had said to Peter, "Whither I go, thou canst not follow Me now; but thou shalt follow Me afterwards." To this Peter had replied, "Lord, why cannot I follow Thee now? I will lay down my life for Thy sake." John 13:36, 37. He failed when the test came, but again he was to have opportunity to prove his love for Christ. That he might be strengthened for the final test of his faith, the Saviour opened to him his future. After a life of usefulness, when age was telling on his strength, he would indeed follow his Lord. Jesus said, "When thou wast young, thou girdedst thyself, and walkedst whither thou wouldest: but when thou shalt be old, thou shalt stretch forth thy hands, and another shall gird thee, and carry thee whither thou wouldest not. This spake He, signifying by what death he should glorify God."

Jesus thus foretold the stretching forth of Peter's hands on the cross. Again He bade His disciple, "Follow Me." Peter was not disheartened by the revelation. He felt willing to suffer any death for his Lord.

Heretofore Peter had loved Christ as a man; he now

loved Him as God. Now he was prepared to share in his Lord's mission of sacrifice. When at last brought to the cross, at his own request he was crucified with his head downward. He thought it too great an honor to suffer in the same way as his Master did.

Hitherto Peter had tried to plan for the work of God instead of waiting to follow out God's plan. But Jesus bade him, "Follow Me." Do not run ahead of Me. Let Me go before you, and you will not be overcome by the enemy.

As Peter walked beside Jesus, he saw that John was following. A desire came over him to know *his* future, and he "saith to Jesus, Lord, and what shall this man do? Jesus saith unto him, If I will that he tarry till I come, what is that to thee? follow thou Me." Peter should have considered that his Lord would reveal to him all that it was best for him to know. In saying of John, "If I will that he tarry till I come," Jesus gave no assurance that this disciple should live until the Lord's second coming; but even if He should will this to be so, it would in no way affect Peter's work. Obedience was the duty required of each.

How many today are interested in the affairs of others, anxious to know their duty, while in danger of neglecting their own! It is our work to look to Christ and follow Him. Beholding Him, we shall become transformed.

John lived to witness the destruction of Jerusalem and the ruin of the temple—a symbol of the final ruin of the world. To his latest days he closely followed his Lord. Peter had been restored to his apostleship, but the honor he received from Christ had not given him supremacy over his brethren. This Christ made plain in answer to Peter's question, "What shall this man do?" He had said, "What is that to thee? follow thou Me." Peter was not honored as the head of the church. He had much influence in the church, but the lesson Christ taught him by the Sea of Galilee Peter carried with him throughout his life.

Writing to the churches, Peter said: "I exhort the elders among you, as a fellow elder and a witness of the sufferings of Christ, . . . Tend the flock of God . . . not as domineering over those in your charge but being examples to the flock. And when the Chief Shepherd is manifested you will obtain the unfading crown of glory." 1 Peter 5:1-4, RSV.

86 / "Go . . . Teach All Nations"

Standing but a step from His heavenly throne, Christ gave the commission: "All power is given unto Me in heaven and in earth. Go ye therefore, and teach all nations." "Go ye into all the world, and preach the gospel to every creature." Mark 16:15. Again and again the words were repeated, that the disciples might grasp their significance. Upon all the inhabitants of the earth was the light of heaven to shine in clear, strong rays.

The commission had been given to the Twelve in the upper chamber, but it was now to be given to a larger number. At the meeting on a mountain in Galilee, all the believers who could be called together were assembled. The angel at the tomb reminded the disciples of His promise to meet them in Galilee. The promise was repeated to the believers at Jerusalem during Passover week, and through them it reached many who were mourning the death of their Lord. With intense interest all looked forward to the interview. From every direction, with wondering hearts they came.

At the time appointed, about five hundred believers collected in little knots on the mountainside, eager to learn all that could be learned from those who had seen Christ since His resurrection. From group to group the disciples passed, telling all they had seen and heard of Jesus, and reasoning from the Scripture as He had done with them.

Suddenly Jesus stood among them. No one could tell whence or how He came. Many had never before seen Him, but in His hands and feet they beheld the marks

This chapter is based on Matthew 28:16-20.

of the crucifixion; and when they saw Him, they worshiped Him.

But some doubted. So it will always be. There are those who find it hard to exercise faith, and they place themselves on the doubting side. They lose much because of their unbelief.

This was the only interview that Jesus had with many of the believers after His resurrection. His words, falling from lips that had been closed in death, thrilled them. Now He declared that "all power" was given to Him. The minds of His hearers were lifted to the highest conception of His dignity and glory.

Christ's words were the announcement that His sacrifice in behalf of man was full and complete. The work for which He came to this world had been accomplished. He was on His way to the throne of God. He had entered upon His mediatorial work. Clothed with boundless authority, He gave His commission: "Go therefore, and make disciples of all nations, baptizing them in the name of the Father and of the Son and of the Holy Spirit, teaching them to observe all that I have commanded you; and lo, I am with you always, to the close of the age." Matthew 28:19, 20, RSV. He commissioned His disciples to proclaim a faith that would have in it nothing of caste or country, a faith adapted to all peoples, nations, all classes of men.

Christ plainly stated the nature of His kingdom. His purpose was to establish a spiritual kingdom, not to reign as an earthly king on David's throne. He said, You see that all I revealed to you concerning My rejection as the Messiah has come to pass. All I said in regard to the humiliation I should endure and the death I should die, has been verified. On the third day I rose again. In all these things the specifications of prophecy have been fulfilled.

Christ commissioned His disciples to do the work He had left in their hands, beginning at Jerusalem. Jerusalem had been the scene of His amazing condescension for the human race. Few had discerned how near heaven came to earth when Jesus was among them. At Jerusalem the work of the disciples must begin.

The disciples might have pleaded for a more promising field, but they made no such plea. Christ had scattered the seed of truth, and the seed would yield an abundant harvest. The first offers of mercy must be made to the murderers of the Saviour.

Many in Jerusalem had secretly believed on Jesus, and many had been deceived by the priests and rulers. These also were to be called to repentance. While all Jerusalem was stirred by the thrilling events of the past few weeks, the preaching of the gospel would make the deepest impression.

But the work was not to stop here. It was to be extended to earth's remotest bounds. To His disciples Christ said, Although Israel has rejected Me as the Scriptures foretold, they shall have still another opportunity to accept the Son of God. To you, My disciples, I commit this message of mercy. It is to be given to Israel first, then to all nations, tongues, and peoples. All who believe are to be gathered into one church.

The Holy Spirit Makes Their Work Effective

Through the Holy Spirit, the disciples' testimony was to be confirmed by signs and wonders. Miracles were to be wrought not only by the apostles, but by those who received their message. "In My name shall they cast out devils; they shall speak with new tongues; they shall take up serpents; and if they drink any deadly thing, it shall not hurt them; they shall lay hands on the sick, and they shall recover." Mark 16:17, 18.

At that time unscrupulous men did not hesitate to remove by poisoning those who stood in the way of their ambition. Jesus knew that many would think it doing God service to put His witnesses to death. He therefore promised them protection from this danger.

And a new endowment was promised: the disciples were to preach among other nations, and they would receive power to speak other tongues. The apostles and their associates were unlettered men, yet through the outpouring of the Spirit on the day of Pentecost, their speech, whether in their own or a foreign language, became pure and accurate, both in word and accent.

Thus Christ gave His disciples full provision for the prosecution of the work, and took on Himself the responsibility for its success. Go to all nations, He bade them. Go to the farthest part of the habitable globe, but know that My presence will be there. Labor in faith and confidence.

The Saviour's commission includes all believers to the end of time. It is fatal to suppose that the work of saving souls depends on the ordained minister alone. For this work, the church was established, and all who take its vows are pledged to be co-workers with Christ. Whatever one's calling in life, his first interest should be to win souls for Christ. He may not be able to speak to congregations, but he can work for individuals. Nigh and afar off are souls weighed down by guilt. It is not hardship or poverty that degrades humanity. It is guilt, wrongdoing. Christ would have His servants minister to sin-sick souls.

Everyone is to begin where he is. In our own families may be souls starving for the bread of life. There are heathen at our very doors. If performed with faith, the work will be felt to the uttermost parts of the earth. God often uses the simplest means to accomplish the greatest results. The humblest worker, moved by the Holy Spirit, will touch invisible chords, whose vibrations will make melody through eternal ages.

The gifts of the Spirit are promised to every believer according to his need for the Lord's work. The promise is just as trustworthy now as in the days of the apostles.

Christ came to heal the sick, to proclaim deliverance to the captives of Satan. He imparted His life to the sick and those possessed of demons. He knew that those who petitioned Him for help had brought disease on themselves, yet He did not refuse to heal them. And many were healed of their spiritual disease as well as their physical maladies. The gospel still possesses the same power. Christ feels the woes of every sufferer. When fever is burning up the life current, He feels the agony. He is just as willing to heal now as when He was personally on earth. He desires through His servants to exercise His power.

Healthful Living a Part of the Gospel

In the Saviour's manner of healing there were lessons for His disciples. The cure could be wrought only by the power of the Great Healer, but Christ made use of simple and natural remedies. He taught that disease is the result of violating God's laws, both natural and spiritual. The great misery in the world would not exist if men lived in harmony with the Creator's plan. He taught that health is the reward of obedience to the laws of God. The Great Physician had spoken to His people from the pillar of cloud: "If thou wilt diligently hearken to the voice of the Lord thy God, and wilt do that which is right in His sight, . . . I will put none of these diseases upon thee, . . . for I am the Lord that healeth thee." Exodus 15:26.

For the sick we should use the remedies God has provided in nature and point them to Him who alone can restore. We should teach them to believe in the Great Healer, to take hold upon His strength.

Only by partaking of Christ's love, through faith, can the life-giving energy flow from us to the people. There were places where the Saviour Himself could not do many mighty works because of their unbelief. So now unbelief separates the church from her divine Helper. By her lack of faith, God is disappointed and robbed of His glory. The very life of the church depends on her faithfulness in fulfilling the Lord's commission. Where there is no active labor for others, love wanes, and faith grows dim.

Angels marvel at man's shallow appreciation of the love of God. How would a mother and father feel if they knew that their child lost in the cold and the snow had been left to perish by those who might have saved it? The sufferings of every man are the sufferings of God's child, and those who reach out no helping hand to their perishing fellow beings provoke His righteous anger.

How the Gospel Has Power

Christ gave His disciples their message. Teach the people, He said, "to observe all things whatsoever I have commanded you." That which He had spoken, not only in person but through all the Old Testament, is here included. There is no place for tradition, man's theories, or laws ordained by ecclesiastical authority. "The law and the prophets," with the record of His own words and deeds, are the treasure to be given to the world.

The gospel is to be presented, not as a lifeless theory, but as a living force to change the life. Those whose course has been most offensive to Him He freely accepts. When they repent, He imparts to them His divine Spirit and sends them into the camp of the disloyal to proclaim His boundless mercy. Through His grace men may possess a Christlike character and rejoice in His great love.

He is not content merely to announce these blessings; He presents them in the most attractive way, to excite a desire to possess them. So His servants are to present the riches of the unspeakable Gift. The wonderful love of Christ will melt and subdue hearts, when the mere reiteration of doctrines would accomplish nothing. Words alone cannot tell it. Let it be manifested in the life. Christ is sitting for His portrait in every disciple. In every one, His longsuffering love, His mercy and truth are to be manifested to the world.

The first disciples prepared themselves for their work. Before Pentecost, they met together and put away all differences. Of one accord they prayed in faith, weighted with the burden for souls. Then it was that the Holy Spirit was poured out, and thousands were converted in a day.

So it may be now. Let the Word of God be preached. Let Christians put away their dissensions, and give themselves to God for saving the lost. Let them in faith ask for the blessing, and it will come. The outpouring in apostolic days was the "former rain," and glorious was the result, but the "latter rain" will be more abundant. See Joel 2:23.

All who consecrate soul, body, and spirit to God will be constantly receiving a new endowment of physical and mental power. Through cooperation with Christ, in their human weakness they are enabled to do the deeds of Omnipotence.

The Saviour longs to manifest His grace and stamp His character on the whole world. He desires to make men free and pure and holy. Through the blood shed for the world there are triumphs to be achieved that will bring glory to God and the Lamb. Christ "shall see of the travail of His soul, and shall be satisfied." Isaiah 53:11.

87 / Christ's Triumphal Entry Into Heaven

The time had come for Christ to ascend to His Father's throne as a divine conqueror. After His resurrection He tarried on earth for a season, that His disciples might become familiar with Him in His glorified body. Now He was ready for the leave-taking. His disciples need no longer associate Him with the tomb. They could think of Him as glorified before the heavenly universe.

As the place of ascension, Jesus chose the spot so often hallowed by His presence while He dwelt among men—the Mount of Olives. Its groves and glens had been consecrated by His prayers and tears. In the garden of Gethsemane at its foot He had prayed and agonized alone. On its summit His feet will rest when He shall come again as a glorious king, while Hebrew hallelujahs mingle with Gentile hosannas, and a mighty host shall swell the acclamation, Crown Him Lord of all!

Now with the eleven disciples Jesus made His way toward the mountain. As they passed through the gate of Jerusalem, many wondering eyes looked on the little company, led by One whom a few weeks before the rulers had crucified. The disciples knew not that this was to be their last interview with the Master. Jesus spent the time in conversation with them, repeating His former instruction. As they approached Gethsemane, He paused. He looked on the vine by which He had represented the union of His church with Himself and His Father. Again He repeated the truths He had then unfolded.

This chapter is based on Luke 24:50-53; Acts 1:9-12.

552

In the world for thirty-three years, Christ had endured scorn, insult, and mockery. He had been rejected and crucified. Now as He reviewed the ingratitude of the people He came to save, would He withdraw from them His sympathy and love? No; His promise is, "I am with you alway, even unto the end of the world." Matthew 28:20.

On reaching the Mount of Olives, Jesus led the way across the summit to the vicinity of Bethany. Here He paused, and the disciples gathered about Him. He looked lovingly on them. He upbraided them not for their faults and failures; words of deep tenderness were the last that fell from the lips of their Lord. With hands outstretched in blessing, as if in assurance of His protecting care, He slowly ascended from among them, drawn heavenward by a power stronger than any earthly attraction. As He passed upward, the disciples strained for the last glimpse of their ascending Lord. A cloud of glory hid Him, and the words came back as the cloudy chariot of angels received Him, "I am with you alway." At the same time there floated down to them the sweetest and most joyous music from the angel choir.

Received by Chariots of Angels

While the disciples were still gazing upward, two angels in the form of men spoke, saying, "Men of Galilee, why stand ye gazing up into heaven? this same Jesus, which is taken up from you into heaven, shall so come in like manner as ye have seen Him go into heaven."

These angels, the most exalted of the angel throng, were the two who had come to the tomb at Christ's resurrection. They longed to join the heavenly throng that welcomed Jesus, but in sympathy for those whom He had left, they waited to give them comfort.

Christ had ascended in the form of humanity—the same Jesus who had broken bread with them and who had that very day toiled with them up the ascent of Olivet. The angels assured them that the very One whom they had seen go into heaven would come again even as He had ascended. He will come "with clouds; and every eye shall see Him." "The Lord Himself shall descend from heaven with a shout, with the voice of the Archangel, and with the trump of God: and the dead in Christ shall rise." "The Son of man shall come in His glory, and all the holy angels with Him, then shall He sit upon the throne of His glory." Revelation 1:7; 1 Thessalonians 4:16; Matthew 25:31.

Thus will be fulfilled the Lord's own promise to His disciples: "If I go and prepare a place for you, I will come again, and receive you unto Myself; that where I am there ye may be also." John 14:3.

After the trial and crucifixion, the disciples' enemies expected to see on their faces an expression of sorrow and defeat. Instead of this there was gladness and triumph, their faces aglow with a happiness not born of earth. With rejoicing they told the wonderful story of Christ's resurrection and ascension, and their testimony was received by many.

The Disciples' Fear Was Gone!

The disciples no longer had any distrust of the future. They knew that Jesus was in heaven and that His sympathies were with them still. They knew that they had a friend at the throne of God, and they were eager to present their requests in the name of Jesus. In awe they bowed in prayer, repeating the assurance, "If you ask anything of the Father, He will give it to you in My name. . . . Ask, and you will receive, that your joy may be full." John 16:23, 24, RSV. And Pentecost brought them fullness of joy in the presence of the Comforter, as Christ had promised.

All heaven was waiting to welcome the Saviour. As He ascended, He led the way, and the multitude of captives set free at His resurrection followed. As they drew near to the city of God, the challenge was given by the escorting angels—

Lift up your heads, O ye gates;
And be ye lift up, ye everlasting doors;
And the King of glory shall come in.

Joyfully the waiting sentinels responded—

Who is this King of glory?

This they said, not because they knew not who He was, but because they would hear the answer of exalted praise—

The Lord strong and mighty,
The Lord mighty in battle!
Lift up your heads, O ye gates;
Even lift them up, ye everlasting doors;
And the King of glory shall come in.

Then the portals of the city of God were opened wide, and the angelic throng swept through the gates amid a burst of rapturous music. The commanders of the angel hosts, the sons of God representing unfallen worlds, were assembled to welcome the Redeemer and to celebrate His triumph.

But He waved them back. Not yet. He entered into the presence of His Father. He pointed to His wounded head, the pierced side, the marred feet; He lifted His hands bearing the print of nails. He presented those raised with Him as representatives of that great multitude who shall come from the grave at His second coming. Before the foundations of the earth were laid, Father and Son had clasped hands in a solemn pledge that Christ should become the surety for the human race. When on the cross Christ cried out, "It is finished," He addressed the Father. The compact had been fully carried out. Now He declared, Father, I have completed the work of redemption. "I will that they also, whom Thou hast given Me, be with Me where I am." John 17:24.

The voice of God proclaimed that justice was satisfied, that Satan was vanquished. Christ's toiling, struggling ones on earth were "accepted in the beloved." Ephesians 1:6. The Father's arms encircled His Son and the word was given, "Let all the angels of God worship Him." Hebrews 1:6.

Heaven seemed to overflow with joy and praise. Love had conquered. The lost was found. Heaven rang with voices in lofty strains proclaiming, "Blessing, and honor, and glory, and power, be unto Him that sitteth upon the throne, and unto the Lamb forever and ever." Revelation 5:13.

From that scene of heavenly joy, there comes back to us on earth the echo of Christ's words, "I ascend unto My Father, and your Father; and to My God, and your God." John 20:17. The family of heaven and the family of earth are one. For us our Lord ascended, and for us He lives. "Wherefore He is able also to save them to the uttermost that come unto God by Him, seeing He ever liveth to make intercession for them." Hebrews 7:25.